CONSTITUTIONAL CONFLICTS IN CONTEMPORARY MALAYSIA

Constitutional Conflicts in Contemporary Malaysia

Second Edition

HP LEE

Emeritus Professor of Law
Monash University

OXFORD
UNIVERSITY PRESS

OXFORD
UNIVERSITY PRESS

Great Clarendon Street, Oxford, OX2 6DP,
United Kingdom

Oxford University Press is a department of the University of Oxford. It furthers the University's objective of excellence in research, scholarship, and education by publishing worldwide. Oxford is a registered trade mark of Oxford University Press in the UK and in certain other countries

First Edition published 1995

Second Edition published 2017

Published in the United States of America by Oxford University Press
198 Madison Avenue, New York, NY 10016, United States of America

British Library Cataloguing in Publication Data
Data available

Library of Congress Control Number: 2016963573

ISBN 978-0-19-875599-9

Cover illustration: © iStock.com / AzriSuratmin

To the people of Malaysia who struggle valiantly to realize the vision of Tunku Abdul Rahman that Malaysia 'shall be forever a sovereign democratic and independent State founded upon the principle of liberty and justice and ever seeking the welfare and happiness of its people and the maintenance of a just peace among all nations'

In memory of
TUN MOHAMED SUFFIAN
Lord President of Malaysia, 1974–1982

'When you see a superior man, imitate him;
when you see a small man, compare yourself'

—Confucius

Foreword

When I was at school, I learned a great deal about Malaya. At the time, it was part of the British Empire, on which the sun never set. That Empire brought to Malaya, as to Australia, many disadvantages: including colonialism, imperialism, and attitudes to race, gender, sexuality, and patriarchy that needed to be reconsidered for the modern world of universal human rights, economic juristic, and the quest for global peace and security under the United Nations.[1]

Nevertheless, with British rule also came a number of advantages that survive into the current age. These advantages included the English language, with its vast treasury of literature and other writings; the legacy of constitutional struggles; and the strong traditions of the rule of law. With these traditions came the idea of independent and apolitical judges who would serve as neutral guardians of the law, including constitutional law. However, those judges could not perform their duties with professionalism, impartiality, and independence, without the support and stimulus of an independent legal profession. Moreover, the provision of fundamental human rights (such as free expression and the power to criticize officials without fear of retaliation) was fundamental to the notion of constitutionalism. It is against the background of these features of Malaysia's independent existence as a federal nation that Professor HP Lee has written this book. It represents the latest edition of a text that has come to assume an important role in chronicling the evolution of Malaysian constitutionalism.

The first edition of this book, *Constitutional Conflicts in Contemporary Malaysia*, was published in 1995. In the intervening 20 years, Malaysia has experienced a number of significant political and legal developments. Some of them pose concerns for those of Malaysia's people and neighbours who subscribe to a vision of a diverse country, joining the vibrant and prosperous democracies of the region and the world.

When Malaysia won its independence from Britain in August 1957, it adopted a carefully crafted constitutional charter. Initially, that document established the Federation of Malaya. It was later amended to provide for the enlarged Federation of Malaysia. This book explores some of the problems that quickly confronted Malaysia. Every country, without exception, faces problems, including problems of a constitutional character. As this book shows, Malaysia seems to have had more than its fair share.

Following independence, or '*Merdeka*', the formal bonds of Empire were severed. A new independent nation emerged with its own rich heritage and its culture freed from most of the colonial presuppositions. One of the greatest jurists

[1] This Foreword is adapted from the version published with the first edition of this book. It has been updated and revised. It contains the personal views of the writer.

in the English-speaking world in the twentieth century, Lord Reid, chaired the body that advised the form of the Constitution. Among the members of the 'Reid Constitutional Commission' was a distinguished scholar of Cambridge University, Sir Ivor Jennings. Despite their backgrounds, Reid, the Scot, and Jennings, the Englishman, recommended the adoption of an autochthonous approach to the selection of the constitutional Head of State of the new nation. He was to be chosen from among the Malay Rulers. The Constitution had also to deal with the protection of the special position of the Malay people. It had to defend the legitimate interests of other ethnic communities in the new Federation.

Soon after its creation, the new state was challenged by problems presented by the enlargement of its component parts; the hostile Indonesian policy of *Konfrontasi* that followed; and the subsequent withdrawal of Singapore from the Federation. Through all those changes, the Constitution endured. However, the challenges continued to present. Professor Lee has offered a description of how the Constitution came about and how successively, it has been shaped by tests and trials. In some of these, Professor Lee feels that constitutionalism has itself been shaken and sometimes found wanting. At different times, each of the principal organs of Malaysia's polity has come under attack.

The book records a number of the constitutional battles that arose between the executive arm of government and the hereditary Malay Rulers over the royal prerogative to assent to legislation and the demand for a raft of royal immunities. It then focuses on the struggle between the executive and the judiciary. Undoubtedly, the outcomes of these constitutional struggles have had significant and long-term consequences for the constitutional law and practice of the nation that has now reached the 60th year of its independence. In this new edition of his work, Professor Lee highlights the rejuvenation of the Malay Rulers. He reviews the present and potential importance of their role as guardians of the national interest.

Professor Lee offers a lucid account of the crisis in the Malaysian judiciary in 1988, when Lord President Tun Mohamed Salleh Abas and two other members of the apex court were removed from office. This event left scars, which the author feels weakened the culture of the judiciary, including the capacity of its members always to act 'without fear or favour, affection or ill will'.

Professor Lee elaborates the trajectory that followed the crisis of 1988 and the attempts by Prime Minister Tun Abdullah Ahmad Badawi to restore public trust in the integrity and impartiality of the judicial institution. He critically analyses the efficacy of the legislative reforms affecting the judiciary that were aimed to restore public confidence in what had initially been a highly respected institution.

It is against this background that in this present edition, Professor Lee has added reflections to the judicial role in the successive trials of Malaysia's former Deputy Prime Minister Anwar Ibrahim. The chronicle of the first trial and the appeal and discharge of Anwar and his second conviction since confirmed have attracted a sharp light of international attention upon the relationship between the government and the judiciary in Malaysia. This has not always reflected well on each of those institutions nor on the legislature that has left in place one of the least attractive remnants of British colonialism: the sodomy offence that lends itself to blackmail and official misuse.

Another new chapter has been added and elaborated by Professor Lee. It concerns the 'Islamization phenomenon', which is described as a 'new constitutional battlefront'. Professor Lee perceives this development against the background of the struggle to maintain the secular character of the Malaysian polity in the context of global developments affecting religious beliefs. He highlights a number of incidents that have raised concern about the long-term trajectory of Malaysia as it struggles to combat the scourge of corruption, to provide transparency and accountability in government, to uphold the secular character of the Constitution, and to advance and defend the rule of law.

As I read this book, it brought home to me the many features of the inherited colonial legal system that have been preserved in Malaysia, where, elsewhere in the crimson lands of Empire, they were allowed to fade away. The laws of sedition, originally devised to defend an imposed colonial ruler, are now available to control the public expression of opinions, which, in other modern countries, would be regarded as legitimate viewpoints and attributes of the exercise of political freedom. Many friends of Malaysia feel that the nation needs, at last, to throw off all of these lingering relics of colonial government. The prospect that this might happen has been promised by governmental leaders, but it has not yet been delivered.

This book is thus important because it demonstrates and illustrates the critical necessity of maintaining the doctrine of the separation of powers in Malaysia. The conflicts portrayed in these pages present a phenomenon that is found in many lands, namely the rising power of the elected executive government as the countervailing powers of the legislature and the courts decline. Yet, as Professor Lee shows, there are courageous voices that are lifted in defence of the cause of human rights, the rule of law, diversity of opinion, legitimate criticism, and secularism. These voices need to be nurtured. They carry the seeds of a greater and more enduring freedom, if they can be allowed to take root in Malaysia's rich and promising soil.

The new conflicts recounted by Professor Lee in this further edition have been fought out within the boundaries marked by the Malaysian Constitution. The enlargement of executive powers at the expense of the powers of the other branches of government is certainly a matter of concern. It is worthwhile to point out the importance to a nation of being governed under the rule of law. It is vital for the peace, order, and good government of the nation. But it is also essential to its long-term economic, social, and cultural success.

By describing the challenges that have been faced by Malaysia over the past 60 years, Professor Lee has not only performed a service to overseas friends and observers of Malaysia, a land with many admirers and well-wishers in the region and beyond. He has also held up a mirror, as it were, so that Malaysians themselves can see their own constitutionalism as others sometimes see them. Out of this perception may grow a recognition of the constant need for restraint in the exercise of governmental powers. And the necessity to respect the abiding values that constitutionalism ultimately safeguards in the lands that are blessed with its secure operation.

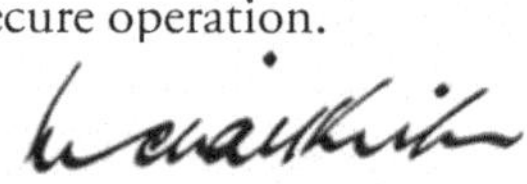

Michael Kirby
Sydney, 1 October 2016

Michael Kirby was a Justice of the High Court of Australia (1996–2009). Earlier he served as President of the Court of Appeal of New South Wales (1984–96), President of the Court of Appeal of Solomon Islands (1995–96), Judge of the Federal Court of Australia (1983–84), and Deputy President of the Australian Conciliation and Arbitration Commission (1975–83). He was elected as a Commissioner and later President of the International Commission of Jurists (1985–95), and to many national and international bodies. In 2009–10, he was a member of the Eminent Persons Group (EPG) of the Commonwealth of Nations (chaired by Tun Abdullah Badawi). This reported on the future of the Commonwealth of Nations. On the initiative of its chair, it recommended the adoption of the *Commonwealth Charter*. The first version of that instrument was drafted by Michael Kirby and appended to the EPG report. In modified form, it was adopted by the Commonwealth as expressing its core beliefs. The *Charter* was signed by Queen Elizabeth II, as Head of the Commonwealth, at Marlborough House. London, on Commonwealth Day, 11 March 2013. It expresses and elaborates sixteen core values. These include democracy; human rights; tolerance, respect, and understanding; freedom of expression; separation of powers; the rule of law; good governance; and gender equality. Each and every one of these values merits consideration in its application to Malaysia, as described in Professor Lee's book.

Preface

The first edition of this work, published in 1995, cast the spotlight on the constitutional dimensions of the major political conflicts and controversies that erupted when Mahathir Mohamad was at the prime ministerial helm (1981–2003). The confrontations with the Malay Rulers over royal assent to legislation and royal immunities, as well as attacks on the judiciary, were of such seismic magnitude that they captured the attention of the Malaysian public. A consolation for the Malaysian nation is that Malaysia, during those trying times, managed to avoid the fate of many other emergent nations where the civil power had been supplanted by the military. The conflicts had been fought and resolved within the literal wording of the Malaysian Constitution. Nevertheless, when the legacy of the Mahathir era is assessed, the economic achievements under his leadership will have to be balanced against the recorded destruction of those checks and balances crucial for the vitality of a nation founded upon the belief of 'government by law and not by men'.

Professor Andrew Harding observes that in contemporary Malaysia, there is 'a heady mix of a lively democracy in perpetual motion; authoritarian nationalism; rapid economic development and urbanisation; and ethnic tension heightened by religious conflict'.[1] He adds, 'All of these elements have deeply affected the contours of the Constitution. More than this, it is the Constitution which has also shaped, as well as providing a battlefield for, continued political struggle.'[2]

In this second edition of the book, the analysis of the constitutional conflicts traversed in the first edition is amplified by the inclusion of political and constitutional developments that have occurred since the first edition was published. The three major crises dealt with in the first edition still have ongoing significance for the state of constitutionalism in Malaysia. Upon his retirement, Mahathir Mohamad was succeeded by Abdullah Badawi, who resigned in 2009. He was succeeded by the current Prime Minister, Najib Razak, whose father, Abdul Razak, was the second Prime Minister of Malaysia. A number of significant legal and constitutional conflicts have arisen since the publication of the first edition, especially the new constitutional battlefront that has opened up concerning the future prospects of the secular nature of the Malaysian Constitution. The Constitution comes to the fore with the rise of the Islamization phenomenon.

An aspect which is not traversed in the book is the current state of the election system. In the 2013 general election, the ruling BN coalition managed to retain power by winning a majority of seats despite the opposition winning a majority of votes. For the will of the people to be accurately reflected it is necessary for the

[1] Andrew Harding, *The Constitution of Malaysia—A Contextual Analysis* (Hart Publishing 2012) 2–3.
[2] ibid.

election system to be reformed and effective safeguards introduced to ensure clean elections. It may be that in the foreseeable future, electoral challenges will become new constitutional battlegrounds.

Undoubtedly, Malaysia is at a crossroads. I hope that this new edition can elucidate the trajectory of the developing constitutional enterprise in Malaysia.

Acknowledgements

The book in revised form either incorporates or draws on the author's following articles: 'Constitutional Amendments in Malaysia: Part I. A Quick Conspectus' (1976) 18 Malaya Law Review 59–74; 'The Malaysian Constitutional Crisis: King, Rulers and Royal Assent' (1984) Lawasia 22–44; 'A Fragile Bastion under Siege: The 1988 Convulsion in the Malaysian Judiciary' (1990) 17 Melbourne University Law Review 386–417; 'Hereditary Rulers and Legal Immunities in Malaysia' (1993) 12 University of Tasmania Law Review 323–36; 'Constitutional Developments in Malaysia in the First Decade of the Twenty-First Century: A Nation at the Crossroads' in Albert HY Chen (ed), *Constitutionalism in Asia in the Early Twenty-First Century* (CUP 2014) 244–69; 'The Islamisation Phenomenon and the Rule of Law in Malaysia' in Guiguo Wang and Fan Yang (eds), *The Rule of Law: A Comparative Perspective: Festschrift for Anton MJ Cooray* (City University of Hong Kong 2013) 139–58. I wish to thank the various law reviews, Ms Finola O'Sullivan of Cambridge University Press, Professor Guiguo Wang, and Dr Fan Yang for permitting me to weave these materials into a coherent account of significant constitutional developments that have been subjected to exegesis in this book.

I place on record my appreciation and thanks to Natasha Flemming, Jamie Berezin, and staff members of Oxford University Press, and Lakshmi Shree for their efficient assistance in bringing out the second edition of the book. I thank Richard Foo for his perceptive comments and suggestions in relation to Chapters 1, 6, and 7, and Amber Tan in relation to Chapter 8. I benefited considerably from discussions with both of them.

I am extremely grateful to one of Australia's most highly respected jurists, the Honourable Michael Kirby AC CMG, who, despite the many demands on his time, has once again kindly agreed to provide a foreword to the second edition of the book.

HP Lee
Emeritus Professor of Law
Monash University
Clayton, Victoria, Australia

Contents

Table of Cases

Table of Statutes

PERAK

SABAH

SARAWAK

UNITED KINGDOM

WESTERN NIGERIA

Abbreviations and Glossary

1MDB	1 Malaysia Development Berhad
AC	Appeal Cases
AIR	All India Reporter
App Cas Law	Reports Appeal Cases
BN	Barisan Nasional (National Front); governing coalition
Bumiputera	'son of the soil'; a term used to embrace the Malays and certain non-Malay indigenous peoples of Malaysia.
CJSS	Chief Judge of the High Court in Sabah and Sarawak
CLJ	Current Law Journal
Cobbold Commission	Commission of Enquiry, North Borneo and Sarawak, 1962; headed by Lord Cobbold
Cox CC	Cox's Criminal Cases.
Dato'	An honorific title.
Dato' Seri	An honorific title.
Dewan Negara	Senate
Dewan Rakyat	House of Representatives
FCR	Federal Court Reports
ICJ	International Commission of Jurists
ISA	Internal Security Act 1960
JAC	Judicial Appointments Commission
JMF	Johor Military Forces
KB	Law Reports, King's Bench
LlLR	Lloyd's Law Reports
MLJ	Malayan Law Journal
NCS	National Security Council
NRD	National Registration Department
NUCC	National Unity Consultative Council
PAS	Parti Islam Se Malaysia (formerly Parti Aislam Sa-Melayu or Pan-Malayan Islamic Party).
PBS	Parti Bersatu Sabah
PCA	President Court of Appeal
PKR	Pakatan Keadilan Rakyat
PMIP	Pan-Malayan Islamic Party (*see* PAS)
PR	Pakatan Rakyat
QB	Law Reports, Queen's Bench
Reid Commission	Federation of Malaya Constitutional Commission, 1957; headed by Lord Reid
SOSMA	Security Offences (Special Measures) Act 2012
Tan Sri	An honorific title
Tun	An honorific title
UEM	United Engineers (Malaysia)
UMNO	United Malays National Organization
UMNO Baru	New United Malays National Organization
USNO	United Sabah National Organisation
WLR	Weekly Law Reports
WSJ	Wall Street Journal

Introduction

> We can observe that constitutionalism generally takes shape only through struggle, controversy and disagreement, seemingly changing its meaning and appearance over time. Nowhere, perhaps, is this truer than in Malaysia, where it is apparent that public life often resembles a fierce struggle over the Constitution itself, a struggle in which every issue, it seems, is capable of being framed as a constitutional issue or one that calls into question the true meaning of constitutionalism.
>
> Andrew Harding, *The Constitution of Malaysia—A Contextual Analysis* (Hart Publishing 2012) 3.

The Constitution of the Federation of Malaya promulgated originally as the supreme document of the Federation of Malaya and subsequently amended to cater for the enlarged Federation of Malaysia was envisioned to operate for a diverse society. The Constitution continues to function, albeit in a much amended form, for an ever-increasing population reported in 2010 to be 28.3 million. The ethnic groups comprised of Malay (53.3%), Chinese (26.0%), indigenous (11.8%), Indian (7.7%), and others (1.2%). Its diversity of religions is as follows: Islam (60.4%), Buddhism (19.2%), Christianity (9.1%), Hinduism (6.3%), and other/none (5.0%). The languages in the country are Bahasa Melayu (official), Chinese (various dialects), English, Tamil, and indigenous.[1] Muslims in Malaysia are followers of the *Sunni* sect (the *Shafi'i* school). By 2015, the population had grown to 30.26 million.[2]

The Malaysian Constitution has weathered remarkably a number of crises and controversies. The important feature is that these crises had been surmounted without setting aside permanently the foundation document of the Malaysian nation. However, the Constitution has not emerged fully unscathed from these crises. Nevertheless, despite the truncation of the Constitution by a broad spectrum of amendments, parliamentary government, rather than martial rule, remains in place.

An overview of constitutional developments since 1957, the year when the Federation of Malaya became independent, indicates that the major crises that

[1] US Department of State: http://www.state.gov/r/pa/ei/bgn/2777.htm (dated 28 January 2011).

[2] For 2015, the population in Malaysia comprised of Malay (50.33%); other Bumiputera (11.80%); Chinese (21.76%); Indian (6.52%); other (0.87%); and non-Malaysian Citizen (8.72%)—see http://penangmonthly.com/demographics-of-a-diverse-malaysia/.

attracted international publicity occurred when Tun Dr Mahathir Mohamad was at the helm of the government.[3] He entered the Malaysian Parliament in 1964 but lost his seat in 1969. He was then expelled from the United Malays National Organisation (UMNO)[4] by Tunku Abdul Rahman, the architect of the independence of the then Federation of Malaya and 'father' of the enlarged Federation of Malaysia. His political fortunes revived with the assistance of Tun Abdul Razak, who had taken over the reins of government from Tunku Abdul Rahman in the wake of the racial riots of 13 May 1969. On 16 July 1981, when Tun Abdul Razak's successor, Tun Hussein Onn, stepped down because of ill health, Dr Mahathir became the fourth Prime Minister of Malaysia. He tenaciously fought off a challenge from his rival, Tengku Razaleigh Hamzah, in the 1987 UMNO presidential election, consolidated his control over the party after protracted political and legal wrangling, and triumphed in his tussles with the hereditary Malay Rulers in 1983 and 1992–1993 and the judiciary in 1988.[5] Mahathir Mohamad's period in office has witnessed a fundamental tilt in the balance of governmental powers under the Constitution.[6] Since Mahathir's retirement from the office of Prime Minister and during the period of office of Tun Abdullah Ahmad Badawi and that of the current Prime Minister, Datuk Seri Najib Razak, significant political and constitutional developments have occurred that place great strains on the Constitution.

To appreciate the shift in the balance of powers it is necessary to highlight the fact that the Malaysian Constitution envisages a separation of powers doctrine. Different governmental powers are reposed in different organs of the government. Legislative power resides in the Federal Parliament by virtue of Article 66(1), whereas the judicial power, before 1988, was vested in the judiciary. The executive authority of the Federation is vested by Article 39 in the Yang di-Pertuan Agong (or King) and is exercisable, subject to the provisions of any federal law and of the Second Schedule of the Constitution, by him or by the Cabinet or any minister authorized by the Cabinet.[7] The Australian Constitution similarly provides for the vesting of the different categories of powers in different organs of government, with Chapter I of the Constitution dealing with the federal legislative power; Chapter II with the executive power; and Chapter III with the judicial power. Such a structuring led Sir Owen Dixon, regarded as Australia's pre-eminent jurist and a former Chief Justice of Australia, to conclude:

> If you knew nothing of the separation of powers, if you made no comparison of the American instrument of government with ours, if you were unaware of the interpretation it had received before our Constitution was framed according to the same plan, you would still

[3] See, generally, Gordon P Means, *Malaysian Politics: The Second Generation* (Oxford University Press 1991); Barry Wain, *Malaysian Maverick – Mahathir Mohamad in Turbulent Times* (2nd edn, Palgrave 2012).

[4] UMNO or United Malays National Organisation was formed by Dato' Onn bin Jaaffar, in 1946, to present a united front of all the Malays against the implementation of the Malayan Union.

[5] Hasan Hj Hamzah, *Mahathir: Great Malaysian Hero* (2nd edn, Media Print Publications 1990).

[6] RH Hickling and David A Wishart, 'Malaysia: Dr Mahathir's Thinking on Constitutional Issues' (1988–89) Lawasia 47.

[7] Article 39.

feel the strength of the logical inferences from Chapters I, II and III.... It would be difficult to treat it as a mere draftsman's arrangements.[8]

The equivalent strength of the 'logical inferences' can be felt when the structure of the Malaysian Constitution is perused.[9]

The division of powers amongst the different organs of government provides for a system of checks and balances. Consequently, constitutional theory envisages an oversight of the executive arm of government by the legislature. In accordance with the Westminster model, a government remains in power as long as it continues to command the confidence of a majority of members of the House of Representatives. Because of the constitutional requirement that a person, in order to be appointed Prime Minister or a minister, must be a Member of Parliament, the system of checks and balances is very weak.[10] As Tun Mohamad Suffian succinctly puts it: 'Thus in a parliamentary democracy there is no real separation of powers between the legislature and the executive, as there is between these two branches on the one hand, and the judiciary on the other.'[11] This is aggravated by the existence of a Senate where the majority of senators are appointed by the government.

The separation of powers doctrine operates at its best when the judicial arm of government is truly independent. The quality of judicial independence, therefore, is a vital ingredient of a vigorous democracy. If the judiciary is cowed by the government of the day, it paves the way for unbridled exercise of authoritarian powers. It can be generally asserted that until 1988, the Malaysian judiciary was well regarded as an independent institution. Although it traversed the path of strict legalism or literalism, its integrity was never questioned.

An institution that is unique to Malaysia, and which constitutes part of the system of checks and balances, is the Conference of Rulers, which comprises nine Rulers and four Governors. The nine hereditary Rulers, every five years, choose one of their own to be the Yang di-Pertuan Agong or 'Supreme Head of the Federation'.[12] To be elected to or dismissed from the office of Yang di-Pertuan Agong, the votes of at least five State Rulers are necessary.[13] Because of this, the Yang di-Pertuan Agong has to take into account the wishes of, at least, a majority of the Conference of Rulers. The Constitution dictates that the Yang di-Pertuan Agong acts on the advice of the Cabinet or a minister acting under the general authority of the Cabinet.[14] A discretion is reposed in the Yang di-Pertuan Agong in respect of some matters specified in the Constitution.[15] The Yang di-Pertuan Agong is head of Islam in his

[8] *R v Kirby; ex p Boilermakers' Society of Australia* (1954) 94 CLR 254, 275.

[9] HP Lee, 'The Judicial Power and Constitutional Government: Convergence and Divergence in the Australian and Malaysian Experience' (2005) 1 Journal of Malaysian and Comparative Law 2–3.

[10] Article 43(2).

[11] Tun Mohamed Suffian, *An Introduction to the Legal System of Malaysia* (Penerbit Fajar Bakti Sdn Bhd 1988) 43.

[12] ibid. [13] Article 38, Third Schedule, clauses 1(2) and 8. [14] Article 40(1).

[15] Article 40(2) provides as follows:

> The Yang di-Pertuan Agong may act in his discretion in the performance of the following functions, that is to say -
> (a) the appointment of a Prime Minister;

home State, in those States with Governors, and in any federal territory. Each Ruler remains head of Islam in his own State. This role enables the Rulers to exert considerable influence amongst the Malays who are also Muslims, given their traditional affinity to their Rulers.

The constitutional conflicts that captured national and international attention in 1983, 1988, and 1992–93 have altered the equilibrium in the balance of powers by eroding the influence of the Rulers and the judiciary. Each of these episodes will be considered separately, to highlight the struggle for power fought aggressively within the parameters of the Constitution. The aftermath of the struggle will be analysed. In that connection, the rejuvenation of royal influence and the efforts to restore the battered reputation of the judiciary will also be considered. Constitutional struggles in Malaysia have moved to a new battlefront. The rise of the 'Islamization phenomenon' is generally perceived as a challenge to the secular nature of the Malaysian constitutional polity. The overall effect of all these struggles on the state of constitutionalism in contemporary Malaysia is evaluated.

Malaysian society is in a constant state of flux. Since the attainment of independence in 1957, the many conflicts that have arisen are reshaping the contours of the Constitution. The tale of this reshaping is the nub of the chapters that follow.

(b) the withholding of consent to a request for the dissolution of Parliament;
(c) the requisition of a meeting of the Conference of Rulers concerned solely with the privileges, position, honours and dignities of Their Royal Highnesses, and any action at such a meeting, in any other case mentioned in this Constitution.

1

Constitutional History and Political Developments

> We have now reached the end of the journey and before us we see the gate of freedom ready to admit us. Let us pass through this gate with real joy in our hearts on 31st day of August 1957.
>
> Tunku Abdul Rahman, Federal Legislative Council, 15 July 1957, Clmn 314, as cited in Rais Yatim, 'The Road to Merdeka' in Andrew Harding and HP Lee (eds), *Constitutional Landmarks in Malaysia – The First 50 Years 1957–2007* (LexisNexis 2007) 21.

The evolution of a national constitution generally reflects the history of the birth of a nation. As with most cases of territories that had managed to shake off the shackles of colonialism, the emergence from the colonial cocoon to adult statehood is usually proclaimed with the simultaneous promulgation of a written constitution. This written document symbolizes the beginning of a new era for a newborn nation. Malaysia is no exception. To the ringing chants of 'Merdeka',[1] an independent Federation of Malaya came into being on 31 August 1957.[2] Though described as a 'Federal' constitution of an 'orthodox' nature,[3] the chequered history of the birth of the then Malayan Constitution indicated that the negotiations were concerned not so much with the distribution of Federal and State powers but rather with the tortuous hammering out of acceptable terms and compromises among the various racial components of the Malaysian society, especially on matters of communal interests.[4]

[1] This is a Malay word that denotes *free* or *independent.*

[2] Zelman Cowen, 'The Emergence of a New Federation in Malaya' (1958) 1 Tasmanian University Law Review 46–67.

[3] LA Sheridan (ed), *Malaya and Singapore, the Borneo Territories: the Development of their Laws and Constitutions* (Stevens and Sons 1961) 47.

[4] Rais Yatim, 'The Road to Merdeka' in Andrew Harding and HP Lee (eds), *Constitutional Landmarks in Malaysia: The First 50 Years 1957–2007* (LexisNexis 2007) 1–24; Andrew Harding, *The Constitution of Malaysia: A Contextual Analysis* (Hart 2012) 9–50.

Malayan Union

Malaysian constitutional history recorded its first major challenge with the uproar over the setting up of the Malayan Union. This outburst saw the emergence of simmering Malay nationalism, which had existed in an unorganized form before the Japanese invasion in December 1941.

Before the Second World War, the political structure that had existed in peninsular Malaya comprised a varied grouping of states. There were nine protected Malay States, of which, four were grouped together to form the Federated Malay States: Perak, Selangor, Negri Sembilan, and Pahang. The remaining States of Johor, Kedah, Kelantan, Perlis, and Terengganu comprised the Unfederated Malay States. Penang, Malacca, and Singapore, at that time, were part of the Straits Settlements.[5] North Borneo and Sarawak existed as protected states in Borneo, whilst Brunei remained a sultanate receiving British protection.

Japanese forces invaded Malaya on 8 December 1941 and shortly thereafter, the British army surrendered in Singapore on 15 February 1942. From 1942 to 1945, the Malay Peninsula and Singapore came under Japanese occupation. The end of the Second World War saw the return of British rule and the disbanding of the Straits Settlements. Penang and Malacca were grouped together with the Malay States in 1946, under a new political body called the Malayan Union. Singapore, however, was left to exist as a separate Crown Colony on its own.[6] The Malayan Union's brief and contentious existence lasted until 1948 when it was replaced by the Federation of Malaya.

The failure of the Malayan Union could be attributed to two main factors: the position of the Malay Rulers and the question of citizenship. The opposition by the Malays on these grounds was the pointer to the sensitive areas of agreement, which had to be forged in the spirit of compromise to give rise to the 'Merdeka' Constitution in 1957. Under the concept of the Malayan Union, the Malay Rulers were relegated to the status of mere 'social and religious leaders'. Their relegation in status was brought about through a series of treaties entered into between the Malay Rulers and Sir Harold MacMichael, on behalf of the Crown, whereby the Malay Rulers ceded full jurisdiction over their state territories to the British Crown. The sole legislative powers of the Malay Rulers were in matters concerning the Muslim religion. It was no wonder, therefore, that the Malay Rulers started to voice their dissent even before 'the ink of the signatures endorsing the MacMichael Treaties was hardly dry'.[7] The other major reason for the opposition by the Malays

[5] The Colony of Straits Settlements also included the Cocos-Keeling Islands, Labuan Islands, and Christmas Island.

[6] Great Britain, *Malayan Union and Singapore: Statement of Policy on Future Constitution* (Cmd 6724, 1946) 3. The British Government expressed that for the time being, the distinct social and economic interests of Singapore warranted a separate government. Also see B Simandjuntak, *Malayan Federalism 1945–63: A Study of Federal Problems in a Plural Society* (OUP 1969) 40.

[7] ibid (n 6) 41.

to the Malayan Union was the feeling of insecurity that had arisen from the proposed creation of a common citizenship. Any person could qualify as a citizen of the Malayan Union by the very fact of being born in Malaya or in Singapore and, in other cases, by fulfilling a requirement of a 10-year period of residence in Malaya or in Singapore, out of the 15 years preceding 15 February 1942. With such intense opposition, the concept of a Malayan Union was scuttled before it was fully implemented. In 1948, a new constitution was effected and, in consequence, the Federation of Malaya was established.

The Federation of Malaya

The Federation of Malaya Agreement of 1948 signalled the constitutional progress towards eventual self-government. The aborted Malayan Union experiment had resulted in the setting up of a Working Committee under the chair of Malcolm MacDonald, the first Governor-General of the Malayan Union, Singapore, and the British territories in North Borneo. Representatives of the Malay Rulers and UMNO participated in the discussions, and it was only in the closing stages of the negotiations that the views of the other communities were canvassed.[8] The Working Committee published its report on 24 December 1946,[9] and the final product of all of the negotiations was the Federation of Malaya Agreement, which came into being on 1 February 1948.

The Federation of Malaya comprised the nine Malay States, as well as Penang and Malacca. Singapore remained as a separate Colony 'in deference to the fears of the Malays that they would be dominated by the Malayan Chinese if Singapore's one million Chinese acceded to Malaya'.[10] A Federal government was set up in Kuala Lumpur under a British High Commissioner. Another feature of the Federation of Malaya Agreement was the establishment of a Federal Legislative Council in which the Malays were to be strongly represented. The Council also contained representatives from other races.

On matters of immigration, the High Commissioner had to consult a Council of Malay Rulers called the 'Majlis Raja-Raja Negri Melayu'. In matters of citizenship, there was a retreat from the liberal provisions of the Malayan Union. The addition of stiffer qualifications rendered it more difficult for the other races to acquire citizenship. For instance, all persons other than Malays could only become Federal citizens if they were born as British subjects *and* if their fathers were either State citizens or Federal citizens. For the former Straits Settlements of Penang and Malacca, it was sufficient if they were born as British subjects. The Federation of Malaya Agreement

[8] ibid 45.

[9] Malayan Union, *Constitutional Proposals for Malaya: Report of the Working Committee Appointed by a Conference of His Excellency the Governor of the Malayan Union, their Highnesses the Rulers of the Malay States and the Representatives of the United Malays National Organisation* (Kuala Lumpur 1946).

[10] See Simandjuntak (n 6) 53. See also MN Sopiee, *From Malayan Union to Singapore Separation* (Penerbit Universiti Malaya 1974) 106.

did not attract very warm support from the other racial communities. In 1952, a liberalization of the citizenship requirements was initiated as one of the means of countering the communist insurrection of 1948, which had resulted in a state of emergency being declared. It was only in 1960 that the Emergency was lifted.[11] During the years when efforts were marshalled to battle the communist terrorism, the trek towards independence continued unabated.

In July 1955, the first Federal elections were held for seats on the new Federal Legislative Council. Out of the fifty-two unofficial seats, the Alliance captured fifty-one.[12] The Alliance, founded in 1953, originally consisted of UMNO and the MCA (Malayan, later Malaysian, Chinese Association). Two years later, it included the MIC (Malayan, later Malaysian, Indian Congress). Tunku Abdul Rahman who had succeeded Dato' Onn bin Jaffar as President of UMNO, as head of the Alliance, assumed the office of Chief Minister in 1955.

Notwithstanding the prevailing emergency conditions, Tunku Abdul Rahman headed a Merdeka Mission to London to negotiate for independence. From 18 January to 6 February 1956, talks were held in London, between a Malayan delegation comprising four representatives of the Malay Rulers and four representatives of the Alliance Government, the Colonial Secretary,[13] the High Commissioner,[14] and the British Minister of State. The result of the talks was the appointment of an Independent Constitutional Commission to draw up a constitution providing for full self-government and independence for the Federation of Malaya.[15]

The Reid Commission

The independent Constitutional Commission, which was subsequently set up under the chairmanship of Lord Reid,[16] comprised Sir Ivor Jennings,[17] Sir William McKell,[18] B Malik,[19] and Justice Abdul Hamid.[20] The Canadian Government was unable to make a nomination.[21] Dr Joseph Fernando observed:

[11] In 1955 in an attempt to end the Emergency, an amnesty was offered to the terrorists. The failure of the Baling Talks between Tunku Abdul Rahman (who was accompanied by Tun Tan Cheng Lock and David Marshall) and the leader of the Communists, Chin Peng, resulted in the amnesty being withdrawn.

[12] The sole remaining seat was won by the Pan-Malayan Islamic Party (PMIP) in the Krian constituency.

[13] Lennox Boyd. [14] Sir Donald MacGillivray.

[15] *Report of the Federation of Malaya Constitutional Conference Held in London in January and February 1956* Cmd 9714 (1956).

[16] Nominated by the United Kingdom. [17] Also nominated by the United Kingdom.

[18] Nominated by Australia. [19] Nominated by the Government of India.

[20] Nominated by the Government of Pakistan. He was a Pakistani judge who had also been Secretary to the Law Ministry of West Pakistan.

[21] The Canadian Government nominated a member who withdrew at the last moment on medical grounds. The Canadian Government offered to make a further nomination. Because time was running out before the proclamation of independence in August 1957, this offer was not taken up, as it would have been some other time, for this further nomination and for the new member's arrival in Malaya.

One of the most prominent features of the five members of the Commission was that they were all steeped in English constitutionalism. Despite coming from four different countries, they shared a common background of legal training and experience in Commonwealth parliamentary traditions and constitutions derived largely from English constitutionalism. Hence they were able to debate and discuss the merits and demerits of constitutional provisions with reference to a common code of constitutional norms while bringing practical knowledge of the working of the constitutions in their respective countries. Together, the panel embodied a wealth of experience and balance between legislation-making and the interpretation of the law.[22]

The Commission was an extremely high-powered Commission. Its chairperson, Lord Reid, was described as 'one of the greatest jurists of the century in the English speaking world'.[23] Sir Ivor Jennings 'was one of the most sought-after constitutional experts in the world'[24] and was largely responsible for crafting the draft constitutional document for an independent Federation of Malaya.[25] Andrew Harding described him as the 'dominant intellectual force in the drafting process'.[26] Sir William McKell had been Premier of New South Wales and was the Governor General of Australia 1947–53. B Malik had been Chief Justice of the Allahabad High Court in India, while Justice Abdul Hamid was a Pakistani judge who had also been Secretary to the Law Ministry of West Pakistan.

The Commission was instructed to examine the existing constitutional arrangements throughout the Federation of Malaya and 'to make recommendations for a federal form of constitution for the whole country as a single self-governing unit within the Commonwealth based on parliamentary democracy with a bicameral legislature.' The new constitution was to include provisions for (1) the establishment of a strong central government with the States and Settlements enjoying a measure of autonomy, (2) the safeguarding of the position and prestige of the Malay Rulers, (3) a constitutional Head of State for the Federation to be chosen from among the Malay Rulers, (4) a common nationality for the whole of the Federation, and (5) the safeguarding of the special position of the Malays and the legitimate interest of other communities.

[22] Joseph M Fernando, *The Making of the Malayan Constitution* (MBRAS Monograph No 31)109; Rais Yatim, 'The Road to Merdeka' in Andrew Harding and HP Lee (eds), *Constitutional Landmarks in Malaysia: The First 50 Years 1957–2007* (LexisNexis 2007) 1–24.

[23] Justice Michael Kirby, 'Foreword' to HP Lee, *Constitutional Conflicts in Contemporary Malaysia* (OUP 1995) viii.

[24] H Kumarasingham, *Constitution-Maker: Selected Writings of Sir Ivor Jennings* (Camden Fifth Series, Vol 46, CUP 2014) 3. He wrote, 'The historian Joseph Fernando persuasively reasons that the Malaysian constitution was effectively drafted by one man – Ivor Jennings': ibid 5. Tunku Abdul Rahman, who was a contemporary of Jennings at St Catharine's College, Cambridge, made personal representations which ensured his selection as a member of the Commission: ibid 11.

[25] Joseph Fernando, 'Sir Ivor Jennings and the Malayan Constitution', (2006) 34(4) Journal of Imperial and Commonwealth History 577–97.

[26] Andrew Harding, *The Constitution of Malaysia: a Contextual Analysis* (Hart 2012)31. Private papers of Sir Ivor Jennings contained interesting observations of the personalities and workings of the Commission: ibid 577–96.

The Reid Commission went about its task of collecting data and memoranda[27] from June to October 1956, holding in all 118 sessions.[28] When it had collected all the evidence it needed, the Commission retreated to Rome[29] to prepare its report. The new constitutional framework drawn up by the Commission was devised with two objectives in mind: (1) that there must be the fullest opportunity for the growth of a 'united, free and democratic, nation; and, (2) that there must be every facility for the development of the resources of the country and the maintenance and improvement of the standards of living of the people'.[30] The Reid Commission stated that in making its recommendations it had borne in mind that 'the new provisions must be both practicable in existing circumstances and fair to all sections of the community'. After its completion, the Report of the Reid Commission was submitted to a Working Party.[31] The deliberations by the Working Party, and subsequent new negotiations to settle remaining unresolved issues, culminated in an agreement on a draft constitution. On 31 August 1957, the Federation of Malaya became an independent and sovereign country with an elaborately written constitution.[32]

The Formation of Malaysia

As early as 1961, a concept of a closer association encompassing the Federation of Malaya, Singapore, North Borneo,[33] Sarawak, and Brunei slowly began to take shape.[34] More details were disclosed by the Prime Minister of the Federation of Malaya, Tunku Abdul Rahman, when he requested Parliament to endorse the government's initiative in taking action for the realisation of the concept of Malaysia. The underlying reason for the necessity of Singapore's participation in a closer

[27] The Reid Commission received 131 memoranda. For a list of the names of those who submitted memoranda, see Appendix I of the *Report of the Federation of Malaya Constitutional Commission 1957*, Cmnd 330 (London 1957) (hereafter, called the *Reid Commission Report*) 107.

[28] In addition, numerous meetings of a less formal nature were held by one or more of the members of the Commission.

[29] For reasons as to why the Reid Commission picked on Rome, see *Reid Commission Report*, para 13.

[30] ibid para 14, p 4.

[31] The Working Committee comprised four representatives of the Malay Rulers, four representatives of the Alliance Government, and the High Commissioner, the Chief Secretary, and the Attorney General representing the British Government. The Committee was appointed before the Reid Commission had completed its task.

[32] See, generally: HE Groves, 'The *Constitution* of the Federation of Malaya' (1962) Indian Yearbook of International Affairs 103; LA Sheridan, 'Federation of Malaya's New Constitution', (1957) MLJ xiii. It was observed: 'One of the most remarkable aspects of the grant of independence to Malaya was that it was made at a time at which a guerrilla war was still being waged in the jungle against the Malayan Communist forces.'—Zelman Cowen, 'The Emergence of a New Federation in Malaya', (1958) 1 Tasmanian University Law Review 46, 63.

[33] North Borneo was renamed Sabah after 16 September 1963, and hereafter shall be referred to as such.

[34] See Poh-Ling Tan, 'From Malaya to Malaysia' in Andrew Harding and HP Lee (eds), *Constitutional Landmarks in Malaysia: The First 50 Years 1957–2007* (LexisNexis 2007) 25–46.

association with Malaya was the fear that an independent Singapore would easily succumb to communism and thus 'endanger the peace and security of the Federation'.[35] Such a fear was expressed by the Prime Minister of Singapore, Lee Kuan Yew, in his talks with the Malayan Prime Minister.[36] As to the form of association between the two territories, Tunku Abdul Rahman said, '[It] must be such as to provide protection for the interests of the people in the Federation and at the same time it should provide Singapore with economic security which is the desire of the people of Singapore, and to prevent outside interference and intervention in the affairs of Singapore'.[37]

To realize the Malaysian concept, lengthy negotiations between the British Government and the Malayan Government and representatives of the territories of Singapore, Sarawak, Sabah, and Brunei were conducted. A merger referendum[38] was conducted in Singapore while a Commission of Enquiry, headed by Lord Cobbold, was set up to ascertain the views of the peoples of Sabah and Sarawak in relation to the Malaysian concept, and to make recommendations accordingly. The affirmative results of the referendum in Singapore[39] and the findings of the Cobbold Commission[40] paved the way for the signing of the Malaysia Agreement.[41] Brunei, however, backed out at the closing stages of the negotiations.[42]

In September 1963, the Malayan Parliament passed Act No. 26 of 1963. This Act, known as the Malaysia Act, effected such extensive changes in the Malayan Constitution that it has been described as being responsible for the birth of a new constitution of a new enlarged nation.[43] Amendments were made to accommodate Singapore, Sabah, and Sarawak, within a substantially restructured constitutional framework along the lines of the negotiated terms. The major amendments were

[35] For an in-depth account on the formation of Malaysia, see Sopiee (n 10) chaps V and VI.

[36] Federation of Malaya, *Parliamentary Debates* (Dewan Rakyat) 16 October 1961, col 1590. The Tunku described some of the problems conveyed to him by the Prime Minister of Singapore as 'rather frightening' (col 1595).

[37] ibid col 1598.

[38] See Lee Kuan Yew, *The Battle for Merger* (Government Printing Office 1961). In the referendum, the people of Singapore were given the choice of one of three alternatives: (A) to agree to the Singapore Government's merger proposals, (B) to merge as one of the States in the Federation of Malaya, and (c) to merge on terms no less favourable than those for the Borneo States. In anticipation of a call by the opposition parties to cast 'blank' votes, the National Referendum Bill provided that such blank votes were to be considered as accepting the decision of the Singapore Legislature. See Simandjuntak (n 6) 147–50.

[39] In the referendum, 71% voted for the Singapore government's merger proposals, whereas 25% of the votes were blank.

[40] Federation of Malaya, *Report of the Commission of Enquiry, North Borneo and Sarawak* (Chairman, Lord Cobbold) (1962).

[41] *Malaysia: Agreement concluded between the United Kingdom of Great Britain and Northern Ireland, the Federation of Malaya, North Borneo, Sarawak and* Singapore, Cmd 2094 (1963).

[42] The major reasons speculated upon and attributed to the failure of the talks were the unresolved questions of precedence of the Sultan of Brunei and the financial arrangements concerning Brunei's rich oil revenues. Before this and towards the end of 1962, an open rebellion had broken out, which was led by AM Azahari, the leader of Brunei Party Ra'ayat. The revolt, however, collapsed.

[43] HE Groves, 'The *Constitution* of Malaysia: The *Malaysia Act*' (1963) 5 Malaya LR 245. Cf Ahmad Ibrahim, 'Professor Groves' *Constitution* of Malaysia', (1964) 2 MLJ xcviii.

centred on matters concerning the judiciary, citizenship, financial arrangements, distribution of legislative powers, the public services, and the protection of the 'special interests' of the Borneo States and Singapore.[44]

The teething problems leading up to the birth of Malaysia assumed international proportions with the growing hostility of the neighbouring countries of Indonesia and the Philippines. The latter sought to assert a claim of legal sovereignty over Sabah.[45] Indonesia, on the other hand, voiced its opposition to the formation of Malaysia on the ground that it was a British plot to perpetuate British colonialist designs in South-East Asia. Several meetings[46] were held at various levels between Malaysia, Indonesia, and the Philippines, and these meetings culminated in the signing of the Manila Accord by the Foreign Ministers of the three countries.[47] A further summit meeting of the three Heads of States was held at the end of July 1963 because of a renewed outburst of Indonesian hostility following the signing of the Malaysia Agreement in London. In deference to the accord that was reached at the various meetings, a United Nations mission[48] was permitted to enter Sabah and Sarawak to ascertain the views of the inhabitants of these two territories. As the task of the United Nations fact-finding mission took 3 weeks, the birth of Malaysia was delayed from 31 August to 16 September.[49] Indonesia and the Philippines remained hostile despite the announcement by the United Nations Secretary-General, on 15 September 1963, that the majority of the people in Sabah and Sarawak were in favour of joining Malaysia.[50]

To aggravate the situation, on 10 September 1963, the State of Kelantan proceeded in an unexpected action for a declaration that the Malaysia Agreement, and the subsequent Malaysia Act passed by the Federal Parliament were null and void.[51] The action was based on the grounds, inter alia, that Kelantan should have been

[44] See Groves, 'The *Constitution* of Malaysia: The *Malaysia Act*' 245.

[45] See S Jayakumar, 'The Philippine Claim to Sabah and International Law', (1968) 10 *Malaya LR* 306–35; see also MO Ariff, *The Philippines Claim to Sabah: Its Historical, Legal and Political Implications* (OUP 1970).

[46] A tripartite sub-Ministerial meeting was held in Manila from 9 to 17 April, 1963. A meeting was held in Tokyo (31 May–1 June 1963) between President Sukarno of Indonesia and the Malayan Prime Minister, Tunku Abdul Rahman.

[47] The Conference of Foreign Ministers lasted from 7 to 11 June 1963.

[48] Indonesia, the Philippines, and Malaysia were permitted to send observers to accompany the United Nations fact-finding team. Initially, there was some disagreement over the number of the observers each country was allowed to send, and the matter was finally referred to the United Nations Secretary-General, U Thant.

[49] There was some opposition from Singapore, Sabah, and Sarawak to the change of the planned date of 31 August 1963. September 16 was declared Malaysia Day by the Yang di-Pertuan Agong, in a signed proclamation on 30 August 1963. The fixing of the new date before the United Nations Mission had completed its task was deplored by U Thant and was seized upon by the Philippines and Indonesia as a ground for furthering their resentment against Malaya. In Singapore, however, the Prime Minister, Lee Kuan Yew, ignored the change of date and proclaimed Singapore's independence on 31 August. The legal significance of such a move is highly controversial but academic in nature.

[50] Malaysia, Department of Information, *United Nations Malaysia Mission Report* (1963) vii.

[51] *The Government of the State of Kelantan* v *The Government of Malaya and Tunku Abdul Rahman Putra Al-Haj* (1963) 1 MLJ 355. For an account of this episode, see Johan Shamsuddin Sabaruddin, 'The Kelantan Challenge' in Andrew Harding and HP Lee (eds), *Constitutional Landmarks in Malaysia: The First 50 Years 1957–2007* (LexisNexis 2007) chap. 3.

consulted before the passing of the Malaysia Act and the Ruler of Kelantan should have been a party to the Malaysia Agreement. This would have been a constitutional conflict with serious ramifications if the application had succeeded. It led Thomson CJ to remark: 'Never, I think, has a judge had to pronounce on an issue of such magnitude on so little notice and with so little time for consideration.' He added:

> Today, however the Court is sitting in exceptional circumstances. Time is short and the sands are running out. We cannot close our eyes and our ears to the conditions prevailing in the world around us and a clearer expression of opinion than would be customary is clearly required in a matter which relates to the interests of political stability in this part of Asia and the interests of ten million people, about half a million of them being inhabitants of the State of Kelantan.[52]

He further remarked:

> In doing these things I cannot see that Parliament went in any way beyond its powers or that it did anything so fundamentally revolutionary as to require fulfilment of a condition which the Constitution itself does not prescribe that is to say a condition to the effect that the State of Kelantan or any other state should be consulted.[53]

This remark carries echoes of the Indian Supreme Court's adventurous doctrine of 'basic structure', a doctrine that would have imposed implied restrictions on the power to amend the Constitution.[54]

Thomson CJ, on the eve of Malaysia Day, held that the action had no constitutional merits. With the removal of this last legal obstacle, but in the face of overt Indonesian hostilities, Malaysia came into being on 16 September 1963.[55]

The Separation of Singapore from Malaysia

Between 1963 and 1965, a state of continual friction developed between the Federal Government and the State Government of Singapore. Escalating political events and heightened racial tensions culminated in the expulsion of Singapore from Malaysia on 9 August 1965. Several reasons were proffered for Singapore's exit from 'the hard-fought union with the Federation'.[56] The first reason to do with economics was elaborated by Kevin Tan: '[T]he question of Singapore's contribution to federal and development finance became major bones of contention between the Singapore and Federal Governments.'[57] Other factors lay in 'the vastly different personalities and approaches adopted by the politicians on both sides of the Causeway' and in the 'PAP's attempt to supplant the Malaysian Chinese

52 (1963) 1 MLJ 355, 359.
53 ibid.
54 The 'basic structure' doctrine was expounded in *Kesavananda Bharati v The State of Kerala* [1973] All India Reports SC 1461.
55 On 26 May, Abdul Razak announced that unofficially Indonesian confrontation was over, and in August 1967, normal diplomatic relations with Indonesia were restored.
56 Kevin YL Tan, *The Constitution of Singapore: A Contextual Analysis* (Hart Publishing 2015) 23.
57 ibid.

Association (MCA) as a partner in the Alliance'.[58] The outbreak of communal riots in 1964 also became a trigger for Singapore's separation from the Federation.[59] This separation was effected by the Constitution and Malaysia (Singapore Amendment) Act, 1965.[60] The main tenor of the Act was the inclusion of provisions to allow Singapore to embark on its own course as 'an independent and sovereign State' and to accommodate consequential adjustments. The Act provided for the transfer of executive and legislative powers of the Malaysian Parliament and the sovereignty and powers of the Yang di-Pertuan Agong to the Singapore Government and the Yang di-Pertua Negara of Singapore, respectively. Other provisions of the Act restored the *status quo* in respect of all moveable and immoveable property, rights, liabilities, and obligations, which before Malaysia Day, were the responsibility of the Government of Singapore, but which had been vested in the Government of Malaysia after that day. This restoration of the *status quo* applied to Singapore officers who had been employed by the Government of Malaysia after Malaysia Day. With effect from 9 August 1965, the Senators and Members of Parliament from Singapore ceased to be members of the Malaysian Parliament. The Act also provided for the succession by Singapore to treaties and international agreements entered into before 9 August 1965, between Malaysia and other countries. Specific modifications to the Malaysian Constitution arising from this Act were made by a subsequent instrument, Constitution (Amendment) Act 1966. After the separation of Singapore was completed, there remained in Malaysia thirteen States[61].

1966: The Sarawak Crisis

Malaysia had hardly adjusted itself after the severance of one of its member States when it was buffeted by another crisis. This time the political convulsions occurred in Sarawak, one of the two States in East Malaysia. The crisis was precipitated largely by the Federal government's involvement in Sarawak's political affairs, wherein an assortment of political parties were jostling each other to arrive at certain political alliances.[62]

At the time of the crisis, the Chief Minister of Sarawak was Stephen Kalong Ningkan. He had been appointed on 22 July 1963, and acted as leader of the majority party in the Council Negri or State Legislature of Sarawak. On 16 June 1966, the Governor, Tun Abang Haji Openg, acting on representations said to

[58] ibid. The People's Action Party or PAP was and still is the dominant political party in Singapore.

[59] ibid 25–9.

[60] Act 53 of 1965. For an account on the separation of Singapore, see Sopiee (n 10) chap. VII; Kevin YL Tan, 'Singapore: In and Out of the Federation' in Andrew Harding and HP Lee (eds), *Constitutional Landmarks in Malaysia: The First 50 Years 1957–2007* (LexisNexis 2007) 55–75.

[61] Johor, Kedah, Kelantan, Malacca, Negri Sembilan, Pahang, Penang, Perak, Perlis, Sabah, Sarawak, Selangor, and Trengganu.

[62] See Gordon P Means, *Malaysian Politics* (2nd edn, Hodder and Stoughton Ltd 1976) 381–7; Yash Ghai, 'The Politics of the *Constitution*: Another Look at the Ningkan Litigation' (1986) 7 Singapore LR 147.

have been made to him by the majority of members in the Council Negri that they had lost confidence in their Chief Minister, requested Stephen Kalong Ningkan to resign. Instead of complying with the request, Ningkan urged a reconvening of the Council Negri so that he could be put to the test of no confidence through a formal vote. Upon this noncompliance, the Governor, on 17 June 1966, purported to dismiss Ningkan together with other members of the Supreme Council (or State Cabinet), and appointed Penghulu Tawi Sli as the new Chief Minister.[63] Ningkan thereupon instituted legal proceedings in the High Court at Kuching to have his dismissal declared void and to restrain Penghulu Tawi Sli from acting as Chief Minister.[64] Harley Ag CJ decided in favour of Ningkan and, accordingly, declared the latter's dismissal void.[65]

The main issue on which the outcome of the case was pivoted, was the mode of assessing the lack of confidence in the Chief Minister under the Sarawak Constitution. In this connection, the Governor, Tun Abang Haji Openg, purported to dismiss Ningkan on receipt of a letter signed by twenty-one members of the Council Negri, to the effect that the signatories no longer had any confidence in Ningkan.[66] Harley Ag CJ quoted extensively from the Nigerian case of *Adegbenro v Akintola*,[67] but did not follow the decision of the Privy Council in that case. There, the Privy Council had held that under the Constitution of Western Nigeria, by the use of the words 'it appears to him' in Section 33(10).[68] The judgment as to the measure of support enjoyed by the Premier was left to the Governor's own assessment, and that there was no limitation as to the materials on which he might resort for the purpose. The learned judge opined that the Privy Council's decision was not applicable in respect of the Sarawak Constitution upon the basis of the following five distinctions:

(1) In the Nigerian case, it was mathematically beyond question that more than half of the House no longer supported the Premier.

(2) The measurement in Nigeria was a measurement of 'support', not of 'confidence'. The Sarawak Constitution is dated subsequent to the decision of *Adegbenro v Akintola*, and that the 'confidence' of a majority of members,

[63] Penghulu Tawi Sli was nominated by the Malaysian Alliance National Council and not the Sarawak Alliance Council. See Gordon P Means (n 62) 381–7.

[64] *Ningkan, Stephen Kalong v Tun Abang Haji Openg and Tawi Sli* [1966] 2 MLJ 187. See HP Lee, 'The Ningkan Saga: a Chief Minister in the Eye of a Storm' in Andrew Harding and HP Lee (eds), *Constitutional Landmarks in Malaysia: The First 50 Years 1957–2007* (LexisNexis 2007) 77–87.

[65] ibid.

[66] The letter was addressed from Kuala Lumpur and was produced after an entourage of the dissident members had flown to Kuala Lumpur and held discussions—See Gordon P Means (n 62) 384. Again, it is interesting to note that the Sarawak Council Negri comprised altogether forty-two members, including the Speaker. The question was left open as to whether twenty-one out of forty-two members constituted a majority.

[67] [1963] 3 WLR 63.

[68] Section 33(10) of the Constitution of Western Nigeria provides that: '… the Ministers of the Government of the Region shall hold office during the Governor's pleasure: Provided that—(a) the Governor shall not remove the Premier from office unless it appears to him that the Premier no longer commands the support of a majority of the members of the House of Assembly; …'

being a term of art, may imply reference to a vote such as a vote of confidence or a vote on a major issue.

(3) In Nigeria, it was not disputed that the Governor had express power to remove the Premier from office if he no longer commanded support.

(4) In Nigeria, the Governor had express power to assess the situation 'as it appeared to him'.

(5) In Nigeria, all Ministers, including the Premier, held office 'during the Governor's pleasure', although there was an important proviso to this.

Because of these distinguishing features, Harley Ag CJ concluded that, by the provisions of the Sarawak Constitution, lack of confidence may be demonstrated only by a vote in the Council Negri.[69]

The events arising upon the reinstatement of Ningkan as Chief Minister led to the passing of the Emergency (Federal Constitution and Constitution of Sarawak) Act 1966.[70] Penghulu Tawi Sli, as spokesperson of the Alliance majority in the Council Negri, and the Governor, Tun Abang Haji Openg, had requested Ningkan to convene the Council Negri. This time, the Governor had received signed statutory declarations from twenty-five members stating their loss of confidence in Ningkan. Ningkan, instead of acceding to the request, called for the consent of the Governor to dissolve the Council Negri and to hold direct elections.[71] Under the Sarawak Constitution, the Governor has absolute discretion to withhold his consent.[72] A constitutional impasse was created when the Governor invoked this discretion to refuse consent to Ningkan's request. After much public outcry and publicity by the press of a deteriorating situation, the Yang di-Pertuan Agong proclaimed a state of emergency[73] in Sarawak, and in an emergency session of the Federal Parliament, the Emergency (Federal Constitution and Constitution of Sarawak) Act 1966 was passed.

The Emergency (Federal Constitution and Constitution of Sarawak) Act 1966 was aimed at solving the constitutional deadlock by empowering the Governor of Sarawak to convene Council Negri at his absolute discretion and to dismiss the Chief Minister should the latter fail to resign after a vote of no confidence had been passed against him in the Council Negri.[74] By this time, there had been a shifting

[69] For a critical analysis of the judgment of Harley Ag CJ, see SM Thio, 'Dismissal of Chief Ministers' (1966) 8 Malaya LR 283.

[70] Act 68 of 1966.

[71] Article 7(1) of the Sarawak Constitution reads as follows:

> If the Chief Minister ceases to command the confidence of a majority of the members of the Council Negri, then, unless at his request the Governor dissolves the Council Negri, the Chief Minister shall tender the resignation of the members of the Supreme Council.

[72] Article 10(2) of the Sarawak Constitution reads as follows:

> The Governor may act in his discretion in the performance of the following functions - (a) the appointment of a Chief Minister; (b) the withholding of consent to a request for the dissolution of Council Negri.

[73] *Vide* PU 339A/1966. The proclamation of emergency was issued by the Yang di-Pertuan Agong on 14 September 1966.

[74] Act No. 68 of 1966, ss 4 and 5.

and reshifting of political allegiance and, in consequence, Ningkan found himself outvoted. Ningkan once again resorted to the courts.[75] However, the Privy Council upheld the validity of the Emergency (Federal Constitution and Constitution of Sarawak) Act 1966.[76]

The May Thirteenth Crisis

On 13 May 1969, Kuala Lumpur was convulsed with racial violence of an unprecedented nature and scale. The racial riots were precipitated by the general elections that were held on 10 May. For the first time, the ruling Alliance Party nearly failed to acquire a two-thirds majority in the House of Representatives, whilst the opposition parties made heavy inroads into many Alliance strongholds.[77] The government attributed the outbreak of violence to the inflammatory speeches by political candidates from various parties during the election campaigns, and the 'victory' processions staged by some opposition parties.[78] To contain the situation, a Proclamation of Emergency under Article 150 of the Federal Constitution was issued by the Yang di-Pertuan Agong, Sultan Ismail Nasiruddin Shah.[79] The proclamation was issued at a time when the elections to all the seats in the Dewan Rakyat (House of Representatives) were not yet completed. Acting under Article 150(2), the Yang di-Pertuan Agong promulgated a number of ordinances having the force of law.[80] All uncompleted elections to the Dewan Rakyat and to all State Legislative Assemblies were suspended.[81] By virtue of the Emergency (Essential Powers) Ordinance

[75] *Stephen Kalong Ningkan v Government of Malaysia* [1968] 1 MLJ 119 (FC); [1968] 2 MLJ 238 (PC).

[76] [1968] 2 MLJ 238 (PC).

[77] See also RK Vasil, *The Malayan General Elections of 1969* (OUP 1972).

[78] No independent Commission of Inquiry was held to determine the causes of the racial riots and to trace the sequence of events. The government's version of what took place is contained in *The May 13 Tragedy: a Report of the National Operations Council* (Government Printer 1969). See also Tunku Abdul Rahman, *May 13, Before and After* (Utusan Melayu Press Ltd 1969); Goh Cheng Teik, *The May Thirteenth Incident and Democracy in Malaysia* (OUP 1971); and Kua Kia Soong, *May 13: Declassified Documents on the Malaysian Riots of 1969* (Suaram 2007).

[79] PU (A) 145/1969. See Cyrus Das, 'The May 13th Riots and Emergency Rule' in Andrew Harding and HP Lee (eds), *Constitutional Landmarks in Malaysia: The First 50 Years 1957–2007* (LexisNexis 2007) 103–13.

[80] Article 150(2) provides:

> If a Proclamation of Emergency is issued when Parliament is sitting, the Yang di-Pertuan Agong shall summon Parliament as soon as may be practicable, and may, until both Houses of Parliament are sitting, promulgate ordinances having the force of law, if satisfied that immediate action is required.

[81] Section 7, Emergency (Essential Powers) Ordinance, 1969, PU (A) 146/1969.

> The question may be raised as to whether the Yang di-Pertuan Agong can summon Parliament when elections to all the seats of the Dewan Rakyat are not yet completed. The answer lies in Article 62(2) of the Federal Constitution which provides that 'Each House may act notwithstanding any vacancy in its membership.' See 'On the Legality of Emergency Laws Proclaimed in Pursuance of Article 150 of the Federal Constitution' (1969) III (3) INSAF (Journal of the Malaysian Bar) 31-9.

No. 2 1969,[82] the executive authority of Malaysia and all powers and authorities conferred on the Yang di-Pertuan Agong by any written law, were delegated to a director of operations. Tun Abdul Razak, who was then Deputy Prime Minister, was appointed by the Yang di-Pertuan Agong as the director of operations. A National Operations Council was set up to assist him.[83]

Malaysia, however, managed to weather the crisis, and on 20 February 1971, Parliament was reconvened, following the resumption of the uncompleted elections.[84] After much debate, the reconvened Parliament passed the Constitution (Amendment) Act 1971.[85] The Act embodied many of the conclusions arrived at during the deliberations of the National Consultative Council.[86] The Act imposed restrictions on the right to freedom of speech, abridged the parliamentary privileges of members of the Federal Parliament and the State Legislative Assemblies, defined the scope of official usage of the national language, enhanced the status of the natives of the Borneo States and the Malays, and, finally, entrenched various constitutional provisions.

The May Thirteenth crisis marked a turning point in political and constitutional developments in Malaysia. The event also 'constituted a major turning point in the socio-economic policies the country would see in the years to come'.[87] The fundamental changes to the Constitution sought to curb public discussion of certain sensitive issues and to redress 'the racial imbalance in certain sectors of the nation's life'.[88] In the post-crisis years, the government deployed the new important powers 'to forge major changes in Malaysian society, and in the economy'.[89] Andrew Harding observed:

> These changes were the foundation of a New Economic Policy (NEP), designed to secure 30 per cent ownership of the economy for '*bumiputra*' (sons of the soil, or indigenous Malaysians) within 20 years. At a stroke the *Rukunegara* amendments had redefined ethnic relations and the political economy of Malaysia, the roles of the executive and legislative powers, and the limits of freedom of expression. They had in effect converted a liberal

[82] Emergency (Essential Powers) Ordinance No. 2, 1969, P.U. (A) 149/1969.

[83] There was some confusion as to the respective roles and standing of the Director of Operations, the National Operations Council, and the Cabinet. Tun Abdul Razak claimed that he had 'supreme powers' being responsible to Tunku Abdul Rahman—*Straits Times* (15 May 1969). Tunku Abdul Rahman declared that the Cabinet was 'all powerful' and that it was wrong to say that the National Operations Council was stronger than the Cabinet—*Straits Times* (4 July 1969).

[84] This only occurred after the government was certain that the constitutional amendments that it had proposed would definitely be passed: 'The creation of the Barisan Nasional (BN) to replace the Alliance, and the accession to it of the Sarawak United People's Party (SUPP), gave the Government the likelihood of the two-thirds majority it sought….'—Andrew Harding, *The Constitution of Malaysia: A Contextual Analysis* (Hart 2012) 47.

[85] Act A30 of 1971.

[86] The National Consultative Council was established during the emergency to provide a forum for the frank discussion of various matters relating to the racial riots. It comprised members of all races and political parties (except for the Democratic Action Party, which turned down the invitation to sit on the Council).

[87] See Cyrus Das, 'The May 13th Riots and Emergency Rule' in Andrew Harding and HP Lee (eds), *Constitutional Landmarks in Malaysia: The First 50 Years 1957–2007* (LexisNexis 2007) 103.

[88] *Parliamentary Debates on the Constitution Amendment Bill, 1971* (Government Printers 1972) 3.

[89] Gordon P Means, *Malaysian Politics: The Second Generation* (OUP 1991) 16.

democracy observing basic rights into an authoritarian semi-democratic police state with large exceptions to basic rights.[90]

Post–May Thirteenth Developments

No major constitutional conflicts occurred in the interregnum between Tunku Abdul Rahman's retirement from prime ministership in September 1970, through the periods of government under Tun Abdul Razak and Tun Hussein Onn, and the assumption of office by Dr Mahathir Mohamad, as the fourth Prime Minister of Malaysia, on 17 July 1981. Musa Hitam, who defeated Tengku Razaleigh Hamzah for the post of Deputy President of UMNO, was automatically selected as Deputy Prime Minister.

Political disputes at the state level engendered conflicts between the Federal government and some State governments. In 1977, the Federal government, under Tun Hussein Onn, invoked emergency powers under Article 150 of the Constitution to deal with a political crisis in Kelantan. The Emergency Powers (Kelantan) Act 1977 was enacted to extend Federal executive authority to Kelantan 'in respect of matters which are now within the executive authority of the State of Kelantan'. 'Legislative authority of the State of Kelantan in respect of all matters which are now within the legislative authority of the State of Kelantan' was conferred upon the Ruler of the State of Kelantan, to the exclusion of the Legislative Assembly of that state. The crisis was provoked by internal bickering in Parti Islam Se Malaysia (PAS) (which at that time was a member of the Barisan Nasional),[91] and rivalries between it and UMNO. Political stability was restored by the imposition of Federal rule under the Emergency Powers (Kelantan) Act 1977. PAS was expelled from the Barisan Nasional when it opposed the enactment of this legislation.[92]

In 1985, a constitutional crisis at the state level was played out in Sabah.[93] Parti Bersatu Sabah (PBS), a new party led by Datuk Joseph Pairin Kitingan, won a majority of seats in a snap state election called by Datuk Harris Salleh, who was then the Chief Minister of Sabah and leader of the Berjaya party. Berjaya saw its numbers reduced to six seats, whilst the United Sabah National Organisation (USNO), led by Tun Mustapha Harun, won sixteen seats. The expectation was that Datuk Pairin would be called upon to form the new state government, since his party controlled twenty-six seats in the forty-eight-member Legislative Assembly. A brazen attempt was made to subvert that expectation. As Gordon Means explained:

> At the height of the agony of defeat, Harris Salleh conceived of a scheme to deny his arch-rival and critic, Joseph Pairin Kitingan, of the fruits of victory. Under the Sabah Constitution, as

[90] Andrew Harding, *The Constitution of Malaysia: A Contextual Analysis* (Hart Publishing 2012) 48.

[91] Before 1974, the Barisan Nasional was known as the Alliance.

[92] Gordon P Means, *Malaysian Politics: The Second Generation* (OUP 1991) 61–4. See also Lim Kit Siang, *Time Bombs in Malaysia* (Democratic Action Party 1978) 247–55.

[93] AJ Harding, Turbulence in the land below the wind: Sabah's constitutional crisis of 1984/5' (1991) XXIX JCCP 86.

a relic from the colonial era, the Chief Minister had the power to appoint six non-elected assemblymen. Berjaya, with its 6 elected members, would support Tun Mustapha for Chief Minister, who with USNO's 16 elected members, and the 6 appointed members would constitute a majority of 28 in the 48-member Assembly. By this move, Berjaya would also have the power to force a new election at any favourable moment so as to recoup its losses.[94]

To implement this scheme, Tun Mustapha with a number of his supporters entered the residence of the State Governor[95] in the middle of the night. On 22 April 1985, at about 5:30 a.m., Tun Mustapha was appointed Chief Minister by the Governor. Within the same day, this appointment was revoked and, at about 8:00 p.m., the Governor appointed and swore in Datuk Pairin as Chief Minister. Tun Mustapha sought relief from the courts claiming, among other things, that the Governor's revocation of his appointment as Chief Minister, on 22 April 1984, was *ultra vires* the Sabah Constitution and was, therefore, null and void. Tan Chiaw Thong J of the High Court in 'a careful decision, admirable for its breadth and careful assessment of both facts and law'[96] dismissed the suit filed by Tun Mustapha.[97] In the course of judgment, he said:

> I do not consider that the Constitution envisages or permits that the judgment of the Head of State under art. 6(3) could be made in circumstances which I have found to have occurred here, when the swearing in was not made voluntarily and willingly, but was done under pressure, threat, fright and when the mental and physical condition of the Head of State was such that he could not think properly. In my view, the Constitution envisages that the Head of State should be allowed to make his judgment quietly, freely, independently and impartially, without any influence, pressure, threat or other factors not sought by him which might influence his judgment. It is common knowledge that it is the tradition in all countries having the party system of government based on Parliamentary democracy, and the Constitutions of which follow the Westminster model, that this should be so.[98]

Accordingly, Tan Chiaw Thong J held that, given the circumstances under which the swearing in of Tun Mustapha had taken place, the Governor had made no judgment under Article 6(3) of the Sabah Constitution; the swearing in was, therefore, null, void and of no legal effect. The attempt to question the validity of Datuk Pairin's appointment as Chief Minister was, consequently, unsuccessful. The appeal to the Supreme Court on the basis that the High Court lacked jurisdiction to entertain the action as the matter was a nonjusticiable issue was dismissed.[99]

[94] Gordon P Means, *Malaysian Politics: The Second Generation*, 160.

[95] Tun Datuk Haji Mohamed Adnan Robert.

[96] Philip TN Koh, 'The Sabah Constitutional Cases 1985-1986: Conventions, Justiciability and Democratic Governance' in Andrew Harding and HP Lee (eds), *Constitutional Landmarks in Malaysia: The First 50 Years 1957–2007* (LexisNexis 2007) 165, 166.

[97] *Tun Datu Haji Mustapha Bin Datu Harun v Tun Datuk Haji Mohamed Adnan Robert, Yang di-Pertua Negeri Sabah & Datuk Joseph Pairin Kitingan (No. 2)* [1986] 2 MLJ 420. See Philip TN Koh, 'The Sabah Constitutional Cases 1985–1986: Conventions, Justiciability and Democratic Governance' in Andrew Harding and HP Lee (eds), *Constitutional Landmarks in Malaysia: The First 50 Years 1957-2007* (LexisNexis 2007) 165–72.

[98] ibid 452.

[99] *Tun Datuk Haji Mohd Adnan Robert v Tun Datu Haji Mustapha b Datu Harun; Datuk Joseph Pairin Kitingan v Tun Datu Haji Mustapha B Datu Harun* [1987] 1 MLJ 471.

A footnote to the constitutional conflict in Sabah was the attempt to destabilize the state when Datuk Pairin dissolved the Sabah Legislative Assembly on 24 February 1986 and called a new election. Demonstrations were organized and bombings staged. Tan Chee Khoon observed: 'One very disturbing feature of the demonstration was the use of illegal Filipino immigrants to create unrest in the state capital. These illegal immigrants have been paid to create disturbances that caused damage running into tens of millions!'[100]

The agitators' objective was clear. They hoped that the civil disturbances would result in Federal intervention along the same lines as the Kelantan Crisis of 1977. On this occasion, the government of Dr Mahathir did not so respond as expected. The subsequent elections resulted in an enhanced majority for the party led by Datuk Pairin. Datuk Pairin led his party to another election victory in 1990. On 10 January 1994, he dissolved the State Legislative Assembly and called a snap election that his party won narrowly. He had to maintain a 36-hour vigil outside the State Governor's residence before he was finally sworn in as Chief Minister of Sabah. A number of his party's assemblymen 'defected' to the Barisan Nasional and a petition with the signatures of thirty members of the Assembly was presented to the Governor. On 17 March 1994, he resigned as Chief Minister, 'without there having been any vote or motion of no confidence in him or the State Government in the Assembly'.[101] An action based on the argument that as there had been no vote of confidence in the Assembly, the resignation of Pairin was personal to him was dismissed by Kadir Sulaiman J.[102] Andrew Harding succinctly remarked: '[A] resignation of a Chief Minister on grounds of lack of confidence or support is always a resignation of the entire Cabinet. Any other conclusion defies the deep logic of constitutional convention.'[103]

The Kelantan and the Sabah crises were constitutional conflicts arising from warring political parties. In the main, they did not have lasting impact on the state of constitutionalism in Malaysia, unlike the three major crises that took place in 1983, 1988, and 1992–1993. These three major crises represent struggles for power of titanic proportions; their impact is more lasting.

The 1983 and 1993 Constitutional Crises: Malay Rulers under Siege

No constitutional conflict has been as explosive as the convulsion that occurred in 1983. The constitutional confrontation pitted the Mahathir government against

[100] Tan Chee Khoon, *Sabah: A Triumph for Democracy* (Pelanduk Publications 1986) 162.

[101] See Andrew Harding, 'When is a Resignation Not a Resignation? A Crisis of Confidence in Sabah' (1995) The Round Table 353, 354.

[102] *Datuk Amir Kahar bin Tun Datu Haji Mustapha* v *Tun Mohamed Said bin Keruak, Yang di-Pertua Negeri Sabah & 8 Others* [1995] 1 CLJ 184.

[103] Andrew Harding, 'When is a Resignation Not a Resignation? A Crisis of Confidence in Sabah' (1995) The Round Table 353, 358.

the Malay Rulers. The first phase of the conflict was impelled by the fear that the Malay Rulers would exercise a claimed unfettered discretionary power of not giving the royal assent to legislation. The conflict was divisive but it could not be convincingly said that Mahathir ultimately had a complete triumph. A decade later, the tussle reignited over the treatment meted out by the Sultan of Johor to a hockey coach. This time Mahathir triumphed over the rulers by removing their immunity. Each of these crises will be evaluated in later chapters.

The 1988 Judiciary Crisis

This crisis arose when Mahathir Mohamad's grip on power was under challenge by another team within UMNO led by Tengku Razaleigh. The intra-UMNO political struggle moved into the judicial arena. It ultimately resulted in the removal of Lord President Salleh Abas and two other senior judges of the Supreme Court. This was the most traumatic crisis to afflict the judiciary. Article 125 of the Constitution, which provides for a tribunal mechanism to effect the removal of a judge, was deployed in an unscrupulous manner. That event and ensuing controversies afflicting the judicial institution witnessed the downward spiral in public confidence in the independence and integrity of the judiciary.

The 1988 Constitutional Amendments

A constitutional amendment Act was passed without much fanfare in 1988, which altered Article 121 of the Malaysian Constitution in two major aspects. There was little public airing or parliamentary discussion of the full implications of the amendments. These amendments, which on the face appear to be relatively innocuous, have turned out to be silent time bombs that have now engendered conflict over their interpretation. They carry fundamental significance in the reshaping of the constitutional balance as originally envisioned by the Reid Commission.[104] The first of these 1988 amendments has created uncertainties about the operational effectiveness of a separation of judicial powers doctrine in Malaysia. Before the amendment, the judicial power of the Federation was expressly vested in the High Courts and such inferior courts provided by Federal legislation. The effect of the amendment is to make the High Court and inferior courts receptacles of 'such jurisdiction and powers as may be conferred by or under federal law'. The formula 'such other jurisdiction as may be conferred by or under federal law' now also applies to the Court of Appeal and the Federal Court. The opportunity arose in *Kok Wah Kuan*[105] for the Federal Court to protect the paramount status of the judicial power and entrench a strict separation of judicial power doctrine, but such

[104] Andrew Harding, *The Constitution of Malaysia: A Contextual Analysis* (Hart 2012) 203.
[105] [2007] 5 MLJ 174 (CA); [2008] 1 MLJ 1 (FC).

an opportunity was squandered through a docile and unimaginative construction of the amended Article 121.

The second of the amendments, which involved the insertion of a new Article 121(1A), have now become the constitutional crucible for intense and highly fanatical struggle over the secular nature of the Malaysian polity. The rise of the Islamization phenomenon poses troubling implications for the state of constitutionalism in Malaysia. The insertion of Article 121(1A) was designed to preclude the civil courts from exercising 'jurisdiction in respect of any matter within the jurisdiction of the Syariah courts'. The interpretive approach adopted by the civil courts appears to suggest an abdication of their role as constitutional arbiters whenever they have a whiff of an issue of Islamic Law.

The Anwar Ibrahim Saga and the Rise of *Reformasi*

The Anwar Ibrahim saga is said to 'rank as one of the highest profiled and controversial events'[106] in Malaysian legal history. Although the saga would be viewed as more of a political conflict, it does have constitutional significance when viewed from a broader perspective. The saga engendered widespread public concern over abuses of power and the deteriorating state of constitutionalism in the face of the deployment of unbridled executive power in the carrying out of a strategy of total destruction of a former Deputy Prime Minister. Jesse Wu Min Aun remarked, 'It is often the case that the true constitutional significance of controversial events can only be seen at a distance when the dust has truly settled.'[107]

The saga was prompted in the first instance by fundamental disagreement between Prime Minister Mahathir Mohamad and Deputy Prime Minister Anwar Ibrahim (who was also the Finance Minister) over the strategy to be adopted in coping with the 1997/98 Asian financial crisis, which brought about a recession in Malaysia. The struggle between Anwar and Mahathir may be further viewed 'against the backdrop of the jousting for power apart from disagreements over economic and other policies.'[108] That struggle culminated in the dismissal of Anwar Ibrahim on 2 September 1998, by Mahathir, from all his government posts and his expulsion from UMNO on 3 September, following the release by the Attorney General's office of an affidavit by a senior police officer, which alleged corrupt practices and sexual misconduct involving Anwar Ibrahim.[109] The outburst of spontaneous support across ethnic and religious divide galvanized the holding of many massive rallies across the country. Anwar's call for *Reformasi* struck a chord with the

[106] Jesse Wu Min Aun, 'The Saga of Anwar Ibrahim' in Andrew Harding and HP Lee (eds), *Constitutional Landmarks in Malaysia: The First 50 Years 1957–2007* (LexisNexis 2007) 273. See also Wu Min Aun, 'Anwar Ibrahim: The Fall and Fall of a Favoured Son' [2000/2001] LAWASIA Journal 46–71.

[107] ibid 290. [108] ibid 274.

[109] The affidavit was filed in a prosecution case against a friend of Anwar Ibrahim, S Nallakaruppan, who was later charged with unlawful possession of bullets: Amnesty International, *MALAYSIA Human Rights Undermined: Restrictive Laws in a Parliamentary Democracy* (1999) 26–7.

Malaysian public. The word '*Reformasi*', in the Malay language, was a call for 'social and political reforms' that was in opposition to Mahathir's 'cronyistic' responses to the Asian financial crisis.[110] It was pointed out that Anwar's *Reformasi* declaration echoed the slogan used in neighbouring Indonesia in student-led demonstrations against *kolusi* (collusion), *korupsi* (corruption), and *nepotisme* (nepotism) that resulted in President Suharto's resignation just a few months earlier in May.[111] 'On the evening of 20 September 1998, Anwar was arrested in a most dramatic manner which underlined the fear of the potential threat posed by Anwar Ibrahim to the stranglehold on power of Mahathir himself and of UMNO as the nation's dominant political organisation. Khoo Boo Teik wrote: "[B]alaclava-clad and submachine-gun-toting commandos broke into Anwar's home, arrested Anwar, and whisked him to the national police headquarters in Bukit Aman, Kuala Lumpur." '[112] That night he was served documents informing him that his arrest was made under the Internal Security Act, which provided for the power of preventive detention.

An event which propelled the brutal treatment of Anwar into the gaze of the international community was the image of Anwar with 'a blackened eye and visible bruises to his forehead and face'[113] when he was brought to court. The outrage forced Prime Minister Mahathir to establish a Royal Commission of Inquiry. The Inspector General of Police, Abdul Rahim Noor, admitted to the Commission that he was responsible for the injuries inflicted on Anwar Ibrahim.[114]

Five counts of corruption[115] and five counts of sodomy[116] were levelled against Anwar Ibrahim. On 14 April 1999, Anwar Ibrahim was, after a highly controversial and questionable trial before Justice Augustine Paul of the High Court, found guilty of committing a 'corrupt practice' and sentenced to 6 years imprisonment.[117] A second trial commenced in July 1999 against Anwar Ibrahim in

[110] Khoo Boo Teik, *Beyond Mahathir: Malaysian Politics and Its Discontents* (Zed Books Ltd 2003) 100.

[111] ibid. Amnesty International, *MALAYSIA Human Rights Undermined: Restrictive Laws in a Parliamentary Democracy* (1999) 5.

[112] ibid.

[113] Amnesty International, *MALAYSIA Human Rights Undermined: Restrictive Laws in a Parliamentary Democracy* (1999) 76.

[114] On 30 April 2001, Abdul Rahim Noor was 'convicted of the assault of Anwar and was sentenced to two months imprisonment and fined RM 525'—see Mark Trowell QC, 'Anwar's Long Struggle for Justice', Report on Datuk Seri Anwar bin Ibrahim's Appeal against conviction observed on behalf of the Australian Bar Association and International Commission of Jurists. http://www.austbar.asn.au/wp-content/uploads/2014/02/ABA_Anwar_Appeal_25E109_v3.pdf (accessed 17 October 2016).

[115] Under s 2(1) of the Emergency (Essential Powers) Ordinance No 22, 1970. 'In summary, the charges alleged that Anwar, in his capacity as Deputy Prime Minister and Minister of Finance, committed a corrupt practice in that he directed the investigating officers to obtain from the complainants a retraction of an allegation of sodomy. It was also alleged that he had directed the officers to secure from the parties a written public statement to deny sexual misconduct and sodomy allegedly committed by him for the purpose of protecting himself against any criminal action or proceedings. The complainants, who had written to the Prime Minister were a driver, Azizan bin Abu Bakar, and another person, Umni Hafilda binte Ali.'—Jesse Wu Min Aun, 'The Saga of Anwar Ibrahim' in Andrew Harding and HP Lee (eds), *Constitutional Landmarks in Malaysia: The First 50 Years 1957–2007* (LexisNexis 2007) 273, 278.

[116] Under s 377B of the Penal Code.

[117] *PP v Dato' Seri Anwar Ibrahim* [1999] 2 MLJ 1.

relation to the allegations of sodomy that were raised and dropped in the first trial, and on 8 August 2000, he was found guilty of sodomy and sentenced to 9 years imprisonment.[118] The first phase episode has been described as bearing 'many of the hallmarks of a classic show trial: police brutality, coerced confessions, denial of basic procedural fairness in court, and an absence of judicial impartiality and independence'.[119] Amanda Whiting elaborated:

> Anwar was beaten while in police custody and witnesses were coerced into making confessions incriminating Anwar and themselves. Several defence lawyers were prosecuted when they tried to establish a political conspiracy against Anwar. Anwar's supporters, and participants in the wider movement of Malaysians calling for an end to authoritarian rule, were subject to harassment, police brutality, and some to periods of detention without trial.[120]

The Court of Appeal dismissed Anwar's appeal regarding the sodomy conviction and sentence but these were quashed by the Federal Court on 2 September 2004. Having served out his term of imprisonment on the corruption charge, Anwar led a coalition opposition at the general election on 8 March 2008, although he himself was still barred from standing for political office. The results came as such a rude shock to the government that the description of the election outcome as a 'political tsunami' was freely bandied about. For the first time in Malaysian history, the ruling coalition lost its control of a two-thirds majority in the Dewan Rakyat. According to the Constitution, a two-thirds majority is required in order to amend the Constitution. Out of 222 seats, the Barisan Nasional won 140, while the Pakatan Rakyat won 82. On top of that, the opposition won control of five of the Malaysian states: Kedah, Kelantan, Penang, Perak, and Selangor. The jewel in the crown was the victory in the state of Selangor as it is the richest state in the Federation. The Pakatan Rakyat subsequently lost control of the state of Perak in a controversial constitutional battle that drew in the state Ruler, Sultan Azlan Shah, and the intervention of the courts. The legal and constitutional dimensions of the 'Perak Crisis' are canvassed in a later chapter.[121] The outcome of the 2008 general election led to the subsequent political demise of Prime Minister Abdullah Badawi. A key feature of Abdullah Badawi's term in office was his frank recognition of the continuing low confidence accorded by the public to the judiciary and his preparedness to bring about fundamental reforms to eliminate political interference in the process of appointment of members of the superior courts. His reforms, while well intentioned, were in the end undermined by the powerful 'warlords' within UMNO: in relation to the judicial reforms, it could best be summed up as equivalent to a mountain labouring and ultimately a timorous mouse was born.

[118] [2001] 3 MLJ 193. See Wu Min Aun, 'Anwar Ibrahim: Epilogue' [2002] LAWASIA Journal 45–59.

[119] Amanda Whiting, 'Anwar Ibrahim's conviction lowers the bar on the Malaysian legal system'—http://www.eastasiaforum.org/2015/04/13/anwar-ibrahims-conviction-lowers-the-bar-on-the-malaysian-legal-system/ (accessed 19 November 2016).

[120] ibid. [121] See chap. 4 below.

The stunning success for the opposition also spelt more trouble for Anwar Ibrahim. His disqualification having ended soon after the general election, Anwar could now contest a by-election to regain his old parliamentary seat, which his wife, Dr Wan Azizah Wan Ismail, had comfortably held in his absence. On 28 June 2008, a police report was lodged by Mohammad Saiful Bukhari Azlan, an aide to Anwar Ibrahim. In the report, the aide claimed that he had been forcibly sodomized by Anwar. On 7 August 2008, Anwar thus found himself facing new charges of sodomy, referred to as 'Sodomy II' by commentators, but he still regained his seat on 26 August 2008, becoming the Opposition Leader. On 1 February 2010, the trial commenced. On 9 January 2012, he was acquitted. The government appealed to the Court of Appeal. At the general election held on 5 May 2013, the Pakatan Rakyat increased its seats from eighty-two to eighty-nine, while the Barisan Nasional won 133 out of the 222 parliamentary seats. The Barisan Nasional won a majority of seats despite losing the popular vote to Pakatan Rakyat. For the second time in Malaysian history, the Barisan Nasional was denied a two-thirds majority. Anwar Ibrahim was clearly posing a serious threat to the grip on political power of BN and especially of UMNO. In March 2014, his acquittal was overturned by the Court of Appeal, which sentenced him to 5 years imprisonment. The Court of Appeal handed down its judgment a week before Anwar Ibrahim was to stand for a Selangor state by-election, effectively disqualifying him from standing, and demolishing his plan of becoming the Menteri Besar of the State of Selangor.[122] He was released pending an appeal to the Federal Court. On 10 January 2015, the Federal Court upheld his conviction and the 5-year term of imprisonment. His petition for a royal pardon was rejected by the Yang di-Pertuan Agong acting on advice of a Pardons Board.[123] From a constitutional perspective, observers of the Anwar trials have made reports that reflected adversely on the reputation of the Malaysian judiciary.

A False Dawn of a 'New Era'?

Following the shocking electoral outcome of the 2009 general election, Abdullah Badawi was forced to make way for Najib Razak to assume the prime ministerial role. Najib Razak, the son of the second Prime Minister, Abdul Razak, sought, at the outset of his prime ministership, to project an image of a leader of moderation and one who would spearhead 'an organised and graceful political transformation' and create a Malaysia 'that practises a functional and inclusive democracy'.[124] He articulated this vision in a speech on 15 September 2011, the eve of Malaysia Day. He reiterated the commitment of the government to 'upholding the system of parliamentary Democracy, Constitutional Monarchy, the rule of law, the

[122] Anwar Ibrahim's wife, Dr Wan Azizah Wan Ismail, won the by-election.

[123] Daniel Pascoe, 'What the Rejection of Anwar Ibrahim's Petition for Pardon Tells Us about Malaysia's Royal Pardons System' (2016) 18(1) Asian-Pacific Law & Policy Journal (forthcoming).

[124] 'Full text of PM's Malaysia Day message' *Malaysiakini* (15 September 2011) https://www.malaysiakini.com/news/175970 (accessed 7 July 2016).

philosophy of federalism and the check and balance principle between the three branches of government'.[125] He went on to announce his intention to revoke three Proclamations of Emergency, repeal the Internal Security Act (ISA), and review several pieces of legislation, including the Banishment Act 1959, the Restricted Residence Act 1933, and the Printing Presses and Publications Act 1984.[126] In that same speech, he mentioned that new legislation under Article 149 ('Special Laws against Subversion') of the Federal Constitution would be enacted to 'prevent subversive action, organised violence and criminal acts in order to preserve public order and security'. Article 149 'allows parliament to enact sweeping security provisions that deny basic freedoms'.[127] Although the Proclamations of Emergency were revoked and the ISA was repealed in its entirety, the enactment of the Security Offences (Special Measures) Act 2012 (SOSMA) and accompanying legislation was viewed by observers to be providing for preventive detention by the back door. There was some talk of repealing the Sedition Act and replacing it with a national harmony Act. Yvonne Tew said, 'Optimism over the Prime Minister's reforms, however, was short-lived.'[128] The unfavourable outcome of the 2013 general election led to the jettisoning of the reform fervour of Prime Minister Najib Razak. Apart from introducing new highly contentious laws, the Sedition Act has become a more conspicuous weapon for intimidating and silencing government critics. What is of further concern is the passing of the National Security Council (NSC) Act 2016. The Act empowers the Prime Minister, on advice by a newly created body called the NSC, whose members are appointed by the Prime Minister, to declare an area a security area. Following the declaration, the Prime Minister is able to deploy the security forces and any government agencies in a declared security area. Undoubtedly, the NSC Act provides a loaded gun for possible future invocation in the event an unscrupulous leader seeks to override parliamentary democracy with authoritarian rule. Whether Najib Razak genuinely intended to achieve his vision of a Malaysia to 'be at par with other democratic systems in the world which are underscored by the universal principle from the people, by the people and for the people', or whether it was politically convenient rhetoric, is a matter that has now been shunted into the realm of speculation. Najib Razak's position was considerably weakened by the poor outcome of the 2013 general election. Furthermore, he found himself caught up in a series of controversies and scandals that afflicted his administration.[129] How the turbulence within UMNO will affect the state of constitutionalism in the event of another electoral disaster is a matter of speculation and concern.

125 ibid.

126 See 'Malaysia' (Human Rights Watch, Country Summary, January 2012) https://www.hrw.org/sites/default/files/related_material/malaysia_2012.pdf (accessed 4 July 2016).

127 ibid. Other laws which were enacted at the same time were the Criminal Procedure Code (Amendment) (No 2) Act 2012, the Evidence (Amendment) (No 2) Act 2012 and the Territorial Sea Act 2012.

128 Yvonne Tew, 'On the Uneven Journey to Constitutional Redemption: The Malaysian Judiciary and Constitutional Politics' (2016) 25(3) Washington International Law Journal 1, 2.

129 A particular controversy arose over a strategic state investment fund, the 1 Malaysia Development Berhad (1MDB), which was set up by Najib Razak when he came into office in 2009 to make Kuala

Concluding Observations

In proclaiming independence to the multitude assembled in the Merdeka Stadium in Kuala Lumpur, Tunku Abdul Rahman said:

> Now in the name of God the Compassionate, the Merciful, I, Tunku Abdul Rahman Putra, Prime Minister of the Persekutuan Tanah Melayu, with the concurrence and approval of Their Highnesses the Rulers of the Malay States do hereby proclaim and declare on behalf of the people ... that as from the thirty first day of August nineteen hundred and fifty-seven, the Persekutuan Tanah Melayu ... shall be forever a sovereign democratic and independent State founded upon the principle of liberty and justice and ever seeking the welfare and happiness of its people and the maintenance of a just peace among all nations.[130]

The *Merdeka* vision of Tunku Abdul Rahman for 'a sovereign democratic and independent State founded upon the principle of liberty and justice' is a vision that is held dearly by the Malaysian public. Whether that vision can ever attain complete realization depends on the strength of the separation of powers doctrine in Malaysia. The unfolding story in the subsequent chapters of this book narrates the blurring of the constitutional constraints on powers of various arms of government and the struggles within the political and judicial arenas to clarify and defend those constraints.

The constitutional document that marked the birth certificate of a nation was infused with the spirit of British traditions and law. Rais Yatim remarked:

> With independence, the British legacy in matters having to do with the administration of the country continued, although gradually thereafter things began to take shape into the new Malayan way. The judiciary and administration of criminal justice, land and district administration, the Malayan Civil Service (MCS), police powers in handling security, law and order, the handling of emergency rule, among others, retained much of the British way.[131]

Lumpur into a financial hub. He is also the chair of the board of advisors to 1MDB. *The Wall Street Journal* (WSJ) and the *Sarawak Report* reported the story that a sum of RM 2.6 billion (US$700 million) was traced to bank accounts believed to be controlled by Najib Razak. 'WSJ: 1MDB's RM2.6b found in "PM's accounts"' (3 July 2015) https://www.malaysiakini.com/news/303876 (accessed 29 March 2016). The Deputy Prime Minister (Muhyiddin Yusuf) who called on Najib Razak to answer questions about 1MDB was removed from office. The Federal Attorney General (Abdul Gani Patail) was also removed and replaced by a former Federal Court judge (Mohamed Apandi Ali). Najib Razak has been facing public denunciation and calls to resign, with Mahathir Mohamad leading the charge. A remarkable event occurred when Mahathir Mohamad, 4 days after resigning from UMNO, teamed up with a group of more than fifty prominent politicians and civil society leaders in signing a 'Citizens' Declaration', which urged 'Malaysians to join them in removing Najib Razak through non-violent and legally permissible means'. V Anbalagan, 'For now, Najib's fate in the hands of 222 MPs, says ex-A-G' *Malaysian Insider* (9 March 2016) http://www.themalaysianoutsider.com/malaysia/article/for-now-najibs-fate-in-the-hands-of-222-mps-says-ex-a-g (accessed 9 March 2016).

[130] Tunku Abdul Rahman, 'Proclamation of Independence', Merdeka Stadium, Kuala Lumpur, 31 August 1957.

[131] Rais Yatinm (n 22) 23.

The British legacy was much more extensive than that described by Rais Yatim. The style of government in Malaysia reflects the Westminster model. The doctrine of responsible government permeates through the constitutional framework. The divergence lay in the explicit declaration of the supremacy of the Constitution, instead of subscription to the British doctrine of parliamentary supremacy. Mohamed Suffian captured it succinctly with the statement, 'In Malaysia, only the constitution is supreme.'[132] In consequence, the Malaysian judiciary really has the power to uphold the rule of law by declaring legislation and executive acts that infringe the fundamental guarantees and the constitutional limitations provided by the Constitution to be invalid. Many political conflicts have manifested themselves as constitutional conflicts, thus drawing the courts into sensitive arenas. To perform its role as constitutional guardian, the judiciary has to be able to command the confidence of the public. The true test for the judiciary may arise down the track, when it finds itself at the eye of a constitutional storm, when it becomes blatantly obvious that those who control the levers of power are seeking to obliterate Tunku's vision of 'a sovereign democratic and independent State founded upon the principle of liberty and justice' and replace it with authoritarian rule.

[132] Tun Mohamed Suffian, *An Introduction to the Constitution of Malaysia* (2nd edn, Government Printer 1976) 17.

2

The Constitutional Crisis of 1983

> For so long as the Yang di-Pertuan Agong and Rulers abide by the Constitution and play their part properly as Father of the Nation or, in the case of Rulers, Father of the State, and do not get involved in public chicanery and scandals, the public will continue to respect and love them.
>
> Tun Mohamed Suffian, 'Role of the Monarchy' in *Reflections on the Malaysian Constitution* (Aliran 1987) 41.

Two major confrontations in the life of the Constitution occurred during 1983–93, between the Mahathir government and the Malay Rulers. The 1983 constitutional crisis was predominantly focused on the King's power to assent to legislation in relation to federal legislation and on the State Rulers' equivalent power in relation to State legislation.[1] The 1993 constitutional crisis was centred on a proposed constitutional amendment advanced by the federal government that sought to abrogate the Malay Rulers' personal immunity. These two major confrontations resulted in a bruising victory for the federal government over the Malay Rulers. The State Rulers were forced to confront and defer to the reality that they have to act as monarchs within a representative democracy. The ultimate victory of the Mahathir Government over the State Rulers could be construed as a triumph for constitutionalism.

The constitutional crisis of 1983 should be viewed against the backdrop of the fact that amendments to the Federal Constitution are not uncommon in Malaysia.[2] Given the fact that the government in power has—in the period

[1] HP Lee, 'The 1983 Constitutional Crisis' in in Andrew Harding and HP Lee (eds), *Constitutional Landmarks in Malaysia: The First 50 Years 1957–2007* (LexisNexis 2007) 157–64; S Barraclough and P Arudsothy, 'The 1983 Malaysian Constitutional Crisis: Two Views and Select Documents' (Australia-Asia Papers, No. 32, Centre for the Study of Australian-Asian Relations, Griffith University, 1980); V Lowe, 'Redefining the "Constitutionality" of the Monarchy: The 1983 Constitutional Amendment Crisis in Malaysia' (1984) 2(2) Kajian Malaysia 1–15; HF Rawlings, 'The Malaysian Constitutional Crisis of 1983' (1986) 35(2) International and Comparative Law Quarterly 237–56; AJ Stockwell, 'Princes and Politicians: The Constitutional Crisis in Malaysia, 1983-84' in DA Low, *Constitutional Heads and Political Crises: Commonwealth Episodes, 1945-85* (St Martin's Press 1988) 182–97.

[2] See LA Sheridan and HE Groves, *The Constitution of Malaysia* (3rd edn, Malayan Law Journal Pte Ltd 1979) 14–24; HP Lee, 'The Process of Constitutional Change in Malaysia' in Tun Mohamed Suffian, HP Lee and FA Trindade (eds), *The Constitution of Malaysia: Its Development: 1957-1977* (OUP 1978) 369; HP Lee, 'Constitutional Amendments in Malaysia' (1976) 18 Malaya LR 59; Tan Sri Salleh Abas, 'Amendment of the Malaysian Constitution' (1977) 2 MLJ xxxiv.

since independence until 2008—commanded more than two-thirds of the seats of both Houses of the Federal Parliament, thus enabling it to amend the Constitution without constraints, constitutional amendments hardly engender extreme excitement. However, intense national interest was generated by the refusal of the Yang di-Pertuan Agong, Sultan Ahmad Shah, to assent to the Constitution (Amendment) Bill 1983. What was the significance of the 1983 Amendment Bill? What were the motives of the government in mooting the amendments? An attempt is made in this chapter to review the chain of events and to clarify many of the constitutional issues that were clouded by the confrontation between the dissenting parties.

Some Relevant Provisions of the Constitution

Before the constitutional issues thrown up by the crisis are isolated and analysed, it is necessary to draw attention to some relevant provisions of the Federal Constitution. Article 66 of the Constitution provides for the 'exercise of legislative power'. Article 66(1) provides that the power of Parliament to make laws shall be exercised by Bills passed by both Houses (or, in the cases mentioned in Article 68, the House of Representatives) and assented to by the Yang di-Pertuan Agong. Article 66(5) declares: 'A Bill shall become law on being assented to by the Yang di-Pertuan Agong, but no law shall come into force until it has been published, without prejudice, however, to the power of Parliament to postpone the operation of any law or to make laws with retrospective effect.'

The provision, which is of fundamental importance to the constitutional validity of the Constitution (Amendment) Bill 1983, is Article 38(4), which states that 'no law directly affecting the privileges, position, honours or dignities of the Rulers shall be passed without the consent of the Conference of Rulers'. It is also provided in Article 38(6) that the members of the Conference of Rulers may act in their *discretion* in any proceedings relating to, inter alia, 'the giving or withholding of consent to any law … affecting the privileges, position, honours or dignities of the Rulers'.

Article 159 deals with 'Amendment of the Constitution'. In brief, the general process of effecting changes to the Constitution requires that the amendment Bill must be supported in each House of Parliament by the votes of not less than two-thirds of the total number of members of that House. A number of amendments that do not pertain to the present discussion are excepted from this general process (see Article 159(4)). Article 159(5) states: 'A law making an amendment to Clause (4) of Article 10, any law passed thereunder, the provisions of Part III, Article 38, 63(4), 70, 71(1), 72(4), 152 or 153 or to this Clause shall not be passed without the consent of the Conference of Rulers.' Now, it should be noted that neither Article 66 nor Section 11(3) of the Eighth Schedule is included among the provisions spelt out in Article 159(5), which requires the consent of the Conference of

Rulers. Section 11(3) of the Eighth Schedule, which contains a provision equivalent to Article 66(5), requires the assent of a State Ruler for the enactment of state legislation.

The Constitution (Amendment) Bill 1983

In tracing the events of 1983, one has to look back to the months of July and August of 1983. During that period, the Dewan Rakyat (House of Representatives) and the Dewan Negara (Senate) passed the Constitution (Amendment) Bill 1983 (hereafter also referred to as the '1983 Bill'). The controversy arose from three key provisions of the 1983 Bill: clauses 12(b), 20, and 21.

Clause 12(b)

Clause 12(b) seeks to amend Article 66(5) of the Constitution by substituting it with the following:

> (5) A Bill shall become law on being assented to by the Yang di-Pertuan Agong. If for any reason whatsoever the Bill is not assented to within fifteen days of the Bill being presented to the Yang di-Pertuan Agong, he shall be deemed to have assented to the Bill and the Bill shall accordingly become law.
>
> (5A) No law shall come into force until it has been published, without prejudice, however, to the power of Parliament to postpone the operation of any law or to make laws with retrospective effect.

Thus the thrust of this amendment effected by clause 12(b) of the 1983 Bill is to provide for the royal assent to be 'deemed' to have been given after a lapse of 15 days from the day of presentation to the Yang di-Pertuan Agong.

Clause 21

The substance of clause 21 of the Bill is best explained before clause 20 is dealt with for the very simple reason that the 'deeming' provision, which is sought to be achieved at the Federal level, is intended to apply to assent to State legislation by the State Rulers. Each State Ruler assents to legislation passed by the Legislative Assembly of the state. Clause 21 seeks to amend Section 11(3) of Part I of the Eighth Schedule to the Constitution, which provides that 'a Bill shall become law on being assented to by the Ruler'. Under the proposed amendment, if a Bill passed by the Legislative Assembly of a State is not assented to within 15 days of its being presented to the Ruler, he shall be deemed to have assented to it, and the Bill shall, accordingly, become law. The Federal Parliament is able to alter the state constitutions to bring about this 'deeming' requirement by virtue of Article 71(4). Article 71(4) provides that, if at any time a State Constitution does not contain the provisions set out in Part I of the Eighth Schedule (the essential provisions), or provisions substantially to the same effect, or contains provisions inconsistent with the essential provisions, the Federal Parliament may, notwithstanding anything in the Federal Constitution, by law make provision for giving effect in that state to the essential provisions or for removing the inconsistent provisions.

Clause 20

The thrust of clause 20 of the 1983 Bill is the proposed amendment of Article 150 to provide for the issuance of a Proclamation of Emergency by the Yang di-Pertuan Agong, if the Prime Minister is satisfied that a grave emergency exists, whereby the security or the economic life or public order in the Federation or any part thereof, is threatened. The proposed amendment replaces the 'satisfaction' of the Yang di-Pertuan Agong with the 'satisfaction' of the Prime Minister. The implications of this proposed amendment will be considered at a later stage.

Some relevant background facts

Why did the Government propose these amendments? No official reason was given but it is easy to piece together the picture. The general opinion was that the Constitution (Amendment) Bill 1983 was prompted by the impending change of the (Yang di-Pertuan Agong) in April 1984.[3] As Tan Chee Khoon, in his column 'Without Fear or Favour' in the *Star*, put it: 'In April, the reign of the present King will come to an end. A new one will be elected, with most likely candidates for the throne being the Sultan of Perak and the Sultan of Johor. Both of them are strong-willed and are quite likely to defy the Government. This prospect is not quite relished by the Government and it set about to curb the powers of not only the King but also his brother rulers as well.'[4]

[3] Malaysia's constitutional system of a rotating kingship has been described by the first Prime Minister of Malaysia, Tunku Abdul Rahman, as 'a unique institution'—Tunku Abdul Rahman, *Viewpoints* (Heinemann 1978) 71. The office of the Yang di-Pertuan Agong, a Ruler elected for 5 years by Rulers, is an adaptation of the office of the Ruler (Yang di-Pertuan Besar) in Negri Sembilan. Tunku Abdul Rahman explained: 'When the time came to institute the high office of the Yang Dipertuan Agung, it was difficult to decide whether to appoint the incumbent for the rest of his life or for a term of years. It was then that I conceived the idea of calling the high office of the Yang Dipertuan Agung, which literally means "The Supreme Ruler of All the Rulers", following what had been instituted in Negeri Sembilan where nine chiefs migrated from Minangkabau, Sumatra and founded nine states in Central Malaya, calling them Negeri Sembilan (the nine states).' (*Viewpoints* 72)

In relation to the current system of electing the Ruler of Negri Sembilan, Tun Mohamed Suffian said: '[The Yang Dipertuan Besar] is elected by the Undangs of Sungai Ujong, Jelebu, Johol and Rembau. On his death the four Undangs choose a successor from among his male issue, but they may, if they think that there is no suitable and competent person among his male issue, choose another suitable and competent person, giving preference first to the brothers of the Yang Dipertuan Besar, secondly to his paternal uncles and then to others.' (Tun Mohammed Suffian, *An Introduction to The Constitution of Malaysia* (2nd edn, Government Printer 1976) 35.

[4] Tan Chee Khoon, 'The Will of the People Must Prevail', *The Star* (Penang, 4 January 1984) 20.

Election to the office of Yang di-Pertuan Agong

As there are nine hereditary Rulers in the Malaysian Federation, and as the King is appointed by the hereditary Rulers from among themselves, how can one predict whom the likely Yang di-Pertuan Agong would be? The answer is not difficult to obtain for the election of the Yang di-Pertuan Agong is regulated by the provisions of the Constitution. The Yang di-Pertuan Agong is elected by the Conference of Rulers, which, for this specific purpose, comprises only the nine hereditary Rulers.[5] In exercising the function of electing the Yang di-Pertuan Agong, the Conference of Rulers is required by Article 38(2) of the Constitution to act in accordance with the provisions of the Third Schedule.

Part I of the Third Schedule sets out the prescription for the election of the Yang di-Pertuan Agong. A Ruler is qualified to be elected Yang di-Pertuan Agong unless he is a minor, or has notified the Keeper of the Rulers' Seal that he does not desire to be elected, or the Conference of Rulers by secret ballot resolves that he is unsuitable by reason of infirmity of mind or body or for any other cause to exercise the functions of Yang di-Pertuan Agong.[6] The selection centres on an 'election list'. The election list for the first election in 1957 comprised the Malay States ranked in the order in which the State Rulers recognized precedence among themselves. According to Professor FA Trindade, 'The order of precedence was based on the dates of accession to the thrones of the several States and the list in order of precedence was Johor, Pahang, Negri Sembilan, Selangor, Kedah, Perlis, Kelantan, Terengganu, and Perak.'[7] The office of Yang di-Pertuan Agong is offered to the Ruler qualified for election whose state is first on the election list and, if he does not accept the office, to the Ruler whose State is next on the list, and so on until a Ruler accepts the office. After each election, any state preceding the one whose Ruler was elected shall be transferred (in the order in which they are then on the list) to the end of the list; the state whose Ruler was elected shall be omitted. Whenever there is a change in the Ruler of a state on the list, that state shall be transferred to the end of the list. For the 1984 election of the next Yang di-Pertuan Agong, the election list was headed by Perak and Johor.

Justification for the fears of the Federal Government

Under the rotation system embodied in the Constitution, the likely successor would be the Sultan of Johor, as he was more senior than the Sultan of Perak. HF Rawlings

[5] Section 7 of the Fifth Schedule stipulates that the State Governors 'shall not be members of the Conference of Rulers for the purposes of any proceedings relating to the election or removal of the Yang di-Pertuan Agong or the election of the Timbalan Yang di-Pertuan Agong or relating solely to the privileges, position, honours and dignities of Their Royal Highnesses or to religious acts, observances or ceremonies.'

[6] Section 1(1), Part 1, Third Schedule.

[7] Francis A Trindade, 'The Constitutional Position of the Yang di-Pertuan Agong' in Tun Suffian, Lee and Trindade (eds), *The Constitution of Malaysia: Its Development: 1957–1977* (OUP 1978) 103. See also Tun Suffian, *An Introduction to the Constitution of Malaysia* (2nd edn, Government Printers 1972) chap. 3.

said: '[I]t was reported that at least one of the candidate Rulers had spoken openly of an intention, on assuming the office of Agong, to declare a Proclamation of Emergency under Article 150 of the Constitution and seek to exercise some governmental powers himself.'[8]

In the light of a number of incidents involving the Rulers of some states the Federal Government had, it could be argued, some basis for its fear that it might have to deal with a 'defiant' Yang di-Pertuan Agong. These incidents involved, inter alia, the Rulers of Perak (Sultan Idris) and Johor (Sultan Mahmood Iskandar).[9] The following accounts of incidents concerning these two Rulers and their Chief Ministers (Menteri Besar) were described, extra-curially, by the then Lord President of the Federal Court of Malaysia, Raja Tun Azlan Shah:

> [A]t State level things have not been so smooth sailing. It was well known that the Sultan of Perak and his former Menteri Besar, Tan Sri Ghazali Jawi, were not on good terms. However as the Menteri Besar had the confidence of his party, there was nothing that the Sultan could do to replace him with another Menteri Besar. The Sultan refused to attend any functions where Tan Sri Ghazali was present. The matter got so bad that the Sultan finally decided to sport a beard, and vowed that he would only shave it off after Tan Sri Ghazali had left the office of Menteri Besar. The crisis was solved when the Menteri Besar, on the advice of his party leaders, resigned from office. Another name was submitted to the Sultan and the Sultan appointed him as Menteri Besar.[10]

After referring to a similar incident which occurred in Pahang, and which was solved in the same way as in Perak, Raja Tun Azlan Shah went on to describe the incident involving the Sultan of Johor and the Menteri Besar, Datuk Haji Othman bin Saat:

> From reports in the press it seems that the Sultan could not get along with the Menteri Besar. His Royal Highness even ordered the Menteri Besar to vacate his office premises as he (the Sultan) wanted to occupy the office. The Menteri Besar vacated the premises. But

[8] HF Rawlings, 'The Malaysian Constitutional Crisis of 1983' (1986) 35(2) ICLQ 237, 246. Rawlings, at 246, added: '[T]he Ruler of Johore, at least, had a reputation as a somewhat colourful character, and his high-spirited exuberance had, prior to his accession to the throne of Johore, twice led to criminal convictions for offences involving personal injury to others.' In relation to his prosecution and conviction, see *Public Prosecutor v Tengku Mahmood Iskandar* [1973] 1 MLJ 128; *PP v Tunku Mahmood Iskandar* [1977] 2 MLJ 123.

[9] Tunku Abdul Rahman, in 1977 in commenting on the responsibility of the Rulers, recalled an occasion when he was approached by a Ruler complaining about a Menteri Besar 'who had not considered his application for mining-land' and that he 'would like him replaced with someone else who would be more amenable'. Tunku responded: 'I told the Ruler that the Menteri Besar was the elected representative of the people. It was his duty to uphold the Constitution and to carry out the administration with honour and fairness. If his Royal Highness could prove that he was not doing his duty, then he could be replaced; otherwise he was there until the people chose to displace him.'—Tunku Abdul Rahman, *Looking Back* (Pustaka Antara 1977) 214.

[10] Raja Tun Azlan Shah, 'The Role of Constitutional Rulers: A Malaysian Perspective for the Laity' (1982) 1 Journal of Malaysian and Comparative Law 6 (reproduced as 'The Role of Constitutional Rulers in Malaysia' in Francis A Trindade and HP Lee (eds), *The Constitution of Malaysia: Further Perspectives and Developments* ch 5). It was reported that the royal beard was shaved in full view of photographers when Tan Sri Ghazali left office—*National Times* (18–24 November 1983).

as the general election was just round the corner, the Menteri Besar stayed on. However he did not seek re-election.[11]

Thus as Sultan Idris of Perak and Sultan Mahmood Iskandar of Johor would probably be elected the new Yang di-Pertuan Agong and Timbalan Yang di-Pertuan Agong (Deputy King) respectively, one can understand the impetus behind the Constitution (Amendment) Bill 1983.[12] The Constitution (Amendment) Bill 1983 'constituted the Federal Government's attempt at pre-emptive strike to mitigate the effects of the election of an autocratic or unpredictable Agong'.[13]

The gathering storm burst upon the Mahathir Government when the Constitution (Amendment) Bill 1983, designed to forestall a future crisis, provoked a constitutional crisis 'that rocked the nation to its very foundations'.[14] The crisis stemmed from the refusal of the Yang di-Pertuan Agong to give royal assent to the Bill. Tan Chee Khoon wrote:

> The King had earlier on been briefed by the Prime Minister about the amendments and he had agreed to them. But apparently he did not quite understand the full import of the amendment to the Eighth Schedule or he had not been briefed on them. When his brother Rulers realised the full impact of the amendment to Schedule Eight they were up in arms.

Led by the Sultans of Perak and Johor, they resolved that the Yang di-Pertuan Agong should not give the Royal Assent to the Bill. Then at the Conference of Rulers in Kota Kinabalu in October, the Rulers voted 8 to 0 against the acceptance of the amendments.[15]

The legal issues

The central question in the ensuing controversy was whether the Yang di-Pertuan Agong was constitutionally bound to assent to the legislation. In other words, was the King obligated to assent automatically to any legislation passed by both Houses

[11] Raja Tun Azlan Shah, 'The Role of Constitutional Rulers: A Malaysian Perspective for the Laity' 6. The Sultan of Pahang was another Ruler whose refusal to assent to State legislation for over two years compelled the resignation of the Chief Minister of that State. See *Asiaweek* (24 February 1984) 31–2.

[12] This legislative response was finally triggered off by a dispute over the date to mark the end of the fasting month of Ramadan, i.e. the date for Hari Raya Aidilfitri. Means explained:

> 'The Constitution gave authority over Islamic affairs to each Malay Ruler, but to co-ordinate Islamic policy, the Federal Government in 1968 had formed the National Islamic Religious Affairs Council. The Sultans of Johore and Perak had withdrawn from the Council to preserve their autonomy. When the Council, under federal direction, picked one of two authorized methods to determine the correct date, Johore and Perak proceeded to pick the other method; this produced a different date and created confusion and distress within the Malay community with regard to their most important religious holiday.'—Gordon P Means, *Malaysian Politics: The Second Generation* (OUP 1991) 114. See also AJ Stockwell, 'Princes and Politicians: The Constitutional Crisis in Malaysia, 1983–4' in DA Low (ed), *Constitutional Heads and Crises* (Macmillan 1988) 186.

[13] HF Rawlings, 'The Malaysian Constitutional Crisis of 1983' (1986) 35(2) ICLQ 237, 248.

[14] Tan Chee Khoon, 'The Will of the People Must Prevail' *The Star* (Penang, 4 January 1984).

[15] ibid.

of Parliament? In his essay on 'The Constitutional Position of the Yang di-Pertuan Agong', Trindade said, 'For a Bill to become law it is necessary that it be passed by both Houses of Parliament and be assented to by the Yang di-Pertuan Agong. The Yang di-Pertuan Agong signifies his assent to a Bill by causing the Public Seal to be fixed to the Bill. An air of unreality surrounds the assent of the Yang di-Pertuan Agong because the *assent can never be withheld*.'[16] Trindade also drew attention to the following comments of Justice Abdul Hamid in his note of dissent to the proposals of the Reid Commission:

> If this article is allowed to remain in the draft as it stands the Yang di-Pertuan (Besar) Agong will have no choice in the matter of assent. He shall be bound to assent to the Bill passed by the two Houses. In other words a Bill passed by the two Houses shall become law. If this is the intention, it is far better to approach this subject direct by saying ... that a Bill passed by the two Houses shall become law. No mention of assent is necessary at all. But if assent is to be mentioned the Constitution should give the power to the Yang di-Pertuan (Besar) Agong to accord assent or to withhold assent. In all constitutions the power to accord assent goes with the power to withhold assent.[17]

Trindade went on to say, 'Nevertheless, it does not seem possible for the Yang di-Pertuan Agong to withhold assent to a Bill passed by both Houses of Parliament.'[18]

A similar stand appears to have been taken by Raja Tun Azlan Shah. National attention was focused on the article, 'The Role of Constitutional Rulers', written by him in the *Journal of Malaysian and Comparative Law*.[19] In his article, Raja Tun Azlan Shah referred to the federal constitutional provisions concerning the royal assent and pointed out that 'similar provisions are also to be found in the State Constitutions regarding the Ruler and the State Legislative Assembly'. He said:

> In Malaysia, the role of the Rulers is specifically provided for in the Constitutions and the Rulers have no power to refuse. It is most unfortunate, therefore, that the Regent of Pahang, as reported in the Press recently, because of differences with the Menteri Besar, refused to signify his assent to a Bill passed by the State Legislative Assembly. Such refusal is clearly unconstitutional.[20]

Raja Tun Azlan Shah also referred to the position in England where 'it is only by convention that assent is not withheld. The right of veto has not been exercised since the reign of Queen Anne. It may be said to have fallen into disuse as a consequence of ministerial responsibility.'[21]

In the light of the above assertions, was the Yang di-Pertuan Agong acting unconstitutionally in refusing to assent to the 1983 Bill?[22] It is submitted that the answer

[16] In Tun Mohamed Suffian, Lee and Trindade, *The Constitution of Malaysia: Its Development: 1957–1977* (OUP 1978) 103. Emphasis added.

[17] *Report of the Federation of Malaya Constitutional Commission* (1957) 102.

[18] Tun Mohamed Suffian, Lee and Trindade, *The Constitution of Malaysia: Its Development: 1957–1977* (OUP 1978) 111.

[19] Raja Azlan Shah, 'The Role of Constitutional Rulers: A Malaysian Perspective for the Laity' (1982) 1 Journal of Malaysian and Comparative Law 1.

[20] ibid 14. [21] ibid 13.

[22] The Attorney General, in his opinion to the Prime Minister, appeared to suggest that it was *illegal* for the King to refuse assent for he said, 'It is a *duty* of the Yang di-Pertuan Agong under the

in the Malaysian constitutional context is not clear-cut. At the Federal level, the assertions of Trindade and Raja Tun Azlan Shah are tenable if they are intended to provide for a general but not an absolute rule. It must be remembered that in England there is no written provision equivalent to Article 38(4). The language of Article 38(4) is very clear: 'No law directly affecting the privileges ... of the Rulers shall be passed without the consent of the Conference of Rulers.' To harmonize the operation of different provisions of the Constitution, Article 38(4) must be seen as an exception to the general rule. Thus, if a proposed law is seen to affect the privileges of the Rulers, the obtaining of the consent of the Conference of Rulers is the *prior* step to be taken before it is passed into law.

It may, however, be argued that, even though the 1983 Bill is unconstitutional on the ground of an infringement of Article 38(4), this does not justify a refusal of assent by the Yang di-Pertuan Agong. Otherwise, the Yang di-Pertuan Agong would assume the role of a self-appointed constitutional court, and this could lead to a situation in which the Yang di-Pertuan Agong could refuse assent to *any* Bill on the ground of some supposed unconstitutionality. Such an argument does not preclude the Bill from being invalidated *after* the royal assent has been given. It is submitted that this argument ignores the peculiar nature of the Malaysian Constitution. Under Article 38(2) the Conference of Rulers is entrusted with the function, inter alia, of 'consenting or withholding consent to any law ... which under this Constitution requires the consent of the Conference ...' Article 38(6) furthermore provides that the members of the Conference of Rulers 'may act in their discretion' in any proceedings relating to '(c) the giving or withholding of consent to any law ... affecting the privileges, position, honours or dignities of the Rulers'. To accede to the argument that the Yang di-Pertuan Agong *must* assent to the 1983 bill would lead to an undermining of the provisions of Article 38(2) and (6). The argument also ignores the dilemma of the Yang di-Pertuan Agong when confronted with a decision of the Conference of Rulers to withhold consent. The argument of abuse can be refuted by highlighting Article 130, which provides for resort by the government to the advisory opinion jurisdiction of the Federal Court.

If the view that there must be compliance with Article 38(4) before the royal assent is given is accepted, then it is important to determine whether the proposed law is a law that fulfils the description of a law 'affecting the privileges, position, honours or dignities of the Rulers'. It must also be determined whether the law 'directly' affects these privileges, position, honours, or dignities.

One of the factors contributing to the confusion at the height of the crisis was the failure, by many of the participants, to view the three main proposed amendments

Constitution to assent to any Bill passed by Parliament' (Annexe 1). This statement, with respect, could not be accurate for the existence of a 'duty' depended upon the availability of means to enforce it. At that stage, enforceability was not possible especially in the Malaysian context for the King, before 1993, was not subject to process in court. Article 32(1), in its unamended form, provided that the King 'shall not be liable to any proceedings whatsoever in any court'. The argument would have to proceed based on a breach of a constitutional convention. However, in the case of a breach of convention the redress lay in the political and not the judicial arena.

separately. It is submitted that the case for the invalidity of clause 21 of the 1983 Bill is stronger than for clauses 12 and 20.

The Constitution does not provide for a definition of the terms employed in Article 38(4). The words *privileges, position, honours*, and *dignities* do carry different meanings. Among the many meanings in the second edition of the *Oxford English Dictionary* are the following:

privilege: 'the special right or immunity attaching to some office, rank, or station'
position: 'place in the social scale; social state or standing; status; rank; estate'
honours: 'something conferred or done as a token of respect or distinction; a mark or manifestation of high regard; esp. a position or title of rank, a degree of nobility, a dignity'
dignity: 'worthiness, worth, nobleness, excellence'.

The privileges of the Rulers would encompass the prerogative powers. In relation to the royal assent of the monarch in the United Kingdom, it is regarded as 'a prerogative power of the monarch.'[23] In a recent article, Graham John Wheeler said, 'In principle, then, Royal Assent is a broad discretionary power which lies in the hands of the sovereign. Yet it is truism that this power has been severely cut down over the years, by convention if not by law.'[24] He also states that the literature points to three categories of Bills 'in respect of which Royal Assent might potentially be withheld by a twenty-first century monarch.'[25] The category ('Category 1') which is of significance 'consists of legislation which subverts some fundamental constitutional principle.'[26]

It can be argued that clause 21 of the 1983 Bill, by providing for the assent of the State Rulers to be dispensed with after a lapse of 15 days, would affect the privileges of the State Rulers. However, if the stand taken is based upon the proposition that refusal by the Rulers to assent to legislation is clearly unconstitutional, then what privileges have been affected? How could their 'privileges' have been affected if they have lost nothing? Such an argument can be refuted in the following way. Before the 1983 Bill, the Rulers had an unspecified period to give assent to a Bill. Clause 21 has affected such a privilege by compressing the unspecified period into a period of 15 days. Clause 21, therefore, requires the consent of the Conference of Rulers as it affects the Rulers' privileges.[27]

The constriction of the period for the Rulers to assent to a Bill applies at the Federal level to the Yang di-Pertuan Agong by virtue of clause 12(b). Does this clause require the consent of the Conference of Rulers? The case for this clause is

[23] David Feldman, *English Public Law* (2nd edn, OUP 2009) 29.

[24] Graham John Wheeler, 'Royal Assent in the British Constitution' (2016) 132 LQR 493, 496.

[25] ibid 498. [26] ibid 498.

[27] In his opinion to the Prime Minister, the Attorney General said, 'It is to be noted that this Article [i.e. Article 38(4)] does not relate to the functions and powers of the Yang di-Pertuan Agong or Their Royal Highnesses the Rulers under the Federal Constitution or the State Constitution. One of the functions of the Yang di-Pertuan Agong under the Constitution is to signify assent to any Bill which has been passed by Parliament. That function cannot in my opinion be said to be or deemed to be privileges, position, honours or dignities.' Quaere: If that function attaches to the Yang di-Pertuan Agong by virtue of his office, is not that a 'privilege'?

much weaker. Article 38(4) refers to the privileges, and the like, of the 'Rulers'. Article 160 provides the following definition of 'Ruler':

(a) in relation to Negri Sembilan, means the Yang di-Pertuan Besar acting on behalf of himself and the Ruling Chiefs in accordance with the Constitution of that State; and

(b) in the case of any State, includes, except in Article 181(2) and the Third and Fifth Schedules, any person who in accordance with the Constitution of that State exercises the function of the Ruler.

The Yang di-Pertuan Agong is prohibited by Article 34(1) of the Federal Constitution from exercising his functions as Ruler of his state except those of head of the religion of Islam.[28] The Constitution envisages the Yang di-Pertuan Agong, on his assumption of office, to be a separate and distinct personality from the State Rulers. On that basis, clause 12(b) is not caught by Article 38(4) as it affects the 'privileges' of the Yang di-Pertuan Agong only. This submission can also be reinforced by giving prominence to the word 'directly' in Article 38(4).[29] The arguments in relation to clause 12(b) apply equally to clause 20.

It can also be argued that the amendment of the Constitution is provided for exclusively in Article 159. Article 159(5) provides *expressly* for the consent of the Conference of Rulers in respect of amendments to the following provisions of the Constitution: Clause (4) of Article 10, and any law passed thereunder, the provisions of Part III, Article 38, 63(4), 70, 71(1), 72(4), 152, 153, or 159(5) itself. As Article 159(5) does not include Article 66 and Section 11(3) of the Eighth Schedule to the Constitution, amendments to these excluded provisions, consequently, do not require the consent of the Conference of Rulers. Furthermore, the provisions of the Constitution may be amended by federal law 'subject to the following provisions of this Article [i.e. Article 159] and to Article 161E' only.[30] The amendment process is not expressly subjected to Article 38(4).

Article 38(4) speaks of 'no law ...' 'Law' is defined in Article 160 as including 'written law, the common law in so far as it is in operation in the Federation or any part thereof, and any custom or usage having the force of law in the Federation

[28] Article 34(1). However, nothing in Article 34(1):

shall prevent the Yang di-Pertuan Agong exercising as Ruler of his State any power vested in him either above or in conjunction with any other authority-
(a) to amend the Constitution of the State; or
(b) to appoint a Regent or member of a Council of Regency in the place of any Regent or member, as the case may be, who has died or has become incapable for any reason of performing the duties of the offices of Regent or member of the Council of Regency respectively. Article 34(8).

[29] However, the danger in building up an argument around the word *directly* is that it can lead into a semantic maze. On the one hand, it may be argued that whilst the privileges of the Yang di-Pertuan Agong are affected directly, the privileges of the Rulers are at the most affected indirectly. On the other hand, the direct/indirect dichotomy loses its significance depending on the scope given to the meaning of 'privileges, position etc.' It may be argued that one of the privileges of a Ruler is the privilege of assenting to Federal legislation when elected King. Hence, the privilege is directly affected even though a Ruler can exercise it only when he is elected King.

[30] Article 159(1).

or any part thereof'. Article 160 also defines 'written law' as including 'this Constitution and the constitution of any State'. It can be argued that Article 38(4) catches within its ambit a law that amends the Constitution. The proscription is not confined to an ordinary Act of Parliament. Article 38(4) and Article 159 appear to be inconsistent with one another. Unless the conflict is resolved in favour of an overriding Article 38(4), the protection vested in the Conference of Rulers to preserve their 'privileges, position, honours or dignities' would be negated by a two-thirds majority in the Federal Parliament. While such a construction (i.e. giving overriding effect to Article 38(4)) may be decried as being inconsistent with a parliamentary democracy, it must be acknowledged that the system of government prescribed by the constitutional framework envisages a power of veto vested in the Conference of Rulers in respect of certain specified matters. The problem is not posed by the suggested construction of the constitutional provisions but by having the power of veto in an unelected body in the first place. If such a power is to be abolished the government must, by virtue of Article 159(5), obtain the consent of the Conference of Rulers first in order to bring about a *valid* constitutional amendment.

Resolving the impasse

When the Rulers refused to budge in relation to their opposition to the controversial provisions of the 1983 Bill, despite a meeting with a delegation of the Supreme Council of United Malays National Organisation (UMNO), the Prime Minister 'went barnstorming all over the country'.[31] Mass meetings were held to drum up support for the government's stand. The local news media, which had been reined in for over two months, were allowed to report the crisis.[32] Mass rallies were held by the Prime Minister around the country with extensive media coverage devoted to these rallies but little mention was made of those rallies held in support of the Malay Rulers. 'Several newspapers controlled or owned by UMNO interests published articles on the lavish lifestyles of certain members of royalty.'[33] Eventually, after much negotiation between the government and the Rulers, the Acting Yang di-Pertuan Agong, Tuanku Jaafar Abdul Rahman, signed the 1983 Bill, which became the Constitution (Amendment) Act 1983. This assent was given pursuant to an agreement reached between the Rulers and the government. Apart from a written agreement, it was also reported that there was an 'oral undertaking' agreed to between the government and the Rulers concerning the 15-day royal assent rule in

[31] *The Star* (Penang, 5 January 1984).

[32] The editors of all newspapers were called to a meeting with the Home Affairs ministry and asked 'to play down the issue'—V Lowe, 'Redefining the "Constitutionality" of the Monarchy: The 1983 Constitutional Amendment Crisis in Malaysia' (1984) 2(2) Kajian Malaysia 7–8. The constraint was removed when an UMNO politician (Dato' Senu bin Abdul Rahman) wrote an open letter to the Prime Minister querying the constitutional validity of the proposed amendments.

[33] S Barraclough and P Arudsothy, 'The 1983 Malaysian Constitutional Crisis: Two Views and Select Documents' (Australia-Asia Papers, No 32, Centre for the Study of Australian-Asian Relations, Griffith University 1980) 8.

respect of state legislation. Because of the agreement and oral undertaking, the government introduced a Bill that became the Constitution (Amendment) Act 1984.

The Constitution (Amendment) Act 1984

The Constitution (Amendment) Act 1984 (hereafter referred to as the '1984 Act') contained provisions that have the effect of amending the amendments introduced by the 1983 Act. In the 1984 Act, the government retracted two of the three key proposals objected to by the Rulers: clauses 20 and 21 of the 1983 Bill. On the third proposal contained in clause 12(b) of the 1983 Bill, a compromise was reached.

Assent of the Yang di-Pertuan Agong

The Constitution, as amended by the 1984 Act, now provides that a Bill presented to the Yang di-Pertuan Agong for his assent shall be assented to by him within 30 days after it is presented to him. However, in the case of a Bill that is not a money Bill, he may within such a period of 30 days return the Bill to the House in which the Bill had originated, with a statement of the reasons for his objection to the Bill, or to any provision of the Bill. Under the new Article 66(4B) it is also provided, inter alia, that where the Yang di-Pertuan Agong does neither of these things within the specified period of 30 days, the Bill shall become law at the expiration of that period, in the like manner as if he had assented to the Bill.

Where the Yang di-Pertuan Agong returns a Bill, which is not a money Bill, to the House in which it originated with a statement of the reasons for his objection to the Bill, or to any provision of the Bill, the House shall proceed to reconsider the Bill as soon as possible. If, after such reconsideration, the Bill is passed by the votes of not less than two-thirds of the total number of members of that House in the case of a Bill for making any amendment to the Constitution, other than an amendment excepted pursuant to Article 159, and by a simple majority in the case of any other Bill, with or without amendment, it shall be sent together with the objections to the other House, by which it shall likewise be reconsidered. If the Bill is similarly approved by members of that House, the Bill shall again be presented to the Yang di-Pertuan Agong for assent. The Yang di-Pertuan Agong shall give his assent within 30 days after the Bill is presented to him. The new Article 66(4B) goes on to provide, inter alia, that if the Yang di-Pertuan Agong fails to assent to such Bill within the specified period of thirty days, the Bill shall become law at the expiration of that period, in the like manner as if he had assented to the Bill.

Article 66(5), as amended by the 1984 Act, provides that a Bill shall become law on being assented to by the Yang di-Pertuan Agong, or in accordance with the provisions of the new Article 66(4B). A Bill that thus becomes law shall not come into force until it has been published, without prejudice, however, to the power of Parliament to postpone the operation of any law or to make laws with retrospective effect.

It was felt in some quarters that the 1984 amendments empowered the Yang di-Pertuan Agong to participate directly in the drafting of laws. In fact, the Yang di-Pertuan Agong simply has been provided a longer period to delay giving the royal assent. However, in the case of a Bill for making any amendment to the Constitution, other than an amendment excepted pursuant to Article 159, this holds true only so long as the government commands a two-thirds majority in both Houses of Parliament. An enhanced role for the Yang di-Pertuan Agong may emerge when the government fails to command a two-thirds majority.

In terms of the protection of their privileges, position, honours, or dignities, the Rulers' position has been weakened. On the view taken in the earlier part of this chapter, the consent of the Conference of Rulers is a prerequisite to the making of laws that directly affect the Rulers' privileges, position, honours, or dignities and that the Yang di-Pertuan Agong, in this exceptional situation, can withhold assent to a Federal law in the absence of such consent. Under the new amendments (i.e. the 1984 amendments), even if a law does directly affect the privileges, and the like, of the Rulers and even if they refuse to give their consent, Parliament may choose to override their objection. The objection of the Yang di-Pertuan Agong on behalf of the Conference of Rulers can be ignored by using the new process laid down in the new Article 66. The 'remedy' for the Rulers would then be recourse to the judicial process (e.g. declaratory relief), relying on the courts to invalidate the Act after assent on the ground of infringement of Article 38(4). The Rulers would have to take a punt on the judicial response.

Assent of the rulers in respect of state legislation

The 1984 Act provides for the withdrawal of the amendment effected by the 1983 Act to the Eighth Schedule.[34] The retreat on the 15-day royal assent rule in relation to State legislation was made pursuant to an 'oral undertaking' between the government and the Rulers. Lim Kit Siang, the opposition leader, in commenting on this withdrawal, said, 'Parliament is entitled to know what is the nature and efficacy of such oral undertaking in constitutional law.'[35] The actual terms of the oral undertaking up to now have not been publicized. It would appear that the State Rulers have given some oral assurance that they would not withhold royal assent in respect of State legislation if the 15-day royal assent rule were withdrawn. What is the effect of the oral undertaking even if it is assumed that it satisfies all the necessary legal requirements to constitute a 'contract' between the government of Mahathir Mohamad and the Rulers? Constitutionally, it is possible for the Mahathir Government or any successor government to make use of the new Article 66 to bring about the amendment to the Eighth Schedule, contrary to the terms

[34] The 1984 Act also amends Section 4 of the Eighth Schedule by repealing Section 4(2). In the light of this amendment, the State Legislature is given flexibility to determine by law the number of elected members of the Legislative Assembly as may be appropriate in respect of the State without the need for such number to be a multiple of the number of Federal Constituencies into which the State is divided.

[35] *The Star* (Penang, 10 January 1984).

of the undertaking, although, politically it would be most unwise. However, the point to be made is that, whilst an in-depth analysis of the constitutionality of the oral undertaking must await the publication of the terms of this undertaking, it is clear that an agreement by the Executive to fetter its powers in respect of itself or its successors is in no way effective in law.[36]

Emergency powers

Little mention has been made of the significance of the amendment of Article 150 by the 1983 Act. Attention will now be focused on the amendments effected to Article 150 by the 1983 Act and the repeal of these amendments by the 1984 Act.

Article 150 provides for a comprehensive framework regulating the exercise of emergency powers.[37] The Article had been progressively amended to confer extraordinary powers upon the executive. The Article was subjected to such massive changes in 1981 that it provided the potential for a permanent eclipse of constitutional government.[38] The only restraint was the self-restraint of the government of the day resorting to such powers. The formidable scope of the emergency powers in Article 150 can be illustrated by Article 150(8), which in substance ousts the jurisdiction of the Courts in relation to the invocation of those powers. Before 1983, Article 150(1) declared, 'If the Yang di-Pertuan Agong is satisfied that a grave emergency exists whereby the security, or the economic life, or public order in the Federation or any part thereof is threatened, he may issue a Proclamation of Emergency making therein a declaration to that effect.'

Article 150(2) provides that such a Proclamation of Emergency may be issued before the actual occurrence of the event that threatens the security, or the economic life, or public order in the Federation or any part thereof if the Yang di-Pertuan Agong is satisfied that there is imminent danger of the occurrence of such event. As a result of the 1983 Act, the amended Article 150(1) reads:

> If the Prime Minister is satisfied that a grave emergency exists whereby the security, or the economic life, or public order in the Federation or any part thereof is threatened, he shall

[36] In *Commissioners of Crown Lands v Page* [1960] 2 QB 274, Devlin LJ said:

> When the Crown, or any other person, is entrusted, whether by virtue of the prerogative or by statute, with discretionary powers to be exercised for the public good, it does not, when making a private contract in general terms, undertake (and it may be that it could not even with the use of specific language validly undertake) to fetter itself in the use of those powers, and in the exercise of its discretion.

The principle stated by Devlin LJ has been accepted in a number of authorities, e.g. *Ayr Harbour Trustees v Oswald* (1883) 8 App Cas 623 (HL); *Rederiaktiebolaget Amphritrite v The King* [1921] 3 KB 500; *Board of Trade v Temperley Steam Shipping Co Ltd* (1926) 26 Ll LR 76 and affirmed (1927) 27 Ll LR 230 (CA); *William Cory & Sons Ltd v City of London Corporation* [1951] 2 KB 476 (CA).

[37] See S Jayakumar, 'Emergency Powers in Malaysia' in Tun Mohamed Suffian, Lee and Trindade, *Constitution of Malaysia: Its Development: 1957-1977* (OUP 1978) 328–68; HP Lee, 'Emergency Powers in Malaysia' in Trindade and Lee, *Constitution of Malaysia: Further Perspectives and Developments* (OUP 1986) 133–56.

[38] See Constitution (Amendment) Act, 1981.

advise the Yang di-Pertuan Agong accordingly and the Yang di- Pertuan Agong shall then issue a Proclamation of Emergency making therein a declaration to that effect.

Sweeping changes were also made to the other clauses of Article 150 to accord with the theme that it is the 'satisfaction' of the Prime Minister that is the relevant factor in Article 150 and that the Yang di-Pertuan Agong merely acts on advice.[39]

The motive behind the changes effected to Article 150 by the 1983 Act is a matter for speculation.[40] It can be postulated that the changes were intended to dispel any ambiguity about the scope of the Article. A dispute had arisen among some commentators as to whether a personal discretion resides in the Yang di-Pertuan Agong in relation to the issuance of a Proclamation of Emergency. A view propounding a personal discretion in the Yang di-Pertuan Agong was asserted despite the clear wording of Article 40(1) which stipulates that the Yang di-Pertuan Agong 'shall act in accordance with the advice of the Cabinet or of a Minister acting under the general authority of the Cabinet.'[41] Any such doubt, after the decision of the Privy Council in the 1979 case of *Teh Cheng Poh v Public Prosecutor*,[42] should be cast aside for the Privy Council said:

[The Yang di-Pertuan Agong's] functions are those of a constitutional monarch and except on certain matters that do not concern the instant appeal, he does not exercise any of his functions under the Constitution on his own initiative but is required by Article 40(1) to act in accordance with the advice of the Cabinet. So when one finds in the Constitution itself or in a Federal law powers conferred upon the Yang di-Pertuan Agong that are expressed to be exercisable if he is of opinion or is satisfied that a particular state of affairs exists or that particular action is necessary, the reference to his opinion or satisfaction is in reality a reference to the collective opinion or satisfaction of the members of the Cabinet, or the opinion or satisfaction of a particular Minister to whom the Cabinet have delegated their authority to give advice upon the matter in question.[43]

The 1983 Act provided merely for the advice of the Prime Minister. The possibility of a Prime Minister bypassing the Cabinet on such a fundamental matter existed under the 1983 amendments. It is a welcome relief that the changes effected to Article 150 by the 1983 Act were retracted by the 1984 Act. Despite the retreat on the changes to Article 150, the present state of the Article is a matter that should be of concern to those who are devoted to the cause of constitutionalism.

[39] See Azmi Khalid, 'Emergency Powers & Constitutional Changes' (1983) 3 Aliran Quarterly 5–8.

[40] It was reported that 'at least one of the candidate Rulers had spoken openly of an intention, on assuming the office of Agong, to declare a Proclamation of Emergency under Article 150 of the Constitution and seek to exercise some governmental powers himself'—H F Rawlings, 'The Malaysian Constitutional Crisis of 1983' (1986) 35 ICLQ 237, 246.

[41] RH Hickling, 'The Prerogative in Malaysia' (1975) 17 Malaya LR 207, 223. Cf S Jayakumar, 'Emergency Powers in Malaysia: Can the Yang di-Pertuan Agong Act in His Personal Discretion and Capacity?' (1976) 18 Malaya LR 149.

[42] [1979] 1 MLJ 50.

[43] ibid 52.

An Appraisal

The constitutional conflict of 1983 would not have arisen in the first place if the incidents involving the State Rulers mentioned by Raja Tun Azlan Shah had been confronted head on. Those State Rulers who had exceeded the bounds of constitutional propriety must shoulder the responsibility for the breakdown of trust between the Rulers and the government.

The crisis, in its embryonic stage, could have been averted if Article 130 of the Malaysian Constitution had been resorted to. Indeed, one question that remains a puzzle today is why a mechanism that exists for defusing the situation was never used. Article 130 empowers the Yang di-Pertuan Agong to refer to the Federal Court for its opinion any question 'as to the effect of any provision of this Constitution which has arisen or appears to him likely to arise'. The Yang di-Pertuan Agong in exercising the power under Article 130 is, however, required to act in accordance with the advice of the Cabinet or of a minister acting under the general authority of the Cabinet, except as otherwise provided by the Constitution.[44]

The Yang di-Pertuan Agong was placed in an invidious position. If he went against the wishes of the Conference of Rulers, he could have been removed from office by a resolution of the Conference, if such a resolution was supported by five members of the Conference. By complying with the wishes of the Conference of Rulers, he had to ignore the advice of the government of the day. It was a dilemma that would not have been posed to the Yang di-Pertuan Agong had the government consulted the Conference of Rulers before the passing of the 1983 Bill. The argument that such a consultation would undermine the supremacy of the Federal Parliament is not tenable in the Malaysian context. Tun Mohamed Suffian has said: 'In Malaysia no single institution is supreme, corresponding to the British Parliament. What is supreme in Malaysia is the Constitution itself.'[45] He also added:

> We have an elected King who holds office for five years, nine hereditary Sultans who hold office for life, four appointed Governors, fourteen governments, fourteen legislatures and a host of other bodies established by the Constitution. At first sight it is difficult to imagine why such an elaborate arrangement has been found necessary and more difficult still to imagine how it can possibly work. It is axiomatic that the present does not exist *in vacuo* but arises from the past, and when one considers the history of the country it is not difficult to realise why our Constitution is the long document it is, for each state and each interest insists, and quite properly too, on the writing into the Constitution of safeguards regarding its rights.[46]

[44] An explanation that has been proffered was 'because of a traditional Malay preference for resolving disputes by consensus and accommodation, rather than by submission of issues to third parties by decision': Rawlings, 'The Malaysian Constitutional Crisis of 1983' (1986) ICLQ 237, 249.

[45] Tun Mohamed Suffian, *An Introduction to the Constitution of Malaysia* (2nd edn, Government Printers 1976) 19.

[46] ibid 345.

If, therefore, the safeguard concerning the privileges, position, honours, or dignities of the Rulers is not to be a hollow one, the protection given by Article 38(4) should not be negated by a constitutional convention that the Yang di-Pertuan Agong *must* assent on the advice of his ministers.

If the views expressed in this chapter are not acceptable to those who avow the cause of a genuine parliamentary democracy, then the proper approach is to seek a national consensus on how the present constitutional system in Malaysia can be revamped to accord with modern-day notions of parliamentary democracy. Such a suggested course of action is fraught with difficulties for under the Sedition Act 1948 as amended by the Emergency (Essential Powers) Ordinance No. 45, 1970 it is an offence to question the sovereignty and prerogatives of the Rulers.[47] However, this restriction on public discussion of a 'sensitive' issue no longer applies to members of Parliament because of the Constitution (Amendment) Act 1993.[48] Thus, the obstacle posed by the Sedition Act must be overcome first to pave the way for members of the public, who are not parliamentarians, to participate in a debate on the issue.[49]

There were some bright aspects to the crisis. First, it captured the attention of the entire Malaysian nation. Since independence, never has so much interest been exhibited in the workings of the Malaysian Constitution. Constitutionalism in Malaysia can only stand to benefit from a better-informed public. The second major significance was the retreat by the government from the amendments to Article 150. The 1983 amendments to Article 150 contained the potential for an unscrupulous leader to introduce dictatorial rule. In that regard, the Rulers had rendered a singular service—possibly, unwittingly—to the nation by forcing a governmental retreat on those amendments.

An irony about the whole crisis was that Sultan Idris of Perak suddenly died in the wake of the constitutional convulsion. Raja Tun Azlan Shah was proclaimed the Sultan of Perak on 3 February 1984.[50] In April 1984, Sultan Mahmood Iskandar of Johor assumed the office of Yang di-Pertuan Agong, whilst the newly proclaimed Sultan Azlan Shah assumed the office of Timbalan Yang di-Pertuan Agong.[51] The latter, before his appointment as Sultan of Perak, had occupied the highest judicial

[47] HP Lee, 'The Process of Constitutional Change in Malaysia', in Tun Mohamed Suffian, Lee and Trindade, *Constitution of Malaysia: Its Development: 1957–1977* (OUP 1978) 379–83.

[48] See chap. 8 for a discussion of the Constitution (Amendment) Act 1993.

[49] Tun Mohamed Suffian said, 'It would not, however, be seditious or criminal if any one were to question not the substance of those rights and privileges, but only the implementation of those constitutional provisions' *An Introduction to the Constitution of Malaysia* (2nd edn, Government Printer 1976) 218.

[50] Sultan Idris died of a heart attack on 1 February 1984, and Raja Tun Azlan Shah was made Sultan of Perak on 3 February 1984. Only 7 months earlier, on 1 July 1983, Raja Tun Azlan Shah had been appointed the Raja Muda of Perak. On the 'rotation' system of succession to the throne in Perak, see Khoo Kay Kim, 'Succession to the Perak Sultanate' (1983) 56 Journal of the Malaysian Branch of the Royal Asiatic Society 7; Kobkua Suwannathat-Pian, 'Thrones, Claimants, Rulers and Rules: The Problem of Succession in the Malay Sultanates', (1993) 66 Journal of the Malaysian Branch of the Royal Asiatic Society 1.

[51] Both assumed their duties on 26 April 1984.

office in Malaysia.[52] Trust among the government and the Rulers was restored during the reign of Sultan Mahmood Iskandar. The bond between the King and Mahathir Mohamad was strengthened. However, that bond was subsequently, to wreak havoc on the judiciary.

The Constitution (Amendment) Act 1994: The Last Nail in the Coffin of Royal Assent

The analysis of the constitutional conflicts over royal assent to legislation indicates sharply how the State Rulers have been subjugated by the executive arm of government. The last nail in the coffin of royal assent to legislation was manifested by the enactment of the Constitution (Amendment) Act 1994. The enactment of this Act was an encounter without a showdown. The 1994 constitutional changes did not evoke the outcry of the previous encounters between the government and the Malay Rulers.

One of the aims of the Constitution (Amendment) Act 1994 Act related to the constitutional role of the Rulers. Having been forced into submission over the royal immunity issue a year earlier, the Yang di-Pertuan Agong and the State Rulers are obligated by new express constitutional provisions, in Article 40 and the Eighth Schedule respectively, to accept and act in accordance with advice whenever they are directed constitutionally to act in accordance with advice.

The Act also effected amendments to Clauses (4) and (4A) of Article 66. It should be recalled that the provisions of the clauses were the product of a compromise reached between the government and the Rulers in the 1983 constitutional crisis. The compromise reflected in the provisions of the Constitution (Amendment) Act 1984 provided for the Yang di-Pertuan Agong, in the case of a non-money Bill, to return the Bill to the House in which it had originated with a statement of the reasons for his objection to the Bill. In such an event, the House to which the Bill had been returned was required to reconsider and vote on it again. If the Yang di-Pertuan Agong failed to assent to the Bill again, it would become law upon expiration of thirty days.

The enactment of the Constitution (Amendment) Act 1994 meant that the compromise reached in 1983 has been jettisoned by the government. Article 66 was amended so that any Bill that has not been assented to within 30 days of presentation to the Yang di-Pertuan Agong is deemed to have been assented to by him.

The final humiliating gesture to the Rulers was the amendments effected to the Eighth Schedule to the Constitution to embody provisions similar to the amendments to Article 66, despite the purported oral undertaking in the 1983 constitutional crisis that the State Rulers would not withhold royal assent in respect of State legislation. The *Far Eastern Economic Review* reported, 'Government officials

[52] In 1982, Sultan Azlan Shah was appointed Lord President of the Federal Court, the highest judicial office in Malaysia, in place of Tun Mohamed Suffian, who had retired.

would not say if the Rulers had been informed of the amendments, which provoked a constitutional crisis when proposed in a similar form a decade ago.'[53] If no consent had been secured from the Rulers regarding this amendment, then even if the legislation had finally been assented to by the Yang di-Pertuan Agong a doubt may overhang the constitutional validity of this amendment. However, a future constitutional challenge will have to overcome difficult threshold questions, such as, whether the courts would look behind the assent of the Yang di-Pertuan Agong to determine whether there was consent of the Rulers, as well as the manner of proof of an absence of consent, and whether, in substance, there has been an erosion of the Rulers' privileges given that the amendment was simply an embodiment of an oral undertaking. The disdain with which the government has shown the Rulers by the very enactment of this Act underlines the stranglehold the government has over them. The constitutional amendments represented a total triumph of the Mahathir administration over the Malay Rulers in relation to the hotly contested issue of royal assent to legislation. The Rulers, once they have come to terms with the expectations of the Malaysian people that they are monarchs under the Constitution and have to abide by the rule of law, can play a leading role in promoting a stable and harmonious Malaysian society. Furthermore, the Malay Rulers, by virtue of their acknowledged role as the Heads of Islam in their respective States, can help to counter the resurgence of Islamic fundamentalism that is causing concern in many countries today. Before a truly modernized institution of rulership could emerge, a far more significant constitutional battle over the issue of royal immunity flared up. The Malay Rulers emerged from that titanic conflict with their royal immunities expunged from the Constitution. An excursus of that constitutional conflict is presented in Chapter 3.

[53] Far Eastern Economic Review (19 May 1994) 23.

3

The Battle over Royal Immunity

> Confucius said, 'A sovereign who governs a nation by virtue is like the North Pole Star, which remains in its place and the other stars revolve around it.
>
> Lin Yutang (ed), *The Wisdom of Confucius* (1938)

On 10 December 1992, the following substantive motion was passed unanimously by the House of Representatives of the Federal Parliament:

> That the House which sits today feels extremely sad and views seriously the incident involving a Malaysian citizen, Douglas Gomes, who was injured at the Istana Johor on Nov. 30, 1992 by the Sultan of Johor.
>
> That the House decides that the incident was an abuse of power which goes against the spirit of the Federal Constitution and was contrary to the aspirations of the laws of the country which are based on the system of constitutional monarchy and parliamentary democracy.
>
> That the House resolves that all necessary action be taken to ensure that similar incidents do not recur in the future.[1]

The Prime Minister, Mahathir Mohamad, both in and outside Parliament indicated that the Constitution would be amended if such action were necessary in order to prevent any recurrence of the incident.

Legislative action was deemed necessary when an attempt at a 'consensual approach' failed. The government had sought an agreement of the Malay Rulers that they would abide by a self-regulatory code of conduct. However, the 'Proclamation of Constitutional Principles' dated 4 July 1992 was signed 'only by the Yang di-Pertuan Agong and six of the nine Rulers'.[2] Given the absence of unanimous support of the Rulers to the 'Proclamation of Principles' and the fact that the document was not legally binding, Mahathir Mohamad decided to deal with the problem by amending the Federal Constitution.

[1] The motion was tabled by the then Deputy Prime Minister, Abdul Ghafar Baba: see 'Palace Incident an Abuse of Power', *New Straits Times* (11 December 1992) 2. See generally AJ Harding, 'Sovereigns Immune? The Malaysian Monarchy Crisis' (1993) 327 The Round Table 305; Mark R Gillen, 'The Malay Rulers' Loss of Immunity' (1995) 29(1) UBC Law Review 163; Abdul Aziz Bari, 'The 1993 Constitutional Crisis: A Redefinition of the Monarchy's Role and Position?' in Andrew Harding and HP Lee (eds), *Constitutional Landmarks in Malaysia: The First 50 Years 1957–2007* (LexisNexis 2007) 227–42.

[2] Andrew Harding, *The Constitution of Malaysia: A Contextual Analysis* (Hart 2012) 119.

Background to the Crisis: The 'Gomez Incident'

What apparently triggered off the crisis was a reported assault by the Ruler of Johor, Sultan Mahmood Iskandar, of a school hockey coach. This alleged assault was linked to an earlier chain of events. One of the sons of the Sultan of Johor, Tunku Majid, who was a member of the Johor hockey team, had—after the Johor team lost to the Perak team—allegedly assaulted the Perak hockey goalkeeper. In consequence, Tunku Majid was suspended for 5 years by the Malaysian Hockey Federation's disciplinary committee after it had conducted a hearing that he did not attend. Soon after his suspension, a number of hockey teams from Johor withdrew abruptly from various competitions organized by or associated with the Malaysian Hockey Federation. Douglas Gomez, the college hockey coach of Maktab Sultan Abu Bakar (English College), decided to speak out against the 'forced' withdrawal of his college's hockey players from a prestigious national competition: the Malaysian Hockey Federation—Milo Champion Schools Trophy. He called for the resignation of all Johor Hockey Association office bearers, and bravely said, 'I do not mind taking this stand even if it means putting my neck on the line. I know I will be victimised for my outburst but I am prepared to accept any consequences and will go all the way.'[3]

Shortly after, Gomez was summoned to the Istana Bukit Serene, a palace of the Johor Ruler. It was reported that he was taken by a palace official in a car to the palace and that he was at the palace for 4 hours. In the late afternoon of the same day (Monday, 30 November 1992), Gomez left a handwritten statement in the Johor Baru office of the *New Straits Times* in which he stated, 'I, Douglas Gomez, hockey coach of Maktab Sultan Abu Bakar, Johor Baru, wish to inform you that what has been reported in the Press over the last few days is not true and the situation has been blown out of proportions.'[4]

The next day, Mr Gomez sought medical treatment at a private clinic for 'facial cuts and bruises' and was given medical leave. Subsequently, Gomez, possibly moved by encouragement from the government, lodged a police report alleging that the Sultan of Johor had assaulted him at the palace. Thus was set in motion a major confrontation between the government and the Malay Rulers.

The Remedy Proposed by the Government

The day after the Dewan Rakyat had unanimously passed the motion tabled by the Deputy Prime Minister, Abdul Ghafar Baba, the police were directed by the Federal Attorney General to charge the Sultan of Johor's son in respect of his alleged assault against the Perak hockey goalkeeper and were further authorized to investigate assault charges against the Sultan himself.[5]

[3] 'Hockey Coach Takes a Swipe at JHA', *New Sunday Times* (29 November 1992) 1.

[4] 'Hockey Coach Summoned to Johor Palace', *New Straits Times* (1 December 1992) 2.

[5] On 26 January 1993, Tunku Majid and the Perak goalkeeper agreed to 'compound' the offence: Tunku Majid also paid $1,000(RM) to the goalkeeper. The court consented to the settlement: see

At an urgent meeting, the UMNO Supreme Council resolved that the government should amend the Constitution. This proposal was adopted by the Supreme Council of the Barisan Nasional at an emergency meeting. After chairing the meeting, the Prime Minister announced that a special session of Parliament would be called in a month's time to effect the constitutional changes. On 6 January 1993, the Cabinet unanimously approved a draft of the proposed constitutional amendments.

Why was it necessary to amend the Constitution to deal with a case of criminal assault? The answer lies in Article 181(2), which provides that 'no proceedings whatsoever shall be brought in any court against the Ruler of a State in his personal capacity'. This Article had lain dormant within the Constitution for the first 25 years of independence (since 1957). However, disquiet began to surface regarding the scope of this Article. Tunku Abdul Rahman, the first Prime Minister of Malaysia, as far back as 31 August 1984, had written:

> A Ruler who commits a breach of any Federal law is not subject to the jurisdiction of the courts. At Federal level, therefore, nothing can be done in relation to, for example (taking an extreme case), a Ruler maliciously killing a citizen - although subsequent public outcry may well give rise to a need to amend the law...
>
> What will happen, I repeat, if a Ruler shoots down in cold blood a citizen of the State, or if he in an extreme case of recklessness knocked down a person on the road and injured or killed him? As far as I can see, no action can be taken against him.[6]

He then added:

> In this democratic, egalitarian age it is undesirable that anyone should be completely above the law. If the Ruler is to be made liable, as in the case of a private person, under the provision of the criminal law of Malaysia (which is a Federal law), then appropriate constitutional amendment is necessary.[7]

He called for the appointment of a Royal Commission to review the Constitution.

Tunku Abdul Rahman reiterated his concern when he declared open an Aliran Conference on 'Reflections on the Malaysian Constitution: 30 years after Merdeka' on 15 August 1987. He said:

> What I am concerned about is the position of His Majesty the Yang Di-Pertuan Agong and the Rulers who are above the law, which means that they are free to commit crime without being subject to prosecution under the law.
>
> Firstly I feel that no person should be exempted from the law but a special court might be provided to deal with the offences committed by those above the law. This court should

'Goalkeeper Agrees and Accepts $1,000 in Compensation – Majid Case Compounded', *New Straits Times* (27 January 1993) 1.

[6] Tunku Abdul Rahman Putra, *Challenging Times* (Pelanduk Publications 1986) 36. Khoo Boo Teong wrote, 'In 1986 Daeng Baha Ismail alleged in a suit that he was beaten by the Yang di-Pertuan Agong but the High Court in an unreported judgement of Justice Harun held that the court had no jurisdiction to hear the case because of legal immunity. In 1987, the yang di-Pertuan Agong Sultan Mahmood Iskandar at a golf course hit a caddy on the head leading to his death. The Prime Minister Dr Mahathir took no action at that time.'—Khoo Boo Teong, 'Rule of Law and Fundamental Liberties in Malaysia' (PhD thesis, University of Sydney 1999) 327.

[7] Tunku Abdul Rahman Putra, *Challenging Times* (Pelanduk Publications 1986) 36.

be made up of their brother rulers whose decision shall hold good. This is done in order to protect the fundamental rights of all citizens of this country.[8]

The Proposed Changes

The draft Constitution (Amendment) Bill,[9] which was approved by the Cabinet on 6 January 1993 (hereafter called the First Draft), was submitted to the Malay Rulers during an informal meeting with Dr Mahathir Mohamad and other UMNO leaders on 9 January 1993. The Rulers requested a week to formulate a stand on the proposed constitutional amendments to remove their immunity.

At an informal meeting with the Rulers on 17 January 1993, it appeared that agreement was reached between four Rulers, two Regents,[10] and a government delegation led by Dr Mahathir. It was also reported that the Rulers present had made some proposals to modify some of the proposed amendments, which were agreed to by the government.

The government received a jolt when the next day, 18 January 1993, the Conference of Rulers, at a special meeting, unanimously decided that it was not 'in a position at this stage to give its consent to certain proposals in the original Bill and to the subsequent amendment thereto without further deliberation and consultation with the government.'[11] The Conference of Rulers expressed the view that having regard to the far-reaching consequences of the radical changes on the sovereignty of the Malay Rulers and on the power of the States pertaining to the Malay Rulers, it was desirable that 'a more detailed study of the principles and the mechanisms involved in the proposed amendments incorporated in the Bill be made.'[12]

A major concession made by the government in the second draft was the establishment of a Special Court to try offences committed by the King or a Malay Ruler and all civil cases involving them. The Conference of Rulers responded to this concession as follows:

> The Conference of Rulers is of the view that such a court is not the most suitable forum for such a purpose. The Conference of Rulers recommends that an Advisory Board be established whose function would be to make recommendations to the appropriate State authority for the removal of the Ruler before he is charged or sued.
>
> The mechanics and the details relating to the Advisory Board and of the said State authority, together with its powers and composition are matters which need further consideration

[8] *Reflections on the Malaysian Constitution* (Aliran 1987) 20.

[9] Shad Saleem Faruqi, 'The Sceptre, the Sword and the Constitution at a Crossroad (A Commentary on the Constitution Amendment Bill 1993)' [1993] 1 Current Law Journal xiv–lix.

[10] The Sultans of Kelantan, Johor and Kedah were absent from this informal meeting.

[11] See 'Decision of the Special Meeting of the Conference of Rulers on Jan. 18, '93', *New Straits Times* (19 January 1993) 2, for full text of the statement issued by the Keeper of the Rulers' Seal.

[12] ibid.

and discussion. Such an important issue cannot, in the view of the Conference of Rulers be decided in haste, without mature deliberation and consultation.[13]

Undeterred by this last-minute declaration of its stand by the Conference of Rulers, Mahathir Mohamad proceeded to table the Constitution (Amendment) Bill 1993 at a special sitting of the Dewan Rakyat. The Bill was passed with the requisite two-thirds majority on 19 January 1993, and was passed by the Dewan Negara the next day. The main topic of speculation was whether Sultan Azlan Shah, who had succeeded Sultan Mahmood Iskandar as King, would ultimately assent to the legislation. In response to a journalist's question, Mahathir Mohamad was reported to have replied:

If the King refuses to give his assent, the Bill goes back to Parliament and once approved by both Houses will become law with or without the royal assent.... If the process is disputed, then a decision can be made by the courts. As a government which strongly upholds the rule of law, we will abide by the court's decision.[14]

The Yang di-Pertuan Agong returned the Bill to Parliament with some proposed modifications agreed to by the Conference of Rulers. The Bill, with the proposed modifications (hereafter called the Third Draft), was passed by the Dewan Rakyat on 9 March 1993.[15]

The central aim of the Constitution (Amendment) Bill 1993 was to bring about an *effective* removal of the Rulers' *personal* immunity. The main thrusts of the Bill shall be explained by reference to its third or final draft, and, where relevant, the modifications agreed to by the government shall be highlighted.

1. Clause (1) of Article 32, originally provided as follows: 'There shall be a Supreme Head of the Federation, to be called the Yang di-Pertuan Agong, who shall take precedence over all persons in the Federation and shall not be liable to any proceedings whatsoever in any court.' This clause has been altered by the addition of the following words after 'court': 'Except in the Special Court established under Part XV in respect only of anything done or omitted to be done by him in the exercise or purported exercise of his functions under any written law.' The original Article 32(1) was construed as referring to protecting the Yang di-Pertuan Agong from proceedings against him personally, and not to acts committed in his name. Pike CJ (Borneo) said: 'It cannot be construed to protect the Federal Government from action in the courts in respect of its acts committed in the name of the Yang di-Pertuan Agong, and when the Yang di-Pertuan Agong acts on the advice of the cabinet his act must be deemed to be the act of the Federal Government.'[16] The

[13] ibid. [14] 'Changes to Take its Course', *New Straits Times* (19 January 1993) 1.

[15] The Bill with the modifications was passed by 167 votes out of 180. Six PAS members abstained whilst one was absent; six Semangat 46 members absented themselves from Parliament. See 'Bill on Rulers Passed with 167 Votes', *New Straits Times* (10 March 1993) 1.

[16] *Stephen Kalong Ningkan v Tun Abang Haji Openg and Tawi Sli (No 2)* [1967] 1 MLJ 46, 47. For a discussion, see Francis A Trindade, 'The Constitutional Position of the Yang di-Pertuan Agong'

effect of the change is to make it very clear that the immunity of the Yang di-Pertuan Agong from the legal process relates only to the performance of his official duties.

2. Article 181(2), which was the main bone of contention, was amended to read, 'No proceedings whatsoever shall be brought in any court against the Ruler of a State except in the Special Court established under Part XV in respect only of anything done or omitted to be done by him in the exercise or purported exercise of his functions under any written law.' The removal of the Malay Rulers' personal immunity by the amended Article 181(2) is reinforced by the new Article 181(3) which renders void 'any law which provides for the immunity of the Ruler of a State in his personal capacity from any proceedings whatsoever in any court or attaches sanctity to his residence'.
3. To make the removal of personal immunity of the Malay Rulers effective, it was necessary to effect changes to their power to grant pardons. Under the original terms of Article 42, the Yang di-Pertuan Agong is invested with the power to grant pardons, reprieves, and respites in respect of all offences that have been tried by court-martial and all offences committed in the federal territories.[17] The Ruler or the Yang di-Pertua Negeri of a state has power to grant pardons, reprieves, and respites in respect of all other offences in his state. Under Article 42 in its non-amended form, if, for instance, the son of the Sultan of Johor had been convicted for the assault on the Perak goalkeeper, it was possible for the Sultan to pardon him immediately. Similarly, if the Sultan himself had been convicted for the alleged assault on Gomez, he could have simply pardoned himself. As a result of the new clause (12) to Article 42, a Ruler is precluded from hearing an appeal on his own behalf, and from pardoning himself. In the case of the King or a Ruler or his Consort seeking pardon, the case will be heard and decided by the Conference of Rulers. However, the Conference of Rulers, before arriving at its decision, is obliged to consider any written opinion of the Attorney General. A Ruler is also precluded from hearing an appeal from, or pardoning, his children. In such an instance, the Conference of Rulers will elect another Ruler to hear and decide the matter and he shall act in accordance with the advice of the relevant Pardons Board. In the case of the Yang di-Pertua Negeri of a state, or his wife, son, or daughter, the power to grant pardons, reprieves, and respites is to be exercised by the Yang di-Pertuan Agong, acting on the advice of the Pardons Board constituted for that state, in accordance with the provisions of Article 42.
4. The second thrust of the amendments aimed at securing the effectiveness of the removal of personal immunity was the amendment of Articles 63 and 72

in Suffian, Lee and Trindade, *The Constitution of Malaysia: Its Development: 1957–1977* (OUP 1978) 107–8.

[17] Kuala Lumpur and Labuan.

of the Constitution, which deal with the privileges of the Federal Parliament and the State Legislative Assemblies, respectively. Under these Articles, as amended by the Constitution (Amendment) Act 1971, members of these legislative bodies could not be protected by parliamentary privilege in respect of utterances made in any proceedings of these legislative bodies or their committees, if such utterances constituted an offence under the Sedition Act 1948, as amended by the Emergency (Essential Powers) Ordinance No. 45 1970. The amended Sedition Act 1948 makes it seditious, even in the legislatures, to question the sovereignty or prerogative of the Rulers. Members of these legislatures tread a fine line between permissible speech and sedition in the debates over the legal immunity of the Rulers. Their protection, before this amendment, lay in the fact that the consent of the Attorney General was required before a prosecution for sedition could be initiated. Although the freedom of the elected representatives to criticize the Malay Rulers has now been restored, the freedom does not extend to the advocacy of the abolition of the constitutional position of the Yang di-Pertuan Agong as a Supreme Head of the Federation, or the constitutional position of the Ruler of a state.

5. A concession made to the Rulers was the establishment of a Special Court, after they suggested to the government that they should not be tried in an ordinary court of law.[18] A new Article 182 provides for this Special Court. It shall consist of the Lord President of the Supreme Court, the two Chief Justices of the High Courts, and two other persons who hold or have held office as judge of the Supreme Court or a High Court, appointed by the Conference of Rulers. The Special Court is vested with exclusive jurisdiction to try all offences committed in the Federation by the Yang di-Pertuan Agong or a Ruler, and all civil cases by or against the Yang di-Pertuan Agong or a Ruler. It shall have the same jurisdiction and powers as are vested in the inferior courts, the High Court, and the Supreme Court, by the Constitution or any federal law, and shall apply the practice and procedure of these courts unless Parliament legislates to the contrary. It is also provided in Clause (6) of the new Article 182 that the proceedings in the Special Court shall be decided in accordance with the opinion of the majority of the members. Furthermore, the decision is final and conclusive and shall not be challenged or called in question in any court, on any ground.
6. The final version of the Constitution (Amendment) Bill 1993 contained modifications proposed by the Yang di-Pertuan Agong and which had been agreed to by the Conference of Rulers. The modifications consist of two additions to the Bill. First, a new Article 33A states that if the King is charged with an offence under any law in the Special Court, he ceases to exercise his functions. By adding a new Section 1A to Part I of the Eighth Schedule to the Constitution, the same applies in respect of the Ruler of a State (i.e. he ceases to exercise the

[18] See HP Lee, 'Malaysian Royalty and the Special Court' in Andrew Harding and Penelope (Pip) Nicholson (eds), *New Courts in Asia* (Routledge 2010) 317–26.

functions of the Ruler of the State). These functions, in such an event, are to be exercised by a Regent or a Council of Regency, as the case may be, appointed in accordance with the State Constitution. It is also provided that, where a Ruler is convicted and sentenced to imprisonment for more than 1 day, he shall cease to be the Ruler of the State, unless he receives a free pardon.[19]

7. The second modification consists of a new Article 183, which provides that no action (civil or criminal) can be instituted against the Yang di-Pertuan Agong or the Ruler of a state without the consent of the Attorney General. This modification seeks to ensure that the Rulers 'are not dragged to court by people out to embarrass them or for unfounded reasons.'[20] The new Article 183 also declares that no proceedings whatsoever shall be brought in any court against a Ruler in his personal capacity in respect of anything done by him before the coming into force of this Act. This makes it clear that the removal of personal immunity was to operate prospectively. It would mean that the Sultan of Johor was protected from legal proceedings in respect of his alleged assault of Douglas Gomez.

Reasons for the Rulers' Back-down

It took less than a month for the Rulers to beat a retreat from their unanimous rejection of the Bill on 18 January 1993. The Rulers were in a vulnerable position; all channels of popular communications—the press, the radio, and television stations—were controlled by or under the influence of the government. Every day there were 'revelations of scandalous waste of public funds, misbehaviour of some Rulers and extravagant life-styles.'[21]

[19] The Prime Minister was reported as saying that the Rulers suggested these modifications 'because it would be strange and unacceptable to the public and the Rulers if any one of them continued to exercise his functions after being sentenced or while serving a sentence handed down by the Special Court'. Under Article 71(4), the State Constitutions must accord with the provisions of the Eighth Schedule. If the State governments fail to amend the State Constitution accordingly, the Federal Parliament is empowered by Article 71(4) to legislate to give effect to the provisions of the Eighth Schedule in the States concerned.

[20] 'Kelantan Ruler's Acts Started the Criticisms', *New Straits Times* (9 March 1993) 4.

[21] Government sources were reported as saying that the then King (Sultan Azlan Shah) had spent RM75 million since taking up residence in the National Palace in 1989, of which RM69.32 million was spent on renovating the National Palace. Details were also provided as follows:

$2.5 million on bedspreads
$300,000 on constructing a store to keep the bedspreads
$750,000 for a TV antenna
$220,000 to install a new royal crest.

It was also reported that much of the expenditure was incurred without prior consultation with the government.

The front-page report of the New Straits Times went on to say:

> It is estimated that the RM75 million can buy 3,000 units of low-cost houses or two hospitals ... or 46 rural clinics or 46 primary schools ...' ('Rulers Can Still Live Well', 23 January 1993).

These reports covered matters such as 'white elephant' palaces constructed for some State Rulers, the importation of excessive numbers of luxury cars without paying import duties and obtaining 'approved permits'.[22] Customs officers began to seize luxury cars that had been brought into the country without approved permits. The government also decided to withdraw all benefits and privileges that were not provided for by law.

1. Royal privileges were reviewed by the Foreign Ministry, which decided that only Rulers, Regents, and their consorts would be issued with diplomatic passports. Other 'members of royalty' would be dealt with on a 'deserving cases' basis.[23] This is in contrast to the past practice of freely issuing 5-year diplomatic passports to all members of royalty. Furthermore, the new guidelines forbade foreign missions from entertaining the Rulers' families during private visits abroad, and carrying out such tasks as booking VIP rooms and executing airport formalities.
2. The Deputy Health Minister announced that government nurses attached to palaces would be immediately redeployed if their services were deemed unnecessary.[24] It was reported that four palaces were using the services of at least ten nurses daily. Six nurses were apparently used to babysit the then King's grandchildren around the clock. Underutilized royal wards were to be opened to the public. In one case, a Ruler had used the royal ward for only 45 minutes in a year.
3. Notification was given that services provided by the Royal Malaysian Air Force to fly and maintain aircraft of some Rulers (Johor and Pahang) would be terminated. Apparently, twenty-three Royal Malaysian Air Force pilots and technicians were on secondment to provide such services.[25]
4. Guidelines were issued by the Prime Minister's Department directing Federal and State Government officers to ignore certain royal directives and requests, such as orders to transfer officers, discipline them, or greet returning royalty during working hours.[26]
5. Free postage facilities, previously enjoyed by members of the royal family, would be restricted or withdrawn altogether.
6. Guidelines were issued to the television and radio networks of the Information Ministry to scale down coverage of 'members of the royalty'. Coverage would be restricted to official occasions and by reference to their news value.[27]
7. Public discussion was fostered to discuss the dropping of certain court language and terms that were regarded as degrading and contrary to Islamic teachings.[28]

22 'Sultan Admits Importing Cars without Aps', *New Straits Times* (3 February 1993) 2.
23 'Guidelines on Who Should Get Diplomatic Passports', *New Straits Times* (6 February 1993) 2.
24 'Palace Nurses May be Re-deployed', *New Straits Times* (8 February 1993) 2.
25 'RMAF Services for Sultans to End', *New Straits Times* (5 February 1993) 1.
26 'Orders That Can Be Ignored', *New Straits Times* (5 February 1993) 1.
27 'RTM to Scale Down Coverage of Royalty', *New Straits Times* (27 January 1993) 2.
28 'Don: Stop Using Degrading Terms in Royal Presence', *New Straits Times* (27 January 1993) 2.

The government also made life difficult for the 'recalcitrant' Rulers in many ways. The Sultan of Kelantan rejected the revised amendment on the ground that he had never given his proxy vote to the Sultan of Kedah. The latter disputed this. It was then observed that 'Dr Mahathir thus used his parliamentary speech on the revised amendment to question the legitimacy of the Sultan of Kelantan's succession, and in the following weeks the press was filled with the drama of a pretender, whose father's rights had been lost in 1948 to Tengku Yahya (later Sultan Yahya, who died in 1979, father to ... Sultan Ismail).'[29] In relation to the Sultan of Johor, the government introduced the Johor Military Forces (Disbandment and Repeal) Bill 1994 to provide for the disbandment of the Johor Military Forces (JMF). The principal function of the JMF relates mainly to guarding the royal palaces and the Sultan of Johor and his family. In the end, the government withdrew the Bill on the asserted ground that efforts were being made to absorb the JMF's personnel into other branches of the public service.

Reaping What They Have Sown

The Law Minister, Datuk Syed Hamid Albar, referring to a report that certain members of the royalty had told foreign news agencies that the Malaysian judiciary was not independent, said that members of the royalty should place their confidence in the judicial system and that they should not distrust the system.[30] At the same time, an UMNO Supreme Council member, Datuk Abdul Kadir Sheikh Fadzir, painted a scenario of what could happen if the constitutional amendments were challenged in court. The government would be compelled to substantiate the reasons for the amendments. This would entail a greater revelation of wrongdoings by the Rulers and their families. The government would be compelled to prove these wrongdoings: in cases involving rape or torture, the victims would have to be brought forward; witnesses would have to be produced in open court in relation to these matters and other matters, such as 'smuggling, the refusal to pay loans, cheating and excessive spending.'[31]

The Rulers were confronted with a dilemma. The threat of extensive revelations of misconduct on the part of some of the Rulers and their families diminished their appetite for a court challenge to the constitutional validity of the amendments. There was a clear irony in the whole situation in that Mahathir Mohamad had indicated that if the royal assent was not forthcoming, he would nevertheless have proceeded to gazette the legislation and he would leave it to the courts to decide the matter. The irony was that it was the Ruler of Johor who, when he was the Yang

[29] Roger Kershaw, 'Shattered Symbiosis: The Road to Conflict between Malay Nationalism and Monarchy' (1993) 24 Internationales Asienforum 283, n 52.

[30] 'Place Confidence in Judiciary, Says Hamid', *New Straits Times* (8 February 1993) 2.

[31] 'Kadir: Monarchy at the Crossroads', *New Straits Times* (5 February 1993) 2.

di-Pertuan Agong, contributed to the removal of Tun Salleh Abas as Lord President of Malaysia.[32] The failure by the Conference of Rulers to prevent the erosion of judicial independence during the 'Salleh Abas affair' left them now hoist with their own petard: they were not prepared to place their faith in the judiciary to resolve the matter.

An Evaluation of the Conflict

The resolution of the crisis marks a very important turning point in the shaping of the balance of powers in the Malaysian constitutional system. It also reinforces the clear wishes of the Malaysian people that the Rulers are expected to conduct themselves as constitutional monarchs within a parliamentary democracy.

The confrontation was inevitable. In fact, it could even be said that the conflict was engineered. The less than complete victory over the Rulers in the 1983 crisis must have been a festering irritant with Dr Mahathir. The 'Gomez incident' provided the government with the opportunity to strike. Unlike the 1983 crisis, the government was very well prepared to do battle with the Rulers. In the aftermath of the first confrontation, Dr Mahathir had quietly strengthened his authority.[33] Those UMNO politicians who either had sided with the Rulers or had failed to exhibit sufficient loyal support to Dr Mahathir during the first crisis had eventually been removed from the Cabinet and from the UMNO Supreme Council. A degree of reorganization was effected within the military.[34] With the dismissal of Tun Salleh Abas and two senior judges, the judiciary had been brought to heel. With the press, radio, and television fully under governmental control, the odds were heavily stacked against the Rulers.

Unlike the previous prime ministers of Malaysia, Dr Mahathir does not have the same degree of deference towards the Rulers. His deference to the Rulers is subsumed under the basic principle that the Rulers are constitutional monarchs. However, it is clear that Dr Mahathir would not have achieved ascendancy over the Rulers had it not been for the fact that economic development and governmental

[32] See below chap. 5.

[33] See Gordon P Means, *Malaysian Politics: The Second Generation* (OUP 1991) 117–20.

[34] Means said:

> Besides the reallocation of political office to the strong defenders of the administration, there was also a curious shake-up in the military. During the crisis, the Chief of the Army, General Mohd. Zain Hashim, was known to be close to the Agong and had apparently been critical of Dr Mahathir's confrontational tactics to redefine the role of the Malay Rulers. Five days after the agreement on the compromise formula was made, the government announced that General Mohd. Zain Hashim had decided on early retirement in order to go into business. This was followed by about 500 other dismissals and 'early retirements' from the army. Although no reasons were given for this reorganization of command responsibilities in the army, its timing and its extent suggest that there were probably concerns about the political reliability and the commitment of the army to the objectives and policies of the Mahathir Administration—ibid 119–20.

policy have fostered the creation of a large Malay middle class.[35] Moreover, since independence, the Malays have come to realize that their political and material well-being depended on UMNO, the dominant political party in Malaysia. The entry of a number of the Rulers into business also meant competition between the Rulers and politically well-connected Malays. There was a sense of frustration and resentment against these Rulers for the advantages they held.[36] State government ministers and bureaucrats were generally intimidated by their State Rulers. Dr Mahathir, when he initiated action to amend the Constitution, was able to carry the whole party and government with him.[37] The showdown was intended to establish finally that true governmental powers lie with the executive arm of government and not with the hereditary Rulers.

In the aftermath of the confrontation, the Rulers' standing has emerged considerably diminished.[38] This feature cannot be disguised by the 'face-saving' formula embodied in the modifications to the amendment Bill. The diminution was caused, to some extent, by the backing down of the Rulers. However, the major factors were the disclosures in the media of the extravagance of some of the Rulers and their profligate use of public monies, and their vast business ventures.

[35] Dr Chandra Muzaffar spoke with prescience when in 1987 he said:

> [T]he Malay middle-class has expanded rapidly in the last fifteen years or so. With increasing economic strength and political confidence, it is bound to feel that it does not need to bestow so much prestige and privilege upon a symbolic protector like the Sultanates. Since its own political power is the insurance for the well-being of the community, a section of the Malay middle-class may even doubt the role of the symbolic protector. Indeed, if an individual monarch or the monarchical system as a whole, stands in the way of the economic or political ambitions of individuals or groups within the Malay middle-class, it is quite conceivable that the latter would seek to further curtail the powers of the former. Sometimes, a monarch may create difficulties for himself and the Institution by overstepping certain constitutional limits or through behaviour that leads to popular disenchantment with the Sultanates themselves. *Reflections on the Malaysian Constitution* (Aliran 1987) 293.

[36] Criticisms of palace involvement in business and politics resulted in an UMNO-initiated 'Code of Conduct for Rulers' which was accepted by the majority of the Rulers in July 1992. See Cyrus V Das, 'The Monarchy in Malaysia: The Sultanate System – Rights, Privileges, and Relations with the Executive Government', Paper presented at the First Conference of the LAWASIA Comparative Constitutional Law Interest Group, Melbourne, 18-20 November 1992.

[37] Roger Kershaw observed, 'The fact that it was [Dr Mahathir] alone who was able to unleash public criticism and launch the constitutional reform shows the unique concentration of power in his hands.'—'Shattered Symbiosis: The Road to Conflict between Malay Nationalism and Monarchy' (1993) 24 Internationales Asienforum 283.

[38] See AJ Harding, 'The Constitutional Evolution of the Malaysian Monarchy', Working Paper No 4, School of Oriental and African Studies, University of London, June 1993, 20.

4

The Malay Rulers: A Royal Resurgence?

> The [Rulers] must set the best example, or show in Kingship as well as Sultanship that there is much they can do that can be appreciated and expected by their people.... I think the institution of Rulership suits our people, but it must be preserved with honour and dignity. As with all good things people can get tired, and want a change if they feel that all is not well with the institution of Rulers. The best of food can also turn sour; likewise good medicine can do harm if an overdose is taken. So is it not better to keep an eye on one's diet, and follow out exactly the prescription laid down for any good medicine?
>
> Tunku Abdul Rahman, *Looking Back* (Pustaka Antara 1977) 214–15

Mahathir's Triumph over the Rulers

Mahathir Mohamad's triumph over the Malay Rulers in the conflicts over royal assent to legislation and their personal immunity represented a triumph of constitutionalism, by requiring the Yang di-Pertuan Agong and the Malay Rulers to accept and act in accordance with advice, whenever they are directed constitutionally to act in accordance with advice. Since those encounters, the Malay Rulers have started to make a remarkable comeback in terms of earning the respect of the Malaysian public. The retirement of Mahathir Mohamad in 2003 and the weakening of UMNO's grip on power provided positive conditions for the Rulers to burnish their credentials and redefine their role within a rapidly changing Malaysian society. On some occasions, the Rulers have even flexed their royal muscles boldly. Andrew Harding observes, 'Indeed, whereas previously, especially under the Tunku and Mahathir, it was the task of politicians to guard the Rulers "against weaknesses and follies", it seems now to be, more accurately, the Rulers' perceived role to guard politicians against *their* weaknesses and follies.'[1]

This chapter evaluates the various episodes involving the Rulers and the constitutional dimension of their exercise of discretionary powers, and reflects on the future trajectory of their evolving role.

[1] Andrew Harding, *The Constitution of Malaysia: A Contextual Analysis* (Hart Publishing 2012) 121. See, generally, Kobkua Suwannathat-Pian, *Palace, Political Party and Power: A Story of the Socio-Political Development of Malay Kingship* (NUS Press 2011) 339–44.

A Royal Resurgence of Power?

The role of State Rulers

By 2008, fortunes of the Malay Rulers had revived.[2] It was clear that by the mid-1990s, the power of the Malays Rulers had been considerably diminished following the two major confrontations with the Mahathir government. The Rulers were to keep to their role as constitutional monarchs, functioning under advice unless permitted by the constitutional system to exercise discretionary powers. In an address to the Malaysian Law Conference in 2007 on the fiftieth anniversary of Malaysian independence, the author observed the following:

> With the recognition and acknowledgment that they are now constitutional monarchs required to act on advice of the Prime Minister, in the case of the King, and the state Chief Minister, in the case of the state Rulers, the Rulers could be said to have emerged from the Dark Ages. It is clear that the state and federal monarchies post the two crises now command immense respect and support of the Malaysian people from all walks of life. There is even an expectation on the part of the people that the Conference of Rulers can contribute immensely to good governance by providing the government with their collective wisdom and sound counsel.[3]

Kobkua Suwannathat-Pian, a history professor at Universiti Pendidikan Sultan Idris, observed a 'rejuvenation' of the Malay Rulers, and said, 'The rejuvenation of the Malay royalty was, up to a point, an unqualified success in such a period and perhaps even went beyond royal expectations....'[4] She attributed this rejuvenation to two factors. The first was the stepping down by Prime Minister Mahathir from the presidency of UMNO and the premiership. The other factor was the decline of UMNO political leadership 'through arrogance, corruption, abuse of power, ineffectiveness, and lack of vision and clear and strong direction.'[5]

She elaborated:

> On the surface, the rejuvenation of the royalty has considerably brought much credibility and respect to the Rulers. For the first time in the contemporary history of Malaysia, the

[2] The role and powers of a Regent because of the incapacitation of the Sultan of Kelantan were considered by the courts in suits brought before them. A decision of the Regent of Kelantan to alter the membership of the Kelantan Council of Succession was held to be a non-justiciable issue in an action brought by the Regent's younger brother: *Tengku Muhammad Fakhry Petra Ibni Sultan Ismail Petra v Yang Maha Mulia Pemangku Raja Kelantan & Ors* [2011] 1 MLJ 128 (Mohamad Ariff J). A petition brought by the Sultan questioning the exercise by his son, the Regent, of the powers of revocation and appointment of the members of the Council was dismissed by the Federal Court: *His Royal Highness Sultan Ismail Petra Ibni Almarhum Sultan Yahya Petra v His Royal Highness Tengku Mahkota Tengku Muhammad Faris Petra & Anor and Another Suit* [2011] 1 MLJ 1.

[3] HP Lee, 'The Constitution of Malaysia After 50 Years: Retrospective, Prospective and Comparative Perspectives' (2007) 9(2) Australian Journal of Asian Law 307.

[4] Kobkua Suwannathat-Pian, *Palace, Political Party and Power: A Story of the Socio-Political Development of Malay Kingship* (NUS Press 2011) 410.

[5] ibid.

Malay Rulers have succeeded in presenting themselves to the people as the most credible authority of the land, both in theory and practice. The young generations of Malaysians in particular see the new generation of Rulers and royalty as an impartial non-political power with the ability and credibility to rein in political and administrative excesses committed by discredited and corrupt politicians to the detriment of the common people. However, upon close scrutiny, the resurgence of royal power and its rising credentials among modern Malaysians appear convincing mainly because of the disenchantment of a substantial number of Malaysians, young and not-so-young, by what they consider to be excessive power abuse, disregard for socioeconomic decency and justice, and political leadership bankruptcy. In other words, it is more the politicians themselves who have let self-interests get the better of their social responsibility to the people.[6]

The Rulers and Judicial Appointments

The Constitution provides, in Article 122B(1), that the Chief Justice of the Federal Court, the President of the Court of Appeal, and the Chief Judges of the High Courts and the other judges of these courts 'shall be appointed by the Yang di-Pertuan Agong acting on the advice of the Prime Minister, *after consulting the Conference of Rulers*'.[7] The Prime Minister has to consult the Chief Justice regarding these appointments except in the appointment of Chief Justice of the Federal Court. In the case of the Chief Judge of a High Court, the Prime Minister 'shall consult the Chief Judge of each of the High Courts and, if the appointment is to the High Court in Sabah and Sarawak, the Chief Minister of each of the States of Sabah and Sarawak'. Appointments of judges of the Federal Court, the Court of Appeals, and a High Court, other than the heads of these courts, require consultation with their respective heads.

Lamin PCA, in *Re Dato' Seri Anwar bin Ibrahim*,[8] in his construction of Article 122B(1), said that in the matter of appointment of judges, 'when the Yang di-Pertuan Agong consults the Conference of Rulers, he does not seek its "consent". He merely consults.'[9] He further added that the Yang di-Pertuan Agong 'may consider the advice or opinion' given by the Conference of Rulers but he is not bound by it. Sultan Azlan Shah pointed out the reality of the constitutional practice:

> [T]he statements made by Lamin PCA in this case seem to suggest that the Conference of Rulers gives its advice directly (and only) to the Yang di-Pertuan Agong, and not the Prime Minister. In practice, this is not the case. The Prime Minister submits the names of the candidates to the Conference of Rulers. The Conference then submits its views to the Prime Minister before he tenders his advice to the Yang di-Pertuan Agong. Therefore, the views of the Conference are, strictly speaking, given to the Prime Minister. It is then for him to consider these views before he makes the final recommendation to the Yang di-Pertuan Agong.

[6] ibid 391. [7] Emphasis added.

[8] *In the matter of an oral application by Dato' Seri Anwar bin Ibrahim to disqualify a judge of the Court of Appeal* [2002] 2 MLJ 481 (Court of Appeal).

[9] *In the matter of an oral application by Dato' Seri Anwar bin Ibrahim to disqualify a judge of the Court of Appeal* [2002] 2 MLJ 481 (Court of Appeal) 484.

Only when such a procedure is followed can the Conference of Rulers play an effective role in the 'advising' process.[10]

Sultan Azlan Shah said that the suggestion that the advice of the Conference is given directly to the Yang di-Pertuan Agong would render the entire constitutional process 'meaningless, since when the Prime Minister submits the name to the Yang di-Pertuan Agong, the Yang di-Pertuan Agong is duty-bound, under Art 40(1A), to accept the advice of the Prime Minister.'[11] How efficacious the consultation process is will depend largely on a respectful and harmonious relationship between the Prime Minister and the Rulers. Sultan Azlan Shah elaborated:

> [I]t is generally accepted as good practice that whenever an appointing body receives from another independent and respected body an adverse report on a candidate, such advice should be given serious consideration. In most cases, the advice will provide sufficient and compelling reasons as to why the candidate should not be appointed to the post. If this procedure were complied with, the appointing authority will be in a position to avoid any accusations of bias or favouritism. This mechanism, thus, protects the appointing authority from any allegations of impropriety ...[12]

Sultan Azlan Shah added that it was difficult to 'rationalise why a Prime Minister would not want to consider, or even abide by the views of nine Rulers and four Governors who constitute the Conference of Rulers'. He continued, 'These are independent persons, with vast experiences, and with no vested interest in the nominated candidates. Their duty is to fulfil their constitutional role in ensuring that only the best and most suited candidates are selected for the posts.'[13]

It would seem that the Rulers, in July 2007, played an influential role as a collective body in preventing an extension of the term of retiring Chief Justice Ahmad Fairuz Abdul Halim. In July–August 2007, when Prime Minister Abdullah Badawi nominated Hashim Yusoff FCJ as Chief Justice (Malaya) in a move engineered by Ahmad Fairuz (which meant overtaking a number of more senior judges), the Conference of Rulers held back and the Prime Minister finally agreed with the Rulers to appoint Alauddin Mohamed Sheriff as Chief Judge (Malaya).

The 2009 Perak Crisis

The electoral shock of 2008 and the viable opposition that can form an alternative national government have changed the political fortune of the Rulers, leading some Rulers to become more emboldened to play an active role in the formation of State government.[14] Steven Sim provides an account of two instances in which

[10] Sultan Azlan Shah, 'The Role of Constitutional Rulers and the Judiciary Revisited' in V Sinnadurai (ed), *Constitutional Monarchy, Rule of law and Good Governance* (Professional Law Books 2004) 397–8.

[11] ibid 398. [12] ibid 397. [13] ibid.

[14] See Andrew Harding, 'Crises of Confidence and Perak's Constitutional Impasse' Center for Policy Initiatives (7 June 2009) http://www.loyarburok.com/2009/06/07/crises-of-confidence-and-peraks-constitutional-impasse/ (accessed 7 October 2016).

the Ruler of Terengganu and that of Perlis played an active role in the selection of a Menteri Besar, in the wake of the 2008 General Election. In respect of the former, the Sultan of Terengganu 'chose Ahmad Said over incumbent Menteri Besar Idris Jusoh even though the [UMNO] central leadership supported the latter. All [UMNO] State assembly members even stood behind Idris and some even threatened to resign if he was not made [Menteri Besar]. Ahmad was subsequently sacked by [UMNO] for going against party instructions not to be sworn in. However, the [UMNO] central committee finally relented after a meeting between the then Prime Minister Abdullah Ahmad Badawi and ... the Sultan of Terengganu. Ahmad was subsequently recognised as the MB of Terengganu.'[15] In the case of the latter, he further explains, 'Isa Sabu was appointed as Menteri Besar of Perlis on the claim that he commanded the confidence of the state assembly with eight [UMNO] assemblymen out of the total of 12 against incumbent Shahidan Kassim who had been [Menteri Besar] for 13 years by then. As such, Isa was sworn in by the Raja of Perlis although Shahidan claimed he had the backing of [UMNO]'s central leadership.'[16] In 2014, the Sultan of Selangor was drawn into a protracted saga involving the selection of a new Menteri Besar brought about by internal bickering within PR. The Sultan insisted on three names to be forwarded to him and eventually appointed Azmin Ali over Wan Azizah, the wife of Anwar Ibrahim. It was observed:

> In appointing Azmin Ali as the new Selangor MB, the Sultan of Selangor has arguably charted new and untested course not only for the political discourse in Selangor specifically and Malaysia in general, but indeed in the whole Westminster parliamentary tradition around the world. Conventionally, it was well established that a constitutional monarch does no more than endorsing and formally appointing the nominated leader of a victorious parliamentary party or coalition to head a new government. In the present case, this was manifestly not done.[17]

It was not only a case of conventional behaviour to be expected of the Sultan of Selangor, but, as Aziz Bari rightly pointed out, it was contradicting the express terms of the Proclamation of Constitutional Principles signed in 1992 by the Sultan's father.[18]

A golden opportunity to bolster the prestige of the Malay Rulers as neutral umpires was lost when Sultan Azlan Shah resolved a political impasse in the 'Perak crisis' by dismissing the Perak State government (formed by the opposition PR coalition) and endorsing the formation of a government by the BN coalition, following the 'defection' of three members of the PR to BN.

[15] Steven Sim, 'Can a Menteri Besar be sacked via a press conference?' *FMT News* (22 January 2016) http://www.freemalaysiatoday.com/category/opinion/2016/01/22/can-a-menteri-besar-be-sacked-via-a-press-conference/ (accessed 23 July 2016).

[16] ibid.

[17] Mohamed Nawab Mohamed Osman, Oh Ei Sun, and Afif Pasuni, 'The Selangor Chief Minister Crisis and the Future of Pakatan Rakyat (PR)' (RSIS October 2014) https://www.rsis.edu.sg/wp-content/uploads/2014/10/NL141007_Malaysia_Update.pdf (accessed 23 July 2016).

[18] 'Aziz Bari: Sultan must appoint Azizah due to 1992 deal' http://www.malaysia-today.net/sultan-must-appoint-azizah-based-on-1992-deal/ (accessed 7 October 2016).

The Perak crisis arose from the following set of circumstances.[19] In the State of Perak, following the general elections of March 2008, PR won thirty-one seats in the State Legislative Assembly while BN won twenty-eight seats. PR formed the new State government. In January 2009, a member of BN made a stunning announcement of his intention to defect to PR, which was followed by three of PR's members announcing their resignations from the Legislative Assembly. The defecting BN member re-defected to BN. In consequence, both PR and BN each had twenty-eight seats in the Legislative Assembly. Later the three defecting PR members said that they had withdrawn their resignations and declared their intention to sit as independents but also pledged that they would give their support to the BN in confidential matters.

The Menteri Besar (Chief Minister) from PR, Nizar, requested Sultan Azlan Shah, as Perak's Head of State, to dissolve the Legislative Assembly to enable fresh elections to be held. The then Deputy Prime Minister, Najib Razak, as the chair of the Perak BN, had an audience with the Sultan the next day, and stated that BN had a majority in the Legislative Assembly. Sultan Azlan Shah subsequently met the twenty-eight BN members and the three defecting PR members and 'was convinced that [Nizar] had ceased to command the confidence of the majority of the State Assembly'. Sultan Azlan Shah, invoking Article XVIII (2)(b) of the Perak Constitution refused to dissolve the Legislative Assembly. Instead, Nizar was summoned to the palace and was ordered by the Sultan to resign as Menteri Besar, together with the members of the State executive council, with immediate effect. A press statement issued by the Sultan's office stated, 'If [Nizar] does not resign from his post as Perak Menteri Besar together with the state executive council members, then the posts of Menteri Besar and state executive councillors are regarded as vacant.'[20] This statement was tantamount to a dismissal of Nizar as the Menteri Besar of Perak.[21]

The legality of the actions of the Sultan was considered by the courts.[22] At first instance, the High Court in Kuala Lumpur held Nizar's dismissal was unlawful,[23]

[19] HP Lee, 'Constitutional developments in Malaysia in the first decade of the twenty-first century: a nation at the crossroads' in Albert HY Chen (ed), *Constitutionalism in Asia in the Early Twenty-First Century* (CUP 2014) 244, 252–5.

[20] Office of DYMM Paduka Seri Sultan Perak Darul Ridzuan, 'Sultan Azlan Shah's statement' (Media statement) *The Star* Online (5 February 2009) <http://thestar.com.my/news/story.asp?file=/2009/2/5/nation/20090205173703>.

[21] The Speaker of the Perak Legislative Assembly was subsequently dismissed by the BN controlled Assembly. A challenge to the dismissal was rejected by Azahar Mohamed J of the High Court in *Sivakumar a/l Varatharaju Naidu v Ganesan a/l Retanam* [2010] 7 MLJ 355.

[22] See Andrew Harding, 'Crises of Confidence and Perak's Constitutional Impasse' Center for Policy Initiatives 7 June 2009 http://www.loyarburok.com/2009/06/07/crises-of-confidence-and-peraks-constitutional-impasse/ (accessed 7 October 2016); Andrew Harding, 'The Perak Constitutional Crisis: An Epilogue' in Audrey Quay (ed), *Perak: A State of Crisis* (LoyarBurok Publications 2010) 165–70; NH Chan, 'A prima facie farce in Zambry v Nizar' Malaysiakini 8 July 2009 http://www.malaysiakini.com/news/108046.

[23] *Dato' Seri Ir Hj Mohammad Nizar bin Jamaluddin v Dato' Dr Zambry Abdul Kadir; [2009] 5 MLJ 108, (HC) (Leave Application); (Merits; HC, 11 May 2009).*

but the decision was reversed on appeal by the Court of Appeal[24] and that reversal was supported by the Federal Court.[25] The Sultan, by virtue of Article XVIII (2) of the Perak Constitution 'may act in his discretion' in relation to 'the appointment of a Menteri Besar' and 'the withholding of consent to a request for the dissolution of the Legislative Assembly'. However, the Perak Constitution is silent on the power of the Sultan to remove a Menteri Besar. Article XVI (6) of the Perak Constitution states that if the Menteri Besar 'ceases to command the confidence of the majority of the members of the Legislative Assembly, then, unless at his request His Royal Highness dissolves the Legislative Assembly, he shall tender the resignation of the Executive Council'. Article XXXVI (2) provides that the Sultan may prorogue or dissolve the Legislative Assembly.

The Sultan, who once occupied the highest judicial office, would have been fully familiar with the 1966 case of *Stephen Kalong Ningkan v Tun Abang Haji Openg*.[26] That case reinforced the view that the best test of a failure to command a majority of the members of the House of Representatives is by a vote of no confidence on the floor of Parliament. The provision of the Perak Constitution relating to the failure to 'command the confidence' of a majority of the Legislative Assembly is substantially similar to that of the Constitution of Sarawak under consideration by Harley AG CJ in the High Court in Kuching in 1966. Given the controversial nature of the political tussle, this would have been the better way to protect the neutral image of the Sultan and to enhance constitutional rule in Malaysia.

If a loss of confidence is achieved by defections from the government bench to the opposition, and the Menteri Besar chooses not to resign and instead seeks to dissolve the Legislative Assembly; it places the Sultan in a quandary. Whether to accede to the request of the Menteri Besar for a dissolution of the State legislature is a matter of discretion. The circumstances here would justify the Sultan deciding to dissolve the State legislature and allowing the final say to the people of Perak.

If the Menteri Besar had chosen to neither resign office nor request a dissolution of the Legislative Assembly, a most undesirable situation would have been created, and it would have unnecessarily drawn the Sultan into deciding whether to dismiss the Menteri Besar. The question is whether the Perak Constitution vests a power in the Ruler to dismiss in such circumstances. NH Chan, a retired Malaysian judge, observed:

> After the Sultan has appointed a Menteri Besar under Article 16(2)(a), then, has he the executive power to remove him? The answer is definitely no, because the only executive

[24] *Dato' Dr Zambry bin Abd Kadir v Dato' Seri Ir Hj Mohammad Nizar bin Jamaluddin; Attorney General of Malaysia (Intervener)* [2009] 5 CLJ 265 (CA).

[25] *Dato' Seri Ir Hj Mohammad Nizar Jamaluddin v Dato' Seri Dr Zambry Abdul Kadir; Attorney General (Intervener)* [2010] 2 CLJ 925 (FC).

[26] *Stephen Kalong Ningkan v Tun Abang Haji Openg and Tawi Sli* [1966] 2 MLJ 187; *Adegbenro v Akintola* [1963] 3 All ER 544; *Tun Datuk Haji Mustapha bin Datu Harun v Tun Datuk Haji Mohamed Adnan Robert, Yang di-Pertua Negeri Sabah & Datuk Joseph Pairin Kitingan (No. 2)* [1986] 2 MLJ 420; *Datuk Amir Kahar Tun Mustapha v Tun Mohamed Said Keruak* [1995] 1 CLJ 184.See HP Lee, 'Constitutional Heads and Judicial Intervention' in Wu Min Aun (ed), *Public Law in Contemporary Malaysia* (Longman 1999) chap. 1.

power left for the Sultan in which he 'may act in his discretion'—after a Menteri Besar has been appointed under Article 16(2)(a)—in respect of the Menteri Besar can only be found in Article 18(2)(a) and (b). Apart from Article 18(2)(a) and (b) there is no other executive power bestowed on the Sultan concerning the position and status of the Menteri Besar. The Sultan, therefore, has no executive power under the Perak Constitution to remove a Menteri Besar.[27]

Kevin Tan, adjunct professor of the National University of Singapore, criticized the approach taken by the judges in the Court of Appeal and the Federal Court:

I could not help but note the willingness with which the Court of Appeal judges were prepared to overturn a trial judge's finding of fact. The recounting of facts went on for pages on end, and lamentably, the Federal Court did the same thing. Almost half the Federal Court's judgment was concerned with how the facts should be read.... The Federal Court castigated the High Court judge for being perverse in refusing to believe the evidence of the State Legal Advisor and the documentary evidence before him even though they were not present at the trial.

Reading and re-reading the High Court judgment and those of Raus Sharif and Zainun Ali JJCA in particular, it is not at all obvious that Abdul Aziz J had erred, or if he did, erred to such an extent as to be regarded as 'perverse'.... Unless Abdul Aziz J is openly accused of bias (which was never argued), then what he did was perfectly legitimate and professional. At least he did not make the mistake of taking judicial notice of a supposition of his own making, which the Court of Appeal did. Appellate courts should really confine themselves to doing what they supposedly do best—deliberate on the law, interpret it well and ensure that it promotes the most equitable and just solution in the local context.[28]

Mukhriz Mahathir, the Menteri Besar of Kedah, 'was removed from office when only 17 of the 36 assemblymen expressed their support before the three-man rulers' council.'[29] In view of the decision of the Federal Court in the Perak crisis, the determination of loss of confidence in Menteri Besar, or the Prime Minister at federal level, is not confined to a vote in the legislature.

The Pardoning Power

The Malay Rulers play an influential role in the exercise of the power to grant a pardon or clemency or remission. This power is often described as an exercise of the prerogative power. There has been a debate over the existence of the prerogative in Malaysia. It has been asserted by Professor Hickling that in the case of the territories of Penang, Malacca, Sarawak, and Sabah, over which the Crown had direct

[27] NH Chan, 'The Federal Court in Nizar v Zambry: A Critique' LoyarBurok 19 February 2010 http://loyarburok.com/selected-judgments/the-federal-court-in-nizar-v-zambry-a-critique/ (accessed 23 July 2016).

[28] See Kevin Tan, 'The Final Chapter' in Audrey Quay (ed), *Perak: A State in Crisis* (LoyarBurok Publications 2010) 143–4.

[29] V Anbalagan, 'For now, Najib's fate in the hands of 222 MPs, says ex-A-G' *Malaysian Insider* (9 March 2016) https://sg.news.yahoo.com/now-najib-fate-hands-222-230031144.html (accessed 7 October 2016).

government, the prerogative powers were as extensive as those in England were and they duly devolved on the attainment of independence upon the appropriate successor authority. Referring to the Malay States, Professor Hickling said:

> Given an inheritance of the common law of England, therefore coupled with a transfer of power on independence, it is logical to assume that on 31 August, 1957 there was a transfer from the Crown of both major and minor prerogatives; and the transference of such prerogatives must have been, at the federal level, the [King] and, to such extent, as they affected the Malay States, the Malay Rulers.[30]

Professor AJ Harding, who has asserted a contrary view, stressed that the introduction of the Constitution on 31 August 1957 had the effect of making important redisposition of legislative, executive, and judicial powers. He said:

> Her Majesty's prerogatives ceased to apply, insofar as they had applied, and to the different extents to which they applied (if at all), to the states which joined the Federation. The Head of that Federation was the Yang di-Pertuan Agong; he occupied an office which had never previously existed ... the prerogatives of the Crown at common law merely lapsed when the Malaysian flag was raised in Kuala Lumpur on 31 August 1957, and the Yang di-Pertuan Agong owes nothing to Her Majesty by way of succession.[31]

On the specific prerogative of mercy, the debate is rendered an exercise in futility, given that the Constitution expressly empowers the Yang di-Pertuan Agong, State Rulers, and Governors to grant pardon for certain offences committed in specified territories. The idea of including a pardoning power in the Constitution was influenced by the English prerogative of mercy. The pardoning power is expressly embodied in Article 42 of the Constitution. The drafting of the provisions of this Article was clearly influenced by the provisions of Articles 72 and 161 of the Indian Constitution.

Article 42

Article 42 of the Constitution expressly provides that the Yang di-Pertuan Agong has power to grant 'pardons, reprieves and respites' in respect of all offences which have been tried by court-martial and all offences committed in the Federal Territories of Kuala Lumpur, Labuan, and Putrajaya. It also provides that the Ruler, or a Governor of a State, has power to grant 'pardons, reprieves and respites' in respect of all other offences committed in his State.

The Ruler or Governor of a State is required to exercise the power of pardon on the 'advice' of a Pardons Board constituted for that State. A single Pardons Board is constituted for the Federal Territories of Kuala Lumpur, Labuan, and Putrajaya and is presided by the Yang di-Pertuan Agong. The Constitution does not spell out expressly that the Yang di-Pertuan Agong has to act on the advice of the Pardons Board. The federal legislation prescribing the pardoning function may

[30] RH Hickling, 'The Prerogative in Malaysia' (1975) 17 Malaya Law Review 207.

[31] AJ Harding, 'Monarchy and the Prerogative in Malaysia' (1986) 28 Malaya Law Review 345

make provision requiring the Yang di-Pertuan Agong to 'act in accordance with or on the recommendation of' the Pardons Board.

The Federal Attorney General is a member of all the Pardons Boards. In the case of a State Pardons Board, the other members comprise of the Menteri Besar of the State and three other members appointed by the Ruler or Governor. In the case of the Pardons Board for the Federal Territories, the Minister responsible for the Federal Territories and three other members appointed by the Yang di-Pertuan Agong comprise the other members of the Pardons Board.

Members of a Pardons Board are appointed for a term of 3 years and are eligible for reappointment. A member may resign from the Board at any time. Members of a State Legislative Assembly or of the House of Representatives cannot be appointed to a Pardons Board or exercise temporarily the functions of a member of the Pardons Board. A State Pardons Board is presided by the Ruler or Governor and in the case of the Pardons Board for the Federal Territories, by the Yang di-Pertuan Agong.

The scope of the pardoning power of the Yang di-Pertuan Agong

Only the Yang di-Pertuan Agong has the power to pardon a person tried and sentenced by a court-martial. This power extends to the granting of remission, suspension, or commutation. The reason the Yang di-Pertuan Agong is given the power of pardon for court-martial cases is because the Yang di-Pertuan Agong is, by virtue of Article 41 of the Constitution, 'the Supreme Commander of the armed forces of the Federation'. Article 137 provides that the command, discipline, and administration of the armed forces all be under the general authority of the Yang di-Pertuan Agong.[32]

In exercising the pardoning power in court-martial cases, the Pardons Board has no role to play because there is no statutory provision stating that the Yang di-Pertuan Agong is to act on the advice of a Pardons Board in such cases. The Yang di-Pertuan Agong, in such cases, acts on the advice of the Cabinet or of a Minister acting under the general authority of the Cabinet. This position is in accordance with Article 40(1), which states:

> In the exercise of his functions under this Constitution or federal law the Yang di-Pertuan Agong shall act in accordance with the advice of the Cabinet or of a Minister acting under the general authority of the Cabinet, except as otherwise provided by this Constitution …

[32] With effect from 5 October 1975, the pardoning power in relation to offences under the Internal Security Act 1960 (now repealed) became the exclusive preserve of the King acting on the advice of a Pardons Board specially constituted for security offences by virtue of Regulation 2(1) of the Essential (Security Cases) (Amendment) Regulations 1975 ('ESCAR'). Regulation 2(1) provides as follows: '… the power of the [King] to grant pardons, reprieves and respites or to remit, suspend or to commute sentences under Clauses (1) and (2) of Article 42 of the Constitution shall extend to all security offences wherever committed or tried and such extended power shall be exclusively exercisable by him notwithstanding however the provisions of any written law to the contrary.'

A 'security offence' refers to an offence against various stated provisions of the Internal Security Act 1960, or any offence against any other written law the commission of which is certified by the Attorney General to affect the security of the Federation (Regulation 29(1)).

The Yang di-Pertuan Agong's pardoning power extends also to sentences imposed by the Syariah Courts in the States of Malacca, Penang, Sabah, or Sarawak or the Federal Territories of Kuala Lumpur, Labuan, and Putrajaya. This is because the Yang di-Pertuan Agong is the Head of the religion of Islam in the State.

Subject to the abovementioned categories, the general rule prescribed by the Constitution is that the power of pardon is exercised by the Ruler or Governor of a State in which the offence was committed.

In relation to Anwar Ibrahim's petition to the Yang di-Pertuan Agong for a royal pardon, Daniel Pascoe observes:

> [D]espite the official position being that the Pardons Board deliver politically-impartial advice and that 'the Federal Government has no say in the power of pardon', the implicitly or overtly political representatives serving on the Pardons Board (in the form of the Federal Attorney-general, the local Chief Minister, and perhaps even politically sympathetic lay members) are usually in a position to guarantee recommendations for pardon to the Agong, Ruler or Governor that suit the UMNO-dominated government's agenda.

Daniel Pascoe further points out that Article 42(9) mandates that the Pardons Board '*shall* consider any written opinion which the Attorney-General may have delivered thereon.'[33]

The Rulers as Guardians of the Nation

Andrew Harding has noted that the Rulers 'have clearly started to take a more active and somewhat less formal role in Malaysian society.'[34] Some Rulers can play a vital role in deterring religious extremists seeking to advance a highly conservative religious agenda. They have spoken out loudly against undesirable pressures being exerted by religious fundamentalists. For instance, in April 2016, the Sultan of Johor, Sultan Ibrahim Ibni Almarhum Sultan Iskandar, openly criticized those who sought to replace Malay culture with Arab culture.[35]

In the on-going controversy over the sovereign fund 1MDB, there have been calls for the Yang di-Pertuan Agong, and as a final resort, the Conference of Rulers, to remove Najib Razak from his prime ministerial position. The manner in which the State Ruler had resolved the 'Perak crisis', in which Najib Razak was the pivotal player, may come back to haunt him. Abdul Aziz Bari, a prominent Malaysian constitutional law expert, asserted that the Yang di-Pertuan Agong should monitor developments following the WSJ report and added, 'If the Agong seems not firm enough to handle the matter, the Conference of Rulers can step in.'[36] Mahathir

[33] 'What the Rejection of Anwar Ibrahim's Petition for Pardon Tells Us about Malaysia's Royal Pardons System' (2016) 18(1) Asian-Pacific Law & Policy Journal (forthcoming).

[34] Andrew Harding, *The Constitution of Malaysia: A Contextual Analysis* (Hart Publishing 2012) 123.

[35] Wong Chun Wai, 'Stop trying to be like Arabs, Ruler advises Malays' http://aliran.com/web-specials/2016-web-specials/stop-trying-like-arabs-ruler-advises-malays/ (accessed 6 April 2016).

[36] Hafiz Yatim, 'Can the Agong act to depose a sitting PM?' *Malaysiakini* (7 July 2015) https://www.malaysiakini.com/news/304338 (accessed 29 March 2016).

Mohamad, in calling on Malaysians to sign the Citizens' Declaration calling for the resignation of Prime Minister Najib Abdul Razak, has said that once it has received a million signatures, the 'Save Malaysia' campaign can then petition the Rulers to 'pressure' Najib Razak to resign.[37] Abdul Aziz Bari, while acknowledging that the Yang di-Pertuan Agong cannot dismiss a Prime Minister who still retains the support of a majority of members of the Dewan Rakyat, nevertheless, said that the Yang di-Pertuan Agong 'can instruct the Dewan Rakyat speaker to allow a vote of no-confidence to take place ..., as part of the ruler's duty to protect the Federal Constitution.'[38] The Rulers, who were stripped of their royal immunity in 1993, are now being urged to play a pivotal role in the political life of Malaysia and being accorded the status of constitutional defenders. There is no clearer indication of the royal resurgence than this.

Time to restore royal assent to legislation

As a result of the 1983 confrontation between the Rulers and the Mahathir administration, the Rulers were stripped of the traditional role of giving the royal assent to legislation as the final act of transforming a Bill into an Act of Parliament. It was reported that the controversial National Security Council Bill became law through deeming that royal assent had been given. This reporting, when one reads between the lines appears to suggest that the Conference of Rulers have reservations about aspects of the Bill. By using the deeming provision, any valuable suggestions by the Rulers for a more refined piece of legislation can simply be ignored. It is time for the Constitution to be amended to restore the royal assent to legislation.

Conclusion

Andrew Harding observes, 'The Rulers have realized the limits of their influence, and are clearly aware that, if they do not adapt to the requirements of a modern, democratic Constitution, they run the risk of abolition of their powers.'[39] He describes the transformation of the Malay Rulers as a remarkable 'turn-around',[40] while Suwannathat-Pian refers to it as 'a rejuvenation'.[41] The resurgence of the Malay Rulers is also assisted by the changing political landscape. John Berthelsen points out that in the political vacuum that arose after the weakened national coalition lost the popular vote for the first time since 1969, UMNO 'has found it

[37] 'Agong has a moral duty to act, says constitutional expert' *Malaysiakini* (29 March 2016) https://www.malaysiakini.com/news/335642 (accessed 29 March 2016).

[38] ibid.

[39] Andrew Harding, 'Sovereigns Immune? The Malaysian Monarchy in Crisis' (1993) 327 The Round Table 305.

[40] Andrew Harding, *The Constitution of Malaysia: A Contextual Analysis* (Hart Publishing 2012) 121.

[41] Kobkua Suwannathat-Pian, *Palace, Political Party and Power: A Story of the Socio-Political Development of Malay Kingship* (NUS Press 2011) 410.

expedient to rehabilitate the sultans for political uses' and that this, in turn, 'has resulted in opportunities for the sultans to rebuild their power base'.[42]

After the 2008 general election, when the opposition scored a stunning result, 'a large section of UMNO went all out to prove that they were the true royalists and that parties in the Pakatan coalition were anti-monarchy'.[43] Syed Husin Ali observes:

> It appears that for a long time to come, the institution of the Rulers will continue to be upheld in this country. The question is how will this institution adapt itself or be adapted to the needs of change, progress, modernization, democracy, justice as well as religious and customary values? There is nothing wrong with having a ruling monarch in a political system as long as he is just, kind, humane, god-fearing, intelligent, not selfish or wasteful. A Ruler who has these qualities could serve as a useful check and balance, especially in a political system that is beginning to show authoritarian tendencies or, worse still, is dictatorial, corrupt, and wasteful. But if the Rulers do not possess these qualities, their role at check and balance would be ineffective.[44]

How the Malay Rulers forge their role within the Malaysian Constitution and carve out a special niche in the governance of the Malaysian polity will determine their tryst with destiny.

[42] John Berthelsen, 'Malaysia's Sultans Return to Power' *Asia Sentinel* (18 September 2014) http://www.asiasentinel.com/politics/malaysia-sultans-regain-power/ (accessed 23 July 2016).

[43] Syed Husin Ali, *The Malay Rulers: Regression or Reform?* (Strategic Information and Research Development Centre 2014) 46.

[44] ibid 82. See, also, Abdul Aziz Bari, *The Monarchy, and the Constitution in Malaysia* (IDEAS 2013) 333–50.

5

The Judiciary under Siege: The 1988 Crisis

> An independent Judiciary that is not subservient to the Legislature or the Executive, either in theory or in practice, is often regarded as the bastion of Parliamentary Democracy. That bastion is under siege today.
>
> C Muzzafar 'Press Release' 16 March 1988

> Judicial Independence is a privilege of, and a protection for, the people. It is a fundamental element in our democracy, all the more so now that the citizen's rights against the state are of greater value than his or her rights against other citizens.
>
> Chief Justice Mason, 'The Independence of the Bench; The Independence of the Bar and the Bar's Role in the Judicial System', Keynote address to the 1992 Conference of English, Scottish and Australian Bar Association, London, 4 July 1992, 3

In 1988, as Sultan Mahmood Iskandar was about to enter into the final year of his term of kingship, a constitutional drama of a greater magnitude than the 1983 crisis unfolded in Malaysia.[1] For the first time in Malaysian legal history, the highest judicial officer in the land was suspended and, after an inquiry to determine whether he should be removed for alleged misbehaviour, was subsequently removed.[2] Following

[1] See, generally, Tun Salleh Abas, *The Role of the Independent Judiciary* (Promarketing Publications 1989) (The Sir John Foster Galaway Memorial Lecture delivered at University College, London, on 4 November 1988); Tun Salleh Abas and K Das, *May Day for Justice* (Magnus Books 1989); Andrew Harding, 'The 1988 Constitutional Crisis in Malaysia' (1990) 39 ICLQ 57; RH Hickling, 'The Malaysian Judiciary in Crisis' (1989) Public Law 20; FA Trindade, 'The Removal of the Malaysian Judges' (1990) 106 LQR 51; Lawyers Committee for Human Rights, *Malaysia: Assault on the Judiciary* (New York 1990). The drama evoked considerable international concern—see e.g., Justice Kirby, 'Malaysia: The Judiciary and the Rule of Law' (1998) 41 International Commission of Jurists' Review 40; (1988) Australian Law News (August) 12–16; (1988) New Zealand Law Journal 217–8, 266–7; Resolution adopted by the International Commission of Jurists at its meeting in Caracas, Venezuela, on 20 January 1989 (reproduced in (1989) 1 MLJ cxxii); *The Times* (16, 19. and 23 October 1989). An attempt was made to defend the actions of the government in Peter Aldridge Williams, *Judicial Misconduct* (Pelanduk Publications 1990). The deficiencies in this attempt were highlighted in Raja Aziz Addruse, *Conduct Unbecoming* (Walrus 1990). See also K Das, *Questionable Conduct* (Kuala Lumpur 1990).

[2] *Report of the Tribunal Established under Article 125(3) and (4) of the Federal Constitution. Re: YAA Tun Dato' Hj. Mohamed Salleh Abas* (Government Printer 1988) (hereafter referred to as the *First Tribunal Report*).

this unprecedented development, two other senior judges of the Supreme Court were, after an inquiry by a Second Tribunal, also removed from office.

The subsequent events should be seen in the context of a 'high stakes' political struggle within the ranks of UMNO, Malaysia's dominant political party. It must also be viewed against the relationships and conflicts of a number of prominent personalities: the Prime Minister (Dr Mahathir Mohamed), the then Yang di-Pertuan Agong or King (Sultan Mahmood Iskandar), and the then Lord President of the Supreme Court of Malaysia (Tun Mohamed Salleh bin Abas). Other participants, who were hovering in the wings, included Sultan Azlan Shah (the then Deputy King) and Tan Sri Abu Talib Osman (the then Federal Attorney General). Eventually, the spotlight was also turned on Tan Sri (later Tun) Abdul Hamid Omar (the then Chief Justice of the High Court of Malaya).

This chapter explores the various constitutional and political dimensions of the convulsion that afflicted the Malaysian judiciary in 1988. The political dimension cannot be divorced from the constitutional dimension, for the legal and constitutional manoeuvrings were consonant with the political skirmishing that involved, at one stage, the very political survival of the Prime Minister, Dr Mahathir.

The Backdrop

A Letter to the King

The crisis developed from a letter sent, on 26 March 1988, by Tun Salleh Abas to the King; a copy of which was sent to each of the State Rulers. The contents of the English translation of the letter as reproduced in the *Report of The Tribunal Established Under Article 125(3) and (4) of the Federal Constitution. Re: Y.A.A. Tun Dato' Hj. Mohamed Salleh Abas,*[3] (hereafter referred to as the *First Tribunal Report*), are as follows:

> I as Lord President on behalf of myself and all the Judges of the country beg to express our feelings regarding the development in the relationship between the Executive and the Judiciary.
>
> All of us are disappointed with the various comments and accusations made by the Honourable Prime Minister against the Judiciary, not only outside but within Parliament.
>
> However all of us are patient and do not like to reply to the accusations publicly because such action is not compatible with our position as Judges under the Constitution. Furthermore such action will not be in keeping with Malay tradition and custom. It is to be remembered that we are Judges appointed and given letters of appointment by Duli Maha Mulia Seri Paduka Baginda Yang di-Pertuan Agong and also Duli Yang Maha Mulia the Malay Rulers to preserve, protect and defend the Constitution. As such it is only proper for us to be patient in the interest of the nation.

[3] *First Tribunal Report* (Government Printer 1988).

> Other than that the accusations and comments have brought shame to all of us and left us mentally disturbed to the extent of being unable to discharge our functions orderly and properly. We all feel ashamed because we are not able to avoid from being looked down by those who do not understand our position under the Constitution.
>
> This letter is an effort to convey our feelings to Duli Yang Maha Mulia Tuanku with the hope that all of those unfounded accusations will be stopped.[4]

It must be pointed out that the letter was couched in high Malay, which is the customary mode of writing to the King. Those who are familiar with Malay culture and language describe the letter as quiet, courteous, and dignified. The English translation does not do it justice.[5]

This letter was written in response to a continuing barrage of criticisms levelled by the Prime Minister at the judiciary.[6] As Tun Salleh Abas, himself, explained:

> A judge of the High Court Malaya, who was unable to bear the criticisms of the Prime Minister wrote a letter to me and the Chief Justice Malaya (who is now the Acting Lord President), threatening to go public if the criticisms continued. I therefore immediately called a meeting of judges. There were 20 judges altogether attending the meeting, all Kuala Lumpur judges, including the Acting Lord President. It was then decided that no public speech in reply to the Prime Minister's criticisms should be made, but a letter should be addressed to the King and other Malay Rulers. This was agreed to by all, including the Acting Lord President, although one Supreme Court Judge, Hashim Sani, felt a bit unhappy about the decision. The letters to the King and to the Malay Rulers were all identical in terms except for the addresses. These were drafted by me and a drafting committee, which was set up at the judges' meeting. All judges including those who did not attend the meeting were each given a copy of the letter. I received no objection from any of them but instead a few of them wrote to me positively supporting the move.[7]

The letter sent by Tun Salleh Abas to the King constituted the central 'justification' for the ultimate removal of the Lord President of the Supreme Court. However, a number of significant developments had given impetus to the moves that eventually resulted in his removal. Some of these will now be explored.

[4] ibid Vol I annexure 2.

[5] The author understands that it is traditional for Malays to have direct access to the sovereign, to complain even about the District Officer, or even the highest officer in the land. The complaint even if it had come from a humble villager would have been dealt with, and the writer would not have been punished at all.

[6] The occasions on which the Prime Minister had criticized the judiciary are set out in 'A Report by the Bar Council on the Report of the Tribunal Established in Respect of Tun Mohamed Salleh Abas' (1988) XX (5) INSAF (Journal of the Malaysian Bar) 30, 36–7. Initially, Tun Salleh opted to maintain 'a profile of silence'. However, believing that continued silence in the face of the unending attacks would 'seriously undermine the confidence of the public in the judiciary', he began to reply to the criticisms of the Prime Minister in a speech at an official book-launching ceremony at the Shangri-la Hotel, Kuala Lumpur on 12 January 1988. A copy of this speech is reproduced in *First Tribunal Report* Vol III 32–4.

[7] Tun Salleh Abas, *The Role of the Independent Judiciary* (Promarketing Publications 1989) 15–16. In his book, *May Day for Justice*, Tun Salleh disclosed that the High Court judge who had written to him was Abdul Razak J. The full text of that letter is set out at pp 67–8 of that book.

The Berthelsen Case

The Prime Minister's dissatisfaction with the judiciary intensified with the decision of the Supreme Court in *Berthelsen v Director General of Immigration, Malaysia & Ors.*[8] This case involved an American staff correspondent attached to the Kuala Lumpur office of the *Asian Wall Street Journal*. He had been granted a 2-year employment pass valid until 2 November 1986. However, on 26 September 1986, he was served with a notice of cancellation of his employment pass under the Immigration Regulations 1963.[9] The notice of cancellation stated that the Director General of Immigration was satisfied that Berthelsen had contravened or failed to comply with the Immigration Act 1959–1963 and the Immigration Regulations 1963, that he had failed to comply with the conditions imposed in respect of that pass or the instructions endorsed thereon, and, therefore, his presence in the Federation was or would be prejudicial to the security of the country. Berthelsen sought leave from the High Court to apply for an order of *certiorari* to quash the cancellation of the employment pass, and for an order of prohibition against his expulsion from the country. When leave was refused, he appealed to the Supreme Court.

Abdoolcader SCJ, delivering the judgment of the Court,[10] pointed out that Berthelsen was lawfully in the country under the sanction of an employment pass validly issued for a stipulated period, and that he clearly had a 'legitimate expectation' to be entitled to remain in the country, at least until the expiry of the prescribed duration. Abdoolcader SCJ added, '[A]ny action to curtail that expectation would in law attract that application of the rules of natural justice requiring that he be given an opportunity of making whatever representations he thought necessary in the circumstances.'[11]

It was the conclusion of the Court that as Berthelsen had not been given the opportunity to make representations regarding the cancellation of his employment pass, the requirements of natural justice had not been satisfied. Accordingly, the Court ordered that *certiorari* be issued to quash the cancellation.

The Prime Minister must have taken umbrage at this bold decision of the Supreme Court. In the parliamentary debates on a Constitutional Amendment Bill, Dr Mahathir, after referring to the *Berthelsen* case, was reported to have said that the laws clearly stated that the Minister could decide how long a foreigner could stay in the country and that this decision was final. He was also quoted as saying: 'But the judge overruled this. That was a well-known case. The person was allowed to stay here and the Minister could not do anything.'[12]

[8] [1987] 1 MLJ 134.

[9] Berthelsen was one of two journalists of the *Asian Wall Street Journal* to be expelled. In September 1986, the Malaysian Government had banned the distribution of the journal. Although no specific reasons were given by the Government, it was alleged that the reason for the action against the journal was an article it ran on 'cronyism' in Malaysian banking and mismanagement in economic affairs: See 'Human Rights in the World: Malaysia' (1986) Review International Commission of Jurists 12.

[10] The other members of the Court were Salleh Abas LP and Mohamed Azmi SCJ.

[11] [1987] 1 MLJ 134, 137.

[12] 'Constitutional Change Passed' *New Straits Times* (19 March 1988) 4.

These reported remarks of Dr Mahathir gave an impression of a failure to appreciate the nature of the judicial function. In many countries committed to the rule of law curial constraints imposed upon the exercise of ministerial powers have been accepted as commonplace. Governments do not rail against the judiciary simply because the judiciary has not facilitated the exercise of executive powers: instead, attempts are made to exercise the powers in accordance with the judicial rulings.

Dr Mahathir was misconceiving the thrust of the decision in *Berthelsen*. The Court was not saying that 'the Minister could not do anything.' What the Supreme Court was emphasising was that such cancellation should be in accordance with well-established principles of natural justice. These principles, which have been developed by eminent courts of the common law world, simply reflect a mature and civilized society. All that the Minister was required to do was to provide an opportunity for the accused to tell his side of the story. 'If, having done all this, the [Director General of Immigration] then gives consideration to [Berthelsen's] representations, the requirements of natural justice will have been satisfied and it would be for the [Director General of Immigration] to make his decision whether or not to cancel the employment pass in the exercise of the discretion conferred upon him.'[13]

The remarks of Dr Mahathir were unfortunate. The Supreme Court's decision in *Berthelsen* was clearly impeccable: it was logical and consistent with established authorities.

The contempt of court action against the Prime Minister

Dr Mahathir's annoyance with the *Berthelsen* decision was highlighted soon after in an interview he gave to the international editor and the Bangkok bureau chief of *Time* magazine. Excerpts of the interview were published under the heading 'I Know How the People Feel'. In commenting on the role of the courts, Dr Mahathir observed:

> The judiciary says [to us], 'Although you passed a law with a certain thing in mind, we think that your mind is wrong, and we want to give our interpretation.' If we disagree, the courts will say, 'We will interpret your disagreement.' If we go along, we are going to lose our power of legislation. We know exactly what we want to do, but once we do it, it is interpreted in a different way, and we have no means to interpret it our way. If we find out that a court always throws us out on its own interpretation, if it interprets contrary to why we made the law, then we will have to find a way of producing a law that will have to be interpreted according to our wish.[14]

This passage sparked off a contempt of court action instituted by Lim Kit Siang against the Prime Minister. Harun J (as he then was) of the High Court dismissed the application.[15] Harun J, after scrutiny of the passage from *Time* magazine, was reported to have made a certain remark to which the Prime Minister 'took exception':[16] 'The Prime Minister's real complaint is that laws are not being made fool

[13] [1987] 1 MLJ 134, 138.
[14] *Time* (24 November 1986) 18.
[15] *Lim Kit Siang v Dato' Seri Dr Mahathir Mohamed* (1987) 1 MLJ 383.
[16] Tun Salleh Abas, *The Role of the Independent Judiciary* (Promarketing Publications 1989) 10.

proof, so to speak. The statement is an expression of Dr Mahathir's dilemma that the courts are not able to express the intention of the Government in their decisions because of faulty or slipshod laws made by Parliament.'[17] An appeal by Lim Kit Siang to the Supreme Court was dismissed. The Supreme Court (Salleh Abas LP, Abdul Hamid CJ [Malaya], and Abdoolcader SCJ) regarded the passage as containing statements that stemmed from 'a misconception of the role of the courts.'[18] When viewed 'objectively and dispassionately and in proper perspective', it was simply an articulation of the executive's frustration in not being able to achieve its objects in matters where the intervention of the courts had been sought. It was the conclusion of the Supreme Court that the passage did not amount to a contempt of court.

The UEM case

Another case which affected the Prime Minister's perception of the judiciary was the *UEM* case[19]—a case which was also initiated by Lim Kit Siang in his capacity as 'a Member of Parliament, the Leader of the Opposition in the House of Representatives, a State Assemblyman, a taxpayer, a motorist and a frequent user of highways and roads in the country.'[20] For purposes of the present discussion, it is sufficient to simplify the facts of the case.

The case concerned the privatization of the North-South Highway. Lim Kit Siang instituted proceedings against the United Engineers (Malaysia) Berhad (UEM; a holding company controlled by UMNO), the Government of Malaysia, and two ministers (the Minister of Finance and the Minister of Works). Lim sought from the court a declaration to the effect that the letter of intent, given in December 1986, by the government to UEM in respect of the North-South Highway contract was null and void. He also sought an injunction to restrain UEM from signing the contract for the project with any agent or servant of the government.

On 25 August 1987, the Supreme Court, allowing an appeal from the decision of Edgar Joseph Jr J of the High Court, granted an interlocutory injunction against UEM to restrain it from signing the proposed contract pursuant to the letter of intent pending the final determination of the suit. In its oral judgment, the Supreme Court said, inter alia, 'We have considered a number of authorities both English and local as to the question of *locus standi*. We need only say that on the facts of this case the appellant clearly has *locus standi* to bring this suit.'[21] An appeal by UEM and the government to have the interlocutory injunction set aside was dismissed by the High Court but the appeal by the two ministers to have the suit against them

[17] 'Mahathir's Dilemma', *Star* (29 November 1986) 1. On 5 September 1987, Harun J at a law seminar at Universiti Kebangsaan Malaysia expressed certain views regarding the need to make improvements to the Malaysian Constitution, particularly, the need to revamp the Senate. These reported comments aroused the ire of the Prime Minister. See 'Harun: Some Changes Needed', *New Sunday Times* (6 September 1987) 5.

[18] ibid. [19] *Government of Malaysia v Lim Kit Siang* [1988] 2 MLJ 12.

[20] ibid 43 (per Abdoolcader SCJ).

[21] The oral judgment is quoted in [1988] 1 MLJ 50, 53.

struck out was allowed. Both UEM and the government promptly appealed to the Supreme Court against the dismissal of their respective applications.

Tun Salleh Abas subsequently explained the main thrust of the case as follows:

The case turned upon the issue of *locus standi*. The Supreme Court sat in a panel of 5 judges and was almost evenly divided ... Two judges held that Mr Lim had *locus standi* whilst two others held otherwise. I sided with the latter not so much on the ground that Mr Lim had no *locus standi* but more on the ground that the allegations of frauds and criminal offence should be thrashed out according to criminal law in a criminal law court.[22]

Abdul Hamid Omar CJ described the question of *locus standi* as the 'central issue'[23], whilst Hashim Yeop Sani SCJ described it as 'the crucial question.'[24] Both judges appeared to have sympathy for the argument that the judgment of the Supreme Court on the issue of *locus standi* 'was merely obiter'. It is not difficult to share the annoyance of Abdoolcader SCJ, who described the argument as a 'preposterous contention':

The pronouncement on 25 August 1987 is a judgment of the Supreme Court which unequivocally made a decision on the points in issue before it including that of standing taken by the appellants themselves and crucial to the substratum and basis of the respondent's suit. Any view to the contrary as to the efficacy of that judgment would lay open the door to similar contentions in relation to decisions of this court and indeed of other courts as well in matters where brief oral judgments are delivered at the conclusion of argument.[25]

Abdoolcader SCJ entered a self-described 'vigorous dissent' and endeavoured 'to translate the sting of the thing into language as mild as [he] can mobilise and muster without mincing words.'[26] George Seah SCJ, the other dissenting judge, also argued convincingly that the Court lacked the jurisdiction to review and reverse the decision made by the Supreme Court on 25 August 1987.

The dissenting judges clearly adopted an enlightened view of the rule relating to *locus standi*. In his eloquent judgment, Abdoolcader SCJ dealt with the question of a relator action by describing it as 'a theoretical possibility with no conceivable hope generally for practical purposes of advancing the concrete action beyond that.' He also remarked:

I would think it would be too much to expect process of this nature involving the ventilation of a public grievance to proceed only through this channel, given even the fortitude the incumbent of the office would presumably be endowed with, in view of the rebound where the complaint is against the Government itself and the Attorney General is its legal adviser, as it would surely be expected that if the complaint merited action by the Attorney General or by his *fiat* to a relator, he would himself in the first instance have had the cause of complaint aborted before its overt manifestation.[27]

Undoubtedly, the views of Hamid Omar CJ and Hashim Yeop Sani SCJ (also shared by Salleh Abas LP) represented a retrograde step in the development of

[22] Tun Salleh, *The Role of the Independent Judiciary* (Promarketing Publications 1989) 12.
[23] *Government of Malaysia v Lim Kit Siang* [1988] 2 MLJ 12, 27. [24] ibid 38.
[25] ibid 46. [26] ibid 41–2. [27] ibid 45.

administrative law in Malaysia. To deny *locus standi* to Lim Kit Siang would possibly lead to an enormous sum of public money running into billions of dollars, being spent illegally. Surely, George Seah SCJ's proposition that Lim Kit Siang, as a Member of Parliament, owes a duty not only to his own electorate but also to the Dewan Rakyat and the peoples of Malaysia is uncontroversial. It would constitute an abdication of his judicial duty if he were to hold that Lim Kit Siang lacked the standing to institute the proceedings.

The additional reason advanced by Salleh Abas LP cannot withstand scrutiny: he regarded the complaint as an attempt to enforce the criminal law against the Prime Minister (because UEM belonged to UMNO, of which the Prime Minister is the President), the Minister of Finance, and the Minister of Works. George Seah SCJ gave short shrift to such a view with the succinct rejoinder that Lim Kit Siang did not sue to enforce the criminal law: 'It was a public interest suit calling for judicial review of the legality of the proposed executive action.'[28]

Although the *UEM* case represented a victory for the government, it was, nevertheless, a decision that had likely disconcerted the Prime Minister; the dissenting judgments signalled that some members of the judiciary were prepared to exercise judicial control over executive actions and were not prepared to countenance procedural expedients, such as *locus standi*. The strain in the relationship between the government and the judiciary was further aggravated when on 19 March 1987, the Supreme Court, by a majority, dismissed the appeal of the Public Prosecutor against the decision of High Court judge, Zakaria Yatim J, in *Public Prosecutor v Dato' Yap Peng*.[29] The decision of the Supreme Court provoked the Prime Minister to bring about a legislative undermining of that decision: Parliament enacted the Constitution (Amendment) Act, 1988.[30]

In *Dato' Yap Peng*, the accused was first produced before the Sessions Court at Kuala Lumpur, and was charged with two charges of criminal breach of trust to which he claimed trial. When his case was mentioned again in the Sessions Court, the Deputy Public Prosecutor tendered a certificate under Section 418A of the Criminal Procedure Code, which was signed by the Public Prosecutor himself. The President of the Court thereupon transmitted the case to the High Court. When the accused was charged again in the High Court at Kuala Lumpur, on the same two charges, objection was taken to the transfer of the case from the Sessions Court to the High Court.

In the said case, it was asserted that Section 418A of the Criminal Procedure Code was unconstitutional because it infringed, inter alia, Article 121(1) of the Constitution.[31] Section 418A of the Criminal Procedure Code provided as follows:

[28] ibid 35. [29] [1987] 2 MLJ 311 (High Court) and 316 (Supreme Court).

[30] Act A704.

[31] Previous challenges to the validity of s 418A of the Criminal Procedure Code on the ground of violation of Article 8(1) of the Constitution had been dismissed: by the Federal Court in *Datuk Haji Harun bin Idris v PP* [1977] 2 MLJ 155; and in *PP v Oh Keng Seng* [1977] 2 MLJ 206; by Hashim Yeop A Sani J in *PP v Su Liang Yu* [1976] 2 MLJ 128; by Ajaib Singh J in *PP v Oh Keng Seng* [1976] 2 MLJ 125. Cf Abdoolcader J in *PP v Datuk Harun bin Hj Idris & Ors* [1976] 2 MLJ 116.

(1) Notwithstanding the provisions of section 417, the Public Prosecutor may in any particular case triable by a Criminal Court subordinate to the High Court issue a certificate requiring the Court before which the case is pending to remove it to the High Court at such place as may be specified in the certificate and to cause the accused person to appear or be produced before the said High Court.

Article 121(1) of the Constitution provided that 'the judicial power of the Federation shall be vested in two High Courts of co-ordinate jurisdiction and status ... and in such inferior courts as may be provided by federal law.'

Zakaria Yatim J of the High Court concluded that s 418A of the Criminal Procedure Code did encroach upon the judicial power of the Federation, which, under Article 121(1), was vested in the courts.

The Supreme Court, by a majority, dismissed the appeal by the Public Prosecutor. Abdoolcader SCJ, with whom Lee Hun Hoe CJ (Borneo) agreed, pointed out that what was under challenge was a power at any stage of the proceedings to effect the transfer of any particular case pending before a subordinate court competent to try it to the High Court. Section 418A was 'both a legislative and executive intromission into the judicial power of the Federation'. In colourful language, Abdoolcader SCJ wrote: 'Any other view would *ex necessitate rei* result in relegating the provisions of article 121(1) vesting the judicial power of the Federation in the curial entities specified to no more than a teasing illusion, like a munificent bequest in a pauper's will.'[32] Mohamed Azmi SCJ, to like effect, said that judicial power to transfer cases from a subordinate court of competent jurisdiction could not be conferred on any organ of government other than the judiciary.[33]

Both Salleh Abas LP and Hashim Yeop Sani SCJ dissented. The former was prepared to make a concession: the law under challenge was constitutional to the extent that the Public Prosecutor's power was exercisable before the trial had started. This concession was clarified by Salleh Abas LP: 'If the Public Prosecutor purports to exercise his power under section 418A after the trial has commenced in the Subordinate Court, such exercise, I agree, would be unconstitutional because viewed from the Court's angle it interferes with the Court's function of carrying on with the trial to its conclusion and therefore could be regarded as encroaching upon the judicial power of the Court.'[34]

As a response to the Supreme Court decision, the Constitution (Amendment) Act 1988 was enacted. One of the provisions of this Act sought to excise the vesting of the judicial power of the Federation in the courts. Henceforth the High Courts and inferior courts 'shall have such jurisdiction and powers as may be conferred by or under federal law.' Another provision declared that the High Court in Malaya and the High Court in Sabah and Sarawak 'shall have no jurisdiction in respect of any matter within the jurisdiction of the Syariah courts', a constitutional amendment that opened a new front for constitutional conflicts as Malaysia entered the twentieth-first century.

32 *Public Prosecutor v Dato' Yap Peng* [1987] 2 MLJ 316, 319.
33 ibid 324.
34 ibid 327.

The 'UMNO 11' case

The case that finally galvanized Dr Mahathir into action was the 'UMNO 11' case.[35] The significance of the case must be viewed in the context of the factionalism that had split the ranks of the UMNO. Two opposing factions were vying for the leadership of the party.[36] In Malaysian politics, whoever holds the presidency of UMNO traditionally becomes the Prime Minister of Malaysia. Dr Mahathir won the presidency by a very slim majority (forty-three votes).[37] Eleven dissatisfied members then challenged the validity of the election. The case was argued before Harun J.

In relation to UMNO's structure, branch elections are held each year, whereby delegates are elected, who in turn attend divisional meetings to elect delegates to the general assembly. The kernel of the plaintiffs' case was that a number of branches that had elected delegates to the divisional conferences had not been registered with the Registrar of Societies, and that this was in clear violation of the Societies Act 1966. Harun J delivered a judgment that was described as creating 'great confusion':[38] He simply held that UMNO, by virtue of the existence of the unregistered branches, had become an unlawful society. He added, 'That being so, the plaintiffs as members of UMNO cannot acquire any right which is founded upon that which is unlawful. The court will therefore not lend its aid to the reliefs sought by the plaintiffs.'[39] The plaintiffs had sought, inter alia, a declaration that the general assembly election was null and void.[40]

The plaintiffs, inevitably, appealed to the Supreme Court. In an unprecedented move, the appeal was fixed to be heard by a full bench of nine Supreme Court judges on 13 June 1988. What was placed at stake, in consequence, was the political survival of the Prime Minister himself. In the meantime, Tun Salleh Abas' letter to the King had evoked an unexpected response. Two days after despatching the letter to the King and the Rulers, the Lord President went abroad for medical treatment, only returning on 17 May 1988.[41] In his absence, events rapidly unfolded; the

[35] *Mohamed Noor bin Othman v Mohamed Yusof Jaafar* [1988] 2 MLJ 129.

[36] See 'A Postscript on UMNO' in Goh Cheng Teik, *Racial Politics in Malaysia* (FEP International Sendirian Berhad 1989) 68–75.

[37] Dr Mahathir received 761 votes while his rival, Tengku Razaleigh Hamzah, received 718 votes.

[38] Tun Salleh Abas, *The Role of the Independent Judiciary* (Promarketing Publications 1989) 13.

[39] *Mohamed Noor bin Othman v Mohamed Yusof Jaafar* [1988] 2 MLJ 129, 134. The judgment is a most perplexing one. For instance, Harun J, after denying the plaintiffs the assistance of the court, went on to say ,'In the circumstances of this case although the plaintiffs have lost their case they have succeeded in obtaining a declaration that the 1987 UMNO elections were null and void and the most appropriate order would be to make no order as to costs.' But where is the declaration if the court could not 'lend its aid to the reliefs sought by the plaintiffs'?

[40] In the ensuing confusion, Dr Mahathir managed to secure the registration of his UMNO Baru (new UMNO). His opponents' attempt to register UMNO Malaysia was rejected by the Registrar of Societies. See *Tunku Abdul Rahman Putra Al-Haj v Dato' Seri Dr Mahathir Mohamad* [1989] 1 MLJ 48.

[41] A few days after his return from overseas, Tun Salleh, apart from fixing the appeal in the UMNO 11 case for 13 June 1988, also fixed the appeal in the *Karpal Singh* case for 15 June 1988. Karpal Singh, a prominent member of the opposition and a well-known lawyer, who had been detained under the Internal Security Act successfully applied for habeas corpus in the High Court (Ipoh). Nine hours after his release, he was rearrested. He filed a second habeas corpus application. In the meantime, an appeal

survival of the Lord President had now moved to centre stage. The crisis confronting the judiciary enabled the Prime Minister's political survival problem to be put aside and to be subsequently resolved in his favour.

Chronology of Events

Tun Salleh Abas' letter, which was sent on 26 March 1988, had allegedly so incurred the disapproval of the King that on 1 May 1988 he commanded the Prime Minister 'to take appropriate action' against the Lord President.[42] On 5 May 1988, the Prime Minister in a letter to the King said that, according to the advice of the Attorney General, he could not take any action against the Lord President, except in the circumstances provided for by Article 125(3) of the Federal Constitution. The Prime Minister undertook to investigate and examine the position of the Lord President, and declared: 'If there is evidence of any behaviour or other causes which, in my opinion, clearly show that he is no longer able to discharge his functions as Lord President properly and in an orderly manner, I shall make an appropriate representation to Your Majesty.'[43]

On 25 May 1988, the Prime Minister wrote again to the King, this time informing him that on the ground of the behaviour of the Lord President and other causes, the Lord President should be removed from office.[44] Advice was tendered to the King to appoint a Tribunal to investigate and report to the King. The King was further advised that, pending a referral of the matter to the Tribunal, he should suspend the Lord President with effect from 26 May 1988. The King agreed to the appointment of a Tribunal, and to the suspension of the Lord President.[45]

On 27 May 1988, the Lord President was summoned to the Prime Minister's office where he was informed that the King had taken exception to the letter of 26 March 1988 and had initially wanted him to be replaced, but, on advice, had decided to set up a Tribunal. The Lord President said he would not resign but was willing to face the Tribunal and immediately left the meeting. Present at this meeting were the Deputy Prime Minister (Abdul Ghafar Baba) and the Chief Secretary to the Government (Tan Sri Sallehuddin Mohammed). That same day, the Lord President was served a letter from the Prime Minister, informing him that he had been suspended with effect from the previous day, 26 May 1988.

In most respects, the sequence of events stemming from the fateful day of Friday, 27 May 1988 to 8 August 1988, when the Lord President was removed from office, has not been disputed. There have been, however, contradictory versions of the exchange that took place when the Lord President presented himself in the office

had been lodged against the order of the High Court. The outcome of the second habeas corpus application depended upon this appeal. See Tun Salleh with Das, *May Day for Justice*, 61, 82–3.

42 *First Tribunal Report* Vol I, 4.

43 ibid 5. The English translation of the letter dated 5 May 1988 is set out in Annexure 3 to the Report (Vol II).

44 ibid Vol II Annexure 4.

45 ibid Vol II Annexure 5.

of the Prime Minister on 27 May 1988—a contradiction that was significant in reinforcing the possible motivation behind the whole saga. In the encounter, did the Prime Minister accuse the Lord President of having shown bias in cases involving UMNO?[46] This contradiction is examined in the analysis of the *First Tribunal Report*.

On 28 May 1988 (a Saturday and a half working day), the Lord President wrote to the Prime Minister conveying his decision to take early retirement 'in the national interest.'[47] This decision was accepted by the Prime Minister the same day. The next day (Sunday, 29 May 1988), the Lord President wrote to the Prime Minister to say that 'on careful reflection' he had concluded that his earlier retirement decision 'would be detrimental to the standing of the Judiciary and quite adverse to the interest of the nation.' Hence, he had decided to withdraw his application for early retirement. He ended his letter by saying, 'I shall await the appointment of the Tribunal which, I have no doubt, will clear my name. I have also no doubt that justice will prevail in the end.'[48]

After despatching his letter, the Lord President, on the same day, called a press conference at his residence. The next day, 30 May 1988, he gave an interview to the BBC. These actions were regarded by the Prime Minister as further indication that the Lord President was no longer able to discharge properly his functions as Lord President; thus, the Tribunal was also required to look into this matter.[49]

On 13 June 1988, the composition of the Tribunal was publicly announced. The Tribunal was to be chaired by Tan Sri Abdul Hamid Omar who was then the Chief Justice (Malaya). The other members of the Tribunal were Tan Sri Lee Hun Hoe (Chief Justice of Borneo), Ranasinghe CJ (Chief Justice of Sri Lanka), Sinnathuray J (a Judge of the Singapore High Court), Tan Sri Abdul Aziz (a retired judge of the then Federal Court of Malaysia), and Tan Sri Mohd Zahir (a retired Judge of the High Court of Malaya).

Various criticisms were made in respect of the composition of the Tribunal.[50] In the first place, Tan Sri Abdul Hamid Omar was present at the meeting of the Kuala Lumpur judges, which resulted in the letter being written by the Lord President to the King. Secondly, Tan Sri Mohd Zahir's appointment was inappropriate under the doctrine of separation of powers. Apart from being the Speaker of the House of Representatives, he had also presided at a sitting of the House in which the Prime Minister had criticized the judiciary. It was also 'undesirable' for Tan Sri Abdul Aziz to sit on the Tribunal, as his status was that of a businessman-cum-lawyer. As no change was made by the King to the composition of the Tribunal after the objections were brought to his notice, the Tribunal proceeded with its inquiry. It must be stressed that the judges constituting the Tribunal were chosen by the Prime Minister; the King formally appointed them. The disconcerting feature was that the Prime Minister was also Tun Salleh Abas' accuser.

[46] See Tun Salleh, *The Role of the Independent Judiciary* (Promarketing Publications 1989) 16.

[47] *First Tribunal Report* Vol II, Annexure 6. [48] ibid Annexure 8. [49] ibid 13–14.

[50] See 'A Report by the Bar Council on the Report of the Tribunal Established in Respect of Tun Mohamed Salleh Abas' (1988) XX (5) INSAF (Journal of the Malaysian Bar) 2–3.

Apart from these criticisms, the composition of the Tribunal could be criticized because, except for Ranasinghe CJ, the other members were clearly not of equivalent status to Tun Salleh. The Bar Council rightly pointed out:

> It is felt that when appointing the Members of the Tribunal the principle ought to be followed that Members of the Tribunal as far as possible should be more senior in rank than the person facing the proceedings. In this respect, the Bar Council had brought to the notice of the Government that there were available two retired Lord Presidents, at least one retired Chief Justice and a number of retired Supreme Court Judges who could have been appointed.[51]

The Tribunal rejected the Lord President's application for a public hearing. It also refused his 'application for adjournment so as to enable [his] counsel, Anthony Lester QC, to appear before the Tribunal.'[52] However, the Tribunal was prepared to adjourn the commencement of its hearing from 27 June 1988 to 29 June 1988: an adjournment of a mere 2 days. The whole process smacked of unseemly haste.

A day before the Tribunal was to sit, the Lord President turned to the courts in his quest for a fair hearing. He sought leave from the High Court in Kuala Lumpur to apply for an order of prohibition against the members of the Tribunal, on various grounds, restraining them from making any investigation, report, or recommendation. What was supposed to be a straightforward matter, developed into a paradoxical situation: while the Tribunal was working feverishly to complete its work, the High Court was perceived to be dragging its feet on the application by the Lord President. The application, filed on 28 June 1988, was set down for hearing on 1 July 1988, before Yusoff J. However, the application had to be transferred to Ajaib Singh J because Yusoff J had 'produced a medical certificate.'[53] On Friday, 1 July 1988, Ajaib Singh J, after partly hearing the application, adjourned the matter to the next day. The next day, he further adjourned the hearing until Monday, 4 July 1988. The progress of the Tribunal suggested a strong likelihood that by 4 July 1988, the application would have been rendered academic. The unfolding events looked alarming: Ajaib Singh J had also refused an oral application for a limited stay order against the Tribunal.

Following Ajaib Singh J's rejection of the application for a limited stay, counsel for Tun Salleh Abas approached Wan Suleiman SCJ who, purporting to act under Section 9(1) of the Courts of Judicature Act 1964, convened an immediate special sitting of the Supreme Court just before lunch, again on a Saturday which was a half working day. A bench of five judges unanimously granted the oral application for a

[51] See 'A Report by the Bar Council on the Report of the Tribunal Established in Respect of Tun Mohamed Salleh Abas' 32. For a similar criticism, see Trindade, 'Removal of the Malaysian Judges' 51, 57–8. Trindade has also levelled this criticism in relation to the composition of the Second Tribunal: 69. The Malaysian Constitution embodies the principle that no public servant 'shall be dismissed or reduced in rank by an authority subordinate to that which, at the time of the dismissal or reduction, has power to appoint a member of that service of equal rank': Article 135(1). Surely, this principle must, *a fortiori*, apply by necessary implication to members of the judiciary.

[52] Tun Salleh Abas, *The Role of the Independent Judiciary* 24.

[53] ibid 25.

limited stay, restraining the Tribunal from submitting its report, recommendation, and advice to the King until further order.

The response to the action of these five Supreme Court judges (Tan Sri Wan Suleiman, Datuk George Seah, Tan Sri Azmi Kamaruddin, Tan Sri Eusoffe Abdoolcader, and Tan Sri Wan Hamzah) was swift. After consulting the Prime Minister, Tan Sri Abdul Hamid Omar, the then Chief Justice, made a representation dated 5 July 1988 to the King, complaining of the gross misbehaviour of the five Supreme Court judges and expressing the opinion that the misbehaviour justified their removal from office. The King then ordered that a Tribunal be established to investigate the representation. He also ordered that the five Supreme Court judges be suspended with effect from 6 July 1988. Thus was set in motion the process in Article 125(3) of the Federal Constitution, which culminated in the removal of two of these judges.

The legal barriers were now cast aside to enable a number of developments to take place. On 22 July 1988, a differently constituted bench of five judges set aside the interim order that had been issued by the five suspended judges.[54] Meanwhile, the First Tribunal had wound up its work and on 7 July 1988, completed its report, which recommended the removal of Tun Salleh Abas. On 6 August 1988, a statement issued by the Prime Minister's Department said that the King had agreed with the recommendation of the Tribunal to remove Tun Salleh Abas. The removal was to take effect from 8 August 1988.[55] On 8 August 1988, the 'UMNO 11' appeal was heard and, on the following day, dismissed. The Prime Minister must have been delighted, the ousted Lord President possibly bewildered by the actions of a number of his judicial brethren.

On 12 August 1988, the King appointed the following persons to the Tribunal (hereafter referred to as the 'Second Tribunal') to investigate and report in relation to the conduct of the five suspended Supreme Court judges: Tan Sri Hashim Yeop as Chairman, Datuk Edgar Joseph Jr, Datuk Mohd Eusoff Chin, Dato' Lamin Yunus, Mark Fernando J (a judge of the Supreme Court of Sri Lanka), and P Coomaraswamy J (a judge of the High Court of Singapore).

Subsequently, on 30 August 1988, Tan Sri Hashim Yeop Sani, in the face of vigorous submissions regarding public perception of a real likelihood of bias, withdrew from the Tribunal. Datuk Edgar Joseph Jr was appointed the new chair. In accordance with the recommendations of the Tribunal, the King, on 4 October 1988, ordered the dismissal of Tan Sri Wan Suleiman and Datuk George Seah. The other three suspended judges were reinstated.

On 10 November 1988, Tan Sri Abdul Hamid Omar became the Lord President of the Supreme Court of Malaysia. This elevation of a man who, many believed had violated the fundamental rules of natural justice, underscored the irregularity of the whole episode.

[54] *Tun Dato' Haji Mohamed Salleh bin Abas v Tan Sri Dato' Abdul Hamid bin Omar & Ors* [1988] 3 MLJ 149. The Court comprised the following: Hashim Yeop Sani and Harun SCJJ, Mohamed Yusoff, Gunn Chit Tuan, and Anuar JJ.

[55] See *Sunday Times* (7 August 1988).

The Removal of the Lord President: An Analysis of the First Tribunal Report

Tun Salleh Abas, Tan Sri Wan Suleiman, and Datuk George Seah were all removed in purported exercises of the power conferred by Article 125 of the Malaysian Constitution. It is, therefore, worthwhile to digress slightly and examine the scope of this constitutional provision. The Lord President presides over the Supreme Court of the Federation of Malaysia.[56] He occupies the post at the apex of the Malaysian judiciary. He is appointed by the King on the advice of the Prime Minister, after consultation with the Conference of Rulers.[57] All Supreme Court judges hold office until they attain the age of 65.[58]

A Supreme Court judge at any time may resign his office by writing personally to the King.[59] The removal of a Supreme Court judge can only be effected in accordance with the provisions of Article 125 of the Malaysian Constitution. Article 125(3) provides as follows:

> If the Prime Minister, or the Lord President after consulting the Prime Minister, represents to the [King] that a judge of the Supreme Court ought to be removed on the ground of misbehaviour or of inability, from infirmity of body or mind or any other cause, properly to discharge the functions of his office, the [King] shall appoint a tribunal in accordance with Clause (4) and refer the representation to it; and may on the recommendation of the tribunal remove the judge from office.

The Tribunal must consist of not less than five persons who hold or have held office as a judge of the Supreme Court or a High Court or who hold or have held equivalent office in any other part of the Commonwealth. The Tribunal is to be presided over by the member first in the following order, namely, 'the Lord President of the Supreme Court, the Chief Justices according to their precedence among themselves, and other members according to the order of their appointment to an office qualifying them for membership (the older coming before the younger of two members with appointment of the same date).'[60]

It is also provided by Article 125(5) that pending any reference and report under Article 125(3), the King may, on the recommendation of the Prime Minister and, in the case of any other judge, after consulting the Lord President, suspend a judge of the Supreme Court from the exercise of his functions.

The following provisions of Article 131A(1) should also be noted: 'Any provision made by federal law for the functions of the Lord President of the Supreme Court to be performed, in the event of a vacancy in the office or of his inability to act, by another judge of the Supreme Court may extend to his functions under this Constitution.'

[56] Article 122(1). [57] Article 122B(1).

[58] Article 125(1). The retirement age was changed to 66 by the Constitution (Amendment) Act 1994, Act 885.

[59] Article 125(2). [60] Article 125(4).

Two issues may arise in relation to the invocation of Article 125 for the removal of the Lord President: first, does Article 125 contemplate the removal of the Lord President of the Supreme Court; secondly, what is the scope of the grounds for removal?

As far as the first issue is concerned, a careful reading of the provisions of Article 125 would support the application of that Article to the removal of the Lord President.[61] The opening words of Article 125(3) provide for the referral to the King to be achieved in either of two ways: by a direct reference by the Prime Minister himself or by the Lord President after consultation with the Prime Minister. Thus, in the case of the removal of the Lord President, there is no requirement for consultation with him. The setting out of the order of precedence of members as to who will preside over the Tribunal indicates the possibility that the Lord President may not always be the presiding person. Finally, the provisions of Article 131A(1) contemplate the removal of the Lord President on, inter alia, the ground of 'inability to act', a ground which is set out in Article 125(3). It is thus submitted that the removal of the Lord President is contemplated by the provisions of Article 125.

The second issue is the more difficult and important one, namely the grounds for removal. The Constitution, before 1994, provided for two main grounds: (a) 'misbehaviour', and (b) 'inability, from infirmity of body or mind or any other cause, properly to discharge the functions of his office.' Article 160, which deals with the interpretation of the Constitution, does not contain any definition of the word *misbehaviour*. The First Tribunal favoured the following broad definition: 'Unlawful conduct, or immoral conduct such as bribery [and] corruption, [and] acts done with improper motives relating to the office of a judge or which would shake the confidence of the public in a judge.'[62]

The Second Tribunal, in its report (hereafter referred to as the *Second Tribunal Report*),[63] also endorsed a broad approach.[64] It also canvassed the various attempts at defining *misbehaviour* in various jurisdictions, especially in Australia. Considerable attention was focused on the definition of *misbehaviour* of the Parliamentary Commission of Inquiry appointed in relation to the 'Justice Murphy Affair'.[65] In the end, the Second Tribunal opted for the following broad test as formulated by Sir Richard Blackburn in the 'Justice Murphy Affair': 'Proved misbehaviour means such misconduct, whether criminal or not, and whether or not displayed in the actual exercise of judicial functions, as, being morally wrong, demonstrates the unfitness for office of the judge in question.'[66] The Second Tribunal also insisted

[61] Cf Tun Salleh Abas, *The Role of the Independent Judiciary* 48.

[62] *First Tribunal Report* 50.

[63] *Report of the Tribunal Established Under Article 125(3) and (4) of the Federal Constitution. Re: YA Tan Sri Wan Suleiman bin Pawan* (Government Printer 1988) (hereafter referred to as the *Second Tribunal Report*).

[64] ibid 32–3.

[65] See HP Lee and Enid Campbell, *The Australian Judiciary* (Cambridge UP 2013) 117–20; G Lindell, 'The Murphy Affair in Retrospect' in HP Lee and G Winterton (eds), *Australian Constitutional Landmarks* (Cambridge UP 2003) 280–311.

[66] (1986) 2 *Australian Bar Review* 203, 221.

that proof of improper motive was an essential requirement.[67] It openly acknowledged that a Tribunal, under Article 125(3), had only one course open to it, namely to recommend removal or not to recommend removal; no possibility for an intermediate recommendation existed under that provision.[68]

Coming back to the Tun Salleh Abas saga, a request by him for an open hearing was refused by the Tribunal, which said, 'The majority of the members of the Tribunal were of the view that as several of the allegations to be enquired into involved issues of a sensitive nature, the hearing should not be held in public.'[69] Despite this, the government saw fit to publish not only the findings of the Tribunal but also the transcripts of the proceedings. This publication was a blessing in disguise for it revealed the travesty of justice occasioned against Tun Salleh Abas.

At the outset, the following observations could be made about the Tribunal's report, which has been described as among 'the most despicable document in modern history':[70]

(i) The 'Notes on Proceedings' revealed an utter failure by the Tribunal to appreciate the nature of its role when carrying out the task envisaged for it by the Constitution.

(ii) The questioning of the Chief Secretary to the Government was an indictment of the accumulated years of experience and wisdom of all the members of the Tribunal combined.

(iii) The participation of Tan Sri Abdul Hamid Omar made a mockery of the whole process.

Before these observations are examined more closely, it is necessary to mention the five allegations levelled against Tun Salleh Abas and the deliberations of the Tribunal. In brief, it was alleged that: (1) that in a speech on the occasion of the conferment of the honorary degree of Doctor of Letters at the University of Malaya he had made statements critical of the government; (2) at the launching of a book he had also made statements which sought to discredit the government; (3) he had adjourned *sine die* a case (*Teoh Eng Huat v Kadhi Pasir Mas, Kelantan and Another*),[71] which involved the issue of a minor's choice of religion; (4) he had written the letter of 26 March 1988 to the King, a letter which, amongst other things, was intended to influence the Rulers and the King to take some form of action

[67] *Second Tribunal Report* 37.

[68] ibid 40.

The Tribunal referred to Zelman Cowen and David Derham, 'The Independence of Judges' (1953) 26 ALJ 462.

[69] *First Tribunal Report* 18. Cf 'Basic Principles on the Independence of the Judiciary'—Adopted by the Seventh United Nations Congress on the Prevention of Crime and the Treatment of Offenders held at Milan from 26 August to 6 September 1985 and endorsed by General Assembly resolution 40/32 of 29 November 1985 and 40/146 of 13 September 1985. Basic principle 17 provides that in relation to a charge or complaint against a judge, the examination of the matter at its initial stage 'shall be kept confidential, *unless otherwise requested by the judge*' (Emphasis added).

[70] Geoffrey Robertson, 'Justice Hangs in the Balance', *The Observer* (28 August 1988) 22.

[71] Civil Appeal No 220 of 1986.

against the Prime Minister; and (5) various statements made after his suspension as Lord President contained untruths and were calculated to politicize the issues and to further discredit the government.

In relation to allegations (1) and (2), it was claimed that certain statements of Tun Salleh Abas displayed 'prejudice and bias against the Government', and that these statements were 'incompatible' with his position as Lord President of the Supreme Court. It was also claimed that in his book-launching speech he had also made statements that discredited the government and 'thereby sought to undermine public confidence in the government's administration of this country in accordance with law.'[72] The finding of the Tribunal on these allegations cannot withstand scrutiny if one were to read the speeches as set out in the report[73] and analyse the cursory evidence of the two witnesses (the Director-General of Fisheries and the Deputy-Director of Budget), which was used to substantiate these claims. An insidious aspect of the allegations was the distortion of statements made by Tun Salleh in his book-launching speech to create the impression that he was advocating the acceptance of the Islamic legal system, not only in the interpretation of the civil law of Malaysia but in its general application. Clearly, this distortion was mischievous and it raised serious doubts about whether the Attorney-General had acted fairly. As has been pointed out, 'A reading of the passage in question shows that the Tribunal took the remarks of the Lord President out of context, deleting a crucial sentence at the beginning of the passage in question. In the edited passage, Salleh appears to praise Islamic law, but a reading of the entire passage indicates clearly that he does not do so.'[74]

Allegation (3) involved a case where a father had alleged that he had not consented to his daughter's conversion to Islam. The fact that Tun Salleh Abas had adjourned the case—which had come on appeal to the Supreme Court—*sine die*, was intertwined with the earlier allegation that he was advocating the acceptance of the Islamic Legal System: this somehow or other enabled the Tribunal to accept the contention of the Attorney-General that Tun Salleh Abas had meted out 'discriminatory treatment' to the father and that this was 'deliberately done for extraneous considerations,'[75] Tun Salleh Abas, in a response to the Tribunal's report, said:

This finding of the Tribunal is capricious and, judicially outrageous. In coming to that finding, the Tribunal disregarded all the evidence before it: the Tribunal deliberately ignored –

(a) that the application for adjournment was made by the appellant himself (through his solicitors);
(b) that the other parties to the appeal did not object to the appellant's request for the adjournment;
(c) that it has been the practice of the Supreme Court to grant adjournments requested for by any party for good reasons, without the matter having to be called up on the hearing date;

[72] *First Tribunal Report* 20.

[73] ibid Vol III 21–31 (English translation of his speech at the University of Malaya), 32–4 (his speech in English at the official book-launching ceremony).

[74] *Malaysia: Assault on the Judiciary* (n 1) 46.

[75] *First Tribunal Report* 43.

(d) that the Chief Registrar, in answer to Mr Justice T.S. Sinathuray, agreed that the matter was kept aside 'until such time one or the other party writes in and requests for it to be restored';
(e) that since the adjournment, neither the appellant nor any of the other parties had written in for the appeal to be restored.[76]

It is not difficult to share the view that the finding of the Tribunal on allegation (3) was 'clearly perverse'.[77]

Allegation (4) concerned the letter of 26 March 1988, sent to the King and the Rulers. Tun Salleh Abas was accused of making false representations in his letter: it was alleged that his statement that the letter was from all the judges in the country was an 'untruth' as the letter was written 'after a meeting of all Kuala Lumpur judges.' The Tribunal expressed the view that 'this was not a mistake or an accidental slip ... since as Lord President he knew full well that the number of judges in Kuala Lumpur is less than half the number of judges in the country.'[78] The assertion by Tun Salleh in his letter that he had been patient and had not publicly replied to accusations made against the judges was regarded by the Tribunal as untrue. The Tribunal concluded that Tun Salleh, by sending the letter to the King and the Malay Rulers, was asking them 'to take some action to discipline the Prime Minister.'[79] The finding of the Tribunal on allegation (4) cannot be sustained if the Tribunal had taken into account the circumstances under which the letter was written and the fact that as head of the judiciary Tun Salleh was appointed by the King after consultation with the Malay Rulers.[80] This finding led a commentator to observe, 'How Hamid, the chairman of the tribunal, managed to get through this part of the proceedings without choking is hard to understand, since *he was himself one of the judges at the meeting where the letter was discussed and agreed upon and he made no objection to it or to any other part of the business.*'[81]

Allegation (5) related to various statements made by Tun Salleh Abas after his suspension as Lord President, in particular statements made by him in an interview with the BBC.[82] The Tribunal found that, in the absence of any explanation from Tun Salleh, it was unable to disagree with the submission of the Attorney-General that the 'unfounded statement'—'that he was unjustly removed from office because he had expressed partiality in respect of UMNO cases that have come before the courts'—was made by Tun Salleh Abas 'with a view to politicising the issue of his suspension and to gain public sympathy for himself.'[83] It is difficult for this finding to be sustained when one examines notes of proceedings of the Tribunal: the questioning of the Chief Secretary to the Government was conducted in a most perfunctory manner.

[76] Press Statement by Tun Salleh and reproduced in (1988) XX (5) INSAF (November) 23.
[77] ibid. [78] *First Tribunal Report* 44. [79] ibid 46.
[80] 'A Report by the Bar Council on the Report of the Tribunal Established in Respect of Tun Mohamed Salleh Abas' 43–4.
[81] Bernard Levin, 'Malaysia's Law of the Jungle', *The Times* (19 October 1989).
[82] A transcript of the BBC interview is set out in the *First Tribunal Report*, Vol II Annexure 11 .
[83] ibid 48.

The writing of the letter to the King was generally viewed as providing the pretext for initiating the removal process. The other four allegations were in truth 'afterthought' charges to reinforce the action against the Lord President.[84] Nevertheless, the Tribunal found all allegations had been established against the Lord President. The Tribunal then concluded with the following remarks:

> We very much regret that the respondent chose not to appear before us, even though every reasonable opportunity was afforded to him by us. We have, as has been made clear in this Report, come to the findings which we have arrived at only upon the unchallenged and uncontradicted material placed before us. Needless to say that had we had the benefit of a plausible explanation from the respondent in regard to the several issues which were presented to us for our consideration, our decision may well have been different.[85]

This explanation by the Tribunal exposes the failure by the Tribunal to appreciate its role in relation to the task assigned to it under the Constitution. After noting that Article 125(3) provides for the Tribunal to make a recommendation to the King, the Tribunal observed, 'The obligation and the duty so cast upon us by law is therefore an extremely onerous one, and calls for the most anxious consideration by us. It becomes even more so when the person involved is the Lord President, the head of the Judiciary.'[86] The actions of the Tribunal belied its words. In the absence of the suspended Lord President, it was all the more important for the Tribunal to investigate meticulously and rigorously the material placed before it. The 'extremely onerous' duty was discharged in a most superficial manner. This submission can be illustrated by reference to the contradictory versions of the exchange that took place when Tun Salleh Abas presented himself in the office of the Prime Minister on 27 May 1988. The account of the exchange by Tun Salleh Abas, if established, would provide evidence that the steps taken to remove him were actuated by an improper purpose. In his account, Tun Salleh Abas said, 'At the meeting the Prime Minister told me that the King wanted me to step down because of the letters I wrote to him and the Malay Rulers. When I tried to explain to the Prime Minister why I wrote those letters he cut me short and said that I, through my speeches, had shown bias in UMNO cases. I denied this allegation.'[87]

It should be recalled that present at this meeting were the Deputy Prime Minister (Abdul Ghaffar Baba) and the Chief Secretary to the Government (Tan Sri Sallehuddin Mohammed). The notes of proceedings of the Tribunal contained the following:[88]

[84] It is not intended in this book to recite all the arguments that can be marshalled against the findings of the Tribunal in relation to the five allegations. This task has been lucidly performed by FA Trindade in his article, 'The Removal of the Malaysian Judges' (1990) 106 LQR 51, 59–66. See, also, 'A Report by the Bar Council on the Report of the Tribunal Established in Respect of Tun Mohamed Salleh Abas' (1988) XX (5) INSAF 38–44, and *Malaysia: Assault on the Judiciary* 33–49.

[85] *First Tribunal Report*, Vol I 51. [86] ibid 50.

[87] Tun Salleh Abas, *The Role of the Independent Judiciary* (Promarketing Publications 1989) 16.

[88] *First Tribunal Report* Vol III 17–20.

Tan Sri Abu Talib Othman: Can you please tell the Tribunal whether or not the Prime Minister said that this action was taken because of the fact that he is biased in respect of UMNO cases then pending in court?

Tan Sri Sallehuddin Mohammed: I do not recall what the Prime Minister said, that UMNO cases is the reason for the Agong [i.e. the King] asking the Lord President to relinquish his post.

In response to a question from Tan Sri Hamid Omar, the Chief Secretary recalled that the meeting was quite short, lasting 'roughly 5 to 6 minutes'. The following questions were then directed to the Chief Secretary:

Tan Sri Mohamed Zahir Ismail: Nothing was mentioned about the UMNO cases?
Tan Sri Sallehuddin Mohammed: I cannot recall.
Tan Sri Mohamed Zahir Ismail: Did you take any note?
Tan Sri Sallehuddin Mohammed: Yes, I took note. I had a note book and I jotted down as they were speaking.
Tan Sri Mohamed Zahir Ismail: In your note book was there any mention about UMNO cases?
Tan Sri Sallehuddin Mohammed: No. My note book only mentions two things. That Lord President wrote the letter to the Agong and speeches made against Government interest. These are in my note book. I cannot recall him saying anything about UMNO.
Tan Sri Dato' Abdul Hamid bin Hj Omar: Have you got the note book?
Tan Sri Sallehuddin Mohammed: Yes.
Tan Sri Dato' Abdul Hamid bin Hj Omar: I think that would be all.

It is important to note that the Tribunal was of the view that it lacked the power to administer an oath or affirmation to witnesses testifying before it.[89] Nevertheless, the witnesses appearing before the Tribunal stated that they would tell 'the truth and nothing but the truth.' The formula did not include the telling of the *whole truth*.[90] Therefore, the Tribunal had to be very rigorous in the task of establishing the facts; however, the questions put to the Chief Secretary could hardly be described as searching questions. The Chief Secretary did not answer directly the question whether there was a mention of the UMNO cases. His reply was simply that he had no recollection, which is not the same thing as saying that there was no mention of the matter. How was it possible that a Tribunal, with the collective wisdom of over one 100 years of combined judicial and legal experience, did not do the most obvious thing, namely to take a look in the note book of the Chief Secretary? It is hardly convincing that in a meeting that lasted only 5–6 minutes, the Chief Secretary could remember everything except the mention of the UMNO cases. The Report of the Tribunal thus implicated itself.[91]

[89] ibid Vol I 36. [90] *May Day for Justice* 243.

[91] The First Tribunal, in its report (Vol I, 48), said: 'There is also no evidence that any reference whatsoever was made to the UMNO cases at the meeting between the respondent and the Prime Minister on May 27, 1988.' A commentator, after highlighting this finding of the Tribunal, countered with the following question: 'Is there any evidence that UMNO was not mentioned at the ministry or is the evidence silent on this point altogether?' See A Moosdeen, 'The Tribunal on Tun Salleh Abas - A Hundred Years of Legal Wisdom' (1988) XX (5) INSAF 68, 71.

The other aspect, which is manifest from a reading of the Report, is the failure to articulate the standard of proof which should be adopted, except for the following comment: 'The Tribunal has endeavoured to follow the well-known principles applied and followed in such matters and also in regard to the burden of proof and the standard of proof by similar tribunals in other jurisdictions.'[92] However, a reading of the report indicates that the Tribunal was simply adopting the submissions of the Attorney-General—who had contended that a 'preponderance of the evidence' was sufficient—and then sought to rationalize its stand by pointing to the absence of any explanation from Tun Salleh.

The most deficient aspect of the proceedings was the infringement of one of the twin pillars of natural justice—the rule against bias. As long ago as 1924, Lord Hewart CJ had said: 'a long line of cases shows that it is not merely of some importance but is of fundamental importance that justice should not only be done, but should manifestly and undoubtedly be seen to be done.'[93] Lord Denning elaborated on this requirement: 'The court will not inquire whether he [the judge] did, in fact, favour one side unfairly. Suffice it that responsible people might think he did. The reason is plain enough. Justice must be rooted in confidence and confidence is destroyed when right-minded people go away thinking: "The judge was biased".'[94]

Tan Sri Abdul Hamid Omar should have disqualified himself not only from chairing the Tribunal but also from the Tribunal itself. The arguments for disqualification are obvious. Here was a person who could stand to gain from the removal of Tun Salleh Abas: as Chief Justice of the High Court of Malaya, he would generally be regarded as 'next in line' for the Lord President's post. Furthermore, if the younger Tun Salleh Abas had remained in office until he reached the retirement age of 65, Tan Sri Hamid Omar would not have the opportunity to succeed him, for both were born in 1929.[95] A more fundamental objection was that Tan Sri Abdul Hamid Omar had attended the meeting of 25 May 1988, which led to the decision to send the letter to the King.

Coincidentally, a judgment delivered by the Privy Council 2 months after the Second Tribunal had completed its task supplies strong support (on an analogous level) for the disqualification of Tan Sri Abdul Hamid Omar from the First Tribunal. In *Jeyaretnam v Law Society of Singapore*,[96] the Privy Council allowed an appeal by Jeyaretnam from an order of the High Court of Singapore that the appellant be struck off the roll of advocates and solicitors of the Supreme Court of Singapore. Without going into the intricacies of the facts of the case, it is sufficient to quote from the following passage from the opinion of the Privy Council:

> Their Lordships must record their opinion that the refusal of the appellant's objection to the Chief Justice sitting was both erroneous and unfortunate.... It would be absurd that the

[92] *First Tribunal Report* Vol I 36.

[93] *R v Sussex Justices; Ex parte McCarthy* [1924] 1 KB 256, 259.

[94] *Metropolitan Properties v Lannan* [1969] 1 QB 577, 599.

[95] Tan Sri Abdul Hamid Omar was born on 25 March 1929. Tun Salleh Abas was born on 25 August 1929.

[96] [1988] 3 MLJ 425.

Chief Justice should not be able to disqualify himself from sitting if the advocate and solicitor facing disciplinary charges was either a close relative or a sworn enemy *or for any other good reason*. The refusal of the objection was unfortunate because the court was to be invited to go behind and condemn the Chief Justice's own decision on the appeals from Judge Khoo and his later refusal to reserve questions of law for the Court of Criminal Appeal. It was quite unacceptable that he should preside. Justice might be done, but certainly could not be seen to be done.[97]

In Tun Salleh Abas' case, it could clearly be seen that justice was not done. Tan Sri Abdul Hamid Omar's stand in refusing to disqualify himself from the First Tribunal was contradicted by not only the words of the Privy Council in *Jeyaretnam v Law Society of Singapore*, but also by the following clear utterance of the Second Tribunal: 'The rules and principles governing disqualification for bias or interest *qua* judge are amply prescribed by the common law; they apply to the Lord President and to all judges equally, and no special provision was needed for the Lord President. Those principles of natural justice apply to the exercise of judicial functions, to the task of adjudication; in the broadest sense, to the exercise of powers affecting rights.'[98]

The only justification proffered by Tan Sri Abdul Hamid Omar was that he was not at liberty to disobey a 'royal command'.[99] He also expressed the view that disobedience would amount to an 'act of disloyalty'.[100] This explanation was clearly a most startling one. The 'royal command' in the circumstances of this affair must be subject to the Constitution and the operation of the common law principles of natural justice. It is an unchallengeable proposition that the Malaysian nation in adopting the 'Merdeka' Constitution did not intend to create an absolute monarchy. Tan Sri Abdul Hamid Omar's explanation is also not a tenable one, especially as the King did accede to the wishes of Tan Sri Hashim Yeop Sani to be relieved of the chair of the Second Tribunal.

The Removal of Other Supreme Court Judges: An Analysis of the Second Tribunal Report

As a result of the intervention of the five Supreme Court judges, two of them (Tan Sri Wan Suleiman and Datuk George Seah) eventually paid the heavy price of removal from office. Their removal was effected pursuant to the recommendations of the Second Tribunal. Some aspects of the *Second Tribunal Report* require scrutiny in order to determine whether these recommendations were deficient in any way.

97 ibid 431. 98 *Second Tribunal Report* 46–7.

99 This 'royal command' excuse was reiterated by Tan Sri Abdul Hamid Omar in his letter dated 20 March 1989 and addressed to Mr Niall MacDermot, the Secretary General of the International Commission of Jurists (ICJ). This letter was a response to a resolution adopted by the ICJ at a meeting held in Caracas, Venezuela on 20 January 1989. The exchange of correspondence between the ICJ and Tan Sri Abdul Hamid Omar is reproduced in (1989) 1 MLJ cxxii.

100 See Tun Salleh Abas, 'The Role of the Independent Judiciary' 20.

On this occasion, the judges decided to appear before the Tribunal. The following preliminary observations can be made about this Tribunal:

1. Tan Sri Hashim Yeop Sani, in the first place, should never have been appointed a member of the Tribunal, let alone its chair. It was, therefore, not surprising that at the first sitting of the Tribunal it was submitted that 'there were circumstances from which it might appear to others, and especially to ordinary members of the public, that there was a real likelihood of bias'.[101] Particular reference was made to the fact that he had been a member of the bench of the Supreme Court, which had set aside the order made by the five judges on 2 July 1988. Tan Sri Hashim Yeop Sani, much to his credit, withdrew from the Tribunal; Datuk Edgar Joseph Jr was then made the chair of the Tribunal. The withdrawal of Tan Sri Hashim Yeop Sani demolished Tan Sri Abdul Hamid Omar's justification for refusing to disqualify himself from the First Tribunal.
2. At the outset, the Second Tribunal dealt with the important issue of the burden of proof required in respect of the allegations made in the representation against the five judges. It concluded that proof beyond reasonable doubt was required.[102] This determination of the Tribunal is to be commended (although its application of the burden is questionable). Once again, the contrast with the stand taken by the First Tribunal is very glaring: the First Tribunal had failed to give a clear ruling on this fundamental issue.

The first allegation against four of the judges (Tan Sri Wan Suleiman excepted) was for 'intentionally attending' the Supreme Court sitting 'without the permission or knowledge of the Acting Lord President.'[103] It was alleged that this was in violation of Sections 38(1) and 39(1) of the Courts of Judicature Act 1964,[104] and that such conduct reflected 'an irresponsible and improper attitude', which tarnished the image of the judiciary and was unbecoming of a person holding the office of Supreme Court judge. A similar allegation against Tan Sri Wan Suleiman was for 'intentionally convening and being present' at the 2 July 1988 sitting of the Supreme Court.[105] The Tribunal found that these allegations against the judges had not been established: proof of improper motive was essential and had to be established beyond reasonable doubt. The evidence, according to the Tribunal, showed that the five judges had acted in the honest belief that Tan Sri Wan Suleiman was entitled to convene the special sitting, and that the other four judges were entitled to attend that sitting.[106]

[101] *Second Tribunal Report* 4. [102] ibid 23–9. [103] ibid 71.

[104] Sections 38 and 39 of the Courts of Judicature Act 1964 read as follows:

> 38(1) Subject as hereinafter provided, every proceeding in the Supreme Court shall be heard and disposed of by three judges or such greater uneven number of judges as the Lord President may in any particular case determine.
> (2) In the absence of the Lord President the senior member of the court shall preside.
> 39(1) The court shall sit on such dates and at such places as the Lord President may from time to time appoint: provided that the Lord President may, when he deems it expedient, direct that any appeal be heard at any time and in any place in Malaysia.
> (2) The Lord President may cancel or postpone any sitting of the court which has been appointed under subsection (1).

[105] *Second Tribunal Report* 71.

[106] ibid 74.

Two members of the Tribunal were of the view that if the standard of proof had been one of 'on balance of probabilities' they would have found against Tan Sri Eusoffe Abdoolcader and Tan Sri Azmi.

The second allegation common to all five judges was for 'intentionally hearing' the application at the Supreme Court sitting on 2 July 1988, on a matter still being heard by Justice Dato' Ajaib Singh.[107] Therefore, it was alleged that this showed lack of impartiality and was unbecoming of a person holding the office of a judge. The Tribunal found this allegation to be 'clearly unsustainable'.[108]

There were two additional allegations against Tan Sri Wan Suleiman and one additional allegation against Datuk George Seah. In the case of Tan Sri Wan Suleiman, it was alleged that he had stayed away from a Supreme Court sitting scheduled for 2 July 1988 at Kota Bahru without reasonable cause, and that he had directed both Datuk George Seah and Dato' Harun Hashim to leave the same Supreme Court sitting without proper and reasonable cause.[109] The additional allegation against Datuk George Seah was for staying away from the scheduled Supreme Court sitting at Kota Bahru.

The Tribunal unanimously held that the additional allegations against Tan Sri Wan Suleiman had been established and that they amounted to misbehaviour.[110] The Tribunal, by a majority, recommended that he be removed from office.[111] One member of the Tribunal was of the opinion that removal from office was not justified in the circumstances.[112] The additional allegation against Datuk George Seah was upheld by four members of the Tribunal, three of whom recommended that he be removed from office.[113]

It is unnecessary to deal with the *Second Tribunal Report* in relation to the allegations against the five judges that were dismissed by the Tribunal.[114] Once it was clearly established before the Tribunal that there had been no conspiracy[115] or prior agreement of any kind by the five judges to help Tun Salleh Abas to obtain the interim stay order against the First Tribunal,[116] and once it was accepted that there was nothing wrong in the Supreme Court entertaining the *ex parte* oral application for interim stay even though at very short notice,[117] any other conclusion by the Tribunal would be viewed as perverse.

[107] ibid 62. [108] ibid 70. [109] ibid 77–8. [110] ibid 120.

[111] The majority of the Tribunal, however, recommended that Tan Sri Wan Suleiman should be accorded full pension rights on account of his 'long and hitherto untarnished service as a Judge of the Superior Courts': ibid 122.

[112] ibid 122.

[113] ibid 130–1.

The three members who arrived at the 'inevitable conclusion' that the misbehaviour provided was sufficiently serious to justify removal proffered, at 131, this reason:

> 'To hold otherwise would mean the end of all judicial discipline in the courts of this country - a prospect so alarming that it might at all costs never happen again.'

It is difficult to comprehend how judicial discipline would end, considering that these three members of the Tribunal acknowledged that the circumstances of the case were 'exceptional'!

(Note: It was also recommended that Datuk George Seah be accorded full pension rights.)

[114] An analysis can be found in FA Trindade, 'The Removal of the Malaysian Judges' (1990) 106 LQR 51.

[115] The Tribunal pointed out that the word *conspiracy* was used in para 6 of the English translation of the representation that was first tendered to the Tribunal. The accuracy of this translation was queried and subsequently another translation was tendered: *Second Tribunal Report* 55.

[116] ibid 60. [117] ibid 70.

In so far as the additional allegations against Tan Sri Wan Suleiman and Datuk George Seah were concerned, the adverse finding by the Tribunal could not be sustained. The Tribunal articulated 'six broad strands' in the case against Tan Sri Wan Suleiman.[118] The first strand, which was not accepted by the Tribunal, was based on an improper motive to 'stick his neck out' for Tun Salleh Abas to be inferred from his presence at the meetings of 25 March 1988 and 27 May 1988. The second strand, which was based on his cancellation of a reserved flight to Kota Bahru the day before the scheduled sitting of the Supreme Court at Kota Bahru, and the third strand, which was based on his action in sending his secretary and other court staff to 'monitor' the proceedings in Dato' Ajaib Singh's court enabled the Tribunal to find, 'beyond reasonable doubt', that he was actuated by an improper motive. The second and third strands were, according to the Tribunal, corroborated by the fourth strand, namely, his conduct in cancelling the sitting at Kota Bahru. The Tribunal proceeded to look at the fifth and sixth strands in the case against Tan Sri Wan Suleiman. The fifth strand consisted in 'his eagerness to empanel a seven-judge panel to hear a matter which was then not even pending in the Supreme Court.' The sixth strand 'lay in the events of 2 July 1988 prior to the sittings of the Supreme Court ... when [Tan Sri Wan Suleiman] sent for the Chief Registrar Haidar and said that he was aware of the consequences of his action and was willing to be suspended from office.' The Tribunal expressed the view that the fifth and sixth strands, standing alone, amounted to evidence of a 'slender' kind and, therefore, of 'negligible' value. However, when these strands were taken together with the fourth and fifth strands, they provided further support for the conclusion that the charge of misbehaviour had been made out.

After considering the six strands in the case against Tan Sri Wan Saleiman, the Tribunal said:

> In these circumstances, it was impossible to give the slightest credence to this respondent's explanation that because the sitting at Kuala Lumpur concerned an urgent matter of grave national importance, he gave it priority over the Kota Bahru sitting and not to do so would have amounted to a serious dereliction of his duty and be making a mockery of his oath of office.[119]

It added, 'The alleged belief that he had the power to cancel or postpone or adjourn the sitting before the commencement of the sitting as presiding judge is clearly wrong. He claimed to have had such an honest belief, based on law, convention or practice.' The Tribunal then went on to enumerate the reasons why it found that Tan Sri Wan Suleiman did not have such an honest belief and did not act in pursuance of such belief.[120]

It is unnecessary to rebut the rather unconvincing reasons enumerated by the Second Tribunal.[121] A reference to an absurd reason proffered by the Tribunal is sufficient to highlight the deficiencies of the Report. The Tribunal said:

> It was open to Tan Sri Wan Suleiman to have contacted the Acting Lord President and to have explained that an urgent matter was likely to come up in Kuala Lumpur in which the

[118] ibid 110–15. [119] ibid 115. [120] ibid 116–20.
[121] See Trindade, 'Removal of the Malaysian Judges' 80–5.

Acting Lord President would be a party and so would be disqualified from sitting on it. In that event, Tan Sri Wan Suleiman could have explained that he himself would have to convene the sitting. He could have told the Acting Lord President that for these reasons it was desirable for him (Tan Sri Wan Suleiman) to be in Kuala Lumpur on 2 July 1988 so that it was necessary that the Kota Bahru sitting be cancelled. On that basis, he could have asked the Acting Lord President that he be excused from going to Kota Bahru.[122]

If Tan Sri Wan Suleiman were to seek the permission of Tan Sri Hamid to stay back in Kuala Lumpur, instead of going to Kota Bahru, this would in effect mean that Tan Sri Abdul Hamid Omar was in a position to appoint the judges to decide a case brought by Tun Salleh Abas and in which he (Tan Sri Abdul Hamid Omar) would be a party.[123] The incredulity of the proposition of the Tribunal led the Malaysian Bar Council to comment as follows, 'The Tribunal's conclusion that this would have been a valid excuse for staying away from Kota Bahru defies accepted norms that a litigant should not be consulted about any matter relating to his own case.'[124]

Similarly, the Tribunal's conclusion that the conduct of Datuk George Seah in choosing to return to Kuala Lumpur at the request of Tan Sri Wan Suleiman, despite an explicit directive by Tan Sri Abdul Hamid Omar to remain in Kota Bahru, and his absence 'without reasonable cause' from the Kota Bahru sitting constituted 'misbehaviour', cannot be sustained.[125] Instead of finding a manifest case of 'a clear abdication of responsibility', Datuk George Seah should have been commended for acting in a most proper and responsible manner. The Tribunal accepted as a fact that Datuk George Seah had told Dato' Harun Hashim[126]—who had communicated Tan Sri Abdul Hamid Omar's directive to Datuk George Seah—that he did not wish to speak to the Acting Lord President 'as he did not wish to involve him' as he (i.e. Tan Sri Abdul Hamid Omar) had been named the first defendant/respondent in the application taken out by Tun Salleh Abas.[127]

What ultimately makes the adverse findings against both Tan Sri Wan Suleiman and Datuk George Seah highly questionable was the Tribunal's puzzling failure to render a decision on the proper interpretation of Section 9(1) of the Courts of

[122] *Second Tribunal Report* 118–19.

[123] This point was put in a most cogent fashion (ibid 98–9) by Tan Sri Wan Suleiman when he explained to the Tribunal why he did not seek the permission of Tan Sri Hamid:

> In my case, on this particular occasion, even if I wished to speak to the person officiating as Lord President, Tan Sri Abdul Hamid … I do not think, in the circumstances pertaining at that time, it would be proper for me to do so. He was already a party to the proceedings in respect of which, any sitting of the Supreme Court I should convene under s.9, would have to deal with any application made to us, which I expected would be made shortly. I could not very well ask him 'whether I can sit in Kuala Lumpur to decide on this matter between you and Tun Salleh.' Could I?

[124] Press Statement of 9 October 1988: reproduced in (1988) XX (5) INSAF 78.

[125] For a critical analysis of the Tribunal's findings regarding Datuk George Seah, see Trindade, 'Removal of the Malaysian Judges' 78–80. See, also, Datuk George Seah, '1988 Judicial Crisis: The Hidden Story—Part 4' (2004) 24(7) Aliran Monthly 40.

[126] The third member of the *coram* for the Supreme Court sitting at Kota Bahru.

[127] *Second Tribunal Report* 125–6.

Judicature Act 1964. The Malaysian Bar Council was right when in a press statement it commented, 'This was the crux of the whole matter, and it was incumbent on the Tribunal to come to a decision on the interpretation of this section before they could determine whether or not the judges were wrong to have acted as they did under that provision of the law.'[128] Section 9(1) of the Courts of Judicature Act 1964 provides:

> Whenever during any period, owing to illness or absence from Malaysia *or any other cause*, the Lord President is unable to exercise the powers or perform the duties of his office (including his functions under the Constitution) the powers shall be had and may be exercised and the duties shall be performed by the judge of the Supreme Court having precedence next after him who is present in Malaysia and able to act.

The crucial issue with which the Tribunal was confronted was whether the phrase 'any other cause' included disqualification, because of bias or possible interest in the proceedings. Surely, the interpretation of section 9(1) was pivotal in determining the case against Tan Sri Wan Suleiman, Datuk George Seah, and the other three judges. If section 9(1) carried the inclusion of a 'bias or possible interest' disqualification, Tan Sri Wan Suleiman could have the legal power to perform those acts of which he stood accused. Being the next most senior Supreme Court judge—the Chief Justice of Borneo would also be disqualified, as he was also a respondent in the Tun Salleh Abas case—the power, therefore, rightly devolved on him. If this interpretation of section 9(1) is the proper one, then none of the allegations against the judges could be sustained.

Faced with two opposing submissions on this crucial issue, the Tribunal simply maintained:

> This Tribunal is not constitutionally empowered to interpret s. 9(1) authoritatively, so as to be finally and conclusively binding upon the courts of Malaysia: that function belongs to the Supreme Court alone. In these circumstances, while it is the definite view of this Tribunal that 'any other cause' does not include disqualification on the ground of interest or possible bias, and that this is certainly the better view, it is clear that the other view is not unreasonable.[129]

If Tan Sri Wan Suleiman was acting in accordance with an interpretation of section 9(1), which was accepted by the Tribunal as 'not unreasonable', how could the adverse findings against Tan Sri Wan Suleiman and Datuk George Seah be sustained, let alone a finding based on the test of 'beyond reasonable doubt' be reached? How could the Tribunal, on one hand, avoid a decision on the interpretation of section 9(1) and, on the other hand, have no difficulty in reaching a decision that the language of section 39(2) of the Courts of Judicature Act 1964 was clear and that there was 'no ambiguity' about it? How could the finding that Tan Sri Wan Suleiman could not have held the honest belief that he had the power pursuant to section 39(2) 'to cancel or postpone any sitting of the Court' be sustained when it

[128] See (1988) XX (5) INSAF 78.

[129] *Second Tribunal Report* 48.

could be argued quite logically that this power could vest in Tan Sri Wan Suleiman from the 'not unreasonable' interpretation of section 9(1)? How could the finding against Datuk George Seah that he had 'no reasonable cause' for absence from the Kota Bahru sitting be sustained when the Tribunal had acknowledged that the five judges had acted 'in the honest belief' that Tan Sri Wan Suleiman was entitled to convene the special sitting of the Supreme Court?[130]

It is very difficult to justify the recommendation by the Tribunal that Tan Sri Wan Suleiman and Datuk George Seah should be removed, even if it was assumed that there was 'misbehaviour'. The member of the Tribunal who disagreed with the recommendation for the removal of Tan Sri Wan Suleiman cogently pointed to the following factors against removal:

(a) it is a single isolated incident, which could not have, and which did not, result in a miscarriage or perversion of justice, for the cancellation of the Kota Bahru sitting did not have that consequence;
(b) it was not a case of partisanship;
(c) a long record of service, of unquestioned integrity, and this was the first blemish;
(d) the capacity to administer justice in future, and public confidence in his ability to do so, remain unimpaired; and
(e) none of the precedents suggest that removal in these circumstances could be justified.[131]

These factors were equally applicable to Datuk George Seah.

An analysis of the *Second Tribunal Report* cannot be concluded without a reference to some disturbing observations of the Tribunal. The five judges were suspended and the Second Tribunal was established pursuant to a representation of Tan Sri Abdul Hamid Omar—in his capacity as Acting Lord President—to the King. The representation of Tan Sri Abdul Hamid Omar, upon which the allegation common to the five judges was formulated, appeared to be based 'on nothing more than misinformation and an erroneous inference by the Acting Lord President.'[132] First, the Tribunal pointed out that in paragraph 6 of the English translation of the representation, which was first tendered to the Tribunal, the word *conspiracy* was used. After the accuracy of this translation was queried, another translation was tendered, the accuracy of which was undisputed and which alleged a prior agreement

130 ibid 133. The dissenting member of the Tribunal put it as follows: 'If YA Datuk George Seah's decision that he should attend the Kuala Lumpur sitting was proper (even if only on the basis of an honest belief in its propriety) it cannot be that his absence from Kota Bharu [sic.] was improper.'

131 ibid 137. In the case of factor (b), 'partisanship' was used in the sense as defined in *Grantham's Case* (1906) 160 *Parliamentary Debates*, 4th Series, 394–5 (*Second Tribunal Report* 39). In the case of factor (e), it was pointed out that even in the case of Justice Berger (in Canada) there was no recommendation for removal and that an examination of previous instances (cited in Gerald L Gall, *The Canadian Legal System* 2nd edn, 185–94) from all over the world suggested that removal would not be justified.

132 FA Trindade, 'Removal of the Malaysian Judges' (n 1) 77.

among the five judges to issue the order sought by Tun Salleh.[133] The finding by the Tribunal that there was no conspiracy or prior agreement of any kind rendered this portion of the representation erroneous.[134] Secondly, the Tribunal said, 'The Acting Lord President was without doubt misinformed when he so stated, quoting information given to him, in the opening words of paragraph 6 of the representation to Your Majesty, that they (the five judges) "took the seal from the registry even though the office was closed and the officers had gone home".'[135]

A representation to the King seeking the removal of five members of the Supreme Court must be a matter of an extremely serious nature. It was essential for Tan Sri Hamid Omar to ensure the factual accuracy of the allegations before embarking on such a drastic measure. The following observation of the First Tribunal, which was chaired by Tan Sri Hamid Omar, should be noted: 'Even assuming that [Tun Salleh Abas] was justified in writing to Your Majesty, in the circumstances of this important matter, he should have presented the facts to Your Majesty in good faith and frankness instead of basing his representations on certain facts which were untrue.' If Tun Salleh Abas was condemned for the alleged misrepresentations of fact in a letter to the King, what fate should befall Tan Sri Abdul Hamid Omar for erroneous statements, in a representation pursuant to Article 125(3), to the King?

Concluding Observations

In 1987, Tun Mohamed Suffian, a former Lord President of Malaysia, in delivering a lecture on 'The Role of the Judiciary' said, 'So far the independence of the judiciary has never been in jeopardy, thanks mainly to the fact that our first three Prime Ministers were lawyers who understood the importance of having a judiciary that enjoys public confidence. But what of the future?'[136] This comment could be construed as reflecting a troubled state of mind as to what was in store for the judiciary under the Mahathir Government.[137] While clearly concerned about possible threats to the independence of the judiciary, Tun Mohamed Suffian could not have envisaged the events that unfolded shortly after his comment was made.

In the period from independence in 1957 to the constitutional convulsion in 1988, it was widely acknowledged that the Malaysian judiciary had nurtured a quality of independence that was the envy of judiciaries in many Third World countries. The tragicomic events that led to the removal of the Lord President (Tun Salleh Abas) and the two Supreme Court judges rudely undermined that quality of independence.

133 *Second Tribunal Report* 55. 134 ibid 60. 135 ibid 67.
Tan Sri Hamid, after having received information that Tan Sri Wan Suleiman had decided to convene the special sitting of the Supreme Court, instructed 'that the courtrooms should be kept closed, that the staff should not assist in such sitting, and that the court seal should not be made available' (ibid 72). The Tribunal was satisfied that none of the five judges took the seal from the registry: ibid 67.

136 [1987] MLJ xxiii, xxiv.

137 Dr Mahathir, the fourth Prime Minister, was a medical doctor.

The role of the Conference of Rulers did not appear to feature prominently during the constitutional crisis. It may not be out of place to recall the following words of Sultan Iskandar of Johore, when he was interviewed about two weeks before he ascended the throne of Malaysia: 'I told them all, when they asked me to accept their offer (to make me King). I said, Sir, one thing: our actions and efforts are based on collective decision and collective effort. You ask me to represent you. I am beholden to all of you, your wishes I obey, I accept. If I am King, you are also King; if I am to be His Majesty, you are also His Majesty.'[138] However, in response to another question, 'When you are King, what role do you expect to play', Sultan Iskandar said, 'I shall do whatever the Prime Minister advises me to.'[139] These statements of Sultan Iskandar pose a constitutional dilemma in terms of his relationship with the Conference of Rulers and with the Prime Minister. However, no such dilemma was posed to the King on 1 May 1988 because it was the King who initially commanded the Prime Minister 'to take appropriate action' against Tun Salleh Abas.[140] The net effect of the removal of Tun Salleh Abas is that the checks and balances envisaged for the Malaysian constitutional system have been rendered askew.

Commentators have now questioned the efficacy of the mechanism embodied in Article 125. Trindade, in his analysis of the crisis, said:

> The choice and composition of the two Tribunals, the procedures followed by them (particularly by the Tun Salleh Tribunal) and the broad definition of judicial 'misbehaviour' adopted by those Tribunals might well have left those judges who have been removed with the distinct feeling that these matters should be spelt out in greater detail and that Article 125 in its present form is not the safeguard for judges that it was intended to be. This constitutional provision needs to be looked at again by those concerned with constitutional matters in Malaysia.[141]

Tun Salleh, in questioning the efficacy of Article 125, noted: 'Looking back at our recent Malaysian experience, I am convinced more than ever that removal by a Parliamentary address provides a better safeguard for judges despite being an apparent anachronism, *provided* that there is a reasonably free press.'[142]

It is highly questionable whether, in the context of Malaysia, a parliamentary address is a better safeguard than the mechanism in Article 125.[143] A conspectus of the vast number of fundamental amendments to the Constitution that have been passed by the Malaysian Parliament by a two-thirds majority does not inspire confidence in the parliamentary address system.[144] If the Constitution could be so easily amended, is the fate of one person (albeit the head of the judiciary) likely to

[138] Tan Chee Khoon, *The Monarchy in Malaysia* (Pelanduk Publications 1984) 60.

[139] ibid 53. [140] *First Tribunal Report* 4.

[141] FA Trindade, 'Removal of the Malaysian Judges' 85.

[142] Tun Salleh Abas, *The Role of the Independent Judiciary* 46–7.

[143] See HP Lee and Vince Morabito, 'Removal of Judges: The Australian Experience' (1992) SJLS 40.

[144] See HP Lee, 'Constitutional Amendments in Malaysia' (1976) 18 Malaya LR 59, and 'The Process of Constitutional Change in Malaysia' in Tun Suffian, HP Lee, and FA Trindade (eds), *The Constitution of Malaysia: Its Development: 1957–1977* (OUP 1978) 369; Tan Sri Salleh Abas,

move the government members of Parliament to go against a direction of the Prime Minister?

Those who drafted the Malaysian Constitution regarded a special Tribunal as being a more effective way of securing judicial independence and accordingly deviated from the proposal for a parliamentary address system recommended by the Reid Constitutional Commission.[145] Instead of going back to the drawing board and adopting the parliamentary address as the mode for removing a judge, it would be better to strengthen the provisions of Article 125. It is suggested that the Constitution should be amended to provide explicitly for consultation with the Conference of Rulers on matters of judicial suspension and removal. In terms of the choice and composition of a Tribunal, consideration should be given to some discretionary role for the Conference of Rulers.

In the end, no matter what system is adopted, the safeguards are only effective so long as those who constitute the checks and balances want them to work. The framers of the Constitution did not make a mistake in opting for the removal mechanism in Article 125; their mistake lay in the assumption that the executive arm of government would subscribe to the rule of law. Safeguards require the cooperation of human beings; it is very difficult to safeguard completely against the 'frailty and weakness of human nature.'[146]

The rule of law is eroded when the independence of the judiciary is subverted,[147] leading to dictatorial rule which has characterized many of the Third World countries. Sir Ninian Stephen, a former judge of the High Court of Australia and a former Governor General of Australia, once said:

> What ultimately protects the independence of the judiciary is a community consensus that that independence is a quality worth protecting, the citizen being better served if the judiciary is preserved from domination by those more overtly powerful elements of governments, on whose support the judiciary is dependent, yet whose exercise of power the judiciary is charged with keeping within bounds prescribed by law.[148]

Sir Ninian Stephen also observed that 'an independent judiciary, although a formidable protector of individual liberty, is at the same time a very vulnerable institution, a fragile bastion indeed.'[149] That fragility in the case of the Malaysian judiciary was starkly highlighted by the cataclysmic convulsion in 1988. The failure of the

'Amendment of the Malaysian Constitution' (1977) 2 MLJ xxxiv; L.A Sheridan and HE Groves, *The Constitution of Malaysia* (4th edn Malayan Law Journal [Pte] Ltd 1987) 14–16.

[145] *Second Tribunal Report* 22. See, also, Justice LJ King, 'Minimum Standards of Judicial Independence' (1984) 58 ALJ 340, 345: 'It is at least questionable whether the system of removal by an address of both Houses of Parliament accords to a judge the degree of security which is required by the concept of judicial independence.'

[146] Tun Salleh Abas, *The Role of the Independent Judiciary* 46.

[147] 'An independent Judiciary is an indispensable requisite of a free society under the Rule of Law'; see Clause 1, Report of Committee IV, annexed conclusions to 'The Declaration of Delhi', 10 January 1959.

[148] Rt Hon Sir Ninian Stephen, 'Southey Memorial Lecture 1981: Judicial Independence: A Fragile Bastion' (1982) 13 MULR 334, 339.

[149] ibid 338.

Conference of Rulers to restrain the government from undermining the independence of the judiciary returned to haunt the Rulers 5 years down the track, when the second confrontation between them and the government over the issue of royal immunity arose.

A Belated Recognition of Injustice

The dismissal of Tun Salleh Abas and the other two senior Supreme Court judges immediately attracted international attraction and led to the adoption of a resolution by International Commission of Jurists at a meeting in Caracas, Venezuela, on 20 January 1989. In the resolution, the Commission expressed its 'grave concern' about the removal from office of Tun Salleh Abas and the two Supreme Court judges. The Commission went on to record its 'deep concern' about a number of features of the procedures preceding the removals and suspensions and viewed them as 'apparently illegitimate and unfair procedures.'[150] Two decades on, there is universal consensus that an injustice had been rendered to the dismissed judges That there had been a travesty of justice against the dismissed judges was borne out by a report commissioned on 22 September 2007 in anticipation of the twentieth anniversary of the 1988 judicial crisis by the Malaysian Bar Council, LAWASIA, the International Bar Association and Transparency International.

About a month before the report was released, Dr Mahathir Mohamad stated that the case against Tun Salleh Abas 'was triggered by his letters to the Yang di-Pertuan Agong which were considered by the Agong as being highly improper and insulting to him.'[151] Dr Mahathir Mohamad claimed that Tun Salleh Abas had written a letter to the Yang di-Pertuan Agong to complain about the noise made during some repair work at the palace of the Yang di-Pertuan Agong, which was situated near Tun Salleh Abas' house. He also said that, apart from the fact that the writing of the letter was 'very improper',[152] Tun Salleh Abas had aggravated the problem by sending copies of the letter to the other Rulers. Not much credibility appeared to be given to this self-serving explanation by Dr Mahathir Mohamad.

On 26 July 2008, the Panel of Eminent Persons, which was established to review and report on the crisis, found that 'not only was the Lord President Tun Salleh totally innocent and none of the charges against him had any merit, but in fact, the Lord President Tun Salleh was performing his constitutional duty to uphold and protect the doctrine of separation of powers and the rule of law in the larger

[150] See 'Resolution adopted by International Commission of Jurists on 20 January 1989 and the Honourable Lord President Tan Sri Dato' Abdul Hamid Omar's Reply' reproduced in [1989] 1 MLJ cxxii.

[151] 'Tun Dr Mahathir: The Tun Salleh Saga' (6 June 2008) http://www.malaysianbar.org.my/letters_others/tun_dr_mahathir_the_tun_salleh_saga.html (accessed 22 March 2016).

[152] ibid.

interest of the country.'[153] In relation to the findings and the conclusions of the Second Tribunal and the recommendation for the removal of the two judges, the Panel found them to be 'unjustified and inappropriate'.[154] The Panel said, 'Glaring inconsistencies between enunciation of the legal principles and their application to the facts by the Second Tribunal is indeed incomprehensible.' The Panel noted the widespread perception of an erosion of judicial independence. It said: 'Without impugning the integrity of any individual judge the fact remains that the events of the 1988 judicial crisis have devalued public confidence in the judiciary as a whole. The reputation of the judiciary must be restored and the abuses of 1988 must not be allowed to recur.'[155] In its report, the panel recommended, inter alia,

> 1. It is desirable in the nation's interest to redeem the people's faith in the credibility of the judiciary and the rule of law, for which the wrong done to the Lord President, Tun Salleh and the two Supreme Court judges, Tan Sri Wan Suleiman and Datuk George Seah should be undone, as best and as early as possible. An acknowledgement by the government of the mistake in removing these three judges in 1988 and making suitable amends would be an appropriate gesture to restore confidence in the independence of the judiciary. The panel appreciates the reported recent statements and actions taken by the government in this regard.[156]

The Panel suggested that attention should be paid to the Beijing Statement of Principles of the Independence of the Judiciary in the LAWASIA Region, 1997 and the Bangalore Principles of Judicial Conduct, 2002 as the guidelines for the independence of the judiciary and judicial accountability. The extensive revelations of judicial indiscretions, the scandals relating to the manipulation of the judicial appointment and promotion process, together with the finding of the Panel of Eminent Persons, the extensive revelations about judicial discretions and misbehaviour, and attempts to manipulate the judicial appointments process provided the impetus for Prime Minister Abdullah Badawi to embark on a process to reform the judiciary to restore public confidence in the judicial institution. The reforms are considered in Chapter 6.

[153] *Report of the Panel of Eminent Persons to Review the 1988 Judicial Crisis in Malaysia* (26 July 2008) para 17.3. The Panel comprised of Justice (Retd) JS Verma (formerly, Chief Justice of the Supreme Court of India) (Chairman), Justice (Retd) Fakhruddin G. Ebrahim (formerly, Judge of the Supreme Court of Pakistan), Dr Asma Jahangir (Advocate of the Supreme Court of Pakistan), Tan Sri Dato' Dr Abdul Aziz bin Abdul Rahman (Advocate & Solicitor of the High Court of Malaya), Dr Gordon Hughes (Former President of the Law Institute of Victoria), and Dato' WSW (Bill) Davidson (Barrister-at-Law, Advocate & Solicitor of the High Court of Malaya).

[154] ibid para 22.1.

[155] *Report of the Panel of Eminent Persons to Review the 1988 Judicial Crisis in Malaysia* (26 July 2008) para 24.2.

[156] ibid.

6

Reforming the Judiciary: A Triumph of Form over Substance?

Let us move on. The judiciary must be revitalised to enable it to serve the people in pursuit of justice. The judiciary must be fortified to be an institution that serves the democratic principle of separation of powers. The judiciary must be the guardian of the Constitution and the sentinel of the people's rights.

'Delivering Justice, Renewing Trust' Speech By: Prime Minister Abdullah Ahmad Badawi, Prime Minister of Malaysia, Malaysian Bar Council Dinner, JW Marriott Hotel, Kuala Lumpur, 17 April 2008

Judicial independence has always been a pillar of the Constitution. Judges do not take orders from Parliament, nor do they from the Prime Minister or from anybody in Government. Judges are not civil servants who quite properly take orders from ministers and their seniors in the service.

Tun Mohamed Suffian, 'The Role of the Judiciary' [1987] 2 MLJ xxiii, xxvii.

Introduction

Descending into disrepute

The dismissal of Tun Salleh Abas and two senior Supreme Court judges was not only a traumatic saga from the viewpoint of the dismissed judges but it had a demoralizing effect on the judiciary as a whole and severely dented public confidence in the judiciary. Since that traumatic event, '[t]he judiciary has never been out of the public eye'.[1] In 2008, Chief Justice Dato' Abdul Hamid Mohamad, in addressing a Judges' Conference, said: 'We cannot deny that the Judiciary is now suffering from negative perceptions by the public.... Politicised to the hilt, the full effect is now felt and we bear the burden of trying to redeem those negative perceptions.'[2] The erosion of public confidence plumbed new depths as the judiciary

[1] Andrew Harding, *The Constitution of Malaysia: A Contextual Analysis* (Hart Publishing 2012) 197.

[2] Chief Justice Dato' Abdul Hamid Mohamad, 'Speech at the Malaysian Judges' Conference 2008' (Marriott Putrajaya 8–11 April 2008) <http://www.malaysianbar.org.my/speeches/cjs_speech_at_the_judges_conference_2008.html> (accessed 12 July 2016).

continued to be buffeted by ongoing controversies in the aftermath of the 1988 judiciary crisis.[3] Part I of this chapter contains an excursus on a number of episodes arising in the aftermath of the 1988 judiciary crisis that sapped public confidence in the judiciary as an independent and impartial institution.[4] It is not intended to cover comprehensively every incident involving the judiciary but only the more significant episodes. Part II provides an analysis of the reforms introduced under Prime Minister Abdullah Badawi and considers their efficacy in attaining the aim of restoring public confidence in the judiciary.

Part I

Distrust and hostility

The appointment of Tun Abdul Hamid Omar to fill the post of Chief Justice because of the removal of Tun Salleh Abas generated 'exceptional reactions'.[5] A cordial and close relationship that existed between Tun Abdul Hamid Omar and the legal profession before his appointment as chair of the first tribunal evaporated because of his perceived role in the removal of the Lord President. A resolution was passed by the Malaysian Bar Council calling for his resignation or his removal as Acting Lord President. The Supreme Court was faced with an application by the Bar Council for leave to institute contempt of court against Tun Abdul Hamid Omar but this application was dismissed in *The Malaysian Bar v Tan Sri Dato' Abdul Hamid bin Omar.*[6] An incredulous public looked on as the Secretary of the Bar Council was prosecuted for contempt and found to be so by the Supreme Court in *Attorney-General, Malaysia v Manjeet Singh Dhillon.*[7]

Public confidence in the judiciary from the late 1980s started to slide further because of disquiet arising especially from perceived close links between some judicial officers and some businesspersons. Visu Sinnadurai, a former highly distinguished High Court judge, explained, 'Whilst previously, the fear of executive interference was the main concern, now the apparent interference by businessmen came to the forefront. There were allegations that some judges were associating themselves with some businessmen.'[8]

[3] See Wu Min Aun, 'Judiciary at the Crossroads' in Wu Min Aun (ed), *Public Law in Contemporary Malaysia* (Longman 1999) 76–106. HP Lee, 'Malaysia: The Politics of the Judiciary' in Rainer Grote and Tilman J Roder (eds), *Constitutionalism in Islamic Countries: Between Upheaval and Continuity* (OUP 2012) 305; 'Constitutional developments in Malaysia in the first decade of the twenty-first century: a nation at the crossroads' in Albert HY Chen (ed), *Constitutionalism in Asia in the Early Twenty-First Century* (CUP 2014) 244, 246–7.

[4] The aftermath of the Tun Salleh Abas dismissal is excellently covered in Visu Sinnadurai, 'The 1988 Judiciary Crisis and its Aftermath' in Andrew Harding and HP Lee (eds), *Constitutional Landmarks in Malaysia: The First 50 Years 1957–2007* (LexisNexis, 2007) 173, 186–95. The account ends in 2007.

[5] ibid 173, 186. [6] [1989] 2 MLJ; [1989] 1 SCR 461, SC. [7] [1991] 1 MLJ 167.

[8] Visu Sinnadurai, 'The 1988 Judiciary Crisis and its Aftermath' in Andrew Harding and HP Lee (eds), *Constitutional Landmarks in Malaysia: The First 50 Years 1957–2007* (LexisNexis 2007) 173, 187. Judge Visu Sinnadurai, who had earned an international reputation for his impeccable legal scholarship, was one of the most eminent jurists to be appointed to the Malaysian judiciary. He was formerly a Dean of Law at the University of Malaya and, before his judicial appointment,

The Ayer Molek case

The publicity surrounding the *Ayer Molek* case[9] 'highlighted the sad state of the judiciary'.[10] The plaintiffs, Insas and Megapolitan Nominees Sdn Bhd, applied to the High Court for a mandatory injunction to compel Ayer Molek Rubber Co Bhd (the defendant), to effect the registration of the transfer of over half million shares (540,000) of Ayer Molek to Insas. Without affording a hearing to Ayer Molek, Azmel J of the High Court granted the application and immediately following this decision, the transfer of the shares, said to be worth somewhere in the region of RM 160 million, was registered in the name of Insas. Ayer Molek appealed to the Court of Appeal and sought a stay of the *ex parte* order pending the appeal.

In the Court of Appeal, the appeal judges[11] vigorously criticized Azmel J's decision, and that based on the facts, the decision would 'give the impression to right thinking people that litigants can choose the judge before whom they wish to appear for their case to be adjudicated upon'.[12] The Court of Appeal added:

> This is a case about an injustice which has been perpetrated by a court of law. This is also a case about abuse of the process of the High Court and, it concerns the inherent power which any court of justice must possess to prevent misuse of its procedure and in which the court has a duty to exercise this salutary power.[13]

At that time, the High Courts in Kuala Lumpur were temporarily housed in a building called 'Wisma Denmark'. This led NH Chan JCA to remark: 'These observations are made so that people will not say, "Something is rotten in the state of

Commissioner for Law Revision. He was Judge of the High Court of Malaya 1992–1998. Upon leaving the judiciary, he became the first Asian to be appointed as a Judicial Specialist at the World Bank. Concerns over the parlous state of the judiciary were underlined by the revelation that Visu Sinnadurai had submitted a memorandum on judicial reforms to Prime Minister Mahathir Mohamad and Anwar Ibrahim (who was then the Deputy Prime Minister). According to Anwar Ibrahim, who brought the matter to light in the Federal Court, the Sinnadurai memorandum stated that the Malaysian Judiciary appeared to be in a state of turmoil. It blamed Chief Justice Eusoff Chin for aggravating the loss of public confidence in the Judiciary. Apparently, in respect of the appointment of Judges to the High Court the Chief Justice had not engaged in prior consultation with the Chief Judge, at least of Malaya. The allegation was made that senior judges were not promoted 'either because, it is said, the Prime Minister does not approve of them, or because of quota, or even on the ground that such persons are unsuitable as being anti-establishment.' The Memorandum went on to assert that the image of the judiciary was bad 'because of the perception of biasness, friendly lawyers continue appearing before the Chief Justice and the same judges and "by coincidence or otherwise, these lawyers appear before the same judges and win cases."' <http://www.limkitsiang.com/archive/2000/aug00/lks0436.htm> (accessed 18 July 2016).

[9] *Ayer Molek Rubber Co Bhd v Insas Bhd* [1995] 2 MLJ 734 (CA), [1995] 2 MLJ 841 (FC),

[10] Visu Sinnadurai, 'The 1988 Judiciary Crisis and its Aftermath' in Andrew Harding and HP Lee (eds), *Constitutional Landmarks in Malaysia: The First 50 Years 1957–2007* (LexisNexis 2007) 173, 190.

[11] NH Chan, Siti Norma, and KC Vohrah JJCA.

[12] *Ayer Molek Rubber Co Bhd v Insas Bhd* [1995] 2 MLJ 734, 743. See also Charles Hector, 'Towards an Impartial, Incorruptible and Independent Judiciary' (19 August 2002) <http://www.malaysianbar.org.my/members_opinions_and_comments/towards_an_impartial_incorruptible_and_independent_judiciary.html?date=2015-06-01> [Accessed 30 September 2016].

[13] *Ayer Molek Rubber Co Bhd v Insas Bhd* [1995] 2 MLJ 734, 738.

Denmark".'[14] The Court of Appeal was taken severely to task by the Federal Court. Eusoff Chin CJ delivering the judgment of the Federal Court, in overruling the decision of the Court of Appeal, went on to reprimand the appeal judges for 'bringing the administration of justice into disrepute'. Eusoff Chin CJ added:

> Why should the learned judges of the Court of Appeal go on a frolic of their own and find fault with the High Court judge, criticize the conduct of the applicant's solicitors in a very disparaging manner. Their own conduct would tend to show that they were themselves biased.[15]

In an unprecedented move, he ordered their marks of NH Chan JCA to be expunged from the judgment. However, the Court of Appeal had the last laugh when it was pointed out later on that the Chief Justice had in fact improperly constituted the Federal Court panel. The co-opting of a Judge from the High Court (PS Gill J) to sit in the Federal Court was contrary to the explicit terms of Article 122(2) of the Malaysian Constitution. It is incredulous that the highest judicial officer of the land was either ignorant of the provisions of Article 122(2) or deliberately embarked on a clumsy attempt at 'stacking' of the court.[16] A decade later, a High Court judge expressed the view that, because of non-compliance with the Constitution, the decision of the Federal Court in *Ayer Molek* was a nullity.[17]

There was concern that a habit of 'judge shopping' was becoming conspicuous, arousing suspicion of judicial corruption. The concern was so grave that even the *New Straits Times*, in an editorial, said:[18]

> ... questions are already being asked as to why the courts and judges are speedy in hearing commercial cases, especially when big companies and big businesses were involved, and the apparent ease with which parties choose which courts to go to and which judge to seek out.... This is inevitable when thousands of criminal and civil cases have been held up for years. Some remand prisoners have to languish in jail for years while waiting to stand trial. [19]

A Judge's 'poison letter'

In January 1996, the country was gripped by consternation over the contents of a document that had been circulated anonymously. The document, referred to as a 'poison letter', contained 112 allegations of wrongful conduct against twelve judges. 'Of the said total, 2 were allegations pertaining to the abuse of power, 39 of corruption and 52 of misconduct, immorality and other indiscretions. It claimed corrupt payments of RM 50,000 with recipients graduating to accepting millions from named persons.'[20]

[14] *Ayer Molek Rubber Co Bhd v Insas Bhd* [1995] 2 MLJ 734, 744. [15] ibid 841 (FC).

[16] Wu Min Aun, 'Judiciary at the Crossroads' in Wu Min Aun (ed), *Public Law in Contemporary Malaysia* (Longman 1999) 76, 99.

[17] *Dato' V Kanagalingam v David Samuels, Joff Wild, Menzies Walker & Euromoney Publications PLC* [2006] 5 AMR 402, HC.

[18] 3 September 1995, 13. [19] *New Straits Times* (3 September 1995) 13.

[20] P Ramakrishnan, 'A Royal Commission Is Urgently Needed to Purge the Judiciary of All the Negative Elements Plaguing It' (2005) 25(1) Aliran Monthly. http://aliran.com/archives/monthly/2005a/1i.html (accessed 24 July 2016).

The author of the document was eventually tracked down by the investigating authorities to be a High Court judge, Datuk Syed Ahmad Idid Syed Abdullah Idid. In a vibrant democracy operating under the rule of law, such serious allegations would have been thoroughly investigated by a royal commission or an independent inquiry, given that the reputation and integrity of the judiciary was at stake. The public interest would be better served by determining the veracity of the allegations and immediately taking action to expunge corrupt elements from the judiciary. However, after opaque investigations by the police, the Attorney-General dismissed the allegations as 'wholly untrue and baseless' and said that no action would be taken 'in the public interest and in the interest of justice'. Pertinent questions were asked: 'If that was the case, why was no action taken against the writer for fabrication and false publication? … Was it fear that the writer would spill the beans and reveal details of incriminating evidence that prevented an open trial?'[21] Many years later, Syed Ahmad Idid publicly said that when he was identified as the author of the document, he had been given an ultimatum by the Attorney-General, Mohtar Abdullah, either to resign or be detained possibly under the dreaded Internal Security Act. Syed Ahmad Idid recounted how, later, in a friendly encounter with Mohtar Abdullah, he had asked the latter whether there was a pistol at his neck when he took the particular course of action, Mohtar replied, 'No it was a cannon'.[22]

A Chief Justice in the eye of a storm

On 30 May 2000, while responding to a question during an Australian Radio interview about photographs posted on the internet showing the Chief Justice of the Federal Court, Eusoff Chin, holidaying in New Zealand with lawyer VK Lingam, the Malaysian Law Minister, Datuk Rais Yatim, said, 'We have intimated to the Chief Justice that this was improper behaviour. And this has been intimated to the Chief justice in no uncertain terms … I am not in a position to say whether I approve it or not, but certainly such socialising is not consistent with the proper handling or behaviour of a judicial personality.'[23] This comment sparked controversy and extensive media coverage. In view of the controversy, the Malaysian Bar Council sought to convene an extraordinary general meeting to consider various

[21] ibid.

[22] Santha Oorjitham, 'Interview with Datuk Syed Ahmad Idid' *New Straits Times* (11 June 2008) available at 'Merdeka' (24 June 2006) <http://srenggege.blogspot.com.au/2006/06/interview-with-datuk-syed-ahmad-idid.html>(accessed 18 July 2016). Syed Ahmad Idid was later vindicated when former Court of Appeal Judge KC Vohrah wrote an article 'In the Court of Appeal, during the winds of change' for a publication, *Court of Appeal, Malaysia, 1994–2014: 20th Anniversary*, revealing a number of judicial irregularities. Vohrah who was a member of the three member Court of Appeal in the *Ayer Molek* case recounted how an appeal judge (Vohrah did not disclose the name of the judge) was called by Chief Justice Eusoff Chin to his chambers before the appeal was heard. It was claimed by Vohrah that the Chief Justice, pointing to a pile of files relating to the Ayer Molek case on his table, went on to indicate 'that the appeal had no merit'. See Hafiz Yatim, 'KC Vohrah: Ex-CJ Eusoff Tried to Subvert Judge' (Malaysiakini, 27 February 2015) <https://www.malaysiakini.com/news/290455> (accessed 18 July 2016).

[23] *The New Straits Times* (30 May 2000).

resolutions over the matter. On 19 June 2000, a member of the Malaysian Bar, Raja Segaran, commenced action to restrain the Malaysian Bar from holding the meeting. Finally, in 2008, the plaintiff was held to have no *locus standi*.[24]

Decisional interference

In *Harris Mohd Salleh v The Returning Officer*,[25]an astonishing claim was made by the trial judge (Muhammad Kamil Awang J) in his judgment annulling the election of a BN candidate in Sabah. In his judgment, he said:

> The only guide to a man is his conscience, the only shield to his memory is the rectitude and the sincerity of his action. In my view, it is an insult to one's intelligence to be given a directive over the phone that these petitions should be struck off without a hearing, and above all, it is with prescience conscience that I heard these petitions. God has given me strength and fortitude, as a lesser mortal, to act without fear or favour, for fear of a breach of oath of office and sacrifice justice, and above all to truly act as a judge and not a 'yes-man'.[26]

He did not disclose the identity of the person who had telephoned him and directed him to strike out the election petition. The judge retired 2 weeks after delivering his judgment. Later on, he revealed that the caller was Chief Justice Eusoff Chin. Instead of subjecting the claim to strict independent investigation, Prime Minister Mahathir attacked Muhammad Kamil Awang J for tarnishing the image of the courts.

A Judges' boot camp disclosure

Ian Chin J of the High Court in June 2008 brought to the forefront publicity damaging to the image and standing of the judiciary. In open court, he claimed that after delivering judgments in two cases which earned him the ire of Prime Minister Mahathir Mohamad, he together with selected judges were sent off to a 'boot camp'. At the boot camp, he claimed that the judges were subjected to indoctrination with the message that in arriving at decisions judges should consider the government's interest 'more important than all else'. The ensuing media publicity further eroded public confidence in the judiciary.

Anwar Ibrahim's prosecution

A falling out between Prime Minister Mahathir Mohamad and his anointed successor, Deputy Prime Minister Anwar Ibrahim, in the midst of a global financial crisis,

[24] *Raja Segaran a/l Krishnan v Malaysian* Bar [2008] 4 MLJ 941. An interesting aspect of the judgment of Mohd Hishamudin J was his remark that he was 'unable to agree with the Court of Appeal's interpretation of [Articles 125 and 127] to the effect that only Parliament can discuss the conduct of judges' (970).

[25] [2001] 3 CLJ 161.

[26] [2001] 3 CLJ 161, 183. Cited in Ambiga Sreenevasan, 'Press Statement: Bar Council's immediate response to the Report in the Borneo Post dated June 2008' (The Malaysian Bar, 10 June 2008) <http://www.malaysianbar.org.my/press_statements/press_statement_bar_councils_immediate_response_to_the_report_in_the_borneo_post_dated_10_june_2008.html> (accessed 12 July 2016).

culminated in a saga of explosive political and legal dimensions. In the process of exterminating Anwar Ibrahim as a challenger to his prime ministerial position, the legal and judicial processes were deployed to stultify Anwar Ibrahim's political ambitions. Upon his abrupt removal as Deputy Prime Minister, Anwar Ibrahim was arrested in dramatic fashion and found himself facing charges of sodomy and 'corrupt practice'.

His trial on 'corrupt practice' was presided by Augustine Paul J.[27] This judge had only been transferred to the Criminal Division in Kuala Lumpur a few weeks before the trial began and was also the most junior judge in that division. Anwar Ibrahim was convicted on 14 April 1999 and sentenced to 6 years on each of the four amended charges to run concurrently from the date of conviction without taking into account the 7 months remand since his arrest. On 17 April 1999, RR Chelvarajah, the President of the Malaysian Bar Council, issued a statement that contained, inter alia, the following:

> The unusual manner in which the trial itself was conducted, for example, the refusal of bail; the expunging of evidence given on oath; preventing the accused from raising every possible and conceivable defence and limiting him to particular defences; compelling the defence to state beforehand what evidence the defence sought to adduce through various witnesses; disallowing witnesses from testifying and making rulings as to their relevancy without first hearing their testimony; citing and threatening defence lawyers with contempt proceedings including sentencing a defence lawyer to three months imprisonment for contempt while in the exercise of their legal duties, raise questions impinging on the administration of justice.

The Bar Council also noted with concern the use of intemperate language by the judge in the course of the trial and the fact that the Council was barred from holding a watching brief during the trial and the subsequent proceedings. The Bar Council further pointed out that the trial, which according to law must be held in public was not at all times, public, as there were repeated prohibitions on the publication of crucial evidence given in open court in various instances. Anwar Ibrahim appealed unsuccessfully to the Court of Appeal in 2000 and the Federal Court in 2002.

The manner of arrest of Datuk Seri Anwar Ibrahim, his subsequent assault while in police custody, the lack of immediate medical treatment, the finding of the Royal Commission of Inquiry that the then Inspector General of Police was responsible for assaulting Anwar Ibrahim and the Royal Commission's finding of fact that a normal detention was converted to an ISA detention so as not to expose him to public view are serious matters of profound concern to the citizenry.

In June 1999, Anwar Ibrahim was tried for the offence of sodomy with his wife's driver (this trial was referred to as 'Sodomy I'). Arifin Jaka J, on 8 August 2000, convicted him and sentenced to 9 years imprisonment, to be served consecutively with the sentence for the corrupt practice conviction. The Federal Court in a 2 to 1 decision eventually overturned the sodomy conviction in 2004. All these prosecutions

[27] See Pawancheek Marican, *Anwar on Trial: In the Face of Injustice* (Gerakbudaya Enterprise 2009), which contains a study of the first criminal case against Anwar Ibrahim.

were generally perceived as attempts to destroy a charismatic politician who clearly poses a threat to the hold on power of the ruling BN coalition. The government was shocked by the scale of electoral success of the Pakatan Rakyat (PR) coalition led by Anwar in the general elections of March 2008. Although BN retained government, it failed for the first time in Malaysian history to secure a two-thirds majority in the federal Parliament. Furthermore, the opposition won the government in five of the thirteen Malaysian states (subsequently to lose the state of Perak through defections of three members to BN, and which engendered a political and constitutional crisis in that state). Following this electoral 'tsunami', Prime Minister Abdullah Badawi's position became untenable and he subsequently stepped down as Prime Minister. He was succeeded by Najib Razak, the son of the second Prime Minister, Abdul Razak.

The unprecedented gain in the number of seats in the federal parliament had emboldened the opposition, which had coalesced around Anwar, as their leader. It was clear that the Malaysian public had developed the view that there was an opposition capable of taking over the reins of power. In 2008, allegations were raised against Anwar that he had sodomized a male aide by the name of Mohd Saiful Bukhari Azlan. The circumstances in which the charge had been made raised widespread suspicions that this second trial, nicknamed 'Sodomy II', was another attempt to destroy his political career and impede him from leading the opposition coalition, especially after it was revealed that Saiful had met with Najib Razak before lodging the police report. This only aggravated an angry public who viewed the charge as a blatant manipulation of the legal system to stymie Anwar.

The launch of the 'Sodomy II' prosecution against Anwar in 2008 only reinforced the impression that the prosecution was motivated by political considerations. By pursuing this 'Sodomy II' charge, the government also lost the public relations contest in the domestic and international arena. In January 2012, the High Court in Kuala Lumpur, in a judgment that evoked surprise in the Malaysian nation, acquitted Anwar Ibrahim on the sodomy charge. Then in May 2013, the BN government suffered even worse results than the 2008 elections. The BN government managed to retain a parliamentary majority but it lost the popular vote. When it became clear that Anwar Ibrahim proposed to stand in a by-election with the view of assuming the position of Menteri Besar of the most prosperous state, Selangor, the Court of Appeal brought forward the prosecution's appeal against the High Court's decision in Sodomy II for hearing on 6–7 March 2014. After concluding the hearing on 7 March, the Court retired at 3:36 pm, returned and found Anwar Ibrahim guilty, and after allowing his defence counsel an hour to prepare a plea in mitigation, sentenced him to 5 years imprisonment. This effectively quashed Anwar Ibrahim's plan to become the Chief Minister of Selangor. Ordinary members of the public who looked at the speed of the trial proceedings and the timing of the Court of Appeal's decision could hardly be blamed for harbouring the impression that senior members of the judiciary were keen to act as an instrument of the executive. The collapse of confidence in the independence and integrity of the judiciary was an inevitable outcome of this rush to judgment over the fate of Anwar Ibrahim.

On 10 February 2015, the Federal Court dismissed the appeal by Anwar Ibrahim against the decision of the Court of Appeal. This effectively brought to an end a very long and protracted saga, with the ultimate consequence of depriving the opposition PR of its charismatic leader who clearly posed a threat to the ruling BN coalition's hold on power. This saga did not have the bearings of a direct constitutional conflict. Nevertheless, one cannot ignore the impact of the Anwar trials and tribulations on the state of constitutionalism and the standing of the judiciary.

The VK Lingam video affair

The issue of judicial independence occupied national attention in the lead-up to the 2008 general elections. Alleging illegal interference regarding judicial appointments, former Deputy Prime Minister Anwar Ibrahim, on 19 September 2007, released a 2001 video recording depicting 'images of a person engaged in a phone conversation relating to the appointment of Judges'.[28] It was claimed that the person in the video was a well-connected lawyer, VK Lingam, who was allegedly discussing with Ahmad Fairuz, then holding the top third judicial position (of Chief Judge (Malaya)), about the latter's advance to the top position of Chief Justice of the Federal Court, to which he was eventually appointed in 2003. The video clip also showed purported discussions of judicial promotions of other senior judges. As it was later described:

> The exposure was explosive. It created a chain reaction in the public domain spreading like wildfire across the Malaysian landscape. It became a common topic of conversation and gossip. The judiciary was shaken. The legal fraternity was alarmed. So was the Government. Indeed, so was the whole country.[29]

The breaking of the explosive story over the 'fixing' of judicial appointments led to an emergency meeting on 23 September 2007 of the Malaysian Bar, which decided to hold a protest walk called a 'Walk for Justice' in Putrajaya. On 25 September, the Government decided to set up a Panel to look into the authenticity of the video clip.[30] On 26 September 2007, over 2,000 lawyers marched from the Palace of Justice in Putrajaya to the Prime Minister's Department to present a memorandum to the Prime Minister calling for the establishment of a royal commission into the VK Lingam Tapes and the allegations of judicial impropriety. On 9 November 2007, the Panel reported and recommended that a Commission of Enquiry be established. The Commission of Enquiry on the Video Clip Recording of Images of a Person Purported to be an Advocate and Solicitor Speaking on the Telephone on Matters regarding the Appointment of Judges was set up on

[28] The Commission of Enquiry on the Video Clip Recording of Images of a Person Purported to Be an Advocate and Solicitor Speaking on the Telephone on Matters Regarding the Appointment of Judges, *The Report* (9 May 2008) (hereafter referred to as 'Commission on Video Recording Report') 3.

[29] ibid.

[30] The three-member Panel consisted of Haidar bin Mohamad Noor, Mahadev Shankar, and Lee Lam Thye.

12 December 2007, pursuant to the recommendation of the Panel.[31] Its terms of reference were as follows: '(i) to enquire and ascertain the authenticity of the video clip; (ii) to enquire and identify the speaker, the person he was speaking to in the video clip and the persons he mentioned in the video clip; (iii) to inquire and ascertain the truth or otherwise of the content of the conversation in the video clip; (iv) to determine whether any act of misbehaviour has been committed by person or persons identified or mentioned in the video clip; and (v) to recommend any appropriate course of action to be taken against the person or persons identified or mentioned in the video clip, should person or persons be found to have committed any misbehaviour.'[32]

The Commission presented its report to the King on 9 May 2008. The Commission found the video clip to be authentic and that indeed the speaker was VK Lingam, and that the person to whom he was speaking on the phone was Ahmad Fairuz. The Commission examined the transcript of the conversation in the video clip, which it found to have been 'correctly transcribed except for some very minor details where the words were indecipherable'.[33] It formed the view that 'the central theme that runs through the length and breadth of the conversation in the video clip … turns on the appointment of Judges in the Malaysian Judiciary'.[34]

One specific aspect, according to the Commission, related to the appointment of Ahmad Fairuz as President of the Court of Appeal (PCA). After referring to a number of passages of conversation from the transcript, the Commission said: '[A] compelling inference can be reasonably and conceivably be drawn that [VK Lingam] was actively involved in the appointment of Tun Ahmad Fairus as President Court of Appeal with the possible aim of his further appointment to the post of Chief Justice of the Federal Court. It is clear from the phone conversation that [VK Lingam] was apprising Tun Ahmad Fairuz of his intention, purpose and capability of securing the latter's appointment to the post of President Court of Appeal.'[35]

Regarding Ahmad Fairuz's earlier appointment as the Chief Judge (Malaya), the Commission found that Mahathir Mohamad and Tan Sri Vincent Tan, a business tycoon, 'were friends and that their relationship spanned many years'; that Vincent Tan and Tengku Adnan (the UMNO Executive Secretary and a minister in the Prime Minister's Department) knew each other well; that Vincent Tan and VK Lingam were very good friends; and that Tengku Adnan and VK Lingam had known each other for a long time. The web of friendship among Vincent Tan, VK Lingam and Tengku Adnan 'would have played a significant and active influencing role on the appointment of Tun Ahmad Fairuz as the Chief Judge Malaya

[31] The Commission was composed of Haidar bin Mohamad Noor (retired Chief Judge of Malaya), Steve Shim (retired Chief Judge of Sabah and Sarawak), Mahadev Shankar (retired Court of Appeal Judge), Zaitun Zawiyah binti Puteh (former Solicitor General), and Khoo Kay Kim (Emeritus Professor of Malaysian History, University of Malaya).

[32] Commission on Video Recording Report 4.

[33] ibid 52, para 4.

[34] ibid 52, para 44.

[35] ibid 55, para 51.

at the material time.'[36] The Commission did not find the denial by Mahathir Mohamad 'that he was not influenced by anyone to be entirely convincing'.[37] The Commission went into details regarding the manipulation of promotions for certain High Court Judges, who were aligned to Ahmad Fairuz and examined the allegation that Tun Eusoff Chin, the former Chief Justice, was also involved in the appointment of the judges. To refute Eusoff Chin's denial of a close relationship between him and VK Lingam, the Commission allowed Eusoff Chin to be cross-examined about his New Zealand holiday with VK Lingam and his family. In the end, the Commission concluded that the content of the conversation on the video clip was 'true in substance and material particulars', and that there was sufficient evidence of misbehaviour on the part of certain persons identified or mentioned in the video clip.[38]

The Commission found sufficient cause to invoke the Sedition Act 1948, the Legal Profession Act 1978, the Official Secrets Act 1972 and the Penal Code against various individuals mentioned in the video clip and recommended that matters be referred for prosecution. It is breath-taking to note the names of persons whom the Commission recommended should be investigated and prosecuted: the former Prime Minister Mahathir, the former Chief Justice Eusoff Chin, the lawyer VK Lingam, a prominent businessman, Vincent Tan, and the UMNO power-broker Tengku Adnan. An application by VK Lingam for judicial review of the Commission's findings regarding criminal misbehaviour on his part was ultimately dismissed by the Federal Court.[39] In the end, however, no prosecution whatsoever was levelled at the named individuals.

Some change did result from the Commission's report. The Commission stated:

> Having heard the evidence presented to the Commission in relation to the video clip it would seem clear that the appointment and promotion of Judges to the higher Judiciary is open to interference and manipulation by the Executive and other extrinsic forces including private citizens.[40]

The Commission recommended the establishment of a Judicial Appointments Commission.[41]

Part II

The Abdullah Badawi Reforms: A triumph of form over substance

On 17 April 2008, Prime Minister Abdullah Badawi delivered an important speech at a Malaysian Bar Council dinner. In the audience were Tun Salleh Abas, Tan Sri Azmi Kamaruddin, and Dato' George Seah. In his speech entitled 'Delivering

[36] ibid 58–9, para 57. [37] ibid 59, para 57. [38] ibid 37.

[39] 'Top court says Lingam video RCI findings "cannot be reviewed"' *The Malaysian Insider* (13 September 2011) http://blog.limkitsiang.com/2011/09/13/top-court-says-lingam-video-rci-findings-%E2%80%98cannot-be-reviewed%E2%80%99/ (accessed 17 July 2016).

[40] ibid 175. [41] ibid 38.

Justice, Renewing Trust',[42] Abdullah Badawi lamented the drop in level of trust and respect for the judiciary. He spoke of an earlier era when even the Malaysian judiciary was hailed by some as a model for other countries in the context of it being an independent and credible institution. He added:

> No nation can call itself fair and just without an efficient and trusted judiciary. By 'trusted', I mean a judiciary that delivers justice and is seen to deliver justice. In Malaysia's case, debates and arguments on the state of our judiciary have been heated and protracted. Some of the Malay Rulers have openly voiced their disquiet on what they see as a decline, requiring nothing short of a judicial renaissance. Some retired judges have related troubling tales of impropriety. Politicians on both sides of the aisle have called for reform of this most august institution. Even the Bar Council, true to form, has marched en masse outside my office.[43]

Abdullah Badawi acknowledged, 'To a large extent, the events of 1988 have fuelled much of the disagreement on how to move on.' He announced that the Government, in order to restore public confidence in the judiciary, would effect a change 'to make the process of nominating, appointing and promoting judges more transparent and representative'.[44] The reforms also included innovations to the discipline system in order to improve judges' accountability for misconduct.

Have the reforms achieved their purpose? The answer obviously will depend on whether the reforms have enabled judicial appointments to be insulated from political considerations and whether judicial misconduct can be dealt with by a process that is perceived to operate with integrity, real independence, and impartiality. An analysis of the reforms introduced to-date may suggest that there is still some way to go before the Malaysian judiciary can be set on a course to re-living the glory days of the past.

Prime Minister Abdullah Badawi appointed Zaid Ibrahim as a de facto Law Minister entrusted with the task of effecting reforms to the judiciary. After only 6 months in the job, Zaid Ibrahim resigned his ministerial position, citing opposition to proposed reforms (including the establishment of a Judicial Appointments Commission) by members of the cabinet and his own party, UMNO. Although his replacement (Nazri Aziz) continued with reforms to the judiciary, it was hard to imagine that there could still be any meaningful reforms given that Abdullah Badawi's position was so weakened that he was forced to agree to an accelerated transition of the Prime Minister's post to his deputy, Najib Razak.

The Abdullah Badawi government eventually enacted the *Judicial Appointments Commission Act* 2009 (Act 695). Under the Act, a Judicial Appointments Commission (JAC) was established in relation to the appointment of judges of the superior courts, namely, judges of the High Court, the Court of Appeal and the Federal Court, including the Chief Justice of the Federal Court, the President of

[42] 'Prime Minister: Delivering Justice, Renewing Trust', Speech delivered at the Malaysian Bar Council dinner, JW Marriott Hotel, Kuala Lumpur (17 April 2008) http://www.malaysianbar.org.my/speeches/prime_minister_delivering_justice_renewing_trust.html (accessed 12 July 2016).

[43] ibid. [44] ibid.

the Court of Appeal, the Chief Judge of the High Court in Malaya, and the Chief Judge of the High Court in Sabah and Sarawak.

The JAC consists of nine members and comprises of the following: the Chief Justice of the Federal Court (as chairman), the President of the Court of Appeal, the Chief Judge of the High Court in Malaya, the Chief Judge of the High Court in Sabah and Sarawak, a Federal Court judge[45] to be appointed by the Prime Minister, and 'four eminent persons'[46] who are appointed by the Prime Minister. The Prime Minister can revoke at any time the appointment of any of the 'four eminent persons' 'without assigning any reason'. Section 28 also provides that where 'the Prime Minister has accepted any of the persons recommended by the Commission [for appointment], he may proceed to tender his advice [to the King to appoint such person] in accordance with Article 122B of the Federal Constitution'.

It is clear that the Prime Minister is not obligated to accept the recommendations of the JAC. What makes the reforms highly questionable is that he is not, at the very minimum, required to provide reasons for his rejection of the JAC's recommendations. The Prime Minister can ignore the recommendations of the Commission, without being under any degree of accountability. If the reforms are to be creditable and meaningful, they have to satisfy at the minimum the criteria of transparency and accountability. The judicial appointment process must be revamped to ensure that the mechanism is one of substance and not of form. The executive should not have carte blanche to ignore the recommendation of the JAC without accountability imposed on the executive to explain its rejection of the JAC's recommendations.

A code of ethics regulating the conduct of judges of the Federal Court, the Court of Appeals, and a High Court had been drawn up in 1994. According to Justice James Foong of the Federal Court of Malaysia, the code of ethics 'formalises what exactly a judge can or cannot do' and that the objective of this exercise 'is to enhance transparency and to improve the image and integrity of the judiciary'.[47] The 2008 package of reforms included replacing the Judges' Code of Ethics 1994 and the establishment of a new Judges' Ethics Committee to consider breaches of the code that do not warrant the extreme penalty of removal from judicial office.[48]

The Constitution originally only provided, in Article 124(3), for removal of a superior court judge on the ground of 'misbehaviour' or 'inability, from infirmity of body or mind or any other cause, properly to discharge the functions of his office'. In June 1994, a constitutional amendment resulted in a substitution of 'misbehaviour' with 'any breach of any provision of the code of ethics'. The Judges' Code of Ethics 1994 was introduced, but the only available penalty for a breach of the code remained a removal from judicial office. However, not every breach of

[45] For a period of 2 years, renewable for another term.

[46] For a period of 2 years, renewable for another term.

[47] J Foong, 'The effects of current judicial reform in Asean countries' ASEAN Law Association 10th General Assembly: http://www.aseanlawassociation.org/10GAdocs/Malaysia5-2.pdf.

[48] *Judges' Ethics Committee Act* 2010 (Act 703), 4 March 2010 (PU(B) 96/2010). For critical comments on the Bill, see the Press Release of the Malaysian Bar Council, 'How do we judge the Judges?' 20 March 2009 <http://www.malaysianbar.org.my/press_statements/press_release_how_do_we_judge_judges_.html> (accessed 8 October 2016).

the code would amount to misconduct of sufficient seriousness to warrant removal from judicial office. Because removal was viewed as too harsh for some minor misdemeanours, it had resulted 'in some behaviour having gone unchecked'.[49] Hence, the Constitution was amended in 2006 to provide for the situation where, in a case of a breach of the code of ethics, if the Chief Justice were of the opinion that the breach did not warrant referring the judge to an Article 125(3) tribunal, the Chief Justice could refer the judge to a body 'constituted under federal law to deal with such breach'.[50]

While a new Judges' Code of Ethics 2009 replaced the 1994 Code, the enactment of the Judges' Ethics Committee Act 2010 authorized the creation of an ad hoc body called the 'Judges' Ethics Committee' to deal with breaches that do not warrant removal from office.[51] A complaint regarding breach of the code can be made in writing to the Chief Justice of the Federal Court. Under para 13 of the Judges' Code of Ethics 2009, if the Chief Justice of the Federal Court is of the opinion that the complaint lacks merit, he may, after consultation with the relevant head of jurisdiction, dismiss it or, if the Chief Justice of the Federal Court forms the opinion that the alleged breach does not warrant referral to a tribunal constituted

[49] Ahmad Fairuz bin Dato' Sheikh Abdul Halim, 'Judicial Independence, Accountability, Integrity and Competence: Some Aspects of the Malaysian Position'—Paper presented at the International Conference and Showcase on Judicial Reforms, Shangri-la Hotel, Makati City, Philippines, 28–30 November 2005.

[50] Article 125(3A).

[51] The 2009 version of the Judges' Code of Ethics contains more detailed and explicit guidelines for judicial officers on how to conduct themselves, especially on when to recuse themselves. It provides detailed rules governing how judges should conduct themselves. Paragraph 5, headed 'Upholding the integrity and independence of the judiciary', states that a judge 'shall exercise his judicial function independently on the basis of his assessment of the facts and in accordance with his understanding of the law, free from any extraneous influence, inducement, pressure, threat or interference, direct or indirect from any quarter or for any reason'. This is reinforced by directing a judge to 'act at all times in a manner that promotes integrity and impartiality of the judiciary': para 6(1). That such a direction needs to be embodied shows what a parlous state the judiciary has found itself in. Such a direction is a statement of the obvious and is the underlying substance of the judicial oath which every judge has to take upon taking up judicial appointment. The code lists the following limitations on a judge:

- a judge shall not allow any relationship to influence his judicial conduct or judgment;
- a judge shall not lend the prestige of his judicial office to advance his or others' private interest; and
- a judge shall not convey or permit others to convey the impression to any person that they are in a special position to influence him.

The code requires a judge to perform judicial duties fairly and efficiently, with the judicial duties taking precedence over all other activities of the judge. A judge is required to perform his judicial duties 'without bias or prejudice' and 'fairly, efficiently, diligently and promptly'. Thus, a judge cannot participate in the determination of a case in which any member of the judge's family is representing a litigant or is associated in any manner with the case. He must refrain from giving any public comment about a pending or impending proceedings that may be heard before the judge's court 'in a manner which may suggest to a reasonable person the judge's probable decision in any particular case'. He shall not conduct himself in a manner 'which is not befitting of a judge or which brings or is calculated to bring disrepute to his office as a judge'.

The code spells out the constraints on the performance of non-judicial activities by judges. A judge is required to minimize the risk of conflict with the judge's judicial obligations while conducting his extra-judicial activities. He is thus required to ensure that his extra-judicial duties do not 'cast reasonable doubt on his capacity to act impartially as a judge' or 'interfere with the proper performance of

under Article 125(3), he may refer the matter to the Judges' Ethics Committee. If the committee upholds the complaint, the committee may record an admonition against the judge or suspend the judge from office for a period not exceeding 1 year.

In terms of its composition, the Judges' Ethics Committee must consist of the Chief Justice and other judges or former judges in an odd number, with at least three members. The chair of the Committee is the Chief Justice, with any decision to be determined by a majority vote. The decision is expressly mandated to be 'final and conclusive' and thus is not subject to judicial review.

Unfavourable light was cast on the judiciary when a serving Chief Justice (Zaki Azmi) became the first judicial officer to be confronted with an alleged violation of the code. In an address at a conference soon after his appointment as the new Chief Justice, Zaki Azmi had unwittingly referred to his experience as a private practitioner in 1987 dealing with court officials, saying: 'It took me six months to be nice, to bribe each and every individual to get back into their good books before our files were attended to.'[52] He went on to warn 'all the clerks and all the registries to stop this nonsense'.[53] The next day, Zaki Azmi claimed that his statement had been misreported. However, a senior lawyer and opposition Member of Parliament (Karpal Singh), producing an audio recording of Zaki Azmi's speech, accused the Chief Justice of lying to cover up his admission to criminal corruption. He sent letters of complaint to the Chief Justice, also requiring that the Chief Justice should recuse himself from determining the progress of the complaint under para 13 of the Judges' Code of Ethics 2009.[54] The first letter was sent on 20 August 2010, with a follow-up letter on 1 December 2010. When Zaki Azmi ignored the complaints, Karpal filed proceedings against the Chief Justice seeking an order of mandamus to direct the Chief Justice to respond. Aziah Ali J of the High Court Malaya dismissed the application, concluding that the application for mandamus failed to comply with the conditions prescribed by the Specific Relief Act 1950. In brief, Karpal

his judicial duties'. The code articulates certain restrictions on the association of a judge with individual members of the legal profession, involvement with an organization or participation in any public discussion or political activities. With the written approval of the Chief Justice, a judge can do the following: perform various extra-judicial activities, such as giving lectures, writing, or appearing at public hearings on matters relating to the judicial system; the administration of justice; serve as a member of an official body devoted to the improvement of the law, judicial system, the administration of justice, and related matters or as a member of a body approved by the federal government; write and speak publicly on non-legal subjects and engage in historical, education, cultural, religious, sporting, or social or recreational activities (provided they do not interfere with the performance of non-judicial duties); and participate in civic and charitable activities (but not in charitable fund raising or membership solicitation).

The code requires a judge, on his appointment or at any time as may be required by the Chief Justice, to declare in writing all his assets to the Chief Justice of the Federal Court. Furthermore, a judge shall—on his appointment—cease to have any connection with the firm where he was practising as an advocate and solicitor before appointment.

A judge must comply with any administrative order or direction issued by the head of the Federal Court or the Court of Appeal or the High Courts.

[52] 'Stop it now, corrupt court staff warned', New Straits Times (8 November 2008) 4.

[53] ibid.

[54] Karpal Singh had initially submitted two complaints under para 12 to Chief Justice Zaki complaining about the Chief Justice himself, but to no avail.

Singh lacked the *locus standi* to bring the action for mandamus. The judge also concluded that the application was 'frivolous and vexatious'.[55]

The mechanism set up to handle complaints regarding alleged breaches of the code is not satisfactory. The composition of the Judges' Ethics Committee amounts to a case of judges judging judges, which hardly inspires confidence. The composition of this body must be altered to have, if not a majority of non-judicial members, at the very least, a significant number of public representatives. The chair of the committee should be a public member. Legislation should define the manner of selection and appointment of the public members in order to maintain public confidence in the independence of the committee.

What Has To Be Done

A discussion of reform measures necessitates some reference to the role of the Conference of Rulers.[56] An important question which arises is whether the rulers should be consulted at all in the suspension and the removal of judges. From published accounts,[57] it is clear that in 1988 the Rulers were concerned about Tun Salleh Abas' suspension and the subsequent moves to remove him.[58] If the Rulers were of the view that what had befallen Tun Salleh Abas was wrong, then should the Conference of Rulers have the constitutional power to alter the course of any similar events in future?

Article 38(6) of the Malaysian Constitution provides as follows:

> The members of the Conference of Rulers may act in their discretion in any proceedings relating to the following functions, that is to say –
> (a) the election or removal from office of the Yang di-Pertuan Agong [King] or the election of the Timbalan Yang di-Pertuan Agong [Deputy King];
> (b) the advising on any appointment; …'

It could be argued that construed literally, there is a lacuna in the Constitution: after all, if the Constitution refers to the participation of the Conference of Rulers in

[55] *Karpal Singh Ram Singh v Ketua Hakim Negara* [2011] 4 CLJ 179.

[56] Malaysia is a federation of thirteen States, with hereditary Rulers in nine of the States and with an appointed Yang di-Pertuan Negeri (formerly known as 'Governor') in the remaining States. The King and Deputy King are elected by the nine hereditary Rulers from among themselves for a term of 5 years—see Francis A. Trindade, 'The Constitutional Position of the Yang di-Pertuan Agong' in Tun Suffian, HP Lee, and FA Trindade (eds), *The Constitution of Malaysia: Its Development: 1957–1977* (OUP 1978) 103.

[57] Tun Salleh Abas and K Das, *May Day for Justice* (Magnus Books 1989) 142-44.

[58] See The Australian 8 July 1988, 6. The Malay Rulers, it would appear, did play an unpublicized role in the crisis. According to Tun Salleh, the Rulers had told him that it had been arranged for him to meet the King where he could apologize to the King for his failure to observe proper protocol in sending the letter. Tun Salleh in setting out his version of the Rulers' involvement said, 'They had spoken to His Majesty who had agreed to receive me and accept my explanation and apology.' (Tun Salleh Abas and K Das, *May Day for Justice* (Magnus Books 1989) 142). The 'arrangements' with the King did not unfold as expected by Tun Salleh. An account of the meeting with the King is found in ibid chap. XI.

the matter of 'any appointment' including particularly judicial appointments, then should not the Rulers also act as a constitutional check in the removal of judges?[59] Whatever the appropriate construction of Article 38(6), there is no ambiguity about the general power of the Conference of Rulers under Article 38(2) to deliberate on 'any other matter that it thinks fit'. An intransigent King can be made to accede to the wishes of the Conference through the operation of Article 32(4) and also the provisions of Part III of the Third Schedule which state as follows: 'A resolution of the Conference of Rulers to remove the Yang di-Pertuan Agong from office shall not be carried unless at least five members of the Conference have voted in favour of it.'

The constitutional mechanism to deal with judicial misconduct warranting removal from judicial office must also be strengthened to prevent the Article 125(3) tribunal being used as a rubberstamp of the government. The Constitution provides that a judge of the Federal Court, the Court of Appeal, or a High Court may be removed from office for either a breach of the code of ethics or on the ground of inability, from 'infirmity of body or mind or any other cause, properly to discharge the functions of his office'. The removal is effected by the King upon representation from the Prime Minister or from the Chief Justice after consulting the Prime Minister. A step before removal by the King is the requirement for a tribunal to be appointed by the King. Only in light of the tribunal's recommendation may the King remove the judge from office. The 1988 crisis illustrates that the tribunal system can be cynically manipulated by an unscrupulous government if it is determined to remove a judge.

The formulation of the Judges' Code of Ethics 2009, the establishment of the Judges' Ethics Committee and the creation of the JAC are apparently commendable measures to assist in the restoration of public confidence in the Malaysian judiciary. However, these measures, in the form actually implemented, are still grossly inadequate; and, without other fundamental changes running in parallel with such constitutional and statutory reforms, they do not ultimately revive public confidence in the judiciary. It should be openly acknowledged that at the heart of the crisis of confidence in the judiciary is the perception by reasonable members of the Malaysian citizenry that, with too few exceptions, judges are simply too timid to uphold the rule of law. The courts are seen as either too intimidated by the executive power or as willing participants in subverting the rule of law. Judicial timidity is cloaked by the invocation of a literal reading of fundamental constitutional safeguards or by resorting to a theory of a purely legalistic mode of interpretation or by overstretching the so-called 'four walls' doctrine to exclude from Malaysian constitutional interpretation applicable jurisprudence common to Westminster-model jurisdictions.

The impression that is obtained is that the judicial and legal system, instead of functioning to make government administration compliant with the rule of law and accountable to the public, is being utilized to make life difficult for members

[59] Cf. Abas and Das, *May Day for Justice*, 139–40.

of the opposition, critics of the government and dissidents, such that they become embroiled for much of their time in defending themselves against spurious charges in court. The Malaysian judiciary, if it is to regain the respect of the public, must overcome fear and give loud and courageous affirmation to the rule of law. It can do so in a number of ways. For instance, despite the constitutional amendment to Article 121, the Federal Court need not concede that the separation of powers is at the dispensation of the executive. It requires merely a faithful construction of the amended Article 121(1) in accordance with well-established principles to preserve the separation of the judicial power. The courts should also be as courageous as the highly respected Indian judiciary in expounding a doctrine of 'basic structure' to preclude distortions and the abrogation of fundamental constitutional values and safeguards. In that way, the introduction of a constitutional provision, like the ouster clause in the emergency powers framework could be invalidated. On many occasions, the courts have been only too ready to hide behind the principle of interpretation that constitutional provisions and statutory enactments should be construed with a presumption that it is not the intention of the legislature to encroach upon fundamental rights. The Federal Court and the Court of Appeal, have on a number of occasions been shown up by a display of judicial courage by some judges of the High Courts who truly live up to the creed of doing justice 'without fear, favour, affection, or ill-will'. These unsung heroes placed the virtues of judicial integrity, impartiality, and independence over personal career advancements.

Conclusion

Tun Mohamed Suffian, who served as Lord President of Malaysia, in his Braddell Memorial Lecture in 1982 remarked that nobody reading the judgments where the names of the Malaysian judges had been deleted 'could with confidence identify our race or religion'.[60]

Malaysia is undoubtedly a diverse society with Malays, Chinese, Indigenous, and Indians comprising the main ethnic groups. The diversity of religions comprises Islam, Buddhism, Christianity, and Hinduism. The languages in the country are Bahasa Melayu (the national language), Chinese (various dialects), English, Tamil, and native languages.[61] Sultan Azlan Shah once observed, 'Judging in a diverse society is not an easy task. Judges in many parts of the world face similar difficulties.'[62]

In an essay, published in 1978, surveying constitutional changes in the first 2 decades since the attainment of independence by the Malaysian polity, Professor Hugh Hickling observed how the composition of the Malaysian bench had altered

[60] Tun Mohamed Suffian, 'Four Decades in the Law – Looking Back' in FA Trindade and HP Lee (eds), *The Constitution of Malaysia: Further Perspectives and Developments* (OUP 1986) 216.

[61] US Department of State http://www.state.gov/r/pa/ei/bgn/2777.htm (dated 28 January 2011).

[62] HRH Sultan Azlan Shah, '50 Years of Constitutionalism and the Rule of Law' (Opening address by HRH Sultan Azlan Shah at the 14th Malaysian Law Conference) http://www.malaysianbar.org.my/speeches/opening_address_by_hrh_sultan_azlan_shah_at_the_14th_malaysian_law_conference.html (accessed 29 September 2016).

over those 2 decades. Out of eleven judges in office in 1958, eight (including two acting appointments) were expatriates. However, by 1970 all were Malaysian citizens. In trawling through the Malaysian law reports of the twenty years from 1958, he doubted whether in any case 'we could assert that this judge or that was an English, Scots, Malay, Chinese, or Indian lawyer, on the basis of his judgment'. He added, 'In other words, delete his name as author of the judgment, and you will be unable to identify the ethnic origin of the judge.'[63]

Tun Mohamed Suffian, had in 1978 also pointed out that with the transfer of power to local politicians after Independence, the public service inevitably became politicized. However, according to his observation, a feature of the Malaysian judiciary since Independence was that, 'unlike the civil service, it has remained completely unpoliticised'.[64] Tun Suffian further observed:

> The reputation that [the Malaysian judiciary] enjoys of being able to decide without interference from the executive or the legislature or indeed from anybody, contributes to confidence on the part of the members of the public generally that should they get involved in any dispute with the executive or with each other they can be sure of a fair and patient hearing and that their disputes will be determined impartially and honestly in accordance with law and justice.[65]

By 2004, however, Sultan Azlan Shah had lamented, 'Since Independence, the early judges have always cherished the notion of an independent judiciary and had built the judiciary as a strong and independent organ of government. The public had full confidence in the judiciary and accepted any decision then made without any question. Unfortunately, the same does not appear to be the case in recent years.'[66] Public confidence in the Malaysian judiciary has plummeted ever since the actions of the Mahathir administration which resulted in the dismissal of the Lord President (now entitled Chief Justice) Tun Salleh Abas and two senior judges of the Supreme (now Federal) Court in the judiciary crisis of 1988. Sultan Azlan Shah expressed his 'earnest hope' that the Malaysian judiciary 'will regain the public's confidence and that it will once again be held in the same esteem as it once was held.'[67]

[63] RH Hickling, 'An Overview of Constitutional Changes in Malaysia: 1957–1977' in Tun Mohamed Suffian, HP Lee, and FA Trindade (eds), *The Constitution of Malaysia: Its Development 1957–1977* (OUP 1978), 1, 15–6.

[64] Tun Mohamed Suffian, 'The Judiciary: During the First Twenty Years of Independence' Mohamed Suffian, HP Lee, and FA Trindade (eds), *The Constitution of Malaysia: Its Development 1957–1977* (OUP 1978) above n 1, 231, 241.

[65] ibid 231–62. Quoted in Visu Sinnadurai, 'The 1988 judiciary Crisis and its Aftermath' in Andrew Harding and HP Lee (eds), *Constitutional Landmarks in Malaysia: The First Fifty Years 1957–2007* (LexisNexis, 2007) 173 at 174.

[66] HRH Sultan Azlan Shah, 'The Role of Constitutional Rulers and the Judiciary Revisited' in HRH Sultan Shah, *Constitutional Monarchy, Rule of Law and Good Governance* (Professional Law Books & Sweet and Maxwell 2004) 399–400.

[67] ibid 400. Tun Abdul Hamid Mohamad, on occasion of his appointment as Chief Justice of Malaysia, said:

> I am aware that this appointment is a heavy burden on me. It is more so when it happens at a very challenging time, that is, when public perceptions of the Judiciary are disturbing; when the integrity of the courts in the administration of justice is doubted; when appointments

Nonetheless, the UN Working Group on Arbitrary Detention in its report on Malaysia observed continued to observe in 2011: 'The country does not have a solid, fully independent judiciary based on the principle of separation of powers and composed of independent and impartial judges and magistrates.'[68] Such an observation is not complimentary. However, instead of shying away from it, serious efforts should be made to ensure that the Malaysian people have a judiciary that they can be proud of and that is on par with the prestigious judiciaries of the robust liberal democracies. Prime Minister Abdullah Badawi was right in saying, 'There is still much to do to renew the public's trust in the nation's judiciary and to ensure that justice is consistently delivered.'[69]

The Malaysian judiciary, because of its common law traditions, is in the fortunate position of being able to tap into a rich vein of the historical evolution of judicial independence reaching as far back as 1608, when an angry English monarch, King James I, was told by Chief Justice Coke that 'the King should not be under man, but under God and the Laws'.[70] Dr Yvonne Tew recently concluded:

> The Malaysian courts' journey toward constitutional redemption has, so far, been uneven at best. In order for the Malaysian judiciary to restore its position as a co- equal branch of government, it will need to take firmer steps to assert its commitment to constitutional supremacy and its willingness to protect the fundamental liberties guaranteed by the Constitution.[71]

A solid and truly independent and impartial judiciary is of far greater value to the Malaysian nation than towering concrete edifices. It is far easier to lay the foundations for the latter, as they merely require skilled workers to do the work; it is extremely difficult to achieve the former, as that would require far-sighted, selfless, and uncorrupted political leaders and parliamentarians and courageous judges who are prepared to uphold the rule of law. One saving grace for Malaysia is that there are many people of courage and vision who, despite intimidation and unwarranted prosecution, continue to lift their voices in the common cause of pursuing the aim of an independent and impartial judiciary. I hope that such voices of decent folks will prevail.

> and the behaviour of Judges and their commitments in the discharge of their duties, are all being questioned. The fact that such negative perceptions exist does not necessarily mean such perceptions are all true. But, public perceptions are not formed in a matter of days ... In any event, we cannot simply brush them aside. —*I Will Never Beg* (CLJ Publications 2016) 135–6.

[68] Report of the Working Group on Arbitrary Detention (8 January 2011) at para 12.

[69] 'Delivering Justice, Renewing Trust' Speech By: Prime Minister Abdullah Ahmad Badawi, Prime Minister of Malaysia, Malaysian Bar Council Dinner, JW Marriott Hotel, Kuala Lumpur, 17/04/2008 http://www.malaysianbar.org.my/speeches/prime_minister_delivering_justice_renewing_trust.html (accessed 14 October 2016).

[70] Catherine Bowen, *The Lion and the Throne* (Little, Brown 1956) 305.

[71] Yvonne Tew, 'On the Uneven Journey to Constitutional Redemption: The Malaysian Judiciary and Constitutional Politics' (2016) 25(3) Washington International Law Journal 1, 2.

7

The Islamization Phenomenon: The New Constitutional Battlefront

After all these years of trying to build a genuine multiracial and multireligious Malaysia, we are now confronted with a new danger – Islamic fundamentalism.

Tunku Abdul Rahman, in Hussin Mutalib, *Islam in Malaysia: From Revivalism to Islamic State* (Singapore University Press 1993) 94

The passage of time has blurred the real intentions of the Malaysian framers of the Constitution and some recent scholarly works and discussions have questioned the secular basis of the state. An inadequate examination of the primary documents has largely contributed to these varied interpretations

Joseph M Fernando, 'The Position of Islam in the Constitution of Malaysia' (2006) 37(2) Journal of Southeast Asian Studies 249, 266

Introduction

In Malaysia, the issue of Islam and the Constitution has become 'a crucial aspect of political debate'.[1] The conspicuous feature of the phenomenon is that the Malaysian state itself is at the forefront of the Islamization process as 'its chief architect, orchestrating, shaping and harnessing Islamization as it rejects secularism'.[2] Today, the boundaries between Islamic strictures and the operation of constitutional fundamental guarantees are becoming increasingly blurred. Malaysia becomes an important crucible for the contradictions to be played out. It has been said: 'Conceptually, the contours of Islamism in Malaysia capture the complexities that … are expressed in longstanding debates over the compatibility of Islam

[1] Andrew Harding, 'The Keris, The Crescent and the Blind Goddess: The State, Islam and the Constitution in Malaysia' (2002) 6 Singapore Journal of International & Comparative Law 154, 164. See also: HP Lee, 'Constitutional Developments in Malaysia in the First Decade of the Twenty-First Century: A Nation at the Crossroads' in Albert HY Chen (ed), *Constitutionalism in Asia in the Early Twenty-First Century* (CUP 2014) 244, 261–7; Julian CH Lee, *Islamization and Activism in Malaysia* (Institute of Southeast Asian Studies 2010).

[2] Joseph Chinyong Liow, *Piety and Politics: Islamism in Contemporary Malaysia* (OUP 2009)192.

with democracy, the relationship between Islamists and the state, and the nature of Islamist commitment to mainstream political processes.'[3]

General framework of the Constitution

It is worthwhile to recall that the Federation is governed under a constitution drafted by an eminent Constitutional Commission that was entrusted with the task of drawing up a governing instrument to provide for 'a federal constitution for the whole country as a single, self-governing unit ... based on Parliamentary democracy with a bicameral legislature'.[4]

An essential element of the framework established under the *Merdeka* Constitution is that the legislative powers of the federal and the State legislatures are set out in a respective Federal List[5] and a State List.[6] The Federal List enumerates those matters that only the federal Parliament can legislate on while the State List enumerates those matters with respect to which the State legislatures can make laws. Of the matters set out in the State List, one significant item is para 1 which encompasses:

> Islamic law and personal and family law of persons professing the religion of Islam, including the Islamic law relating to succession, testate and intestate, betrothal, marriage, divorce, dower, maintenance, adoption, legitimacy, guardianship, gifts, partitions and non-charitable trusts; Wakafs and the definition and regulation of charitable and religious trusts, the appointment of trustees and the incorporation of persons in respect of Islamic religious and charitable endowments, institutions, trusts, charities and charitable institutions operating wholly within the State; Malay customs; Zakat, Fitrah and Baitulmal or similar Islamic religious revenue; mosques or any Islamic public places of worship, creation and punishment of offences by persons professing the religion of Islam against precepts of that religion, except in regard to matters included in the Federal List; *the constitution, organization and procedure of Syariah courts which shall have jurisdiction only over persons professing the religion of Islam and in respect only of any of the matters included in this paragraph, but shall not have jurisdiction in respect of offences except in so far as conferred by federal law;* the control of propagating doctrines and beliefs among persons professing the religion of Islam; the determination of matters of Islamic law and doctrine and Malay custom.

A third list, the Concurrent List,[7] sets out matters on which either the federal Parliament or a State legislature can legislate. In the event of a clash between federal and State legislation, supremacy is given to federal legislation. Each of the hereditary State Rulers is head of Islam in his State. In the case of Penang, Malacca, and the Federal Territories, the Yang di-Pertuan Agong is the head of Islam.

[3] ibid 178.

[4] *Report of the Federation of Malaya Constitutional Commission* (Kuala Lumpur 1957) (hereafter the 'Reid Commission Report') para 3.

[5] Ninth Schedule, List I—Federal List.

[6] Ninth Schedule, List II—State List.

[7] Ninth Schedule, List III—Concurrent List.

In the course of the drafting of the Constitution a change pertaining to Article 3, which was described as 'innocuous'[8], has now come become a bone of contention and it is central to the Islamization cause.

Some key provisions

Article 3(1) declares 'Islam is the religion of the Federation' but it goes on to add that 'other religions may be practised in peace and harmony in any part of the Federation'. The principle of equality is contained in Article 8. Article 8(1) declares that all persons 'are equal before the law and entitled to the equal protection of the law'. Article 11(1) guarantees the right of 'every person' to 'profess and practise his religion and, subject to clause (4), to propagate it'. A non-Muslim's right to propagate any religious doctrine or belief is restricted as laws made by a State, or federal laws in the case of the Federal Territories, may restrict the propagation of any religious doctrine or belief among Muslims. However, proselytizing to non-Muslims by members of the Islamic faith is not an offence.

Article 160 defines 'Malay' by reference to a person who professes the religion of Islam, habitually speaks the Malay language, and conforms to Malay custom. Article 160 also contains the following: ' "Law" includes written law, the common law so far as it is in operation in the Federation or any part thereof, any custom or usage having the force of law in the Federation or any part thereof.' It should be noted that Islamic law is not expressly mentioned in the definition.[9]

The jurisdiction and powers of the Syariah Courts are strictly prescribed by the Federal Constitution in the State List para 1. As such, the Syariah Courts would be subject to the judicial review jurisdiction of the Article 121 'civil' courts which are the final judicial arbiters of the Constitution and legislation. Article 121(1A) which was inserted into the Constitution in 1988, however, provides that the civil courts 'shall have no jurisdiction in respect of any matter within the jurisdiction of the Syariah courts'. In seeking to elevate the Syariah Courts to equal status with the civil courts, the government's insertion of Article 121(1A) has opened a can of worms arising from 'two overlapping legal jurisdictions'.[10]

'Religion of the Federation'

The Reid Constitutional Commission deliberated on the question 'whether there should be any statement in the Constitution to the effect that Islam should be the State religion'[11] and said: 'There was universal agreement that if any such provision

[8] *Report of the Federation of Malaya Constitutional Commission*, 'Note of Dissent by Justice Abdul Hamid' para 11.

[9] Ahmad Ibrahim, 'The Position of Islam in the Constitution of Malaysia' in Tun Mohamad Suffian, HP Lee, and FA Trindade (eds), *The Constitution of Malaysia: Its Development 1957–1977* (OUP 1978) 41, 65. He also, at 65, said that in Malaysia 'it is the Constitution which is the Supreme law'.

[10] Aliran, 'The Moorthy Maniam Case: Compassion and Justice Missing' (2005) 25(11) Aliran Monthly http://aliran.com/archives/monthly/2005b/11b.html (accessed 10 July 2016).

[11] *Report of the Federation of Malaya Constitutional Com*mission, para 169.

were inserted it must be made clear that it would not in any way affect the civil rights of non-Muslims.'[12] However, the Malay Rulers 'opposed the establishment clause on federalism grounds: they feared that they would lose their own power as the arbiters of all matters relating to Islam'.[13] It is interesting to note that, as was indeed noted by the Commission, Counsel for the Rulers had said the following to the Commission:

> It is Their Highnesses' considered view that it would not be desirable to insert some declaration such as has been suggested that the Muslim Faith or Islamic Faith be the established religion of the Federation. Their Highnesses are not in favour of such a declaration being inserted and that is a matter of specific instruction in which I myself have played very little part.[14]

Another argument proffered by the Malay Rulers to the Commission was anchored to the then ongoing state of emergency because of the communist insurrection. Professor Kristen Stilt said:

> In the Sultans' written proposals to the Commission, they emphasised that according to the state constitutions the 'Muslim Faith is a matter referred to the States, the Rulers of which exercise the temporal powers of the faith in Their respective territories.... Their Highnesses would point out that one of the results of the constitutional position has been that the loyalty of the overwhelming majority of their Malay subjects has been retained in the face of strenuous efforts to disaffect them in the interests of communism.' They further argued that 'any interference with the present constitutional established position of the Muslim Faith would, at the present times, be fraught with danger to the internal security of the Federation and to the success of the campaign against subversive elements.'[15]

The Commission pointed out that the memorandum submitted by the Alliance after stating that 'the religion of Malaysia shall be Islam' also stated: 'The observance of this principle shall not impose any disability in non-Muslim nationals professing and practising their own religions and shall not imply that the State is not a secular State.'[16] The Commission in its original draft decided not to include a provision for an official religion. Justice Abdul Hamid initially joined in the unanimous view that there should be no establishment clause in the constitution, but when the Commission reassembled in Rome to work on the final draft, he unexpectedly changed his mind. In a separate 'dissenting' note appended to the Report of the Commission, he advocated the adoption of the recommendation submitted by the

[12] ibid.

[13] Kristen Stilt, 'Contextualizing Constitutional Islam: The Malayan Experience' (2015) 13 ICON 407, 415.

[14] *Report of the Federation of Malaya Constitutional Commission* para 169.

[15] Kristen Stilt, 'Contextualizing Constitutional Islam: The Malayan Experience' (2015) 13(2) International Journal of Constitutional Law 407, 416. See, also, Joseph M Fernando, 'The Position of Islam in the Constitution of Malaysia' (2006) 37(2) Journal of Southeast Asian Studies249, 253.

[16] Kristen Stilt (cited in footnote 15), at 416, also said: '[T]here is no evidence that the Alliance intended to achieve substantive legal outcomes of religious law through the establishment clause, which is supported by the ambiguous assertion that Malaya would still be a secular state.'

Alliance.[17] He suggested the insertion of a constitutional provision to the following effect: 'Islam shall be the religion of the State of Malaya, but nothing in this Article shall prevent any citizen professing any religion other than Islam to profess, practise and propagate that religion, nor shall any citizen be under any disability by reason of his being not a Muslim.'[18] Justice Abdul Hamid said that such a provision was 'innocuous' and proceeded to point to a number of Christian and Muslim countries which have a provision of this type entrenched in their constitutions.[19]

In the Working Party, which reviewed the draft of the Reid Commission, there was no objection to the proposal by Tunku Abdul Rahman to include a provision declaring Islam the religion of the Federation. Fernando highlights the minute of the Working Party, which recorded the unequivocal assurance given by Tunku Abdul Rahman that 'the Federation would be a secular state'.[20] According to Fernando, the Colonial Office 'did not object after being assured by the Alliance leaders that they "had no intention of creating a Muslim theocracy and that Malaya would be a secular State" '.[21] Fernando also pointed out that this assurance from the Alliance was recorded in a 'brief prepared for the Secretary of State for the Parliamentary debate in the House of Commons on the Malayan independence bill'.[22]

It is clear today that 'Article 3 is no longer an "innocuous" clause but [lies] at the heart of political and legal debates' as to the character of the Malaysian polity.[23] A stark illustration of revisionism is found in the utterances of a High Court judge:

> Islam is not of the same status as the other religions; it does not sit side by side nor stand side by side. Rather, Islam sits at the top, it walks first, and is placed on a mantle with its voice loud and clear. Islam is like a 'jati' tree – tall, firm and able. Otherwise, Islam will not be the religion of the Federation but just another of the many religions embraced in the country and everybody would be equally free to embrace religions, with none better or more than any other.[24]

The Growing 'Islamization' Phenomenon

The hallmark of Islamism is its 'quintessentially political agenda' involving 'the politicization of Islam through the aligning of structures of governance and society with

[17] See Kristen Stilt, 'Contextualizing Constitutional Islam: The Malayan Experience' (2015) 13(2) International Journal of Constitutional Law 407, 420–2. Joseph M Fernando, 'The Position of Islam in the Constitution of Malaysia' (2006) 37(2) Journal of Southeast Asian Studies 249, 256.

[18] *Report of the Federation of Malaya Constitutional Commission*, 'Note of Dissent by Justice Abdul Hamid' para 11.

[19] Thailand was also specifically mentioned by him as it has a provision enjoining Buddhism to be the religion of the King who is required by the Constitution to uphold that religion.

[20] Joseph M Fernando, 'The Position of Islam in the Constitution of Malaysia' (2006) 37(2) Journal of Southeast Asian Studies 249, 260.

[21] ibid. [22] ibid 261.

[23] Wen-Cheng Chang, Li-ann Thio, Kevin YL Tan, and Jiunn-rong Yeh, *Constitutionalism in Asia: Cases and Materials* (Hart Publishing 2014) 117.

[24] *Meor Atiqulrahman bin Ishak & Ors v Fatimah bte Sihi* [2000] 5 MLJ 375. The passage translated into English from the Malay language judgment was cited in ibid 117, note 189.

Islamic strictures'.[25] In contemporary Malaysia the 'phenomenon of Islamization'[26] puts into the spotlight the reconciliation of this phenomenon with the Malaysian Constitution which was crafted as a governing instrument for a multiracial, multilingual, and multireligious society. The general unease of the non-Muslim segment of Malaysian society was aggravated by a highly publicized pronouncement of Dr Mahathir, Prime Minister (1981–2003), on 29 September 2001 that Malaysia was already an Islamic State.[27] The assertion provoked a storm of controversy. The unease of non-Muslims deepened with the endorsement of the pronouncement on 17 July 2007 by Najib Razak (then Deputy Prime Minister) and its further affirmation on 27 August 2007 by Prime Minister Abdullah Badawi.

What does the Islamization phenomenon involve? The growth of this phenomenon has been attributed by commentators to the1979 Iranian Revolution and was given a boost by Prime Minister Mahathir Mohamad. His publicly articulated policy of inculcating 'Islamic values in government administration' was implemented via a process of 'Islamisation of the state machinery and bureaucracy'.[28] While Mahathir Mohamad might initially have conceived his pro-Islamization agenda as 'solely an attempt to outflank PAS', the present reality is that 'Islamisation soon acquired a dynamics of its own as the UMNO elite derived manifest political advantages from it'.[29] Jaclyn Neo observes:

> Malaysia's economic and educational progress created a favourable environment for the cultivation of an increasingly religiously conscious citizenry. The New Economic Policy (NEP), the programme which actively implemented the special economic privileges to the *bumiputera* in Malaysia, and its major offshoot, the New Education Policy (NEDP) also led to the emergence of a more Islamised Malay elite. The NEDP opened the door for a sizeable number of Malay youths and students to attend local and overseas tertiary institutions, where they were drawn to Muslim student group which provided them social support and placed them in contact with Islamic scholars and personalities who visited Muslim student groups on the campuses. A large number of these Malay Muslim overseas students, particularly those educated in the Middle Eastern universities like Al-Azhar in Cairo, were exposed to radical views of Islam. In 1982, the Mahathir administration launched the International Islamic University in Kuala Lumpur, which contributed to the growth of an educated, Islamically-minded constituency. Muslim organisations in Malaysia have also effectively acted as *de facto* pressure groups in Malaysia in their call for 'more Islam' in the country.[30]

It is now clear that the Islamization genie cannot be put back into its bottle. The unfolding ramifications have placed great strain on the diverse Malaysian society. Controversies from time to time have arisen which call into question the future trajectory of constitutional development in Malaysia. A number of controversial

[25] *Piety and Politics: Islamism in Contemporary Malaysia* (OUP 2009) 6. [26] ibid 17.
[27] ibid 82. [28] ibid 46.
[29] Salah El-Sheikh, 'Implementing Islamic Law within a Modern Constitutional Framework – Challenges and Problems in Contemporary Malaysia' 1.3 Islam and Civilizational Renewal (ICR) http://www.iais.org.my/icr/index.php/icr/article/viewFile/279/271 (accessed 17 May 2016).
[30] Jaclyn Ling-Chien Neo, 'Malay Nationalism, Islamic Supremacy and the Constitutional Bargain in the Multi-ethnic Composition of Malaysia' (2006) 13 International Journal on Minority and Group Rights 95, 104.

episodes have arisen which have engendered concern over this Islamization phenomenon and its adverse impact on constitutionalism in Malaysia.[31]

Moral policing

An area of civil concern relates to acts of 'moral policing' by Islamic authorities. In January of 2005, more than 100 plainclothes officers from the Federal Territories Islamic Department (JAWI) conducted a raid on a Kuala Lumpur nightclub and detained a number of young Muslims.[32] It was reported that the female detainees were subjected to sexual harassment by the officers and that 'non-Muslim patrons, including tourists, who were outside the officers' jurisdiction, also reported being threatened with violence'.[33]

In 2009, a Muslim part-time model, Kartika Sari Dewi Shukarno, aged 32, was sentenced by a Syariah Court to six lashes of the rattan cane and a fine of $5,000 after she had pleaded guilty to drinking beer following a raid on a beach resort in the State of Pahang. At the last minute, the Sultan of Pahang commuted her caning sentence to community service for 3 weeks.

Fatwas relating to trousers and yoga

In 2008, the National Fatwa Council of Malaysia issued a fatwa or religious edict that said that young Muslim women should not wear trousers because by wearing them, they risked becoming sexually active 'tomboys'.[34] The Inspector General of Police (Musa Hassan) was reported to have said that protests against the fatwa would be viewed as a 'security threat'.[35] In the wake of this fatwa, the National Fatwa Council issued another fatwa instructing Muslims 'to avoid yoga because it uses Hindu prayers that could erode Muslims' faith'.[36] The chairman of the National Fatwa Council, Abdul Shukor Husin, said that it was 'inappropriate for Muslims to do yoga and the council has declared that practising yoga when it comes all together with the three elements [physical movements, worshipping and chanting] as *haram* (prohibited)'.[37] To contain the damage, Prime Minister Abdullah

[31] Jaclyn Ling-Chien Neo, 'Malay Nationalism, Islamic Supremacy and the Constitutional Bargain in the Multi-ethnic Composition of Malaysia' (2006) 13 International Journal on Minority and Group Rights 95–118.

[32] Jonathan Kent, 'Malaysia club raid sparks row' (18 February 2005) http://news.bbc.co.uk/2/hi/asia-pacific/4276077.stm (accessed 1 March 2016).

[33] ibid.

[34] 'Tomboy protests a security threat: Malaysia police' (13 November 2008) http://www.reuters.com/article/us-malaysia-tomboys-idUSTRE4AC32Y20081113 (accessed 1 March 2016).

[35] ibid.

[36] 'Malaysia backs down from yoga ban amid backlash' (26 November 2008) http://www.reuters.com/article/us-malaysia-islam-yoga-idUSTRE4AP2CA20081126 (accessed 1 March 2016).

[37] Mazwin Nik Anis, 'Fatwa Council says yoga with worshipping, chanting is prohibited' *The Star* Online (22 November 2008) http://www.thestar.com.my/story/?file=%2F2008%2F11%2F22%2Fnation%2F20081122111842& (accessed 1 March 2016).

Badawi told the national news agency Bernama that 'Muslims could carry on doing yoga but minus the chanting'.[38]

The *Herald*/ 'Allah' case

On 31 December 2009, in *Titular Roman Catholic Archbishop of Kuala Lumpur v Menteri Dalam Negeri and Anor*,[39] Lau Bee Lan J of the High Court lifted a 3-year ban against the Catholic Church using the word *Allah* to refer to the Christian God in its weekly publication, *Herald*—the Catholic Weekly. The ban had been imposed by the Minister pursuant to the Printing Presses and Publications Act 1984 and was directed only to the Malay version of the weekly newspaper. On 14 October 2013, the Court of Appeal[40] allowed the appeal against the decision of the High Court judge.[41] The Court of Appeal stated that the purpose and intention of the phrase 'in peace and harmony' in Article 3(1) was to protect the sanctity of Islam as the religion of the country and that its usage in the Malay version of the *Herald* 'has the potential to disrupt the even tempo of the life of the Malaysian society'.[42] It also found that word or name *Allah* was not an integral part of the faith and practice of Christianity, in particular that of the Roman Catholic Church. The appellate court also ruled that the Home Minister had acted within his powers in banning the *Herald* from using the word. The Court of Appeal said that the use of 'Allah' in the *Herald* would 'create confusion among the Muslims' and thus justified the ban on the grounds of national security and public order.[43] Mohamed Apandi Ali JCA said, '[I]t is not for the court to probe for strong evidential proof of national security. It must be inferred that the Minister's decision, involving national security, is rational.'[44] On 23 June 2014, the Federal Court, in a narrow 4 to 3 decision, rejected an application for leave to appeal against the Court of Appeal decision.[45] The Federal Court later rejected an application to review its earlier decision.[46]

[38] 'Malaysia backs down from yoga ban amid backlash' (26 November 2008) http://www.reuters.com/article/us-malaysia-islam-yoga-idUSTRE4AP2CA20081126 (accessed 1 March 2016).

[39] [2010] 2 MLJ 78.

[40] Mohamed Apandi Ali JCA, Abdul Aziz Rahim JCA, and Mohd Zawawi Salleh JCA. For a critical analysis of the Court of Appeal's decision, see Jaclyn Neo, 'What's In a Name? Malaysia's "Allah" Controversy and the Judicial Intertwining of Islam with Ethnic Identity', NUS Law Working Paper Series, Working Paper 2014/008, June 2014, http://law.nus.edu.sg/wps.

[41] *Menteri Dalam Negeri & Ors v Titular Roman Catholic Archbishop of Kuala Lumpur* [2013] 6 MLJ 468 (CA).

[42] *Menteri Dalam Negeri & Ors v Titular Roman Catholic Archbishop of Kuala Lumpur v* [2013] 6 MLJ 468, [42] (CA) per Mohamed Apandi Ali JCA.

[43] Boo Su-Lyn, 'Three things we learned from: The Allah case' *Malaymail* http://www.themalaymailonline.com/malaysia/article/three-things-we-learned-from-the-allah-case#sthash.EBwLxIuK.dpuf (accessed 11 October 2016).

[44] *Menteri Dalam Negeri & Ors v Titular Roman Catholic Archbishop of Kuala Lumpur* [2013] 6 MLJ 468, 494.

[45] *Titular Roman Catholic Archbishop of Kuala Lumpur v Menteri Dalam Negeri & Ors* [2014] 4 MLJ 765 (FC). See Wilson Tay Tze Vern, 'The Use and Misuse of Article 4(3) and 4(4) of the Federal Constitution' [2015] 2 MLJ cliv.

[46] Ida Lim and Shaun Tan, 'Last nail in Catholic Church's "Allah" case as Federal Court again says no' *Malaymail* Online (21 January 2015) http://www.themalaymailonline.com/malaysia/article/last-nail-in-catholic-churchs-allah-case-as-federal-court-again-says-no (accessed 16 May 2016).

Apostasy and freedom of religion

In 1988,[47] a new Article 121(1A) was inserted into the Constitution through a constitutional amendment.[48] It is doubtful whether the serious ramifications of the constitutional amendment had been thought through. The history of constitutional amendments in Malaysia is a pathetic tale of hasty changes, with little opportunities afforded to members of the public and opposition parliamentarians to comment. The Aliran intoned:

> The 1988 Constitutional Amendment Bill was rushed through Parliament without giving adequate time for MPs and the country to study and debate their far-reaching implications. The Bill was tabled in Parliament for first reading on 17 March 1988 and passed the next day on 18 March 1988 by a margin of 142 for and 18 against.[49]

Professor Salah El-Sheikh observed, 'It was hurriedly passed through Parliament under controversial circumstances, as many vocal non-Muslim opposition parliamentarians were then confined under the Internal Security Act (ISA) following the Operation Lalang crackdown in October 1987.'[50] The new provision, which states that the High Courts and inferior courts 'shall have no jurisdiction in respect of any matter within the jurisdiction of the Syariah Courts', was purportedly designed to ensure that the Syariah Courts would be freed 'from interference by the civil courts'.[51] It created, according to Professor Horowitz, 'two parallel, relatively autonomous systems, one secular and one Islamic'.[52] Such a conclusion—which, if true, would have disturbing constitutional consequences—is by no means certain. The amendment 'has created an interpretive quandary'[53] and has engendered 'continuing legal controversy and public concern over its scope, effects, and implications.'[54]

[47] See Mohamed Azam and Mohamed Adil, 'Law of Apostasy and Freedom of Religion in Malaysia' (2007) 2(1) Asian Journal of Comparative Law 1.

[48] Constitution Act A704/88.

[49] Aliran, 'The Moorthy Maniam Case: Compassion and Justice Missing' (2005) 25(11) Aliran Monthly http://aliran.com/archives/monthly/2005b/11b.html (accessed 10 July 2016).

[50] Salah El-Sheikh, 'Implementing Islamic Law within a Modern Constitutional Framework – Challenges and Problems in Contemporary Malaysia' 1.3 Islam and Civilizational Renewal (ICR) http://www.iais.org.my/icr/index.php/icr/article/viewFile/279/271 (accessed 17 May 2016). 'At the time the bill was passed, seven DAP MPs—including some of the most vocal parliamentarians such as Lim Kit Siang, Karpal Singh, and Lim Guan Eng as well as the late P Patto and V David—were under ISA detention at the Kamunting Detention Centre following Operation Lalang in October 1987—Aliran', 'The Moorthy Maniam Case: Compassion and Justice Missing' (2005) 25(11) Aliran Monthly http://aliran.com/archives/monthly/2005b/11b.html (accessed 10 July 2016).

[51] Ahmad Ibrahim, 'The Amendment to Article 121 of the Federal Constitution: Its Effect on Administration of Islamic Law' (1989) 2 Malayan Law Journal xvii, xx.

[52] D Horowitz, 'The Qu'ran and the Common Law: Islamic Law Reform and the Theory of Legal Change' (1994) 42 American Journal of Comparative Law 233, 236, 259–60.

[53] Vanitha Sundra Karean, 'The Malaysian Constitution and its Identity Crisis: Secular or Theocratic?' [2006] LAWASIA Journal 47, 51.

[54] Li-ann Thio, 'Jurisdictional Imbroglio: Civil and Religious Courts, Turf Wars and Article 121(1A) of the Federal Constitution' in Andrew Harding and HP Lee (eds), *Constitutional Landmarks in Malaysia: The First 50 Years 1957–2007* (LexisNexis 2007) 197.

It is clear that, as asserted by Professor Li-ann Thio, that Article 121(1A) 'has failed to remove civil-religious court jurisdictional conflicts'.[55] There have been many reported cases that illustrate the jurisdictional imbroglio arising from Article 121 (1A). It is not within the purview of this discussion to provide a comprehensive study of the case law.[56] A few instances will be highlighted. One controversial case involved Moorthy Maniam, who achieved 'national hero' status as a member of a Malaysian team that successfully climbed Mount Everest. Upon his death, his widow, Kaliammal, sought to prevent Moorthy from being buried according to Muslim rites.[57] She sought a declaration from the High Court to the effect that Moorthy, at the time of death, was a Hindu and, therefore, should be buried according to Hindu rites. The religious authorities, however, had obtained from the Syariah Court an order stating that Moorthy had become a Muslim without the knowledge of his family. The widow, being a non-Muslim, had no standing in the Syariah Court to contest the order. On the other hand, the High Court stated that it lacked jurisdiction over the matter. The result was that Moorthy's widow was left without any legal remedy.[58]

In 2007, the Federal Court's majority ruling in *Lina Joy v Federal Territory Islamic Council*[59] contained troubling ramifications for non-Muslims in Malaysia. *Lina Joy*, which attracted widespread international publicity, involved a Malay woman who was brought up as a Muslim. Her name before her conversion to Christianity was Azalina Jailani. She applied to the National Registration Department (NRD) to have her name changed to Lina Lelani, but her application was rejected without any reason being given. She applied a second time to change her name to Lina Joy and stated that she had converted to Christianity. She was eventually issued a new identity card but the card still specified Islam as her religion. She then applied to

[55] ibid 198.

[56] See Li-ann Thio, 'Jurisdictional Imbroglio: Civil and Religious Courts, Turf Wars and Article 121(1A) of the Federal Constitution' in Andrew Harding and HP Lee (eds), *Constitutional Landmarks in Malaysia: The First 50 Years 1957–2007* (LexisNexis 2007) 197–226; Poh-Ling Tan, 'Paying the Price for Religious Freedom: A Non-Muslim Perspective' in Wu Min Aun (ed), *Public law in Contemporary Malaysia* (1999) 134–77; Vanitha Sundra Karean, 'The Malaysian Constitution and its Identity Crisis: Secular or Theocratic?' [2006] LAWASIA Journal 47–61.

[57] See Li-ann Thio, 'Jurisdictional Imbroglio: Civil and Religious Courts, Turf Wars and Article 121(1A) of the Federal Constitution' in Andrew Harding and HP Lee (eds), *Constitutional Landmarks in Malaysia: The First 50 Years 1957–2007* (LexisNexis 2007) 199.

[58] *Kaliammal a/p Sinnasamy v Pengarah Jabatan Agama Islam Wilayah Persekutuan* [2006] 1 MLJ 685. See also Aliran, 'The Moorthy Maniam Case: Compassion and Justice Missing' (2005) 25(11) Aliran Monthly <http://aliran.com/archives/monthly/2005b/11b.html> (accessed 10 July 2016).

[59] *Lina Joy v Majlis Agama Islam Wilayah & Anor* [2007] 4 MLJ 585 (FC). Li-ann Thio, 'Jurisdictional Imbroglio: Civil and Religious Courts, Turf Wars and Article 121(1A) of the Federal Constitution' in Andrew Harding and HP Lee (eds), *Constitutional Landmarks in Malaysia: The First 50 Years 1957–2007* (LexisNexis 2007) 197–226; Thio Li-ann, 'Apostasy and Religious Freedom: Constitutional Issues Arising from the Lina Joy Litigation' (2006) 2 MLJ I; Dawson B and Thiru S, 'The Lina Joy Case and the Future of Religious Freedom in Malaysia' [2007] LAWASIA Journal 151; Dato' Cyrus Das, 'Constitutional Supremacy & The Lina Joy Decision' in Samuel Ang, Lee Min Choon, and Lim Siew Foong (eds), *Religious Liberty After 50 Years of Independence* (NECF Malaysia Research Commission 2008) 41–50; Nathaniel Tan and Lee John (eds), *Religion Under Siege? Lina Joy, the Islamic State and Freedom of Faith* (Kinibooks 2008).

have that description deleted from her card but the NRD rejected her application on the ground that she had not first obtained a certificate from the Syariah Court, officially approving her apostasy from Islam, even though there was no provision in the NRD regulations requiring a person to obtain such an order from the Syariah Court. It was clear to her that obtaining any such approval was impossible. Lina Joy failed in the High Court, with Faiza Tamby Chik J saying:

> Therefore a person as long as he/she is a Malay and by definition under art. 160 cl (2) is a Muslim, the said person cannot renounce his/her religion at all. A Malay under art. 160 (2) remains in the Islamic faith until his or her dying days ... Even if one is non-Malay and embraces Islam and becomes a Muslim convert (mualaf) and later decides to leave the Islamic faith he or she is still required to report and see the relevant State Islamic authority who will decide on her renunciation of Islam ... '[60]

The High Court judge held that Lina Joy was still a Muslim and that the issue of finality of her decision to convert out of Islam was a matter for the Syariah Court and not the civil courts.

On appeal, a 2 to 1 majority of the Court of Appeal held that the NRD was 'right in law in rejecting [Lina Joy's] application ... to have the statement of her religion as "Islam" deleted from her NRIC and in requiring a certificate and/or order from the Syariah Court'.[61] The majority judges comprised Abdul Aziz Mohamad JCA and Arifin Zakaria JCA, whereas Gopal Sri Ram JCA dissented. The Federal Court dismissed her appeal from the decision of the Court of Appeal.[62] Ahmad Fairuz CJ and Alauddin Mohd Sherif FCJ comprised the majority while Richard Malanjum CJ (Sabah and Sarawak) dissented.

The substantive effect of the judicial decisions is that a Muslim cannot exit the Islamic faith without first obtaining the approval of the Syariah Court. The stance of the majority derogated from the declared supremacy of the Constitution. It denied Muslim Malaysians the guarantee of Article 11(1) that 'Every person has the right to profess and practise' a religion of his or her choice, by interposing a third party whose approval had to be first obtained in order for Muslims to change their religion. Richard Malanjum CJ (Sabah and Sarawak) delivered 'an intellectually rigorous dissent', which 'demonstrated fidelity to constitutional supremacy'.[63] He adopted an 'originalist' approach in his construction of the Constitution by saying:

> Sworn to uphold the Federal Constitution (the constitution), it is my task to ensure that it is upheld at all times by giving effects to what I think the founding fathers of this great nation had in mind when they framed this sacred document. It is ... my view that when considering an issue of constitutional importance it is vital to bear in mind that all other interests and feelings, personal or otherwise, should give way and assume only a secondary role if at all[64]

[60] *Lina Joy v Majlis Agama Islam Wilayah & Anor* [2004] 2 MLJ 119, 143 (HC).

[61] [2005] 6 MLJ 193 (CA). [62] [2007] 4 MLJ 585 (FC).

[63] Li-ann Thio, 'Jurisdictional Imbroglio: Civil and Religious Courts, Turf Wars and Article 121(1A) of the Federal Constitution' in Andrew Harding and HP Lee (eds), *Constitutional Landmarks in Malaysia: The First 50 Years 1957–2007* (LexisNexis 2007) 197, 225.

[64] *Lina Joy* [2007] 4 MLJ585, [22]–[24] (FC).

He also pointed out that it would be unreasonable 'to expect [Lina Joy] to apply for a certificate of apostasy when to do so would likely expose her to a range of offences under the Islamic law'.[65]

Other persons in an equivalent position to Lina Joy might be placed in an impossible situation by the majority decision. Apostasy from Islam is a criminal offence in some of the Malaysian states, attracting punishments of up to a RM3000 fine or imprisonment of up to three years and mandatory detention in a 'rehabilitation' centre for up to 36 months, like the offences created in Perak, Terengganu and Kelantan.[66] Ambiga Sreenevasan, the President of the Malaysian Bar, in a public statement of 31 May 2007, highlighted the case of Revathi Masoosai in Malacca who had been born as Siti Fatimah to Muslim parents. She was deprived of her liberty and access to her husband and minor child'[67] after her husband contended that she was no longer a Muslim but a practising Hindu. Revathi was charged with committing apostasy. In consequence, she was sent to a 'rehabilitation' centre for almost 100 days, and her detention was subsequently extended by another 80 days.[68]

Andrew Harding described the *Lina Joy* case as creating 'an unprecedented degree of passion among the public'. He added, 'For many Muslims the suit represented an attack on Islam that could lead to unrestricted apostasy. For many non-Muslims the decision undermined the secular state and their constitutional right to freedom of religion.'[69] The outcome is that in these recent cases the jurisdiction of the Syariah Courts has been increased by resolving any doubts in their favour.

Conversion and child custody

Another area in which the Malaysian polity is afflicted by tensions involves situations where one parent (usually the father in the cases that have attracted national attention) quietly converts to Islam and officially converts the minor children of the marriage without the knowledge of the other parent. Typically, a case involves a tussle over the custody of the children who have been purportedly abducted by their Muslim-converted father, where the non-Muslim wife finds herself in a legal 'limbo'. When the Syariah Court purports to grant an order of custody to the Muslim father, the mother, not being a Muslim, has no recourse to the Syariah Court and, in fact, is not subject to the Syariah Court's jurisdiction. When she goes

[65] ibid 632 [90] (FC).

[66] Mohamed Azam and Mohamed Adil, 'Restrictions in Freedom of Religion in Malaysia: A Conceptual Analysis with Special Reference to the Law of Apostasy' (2007) 4(2) Muslim World Journal of Human Rights 1, 24.

[67] Bar Council, 'Federal constitution must remain supreme' in Nathaniel Tan and John Lee (eds), *Religion under Siege?* (Kinibooks 2008) 34.

[68] 'Doing the Impossible: Quitting Islam in Malaysia' *Asia Sentinel* (27 April 2007) http://www.asiasentinel.com/society/doing-the-impossible-quitting-islam-in-malaysia/ (accessed 11 July 2016). See, also, 'Hindu hubbies on warpath with Islamic authorities' (Malaysiakini, 20 April 2007) at https://m.malaysiakini.com/news/66226 (accessed 11 July 2016).

[69] Andrew Harding, 'Constitutionalism, Islam and National Identity in Malaysia' in Rainer Grote and Tilman J Roder (eds), *Constitutionalism in Islamic Countries: Between Upheaval and Continuity* (OUP 2012) 201, 216.

to the civil court for a remedy, she finds that court disclaiming jurisdiction on the argument that the civil courts, by virtue of Article 121(1A), 'shall have no jurisdiction in respect of any matter within the jurisdiction of the Syariah courts'.

The jurisdictional imbroglio is underscored by the readiness of the superior civil courts to abandon the field whenever the jurisdiction of the Syariah Court is claimed. In *Shamala Sathiyaseelan v Dr Jeyaganesh C Mogarajah*,[70] the High Court held that 'a non-Muslim mother could not seek redress of her parental rights in the High Court where her newly converted Muslim husband had in a clandestine manner unilaterally converted their minor children into Islam'.[71]

Another case which illustrates the hardship arising from such jurisdictional imbroglio is that, in 2009, of Indira Gandhi whose husband converted to Islam and also converted their three children—then aged 12 years, 11 years, and 11 months—without Indira's knowledge and without the children being present before the Islamic authorities to recite the confession of faith necessary for their conversion (obviously, the youngest child was incapable of such act). He then obtained a custody order from a Syariah Court for all three children although the High Court had already granted interim custody to Indira.[72] The High Court (Lee Swee Seng JC) quashed the children's conversion as unlawfully done[73] but, in 2015, the Court of Appeal (Balia Yusof Wahi and Badariah Sahamid JJCA, Hamid Sultan Abu Backer JCA dissenting) overturned that decision and maintained that only a Syariah Court could determine if the children's conversion to Islam was valid.[74] Centre For A Better Tomorrow (CENBET) Co-President Gan Ping Sieu pointed out that the Syariah Court has no jurisdiction over non-Muslims and as such, Indira could not seek legal redress there. He said, 'The creeping judicial inclination in cases of this nature has created a gap in Malaysia's justice system, when a case like Indira's was essentially a family dispute that has become a racial-religious monster driving deeper wedges between the different communities and providing a fertile ground for rising extremism.'[75]

In the same case, the husband was also found to be 'in contempt of a custody order for refusing to hand over one of their three children to the wife'.[76] Malik

[70] [2004] 2 MLJ 648. For another similar case, see *Subashini a/p Rajasingam v Saravanan a/l Thangathoray* [2007] 4 MLJ 97.

[71] Vanitha Sundra Karean, 'The Malaysian Constitution and its Identity Crisis: Secular or Theocratic?' [2006] LAWASIA Journal 47, 53.

[72] 'Civil courts failed duty, group says after Indira Gandhi case' *Malaymail* Online (1 January 2016) http://www.themalaymailonline.com/malaysia/article/civil-courts-failed-duty-group-says-after-indira-gandhi-case (accessed 1 March 2016).

[73] *Indira Gandhi v Pengarah Jabatan Agama Islam Perak* [2013] 5 MLJ 552.

[74] *Pathmanathan a/l Krishnan (also known as Muhammad Riduan bin Abdullah) v Indira Gandhi* [2016] 4 MLJ 455.

[75] He also said that 'the government should abide by the April 2009 Cabinet decision that said that the children of divorced parents should be raised in their religion at the time of the marriage, regardless of whether a parent had converted or not.': 'Civil courts failed duty, group says after Indira Gandhi case' *Malaymail* Online (1 January 2016) http://www.themalaymailonline.com/malaysia/article/civil-courts-failed-duty-group-says-after-indira-gandhi-case (accessed 1 March 2016).

[76] *Indira Gandhi a/p Mutho v Patmanathan a/l Krishnan* [2015] 7 MLJ 153. See also Malik Imtiaz Sarwar, 'Constitutionalism, the Rule of Law and Religious Freedom in Malaysia' in Marco Bünte, and Björn Dressel (eds), *Politics and Constitutions in Southeast Asia* (Routledge 2017) 331, 347.

Imtiaz Sarwar elaborated on subsequent developments, 'When the High Court granted a committal recovery order, the Inspector General of Police refused to execute it.'[77] The High Court then issued a mandamus order 'to compel the Inspector General to execute the previous order'.[78] The High Court's decision[79] was overturned by the Court of Appeal.[80]

The Civil Courts: A reawakening?

A few recent decisions provide a glimmer of hope that some superior court judges are now recognizing that the civil courts might have abdicated their role too readily and that it is necessary to draw a line in the sands to make it clear to the authorities involved that they operate under the rule of law and under the Malaysian Constitution.

In April 2016, the Federal Court restored the mandamus order in Indira Gandhi's case and ordered the Inspector General of Police to execute a warrant of arrest against the husband.[81] In May 2016, the Federal Court also granted Indira leave to appeal against the Court of Appeal's decision as regards the children's conversion.[82] The outcome remains to be seen.

In 2012, a High Court judge ordered the authorities to pay compensation for demolishing a chapel built by a Christian *orang asli* (indigenous people) group in the State of Johor, affirming their constitutional right to practise their religion.[83] The Court of Appeal struck out an appeal from the decision of the High Court decision.[84]

In 2013, the Federal Court upheld the decisions of the High Court and Court of Appeal and lifted a ban on a book published by the group Sisters in Islam, entitled *Muslim Women and the Challenge of Islamic Extremism*. The Home Minister had banned the book as being 'prejudicial to public order' after religious authorities alleged that the book (a compilation of scholarly essays highlighting problems in the administration of Islam in Malaysia affecting Muslim women's rights) would 'confuse Muslims, particularly Muslim women' and 'those with shallow knowledge' of Islam.[85]

[77] Malik Imtiaz Sarwar, 'Constitutionalism, the Rule of Law and Religious Freedom in Malaysia' in Marco Bünte and Björn Dressel (eds), *Politics and Constitutions in Southeast Asia* (Routledge 2017) 331, 347.

[78] ibid. [79] *Indira Gandhi a/p Mutho v Ketua Polis Negara* [2015] 9 MLJ 301 (HC).

[80] *Ketua Polis Negara v Indira Gandhi a/p Mutho* [2015] 2 MLJ 149 (CA).

[81] Maizatul Nazlina and Austin Camoens, 'Federal Court orders IGP to arrest Indira's ex-husband' *The Star* (30 April 2016) http://www.thestar.com.my/news/nation/2016/04/30/federal-court-orders-igp-to-arrest-indiras-exhusband/ (accessed 21 October 2016).

[82] Qishin Tariq, 'Federal Court: Indira Gandhi can question validity of children's unilateral conversion' *The Star* (19 October 2016) http://www.thestar.com.my/...s/nation/2016/05/19/federal-court-allows-indira-gandhi-to-question-validity-of-childrens-unilateral-conversion/ (accessed 19 October 2016).

[83] *Pengarah Tanah dan Galian Johor v Khalip bin Bachik* [2013] 1 MLJ 799 (Zakiah Kassim JC).

[84] *Johor Baru City Council (MBJB) v Khalip Bachik* (8 August 2012). For more details, see Hafiz Yatim, 'JB City Council Loses Appeal in "Chapel Demolition" Case', *Malaysiakini* (30 July 2012) www.malaysiakini.com/news/204997 (accessed 1 May 2013).

[85] *SIS Forum (Malaysia) v Dato' Seri Syed Hamid bin Syed Jaafar Albar (Menteri Dalam Negeri)* [2010] 2 MLJ 385 (Mohamad Ariff J) affd [2012] 6 MLJ 340 (CA) (Abdul Wahab Patail, Clement

In 2016, the Federal Court reaffirmed the law that, even when one spouse in a non-Muslim marriage has converted to Islam, the civil courts retain the exclusive jurisdiction to make orders regarding divorce and custody of children. However, the decision has deeply troubling aspects. In *Deepa*'s case,[86] her husband Izwan converted to Islam and, behind her back, officially converted their two children also (a daughter aged 10 years and a son aged 8 years) and obtained Syariah Court orders for a divorce and his custody of the children. Deepa commenced proceedings in the High Court, which Izwan opposed. The High Court (Zabariah Mohd Yusof J), holding that the Syariah Court had no jurisdiction to make those orders, made its own orders dissolving the marriage and granting Deepa custody. After Izwan abducted their son, the High Court issued a further 'recovery order' for the police to retrieve the child for Deepa but the police demurred. The Court of Appeal[87] unanimously upheld the High Court's custody and recovery orders. The Federal Court confirmed that the Syariah Court had no jurisdiction to make its orders. However, the Court overturned the High Court's recovery order. It held that, although the Syariah Court had no jurisdiction to grant Izwan custody, that order remained 'a valid order until it is set aside',[88] and the High Court ought not to have disregarded the Syariah order in issuing its recovery order. The five Federal Court judges[89] did not explain the basic point how Deepa (a Hindu) could have any standing in a Syariah Court to set aside an order. The Federal Court then varied the High Court's custody order, ruling that the children's welfare now required that Izwan should have custody of the son. The decision, which effectively sanctioned the Syariah Court's incompetent order and Izwan's defiance of the High Court's competent orders, would allow future Syariah Courts and convert spouses to act unlawfully with impunity, with no remedy available to non-Muslim spouses. The religious status of the daughter in Deepa's custody also remains problematic. She exercised no personal choice in being converted. But given *Lina Joy*'s decision, she would be unable to disavow Islam as her designated religion without a Syariah Court order, and given the Federal Court's attitude in this case, no solution to the jurisdictional imbroglio remains in sight.

Lessons from the Malaysian Experience

Malaysia emerged from the colonial cocoon in 1957. When compared with the countries that obtained their independence after the Second World War, its development into a stable polity has been regarded as quite impressive. However, an

Skinner JJCA and Mah Weng Kwai J); Hafiz Yatim, 'Federal Court upholds lifting of ban on SIS book', *Malaysiakini* (14 March 2013) http://www.malaysiakini.com./news/223858 (accessed 19 October 2016).

86 *Viran a/l Nagapan v Deepa a/p Subramaniam* [2015] 3 MLJ 209 (CA), revd [2016] 1 MLJ 585 (FC).

87 Abdul Aziz Abdul Rahim, Tengku Maimun, and Ahmadi Asnawi JJCA.

88 *Viran a/l Nagapan v Deepa a/p Subramaniam* [2016] 1 MLJ 585, 608[55] (FC).

89 Raus Sharif PCA, Zulkefli CJ(M), Abdull Hamid Embong, Suriyadi, and Azahar Mohamed FCJJ.

assessment of the Malaysian polity cannot ignore some harsh realities. The diverse nature of the polity in terms of the varied ethnic, lingual, and religious dimensions gives rise to simmering tensions. Those dimensions, until 2008, have been managed through governance by a coalition that represents the major races in Malaysia. Playing on the fear of a possible recurrence of a May Thirteenth tragedy whenever the government's racial or religious policies are questioned, the Barisan Nasional coalition has managed to achieve a two-thirds majority in every of the general elections until 2008. In that year, for the first time, the PR opposition was able to forge a loose alliance of PKR, PAS, and DAP under the leadership of Anwar Ibrahim and came very close to wresting power from the Barisan Nasional. In the general elections of 2013, the PR opposition improved further on its electoral performance and doubts had persisted as to whether the government had resorted to widespread vote rigging to retain power.

Concerns pertaining to the Islamization of the Malaysian polity intended by the framers of the Constitution to be a 'secular' entity continue to simmer. Competing interpretations of the provisions of the Malaysian Constitution, especially Articles 3 and 11, 'have become urgent and divisive matters of political and legal controversy'.[90] Dr Liow stated that there 'should be little doubt that Islamisation is gaining momentum in Malaysia and will continue to do so' and provided the sombre assessment that 'the extent of penetration of Islamic consciousness into conceptions of order and governance' is such that 'the main debate is no longer the question of whether Malaysia is an Islamic or secular state, but what type of Islamic state Malaysia is today and will be in the future'.[91]

Civil society has a very important role to play in resisting the tide of this phenomenon. Such a phenomenon not only undermines the secular status of the Malaysian Constitution; it has serious consequences for moderate and progressive Muslims because it allows a radical or highly conservative form of the Islamic religion to prevail over them. On this score, the Muslims in Malaysia are really the ones who can ensure their enjoyment of the fundamental liberties. It requires moderate and progressive Muslims to articulate publicly their cause, despite a 'campaign of intimidation'.[92] The Honourable Justice Michael Kirby, in his Griffith Lecture analysing the *Lina Joy* case, also said:

> The world has the strongest interest in the reconciliation of the religion of Islam with modern tolerance and acceptance of diverse reality. There is a need for the Luthers of Islam to emerge and to help forge the reconciliation of their religion with modernity and diversity. This cannot be done effectively by Christians or by people of other religions.[93]

[90] Amanda J Whiting, 'Secularism, the Islamic State and the Malaysian Legal Profession' (2010) 5(1) Asian Journal of Comparative Law 1, 2.

[91] Joseph Chinyong Liow, *Piety and Politics: Islamism in Contemporary Malaysia* (OUP 2009) 192.

[92] Amanda J Whiting, 'Secularism, the Islamic State and the Malaysian Legal Profession' (2010) 5(1) Asian Journal of Comparative Law 1, 5: '... alternative and dissenting Muslim voices are sidelined, chastised or silenced by authoritarian elements within both government and the opposition that claim exclusive authority and capacity to interpret Islam'.

[93] Michael Kirby, 'Fundamental Human Rights and Religious Apostasy: The Malaysian Case of *Lina Joy*' (2008) 17(1) Griffith Law Review 151, 177. Organizations such as SIS and the heads of Islam

Prominent Malay Muslims are now emerging courageously to speak out and ensure that the public sphere is not monopolized by Islamic fundamentalists. On 10 December 2014, twenty-five prominent Malays (the 'G25') signed an open letter that called for open debate and a rational dialogue on Islamic law. They referred specifically to 'the current situation where religious bodies seem to be asserting authority beyond their jurisdiction; where issuance of various *fatwa* violate the Federal Constitution and breach the democratic and consultative process of *shura*'. They rejected 'supremacist' groups which labelled their detractors as 'anti-Islam, anti-monarchy and anti-Malay' and decried the use of the Sedition Act 'as a constant threat to silence anyone with a contrary opinion'. They continued:

> These developments undermine Malaysia's commitment to democratic principles and rule of law, breed intolerance and bigotry, and have heightened anxieties over national peace and stability.
>
> As moderate Muslims, we are particularly concerned with the statement issued by Minister Datuk Seri Jamil Khir Baharom, in response to the recent Court of Appeal judgement on the right of transgendered women to dress according to their identity. He viewed the right of the transgender community and Sisters in Islam (SIS) to seek legal redress as a "new wave of assault on Islam" and as an attempt to lead Muslims astray from their faith, and put religious institutions on trial in a secular court.
>
> Such an inflammatory statement from a Federal Minister (and not for the first time) sends a public message that the Prime Minister's commitment to the path of moderation need not be taken seriously when a Cabinet minister can persistently undermine it.
>
> These issues of concern we raise are of course difficult matters to address given the extreme politicisation of race and religion in this country. But we believe there is a real need for a consultative process that will bring together experts in various fields, including Islamic and Constitutional laws, and those affected by the application of Islamic laws in adverse ways.
>
> We also believe the Prime Minister is best placed with the resources and authority to lead this consultative process. It is urgent that all Malaysians are invested in finding solutions to these long-standing areas of conflict that have led to the deterioration of race relations,

in the States play a key role in shaping the public discourse on this phenomenon and countering the posturing of PAS and UMNO in trying to outdo each other in displaying their Islamic credentials. Azrul Mohd Khalib in an opinion piece published in *The Malaysian Insider* said:

> In our country, we find that a small minority of unelected individuals who bestow upon themselves as champions of the faith and feel that they are unaccountable to anyone, are basically attempting to hijack relations and sow distrusts and fear between communities particularly between Muslims and Christians. They have intruded into public policy making far beyond their scope and mandate of religious affairs. Where and when does it stop? Where is the separation of mosque and state?
>
> The paranoia that exists is one of our own making. We have allowed a group of ill-informed, ignorant and bigoted individuals to lead us down the yellow brick road towards their vision of a future where one ethnic group and one faith dominates above all.

Azrul Mohd Khalib, 'Separation of mosque and state' *The Malaysian Insider* (2 April 2012) http://www.themalaysianinsider.com/opinion/article/separation-of-mosque-and-state/ (accessed 1 March 2016). He was criticizing the holding of a seminar by a religious body in conjunction with a Johore State agency. The seminar was originally entitled 'Pemantapan Aqidah, Bahaya Liberalisme dan Pluralism Serta Ancaman Kristianisasi Terhadap Umat Islam. Apa Peranan Guru? (Strengthening the Faith, the Dangers of Liberalism and Pluralism and the Threat of Christianity towards Muslims. What is the Role of Teachers?)'. The seminar involved 300 teachers from Johore.

eroded citizens' sense of safety and protection under the rule of law, and undermined stability.[94]

The group went on to list the many pressing issues that would need 'the urgent leadership and vision of the Prime Minister, the support of his Cabinet and all moderate Malaysians'. They emphasized an urgent need to review the Syariah Criminal Offences Laws of Malaysia, which 'have led to confusion and dispute in both substance and implementation'. There is a 'lack of public awareness, even among top political leaders, on the legal jurisdiction and substantive limits of the powers of the religious authorities and administration of Islamic laws in Malaysia'. They stressed the 'need to ensure the right of citizens to debate the ways Islam is used as a source of public law and policy in this country'. They underlined the 'need to promote awareness of the rich diversity of interpretive texts and juristic opinions in the Islamic tradition'. They called on the Prime Minister 'to assert his personal leadership as well as appoint key leaders who will, in all fairness, champion open and coherent debate and discourse on the administration of Islamic laws … to ensure that justice is done'.[95]

Marina Mahathir, a social reformist and writer, in an interview with the Malay Mail Online, openly criticized 'the "Arabisation" of Islam in Malaysia amid the institutionalisation and growing conservatism of the faith here.'[96] Hitting out at what she described as a form of 'Arab colonialism', Marina was critical of the government's repeated calls for Muslims to unite and conform, which did not allow room for individuality. She also highlighted the double standards in the treatment of Muslim men and women, citing recent controversies when Muslim women had

[94] 'Group of prominent Malays calls for rational dialogue on position of Islam in Malaysia' *The Star* Online (7 December 2014) <http://www.thestar.com.my/news/nation/2014/12/07/group-prominent-malays-calls-for-moderation/> (accessed 8 October 2016). The twenty-five signatories comprise Tan Sri Datuk Abdul Rahim Haji Din, former Secretary General, Home Affairs Ministry; Tan Sri Ahmad Kamil Jaafar, former Secretary General, Foreign Affairs Ministry; Tan Sri Dr Aris Othman, former Secretary General, Finance Ministry; Tan Sri Dr Ismail Merican; former Director-General, Health Ministry; Tan Sri Mohd Sheriff Mohd Kassim, former Secretary General, Finance Ministry; Tan Sri Dr Mustaffa Babjee, former Director General, Veterinary Services Department; Tan Sri Nuraizah Abdul Hamid, former Secretary General, Energy, Communications and Multimedia Ministry; Tan Sri Dr Yahya Awang, cardiothoracic surgeon and core founder, National Heart Institute; Datuk Seri Shaik Daud Md Ismail, former Court of Appeal Judge; Datuk' Abdul Kadir Mohd Deen, former Ambassador; Datuk Anwar Fazal, former senior regional advisor, United Nations Development Programme; Datuk Dali Mahmud Hashim, former ambassador; Datuk Emam Mohd Haniff Mohd Hussein, former ambassador; Datuk Faridah Khalid, representative of Women's Voice; Datuk Latifah Merican Cheong, former Assistant Governor, Bank Negara; Lt Gen (Rtd) Datuk Maulob Maamin, Lieutenant General (Rtd); Datuk Noor Farida Ariffin, former ambassador; Datuk Ranita Hussein, former Suhakam Commissioner; Datuk Redzuan Kushairi, former ambassador; Datuk Dr Sharom Ahmat, former Deputy Vice-Chancellor, Universiti Sains Malaysi; Datuk Syed Arif Fadhillah, former ambassador; Datuk Zainal Abidin Ahmad, former Director-General, Malaysian Timber Industry Board; Datuk Zainuddin Bahari, former Deputy Secretary-General, Domestic Trade, Co-operatives and Consumerism Ministry; Datin Halimah Mohd Said, former lecturer, Universiti Malaya and President, Association of Voices of Peace, Conscience and Reason (PCORE); Puan Hendon Mohamad, Past President, Malaysian Bar.

[95] The G25 also arranged for the publication of a book, *Breaking the Silence: Voices of Moderation* (Marshall Cavendish 2016).

[96] She is the eldest child of former Prime Minister Mahathir Mohamad. See Boo Su-Lyn, 'Marina Mahathir: Malaysia undergoing "Arab colonialism"' *Malaymail* Online (23 May 2016) http://www.themalaymailonline.com/malaysia/article/marina-mahathir-malaysia-undergoing-arab-colonialism (accessed 1 March 2016).

been criticized for going against the norm (when Muslim girls in headscarves at a K-pop concert hugged the Korean artistes; when a female radio journalist had questioned *hudud* (punishments under Islamic law); and when women in *tudung* (a head scarf) had been seen touching dogs at a public pat-a-dog event.)[97] The Sultan of Johor, in a published interview, also criticized those Malays who sought to imitate Arab culture, remarking that if they chose not to follow Malay customs and traditions, they were welcome 'to live in Saudi Arabia'.[98]

The 1988 constitutional amendment in providing for the new Article 121(1A) that apparently precludes the civil courts from having 'jurisdiction in respect of any matter within the jurisdiction of the Syariah Courts' has provided a convenient cover for the civil courts to refuse to hear certain cases or provide remedies, even where one of the parties is non-Muslim and not subject to the Syariah system. It has been pointed out in *Lina Joy* 'that of the seven judges—from the High Court to the Court of Appeal and then the Federal Court—who heard Ms Joy's originating summons, the five who found against her were all Muslims, but the two who found in her favour were from non-Muslim minorities'.[99] The civil courts which 'appear to have gone along for the ride' in the face of 'greater Islamic fundamentalism'[100] must develop a stiffer backbone. Professor Thio Li-ann said:

> When religious freedom rights clash with the rights of others and state interests, it falls to impartial judges to adjudicate upon the legitimacy of a restriction. In so doing, they are bound to protect both constitutional rights and principles informing the constitutional order, such as secularism and multi-culturism.[101]

In an essay, published in 1978, surveying constitutional changes in the first two decades since the attainment of independence by the Malaysian polity, the late Professor Hugh Hickling observed:

> Taking a trawl through the Malaysian law reports of the last twenty years, I doubt whether in any case we could assert that this judge or that was an English, Scots, Malay, Chinese, or Indian lawyer, on the basis of his judgment. In other words, delete his name as author of the judgment, and you will be unable to identify the ethnic origin of the judge.[102]

[97] See more at http://www.themalaymailonline.com/malaysia/article/marina-mahathir-malaysia-undergoing-arab-colonialism.

[98] 'Stop aping Arabs, Johor Sultan tells Malays' *Malaymail* Online (24 March 2016) http://www.themalaymailonline.com/malaysia/article/stop-aping-arabs-johor-sultan-tells-malays (accessed16 May 2016). 'The Johor sultan's remarks come amid the so-called "Arabisation" of Islam in Malaysia, where there is increasing pressure on Muslim women to wear a headscarf and to cover their "aurat", as well as the growing popularity of Arabic terms and dress like the "jubah".'

[99] ALR Joseph, 'Unfettered Religious Freedom Hangs by the Thread of Minority Dissent in Malaysia: A Review of the Dissenting Judgment of the Federal Court in the *Lina Joy* Case' (2009) 14(2) Review of Constitutional Studies 205.

[100] Kevin Y L Tan, Keynote Address at the 'Law and Society in Malaysia: Pluralism, Islam and Development' Conference, University of Victoria, BC, 15 July 2011.

[101] Thio Li-ann, 'Courting Religion: The Judge between Caesar and God in Asian Courts' [2009] Singapore Journal of Legal Studies 52, 53.

[102] RH Hickling, 'An Overview of Constitutional Changes in Malaysia: 1957-1977' in Tun Mohamed Suffian, HP Lee, and FA Trindade (eds), *The Constitution of Malaysia: Its Development: 1957–1977* (OUP 1978) 1, 15–16.

Tun Mohamed Suffian, a former Lord President of Malaysia, in his Braddel Memorial Lecture in 1982 said:

> In a multi-racial and multi religious society like yours and mine, while we judges cannot help being Malay or Chinese or Indian; or being Muslim or Buddhist or Hindu or whatever, we strive not to be too identified with any particular race or religion—so that nobody reading our judgement with our name deleted could with confidence identify our race or religion, and so that the various communities, especially minority communities, are assured that we will not allow their rights to be trampled underfoot.[103]

The observations of Hugh Hickling and Tun Mohamad Suffian may no longer hold true in the context of cases involving Islamic issues. A number of senior judges of the Muslim faith apparently have found it a struggle to reconcile their personal religious beliefs and affinity with their religious community with their sworn duty to preserve, protect, and defend the Constitution. In 1988, the then former Lord President of Malaysia, Tun Salleh Abas, said that, judges should not allow their personal beliefs to override the constitutional and legal system, but 'we have to set aside our personal feelings because the law in this country is still what it is today, secular law, where morality not accepted by the law is not enjoying the status of law.'[104] In contrast, in 2007, about three months after handing down his decision in *Lina Joy*, Chief Justice Ahmad Fairuz called for 'Islamic law to be honoured in its most deserved position' and advocated the abolition of the English-based common law in Malaysia in order, he said, to discard the vestiges of colonialism.[105]

At the Malaysian Bar Conference celebrating the first 50 years of the Malaysian Constitution, I referred to a 'blessing' enjoyed by the Malaysian polity:

> The common law is a precious legacy of colonial rule. For those who care to be properly informed about the common law, it is a worldwide web of legal principles which provides a bond among the members of the Commonwealth of Nations. It is like a jurisprudential reservoir from which the courts around the world draw on for elucidation of legal problems and which they adapt for local conditions. The common law is not a static creature operating in exactly the same form in all countries with a common law jurisdiction. It can be moulded to suit the circumstances of the countries drinking from this reservoir. To assert that the common law is an outdated colonial relic burdening the legal system of a freed colony is a myopic viewpoint. To assert that the common law should be jettisoned or replaced with some other form of jurisprudence is to exhibit ignorance of this dynamic aspect of the legal

[103] Tun Mohamed Suffian, 'Four Decades in the Law: Looking Back' in FA Trindade and HP Lee (eds), *The Constitution of Malaysia: Further Perspectives and Developments* (OUP 1986) 216. Sultan Azlan Shah once observed, 'Judging in a diverse society is not an easy task. Judges in many parts of the world face similar difficulties.'—HRH Sultan Azlan Shah, '50 Years of Constitutionalism and the Rule of Law' (Opening address by HRH Sultan Azlan Shah at the 14th Malaysian Law Conference) (29 October 2007) http://www.malaysianbar.org.my/speeches/opening_address_by_hrh_sultan_azlan_shah_at_the_14th_malaysian_law_conference.html (accessed 1 March 2016).

[104] *Che Omar bin Che Soh v Public Prosecutor* [1988] 2 MLJ 55, 57, cited with approval by Malanjumm CJSS in *Lina Joy* [2007] 4 MLJ 585, 619.

[105] Joshua Neoh (2008) 'Islamic State and the Common Law in Malaysia: A Case Study of *Lina Joy*' 8(2) Global Jurist (Advances) Art 4 http://www.bepress.com/gj/vol8/iss2/art4 (accessed 1 March 2016).

system which has provided and continues to provide vitality and stability to the development of local jurisprudence.[106]

It can be seen that the place of Islam in the Malaysian polity is dependent on the meaning and scope of provisions in the Malaysian Constitution. The observance of the boundaries set by those provisions will be heavily dependent on the extent to which genuine fidelity is given to the original intention behind those provisions. In the face of a push by advocates of an Islamization agenda, the contours of the constitutional provisions have been deliberately distorted in order advance the cause of Islamisation. The *Lina Joy* decision 'reverberated from the courtroom ... to the wider society' and was said to have 'created two polarized camps in society with regard to the state of the law and the constitution in Malaysia'.[107] This observation is likewise true of the *Herald* case. Professor Andrew Harding said:

> Although feelings have run high, violence is rare and, so far, has affected only property, not persons (threats of violence, explicit and implicit, have, however, been many). The Constitution and the institutions of the common law have provided the means whereby a precarious accommodation between two fundamentally contradictory conceptions of legality, one secular, the other religious, has been maintained. Whether this will continue to be so remains, of course, to be seen.[108]

[106] HP Lee, 'The Malaysian Constitution: Retrospective, Prospective and Comparative Perspectives' (2007) 9(2) Australian Journal of Asian Law 307.

[107] Joshua Neoh (2008) 'Islamic State and the Common Law in Malaysia: A Case Study of *Lina Joy*' 8(2) Global Jurist (Advances) Art 4 http://www.bepress.com/gj/vol8/iss2/art4 (accessed 1 March 2016).

[108] Andrew Harding, 'Malaysia: Religious Pluralism and the Constitution in a Contested Polity' (2012) 4 Middle East Law and Governance Journal 356, 385. See also Andrew Harding, 'Constitutionalism, Islam, and National Identity in Malaysia' in Rainer Grote and Tilmann J Röder (eds), *Constitutionalism in Islamic Countries: Between Upheaval and Continuity* (OUP 2012) 201.

8

Whither Constitutionalism?

The spirit of constitutionalism must be impressed on the hearts and minds of our political masters.

Dato' Param Cumaraswamy, 'Role of the Executive' in *Reflections on the Malaysian Constitution* (Aliran 1987) 135

The major constitutional conflicts discussed in the preceding chapters have affected the system of checks and balances in the Malaysian Constitution. The crises involving the hereditary Rulers have blunted their effectiveness as a behind-the-scenes constraining force vis-a-vis an increasingly powerful executive arm of government. The failure of a number of these Rulers to abide by their proper role as constitutional monarchs forced the government to take actions that, ultimately, diminished the standing of the Rulers in the eyes of the Malaysian public. The two crises between the Rulers and the Mahathir Government enabled the latter to adopt the high ground of defending the constitutional order. But no such high ground, of either principle or morality, could be staked out by the Mahathir Government in respect of the 1988 confrontation with the judiciary. The convulsion in the judiciary has resulted in a massive loss of confidence in the independence of this institution. The transformation of a once highly respected bastion into a timorous institution has meant the loss of another effective fetter on executive powers.

This chapter does not seek to canvass exhaustively the present state of constitutionalism in Malaysia. What it aims to do is to evaluate certain aspects of the constitutional system which have been impinged upon, or which are connected to the major constitutional conflicts. Such an evaluation requires, in the first place, an excursus on the notion of constitutionalism in Malaysia.

Constitutionalism

Constitutionalism gives recognition to the necessity for government. At the same time, it places effective constraints on the powers of government.[1] In many countries, the constraints on government are expressly embodied in a written

[1] BO Nwabueze, *Constitutionalism in the Emergent States* (Hurst & Co 1973) 1.

constitution. Now, it is important to note the relationship between the concepts of constitutionalism and a constitution. A conspicuous feature of a developing country is its brand-new constitution—generally drafted in lofty terms. Nevertheless, it is a document providing for the creation of the organs of government: the legislature, the executive, and the judiciary. The document also provides for limitations on these organs. It provides for rules to regulate their operations. It also provides for rules to circumscribe their powers. To that extent, there is an overlap with the concept of constitutionalism. Constitutionalism also thrives on unwritten rules, including customs or conventions. However, to have a constitution does not mean the existence of constitutionalism; otherwise, many countries under repressive regimes can claim to enjoy constitutionalism.

The constraints often embodied in a written constitution can be of various forms. For instance, in relation to the legislative arm of government, the terms of office of its members are clearly stipulated. Every few years, elections must be conducted. The powers of the legislature are also clearly defined. The boundaries between the exercise of legislative powers and fundamental rights are specifically provided for. Similarly, provisions regulate the judiciary. The provisions are designed to secure the independence of the judiciary and to reinforce the separation of powers doctrine. In relation to the executive, safeguards ensure that there is no perpetuation of authoritarian government. Accountability in high office is reinforced by the observance of constitutional conventions.

Despite all these fine limitations on government provided by the constitutional framework, in many developing countries the constitutional order degenerates into dictatorship, often because of direct military intervention. In other instances, the significant trait of the degenerating constitutional order is the relentless attacks on constitutionalism. The attacks can take many forms. In this chapter, some of the forms that affect the state of constitutionalism in Malaysia will be explored.

Emergency Powers

In the 1983 constitutional crisis, the Rulers forced the government to retreat when it attempted to vest the power to declare a state of emergency in the Prime Minister. Despite the back down by the government on this issue, the present state of the emergency powers provisions in the Constitution leaves much to be desired. This is one area of constitutional law that impacts adversely on the state of Malaysian constitutionalism.

Up to 2011, a number of proclamations of emergencies remained in existence in Malaysia despite the fact that the factual basis underpinning them had long ceased to exist. Powers to cope with emergencies are embodied in Article 150 of the Constitution.[2] The thrust of Article 150 is that if the Yang di-Pertuan Agong is

[2] See S Jayakumar, 'Emergency Powers in Malaysia' in Suffian, Lee, and Trindade (eds), *The Constitution of Malaysia: Its Development: 1957–1977* (OUP 1978) 328–68; HP Lee, 'Emergency Powers in Malaysia' in Trindade and Lee (eds), *The Constitution of Malaysia: Further Perspectives and*

satisfied that a grave emergency exists, he may issue a Proclamation of Emergency. Once such a proclamation is issued, there are virtually no limits on the powers that can be invoked by Parliament or the executive. For instance, the Yang di-Pertuan Agong may promulgate ordinances having the force of law if he is satisfied that immediate action is required. Parliament, notwithstanding anything in the Constitution, may make laws with respect to any matter if it appears to Parliament that the law is required because of the emergency.

Article 150 has been invoked on a number of occasions by the Federal Government to meet various crises in the life of the Malaysian nation. In 1964, a state of emergency was declared in the face of the Indonesian 'confrontation', leading to the enactment of the Emergency (Essential Powers) Act 1964. The 'confrontation' was launched by Sukarno, then President of Indonesia, who was opposed to the formation of Malaysia. Despite the existence of good relations between Malaysia and Indonesia for many decades since the ending of 'confrontation', the 1964 Emergency Proclamation was never formally revoked. A constitutional impasse in Sarawak in 1966 resulted in the invocation of Article 150 in relation to the territories of that state. Another nation-wide state of emergency was declared in 1969 because of the May Thirteenth racial riots. Emergency powers were resorted to in 1977 by the Federal Government to deal with a political crisis in Kelantan. The invocation of the emergency powers provisions on so many occasions since the coming into force of the Constitution poses problems of profound significance for the state of constitutionalism in Malaysia.

The challenge to constitutionalism arises largely from the fact that governments in many developing countries are always looking for excuses, even of the flimsiest kind, to draw on the emergency powers to introduce authoritarian rule. Furthermore, having invoked the emergency powers provisions, these governments are most reluctant to surrender them, even when the 'crises' no longer exist.

The Malaysian government was given a reprimand by the Privy Council in the case of *Teh Cheng Poh v Public Prosecutor*,[3] in which Teh Cheng Poh had been found in possession of a revolver and ammunition in Penang, a 'security area'. He was charged under the Internal Security Act 1960, and tried under a special procedure provided by the Security Cases Regulations[4] (which were made in 1975 by the Yang di-Pertuan Agong pursuant to the Emergency [Essential Powers] Ordinance 1969—an ordinance made in consequence of the 1969 state of emergency owing to the May Thirteenth racial riots). The Security Cases Regulations provided, inter alia, for a special procedure to be adopted in trials for security offences. A person charged with a security offence would be tried by a judge alone without a jury. Furthermore, the preliminary inquiry before a magistrate was dispensed with. Teh was found guilty and sentenced to death by the High Court. His appeal to

Developments (OUP 1986) 135–56; Azmi Khalid, 'Emergency Powers & Constitutional Change' (1983) 3 Aliran Quarterly 5–8.

[3] [1979] 1 MLJ 50. See Victor V Ramraj, 'The Cheng Poh Case' in Andrew Harding and HP Lee, *Constitutional Landmarks in Malaysia: The First 50 Years 1957–2007* (LexisNexis 2007) 145.

[4] Essential (Security Cases) (Amendment) Regulations 1975.

the Federal Court was dismissed. In his appeal to the Privy Council, his trial was declared a nullity.[5]

The decision of the Privy Council has to be understood in the context of the provisions of Article 150 standing at the time of *Teh Cheng Poh* and before the amendment of that Article in 1981. It was then provided, under 150(2), that when a Proclamation of Emergency is issued, the Yang di-Pertuan Agong may 'until both Houses of Parliament are sitting' promulgate ordinances having the force of law, if he is satisfied that immediate action is required. In an earlier case (*Public Prosecutor v Khong Teng Khen & Anor*),[6] it had been held by the then Federal Court that the Security Cases Regulations were valid as they had been made not under Article 150(2) of the Constitution but under Section 2 of the Emergency (Essential Powers) Ordinance 1969.[7] In consequence, 'the fact whether or not at the time they were made Parliament was in existence or was sitting is irrelevant'. Suffian LP further said, 'His Majesty has power to make ordinances under Clause (2) of Article 150 only when Parliament is not sitting. In the case of regulations under Section 2 of the Ordinance, they may be made by His Majesty whether or not Parliament is sitting.'[8] This is tantamount to saying that even though his ordinance-making power had lapsed, the Yang di-Pertuan Agong still retained a power to make 'Essential Regulations' pursuant to a power conferred upon himself by an ordinance promulgated before Parliament sat. This proposition was decisively rejected by the Privy Council which pointed out that such a proposition, if accepted, would result in a situation which would be tantamount to 'the Cabinet's lifting itself up by its own boot straps'. The only other source from which the Yang di-Pertuan Agong could derive powers to make 'Essential Regulations', other than the constitutional source of Article 150(2), would be an Act of Parliament delegating such powers to him.

The decision of the Privy Council cannot be faulted. Its reasoning is compelling. It is difficult to envisage how the Yang di-Pertuan can continue to wield law-making powers of issuing 'regulations' when his very power to promulgate ordinances, having the force of law, is curtailed once Parliament has sat. The constitutional value of the decision lies in the attempt by the Privy Council to revitalize parliamentary government under the Constitution.

In nullifying the trial of *Teh Cheng Poh*, the Privy Council created a conundrum for the Malaysian government. Tun Mohamed Suffian wrote, 'It meant not only that the trial of Teh Cheng Poh was a nullity. There were hundreds of other trials held under the regulations. They too were a nullity. In some of them persons had been sentenced to imprisonment or even death, though fortunately nobody had

[5] The various complex legal and constitutional arguments are discussed in HP Lee, 'Emergency Powers in Malaysia', in Trindade and Lee (eds), *The Constitution of Malaysia: Further Perspectives and Developments* (OUP 1986) 135–56.

[6] [1976] 2 MLJ 166.

[7] Section 2(1) empowered the Yang di-Pertuan Agong to make 'Essential Regulations', which 'he considers desirable or expedient for securing the public safety, the defence of Malaysia, the maintenance of public order and of supplies and services essential to the life of the community'.

[8] [1976] 2 MLJ 166, 169.

yet been executed.'[9] To overcome this problem, the Malaysian Parliament enacted the Emergency (Essential Powers) Act 1979. The Act continued to breathe life into those regulations that had been made during the time of the Indonesian 'confrontation' emergency! It also provided for the *retrospective* validation of all trials that would have been nullified because of the Privy Council decision.

The Privy Council decision in *Teh Cheng Poh* has one disappointing respect, namely, the refusal of the Privy Council to come to grips with a far more important issue. Can a Proclamation of Emergency be considered to have ceased to be in force because the facts that provided the justification for its issuance no longer exist? On an earlier occasion, the Privy Council (in *Stephen Kalong Ningkan v Government of Malaysia*)[10] had refused to decide the issue, contenting itself with saying that the issue is 'a constitutional question of far-reaching importance which, on the present state of the authorities, remains unsettled and debatable.'[11] This issue has been rendered academic because of constitutional amendments enacted in 1981.

The Constitution (Amendment) Act, 1981 gives unbridled power to the executive to declare an emergency at will, and to perpetuate emergency rule. The most fundamental change was the excision of the court's jurisdiction in relation to the validity of a Proclamation of Emergency. Henceforth, the satisfaction of the Yang di-Pertuan Agong relating to an emergency 'shall not be challenged or called in question in any court on any ground'. It is also provided that 'no court shall have jurisdiction to entertain or determine any application, question or proceeding, in whatever form, on any ground' regarding the validity of a Proclamation of Emergency, or an ordinance, or their continued operation thereof. These changes would have been effected because of governmental concern over the disquiet expressed by some Malaysian judges. For instance, Federal Judge HT Ong (as he then was) criticized his judicial brethren for conceding an untrammelled discretion to the Cabinet.[12] His brother, Federal Judge HS Ong, referring to the Security Cases Regulations, described them as 'an abrogation of the Rule of Law'.[13]

Emergency powers are also provided for expressly in the Indian Constitution.[14] On the first two occasions when states of emergencies were proclaimed, it was clearly acknowledged that there was justification for them. The proclamations on these two occasions related to the outbreak of hostilities between China and India, and between Pakistan and India, respectively. Nevertheless, it is also clear that they were continued in force after the circumstances that gave rise to them no longer existed. The third Proclamation of Emergency was the most controversial.[15] On 25 June 1975, the President of India, Fakhruddin Ali Ahmed, signed the following proclamation: 'I, President of India, by this Proclamation declare that a grave

[9] Tun Suffian Mohammed, *Malaysia and India: Shared Experiences in the Law* (VV Chitaley Memorial Lectures, 1980) 88.

[10] [1968] 2 MLJ 238. [11] ibid 242. [12] [1968] 1 MLJ 119, 128.

[13] *Public Prosecutor* v *Khong Teng Khen & Anor* [1976] 2 MLJ 166, 175. The 1975 Emergency Regulations are described in International Commission of Jurists, *States of Emergency: Their Impact on Human Rights* (Geneva 1983) 206.

[14] See Articles 352, 353, 358, and 359 of the Indian Constitution.

[15] *States of Emergency* 178–84.

emergency exists whereby the security of India is threatened by internal disturbance.' Coming in the wake of the decision of the Allahabad State High Court invalidating Prime Minister Indira Gandhi's election to Parliament, many disputed the justification of 'internal disturbance' for the proclamation. That period was described in the following terms: 'With every week that passed, the dark pall of tyranny seemed to descend inexorably over India.'[16]

What were the consequences of the state of emergency? According to the International Commission of Jurists, the immediate consequences were the increased use of preventive detention against political opponents and economic offenders, and suspension of the right to apply to the courts for enforcement of fundamental rights. Among other things, twenty-seven organizations were immediately banned. 'The elimination of access to the Courts had the foreseeable effects: ill-treatment of prisoners, increased corruption and nepotism, and insensitive implementation of government programmes (notably slum clearance and population control).'[17] The emergency represented one of the darkest hours in India's history. 'The tale of misdeeds and crimes committed under the cloak of emergency' is recounted in the reports of the Shah Commission.[18]

The termination of the emergency is now a matter of history. The reaction of the populace, when Indira Gandhi ordered the holding of fresh elections, stands out as an inspiration to those in other countries who advocate the cause of constitutionalism. She was swept out of Parliament and of office. Her party was dealt a crushing electoral defeat. HM Seervai said, 'Fearing that the weapon of the emergency which she had forged, and used, against her opponents might be turned against her and her associates, she advised the President to withdraw the emergency before she left office.'[19]

Unrestrained invocation of emergency powers poses a threat to the rule of law. Unfortunately, the problem is a widespread phenomenon in many Asian, African, and Latin American countries. In 1973, Professor Nwabueze observed that emergencies 'have tended to become the normal order of things, thus replacing constitutional government with emergency administration as the normal system of rule'.[20] In 1983, the Commission of Jurists, in a report on Malaysia, said:

> The fact that emergency measures are intended to be only temporary in character is lost sight of when, as has happened in Malaysia, persons are held in administrative detention for periods exceeding 16 years without any charge being preferred against them and without being

[16] HM Seervai, *The Emergency, Future Safeguards and the Habeas Corpus Case: A Criticism* (NM Tripathi Pte Ltd 1978) vii.

[17] *States of Emergency* 180.

[18] JC Shah, a retired Chief Justice of India, was appointed on 28 May 1977 to inquire into the excesses committed during the emergency.

[19] HM Seervai, *The Emergency, Future Safeguards and the Habeas Corpus Case* viii. For a critical examination of the 1975 emergency, see HM Seervai, *Constitutional Law of India* (2nd edn, NM Tripathi Pte Ltd 1979) Vol III. See also NKF O'Neill, 'How the Indian Supreme Court Survived the Emergency', (1981) Lawasia 362.

[20] Nwabueze, *Constitutionalism in the Emergent States* (Hurst & Co 1973) 174.

brought before a Court. To extend emergency powers in this way is to strip constitutional rule of much of its meaning.[21]

It was therefore a much welcome development when, in November of 2011, following an announcement by Prime Minister Najib Razak, the emergency proclamations of 1966, 1969, and 1977, which had remained extant were revoked.[22] This is a laudable move and much overdue on the part of the Federal government.

Constitutional Amendments to the Emergency Powers Provisions

Article 150 has been extensively amended over the life span of the Malaysian nation. The Article as it now stands contains the potential for authoritarian rule to be introduced by the stroke of a pen. The erosion of safeguards commenced as early as 1960. The Constitution, as it originally stood, provided that a Proclamation of Emergency should cease to have force at the expiration of two months from the date on which it was issued, and similarly, any ordinance promulgated by the Yang di-Pertuan Agong automatically lapsed and ceased to have effect, at the expiration of 15 days from the date on which both Houses of Parliament were first sitting. By virtue of the Constitution (Amendment) Act 1960 (Act 10 of 1960), neither the Proclamation of Emergency nor the ordinance automatically lapses. They have a continuity of life until resolutions are passed by both Houses nullifying them.

The scope of Article 150 was further broadened by the Malaysia Act 1963 (Act No 26 of 1963). Article 150(1) was amended so that it provided the following: 'If the Yang di-Pertuan Agong is satisfied that a grave emergency exists whereby the security or economic life of the Federation or any part thereof is threatened, he may issue a Proclamation of Emergency'. The qualifying words 'whether by war or external aggression or internal disturbances', which appeared after 'is threatened' in Article 150(1), were deleted. Clauses (5) and (6) of Article 150 were replaced with new provisions, whilst a new Clause (6A) was added. Professor HE Groves noted the significance of the amendments:

> Under the previous Constitution those provisions which required the consent or concurrence for a law to become valid, such as the consent of the Conference of Rulers, or which required consultation with respect to the passing of a law, as with the Conference of Rulers, were not affected by a Proclamation of Emergency. An amending provision seeks to make clear that legislation passed during an Emergency is not subject to challenges in the courts on the grounds of constitutionality, except as it relates to religion, citizenship or language. Two matters only on the State List were beyond the reach of Parliament during an Emergency.

[21] International Commission of Jurists, *States of Emergency* 208.

[22] The 1964 emergency proclamation arising from the launch of 'Kronfrontasi' by Indonesia against Malaysia was regarded by the government as having been impliedly repealed.

They were Muslim law and the custom of the Malays. To these inviolable subjects has been added any matter of native law or custom in a Borneo State.[23]

The amendments to Article 150 by the Constitution (Amendment) Act, 1981 have already been adverted to. The constitutional entrenchment of an ouster clause provides the potential for Malaysia to slide into a dictatorship if the reins of power were to fall into the hands of unscrupulous politicians.

Preventive detention

The power to detain a person without a trial was a key weapon used by the authorities to counter the communist insurrection that arose in 1948. When the emergency was terminated on 31 July 1960, the then Malayan government felt it was necessary to retain the power of preventive detention. The power that had originally existed under the authority of an emergency ordinance was retained through the Internal Security Act 1960 as enacted by the Malayan Parliament. It was observed, 'From 1960 to 2012, the Malaysian government and its ruling party used the act and its powers of endless detention to their utmost limits to silence political dissidents and government opponents.'[24]

In October 1987, a large-scale deployment of this power occurred in a dragnet operation called 'Operasi Lalang', purportedly to prevent threats to public order.[25] The concerns about the abuse of the now repealed Internal Security Act (ISA) led Tunku Abdul Rahman to reiterate that the ISA was introduced in 1960 to 'be used solely against the communists'.[26] The Tunku added, 'My Cabinet colleagues and I gave a solemn promise to Parliament and the nation that the immense powers given to the government under the ISA would never be used to stifle legitimate opposition and silence lawful dissent.'[27]

Under the ISA, the Minister was empowered to order the detention of a person for up to 2 years (which can be extended a number of times) 'if the Minister is satisfied' that such detention was necessary 'with a view to preventing him from acting in any manner prejudicial to the security of Malaysia or any part thereof or to the maintenance of essential services therein or to the economic life thereof'.[28] In the area of preventive detention, the courts have withdrawn themselves from an

[23] HE Groves, 'The Constitution of Malaysia: The Malaysia Act' (1963) 5 Malaya Law Review 245, 274.

[24] Tyler James Brent Jeffrey, 'Preventive Detention in Malaysia: Constitutional and Judicial Obstacles to Reform and Suggestions for the Future' (2013) 41 Ga J Int'l Comp L 535, 536.

[25] Andrew Harding, *The Constitution of Malaysia: A Contextual Analysis* (Hart publishing 2012) 173–4: 'Following the escalation of acute racial tensions in Kuala Lumpur over the issue of Chinese education, about 109 persons of different political and ethnic groups, including notable opposition figures such as Lim Kit Siang were detained for periods of several months or longer' (ibid 173).

[26] Tunku Abdul Rahman's affidavit at the habeas corpus hearing of Dr Chandra Muzaffar and quoted in 'The Real Reason: Operation Lalang ISA Arrests October 27, 1987' (DAP 1988) 8. Also cited in HP Lee, 'Constitutional Values in Turbulent Asia' (1997) 23(2) Monash University Law Review 375, 382.

[27] ibid. [28] Section 8(1).

effective judicial role, except when a challenge is based on a procedural flaw.[29] The courts, for a long time, relied on a 'subjective' test in gauging the exercise of discretionary power by the detaining authority.[30] However, when the powerful dissenting judgment of Lord Atkin in the famous case of *Liversidge v Anderson*[31] condemning the subjective test attained universal acknowledgement, the Malaysian government swiftly amended the ISA effectively to oust judicial review of preventive detention orders.[32]

Over the course of time, constitutional safeguards circumscribing the power of preventive detention were diluted by amendments to the Constitution. Before 1960, Article 151 provided that if a person was detained under a law promulgated in pursuance of Part XI of the Constitution ('Special Powers Against Subversion and Emergency Powers') he should be informed of the grounds for his detention and be given an opportunity of making representations against the order of detention as soon as possible. However, if a person were a Malaysian citizen he could not be detained longer than three months 'unless an advisory board ... has considered any representation may by him ... and has reported before the expiration of that period, that there is in its opinion sufficient cause for detention'. Under the original terms of Article 151, if the advisory board decided that there was no sufficient cause for the further detention of a citizen, he must be freed. This decision-making role of the board was reduced by the Constitution (Amendment) Act 1960, when the following new clause was enacted, 'No citizen shall be detained under that law or ordinance for a period exceeding three months unless an advisory board constituted as mentioned in Clause (2) has considered any representations made by him under paragraph (a) and made recommendations thereon to the Yang di-Pertuan Agong.'

An amendment of a fundamental nature was made to Article 151 by the Constitution (Amendment) Act 1976. The change to the principle that no citizen

29 For a lucid analysis of the case-law in this area, see Kevin YL Tan, 'Recent Developments in the Law and Practice of Preventive Detention' in Wu Min Aun (ed), *Public Law in Contemporary Malaysia* (Longman 1999) 307.

30 See Rueban Ratna Balasubramaniam, 'The Karam Singh Case' in Andrew Harding and HP Lee (eds), *Constitutional Landmarks in Malaysia: The First 50 Years 1957–2007* (LexisNexis 2007) 89–102.

31 [1942] AC 206, 244. Lord Atkin's dissenting judgment contains the following celebrated pronouncement: 'I view with apprehension the attitude of judges who on a mere question of construction when face to face with claims involving the liberty of the subject show themselves more executive minded than the executive.... In this country, amid the clash of arms, the laws are not silent. They may be changed, but they speak the same language in war as in peace. It has always been one of the pillars of freedom, one of the principles of liberty for which on recent authority we are now fighting, that the judges are no respecters of persons and stand between the subject and any attempted encroachments on his liberty by the executive, alert to see that any coercive action is justified in law, In this case I have listened to arguments that might have been addressed acceptably to the Court of King's Bench in the time of Charles I.' See also HP Lee, 'Judges and Constitutional Government' [2000/2001] LAWASIA Journal 30, 32–5.

32 A new section 8B(1) was inserted into the Internal Security Act. It provided:

> There shall be no judicial review in any court of, and no court shall have or exercise any jurisdiction in respect of any act done or decision made by the [King] or the Minister in the exercise of their discretionary power in accordance with this Act, save in regard to any question on compliance with any procedural requirement in this Act governing such act or decision.

can be detained beyond 3 months unless his representations were considered and the advisory board had made its recommendations was explained by S Jayakumar:

> The 1976 amendment now no longer linked the period of three months with the detention but instead linked it to the time period within which his representations must be considered. Furthermore, this time period could be extended. The effect of the amendment therefore completely changed the scope of Clause (1)(b): citizens can now be detained beyond three months (or for that matter beyond any other period) so long as their representations (when made) are considered within three months of receipt thereof.[33]

The amendments relating to emergency powers and preventive detention have the effect of enlarging the armoury of legal powers already in the hands of the executive arm of government. Conversely, they narrow the jurisdiction of the courts and diminish their role as the guardians of the Constitution.

New legislation

When the Federal government, in 2011, revoked the emergency proclamations, it also, 'with much fanfare',[34] repealed the ISA. Prime Minister Najib Razak announced plans to institute reforms designed to ensure 'a functional and inclusive democracy where public peace and prosperity is preserved in accordance with the supremacy of the constitution, rule of law and respect for basic human rights and individual rights' 'at par with other democratic systems'.[35] That announcement was widely lauded.

Hopes that a new dawn for a more liberal Malaysia started to evaporate with the enactment of the new Security Offences (Special Measures) Act 2012 (SOSMA) and accompanying legislation (especially amendments to the Penal Code).[36] It was remarked, 'Rather than eliminating the practices that made the ISA so controversial, the new laws have codified the worst of its abuses, and as a result, use of these new laws may lead to even further injustice.'[37]

SOSMA is made applicable to 'security offences'. The definition of such offences encompasses the offence of 'activity detrimental to parliamentary democracy', which is then defined as 'an activity carried out by a person or group of persons designed to overthrow or undermine parliamentary democracy by violent or unconstitutional

[33] S. Jayakumar, 'Emergency Powers in Malaysia' in Suffian and Trindade (eds), *The Constitution of Malaysia: Its Development: 1957–1977* (OUP 1978) 328, 351.

[34] Tyler James Brent Jeffrey, 'Preventive Detention in Malaysia: Constitutional Obstacles to Reform and Suggestions for the Future' (2012–2013) 41 Ga J Int'l & Comp L 535, 538.

[35] 'Prime Minister's Message for Malaysia Day 2011' (15 September 2011) <https://www.najibrazak.com/bm/official-addresses/perutusan-khas-hari-malaysia/> accessed 15 October 2016. See also, HP Lee, 'Constitutional Developments in Malaysia in the First Decade of the Twenty-First Century: A Nation at the Crossroads' in Albert HY Chen (ed), *Constitutionalism in Asia in the Early Twenty-First Century* (CUP 2014) 244, 255–60.

[36] Malik Imtiaz Sarwar, 'The death of civil liberties' *Malaysia Today* (23 April 2012) https://www.malaysiakini.com/news/315248 (accessed 24 May 2016).

[37] Tyler James Brent Jeffrey, 'Preventive Detention in Malaysia: Constitutional Obstacles to Reform and Suggestions for the Future' (2012–2013) 41 Ga J Int'l & Comp L 535, 537.

means'. Concerns were fuelled by the detention of a lawyer, Matthias Chang, and his client under SOSMA. The client, Khairuddin Abu Hassan, a vocal critic of the 1MDB scandal, and Matthias were also barred from travelling to New York to meet with the Federal Bureau of Investigation in relation to the allegations of financial impropriety in connection with the 1MDB scandal.[38]

Unfair trial procedures under the Security Cases Regulations 1975 were mentioned earlier. These procedures have been revived and strengthened in SOSMA. Thus, while SOSMA does away with the old regime of detention without trial by order of the Minister, it has merely replaced this with procedures that ensure 'detention without a proper trial'.[39]

In any event, the power of preventive detention that was jettisoned with the repeal of the ISA was also reinvented via new amendments to the Prevention of Crime Act 1959 and the enactment of the new Prevention of Terrorism Act 2015.

The Process of Constitutional Change

Constitutional changes in Malaysia have been so extensive and frequent that Dr Mahathir, in 1970, said, 'The manner, the frequency and the trivial reasons for altering the Constitution reduced this supreme law of the nation to a useless scrap of paper.'[40]

The Constitution is declared by Article 4(1) to be the 'supreme law of the Federation'. It is further provided that 'any law passed after Merdeka Day which is inconsistent with this Constitution shall, to the extent of the inconsistency, be void'. The Constitution is to be perceived as a kind of 'higher' law, the yardstick against which other laws have to be measured in order to be valid. Hence, judges often refer to such a constitution as a 'sacrosanct' document. If the sanctity of the Malaysian Constitution is to have any meaningful content, amendments to it should be the product of extensive discussions and deliberations.

One of the main complaints commonly voiced by parliamentarians and members of the public is the speed with which amendments are literally pushed through Parliament. Many of the hasty amendments that have been effected were clearly motivated by political ends. It demeans the Constitution if this foundation document of the Malaysian nation is manipulated and distorted for short-term political objectives. An example was the constitutional amendments that were effected in 1993 to bolster the position of UMNO Baru in the State of Sabah.

On 19 May 1993, Dr Mahathir announced the appointment of Tun Mustapha Harun, a Sabah State Assemblyman, as the Federal Minister for Sabah Affairs. Apparently, it was overlooked that, under Article 43(8) of the Malaysian

[38] Steven Thiru, 'Sosma is becoming the new ISA' *Malaysiakini* (10 October 2015) https://www.malaysiakini.com/news/315248 (accessed 24 May 2016).

[39] Amanda Whiting, 'Emerging from Emergency Rule? Malaysian Law "Reform" 2011–2013' (2013) 14(2) Australian Journal of Asian Law Article 1, 9, and 16.

[40] Mahathir bin Mohamad, *The Malay Dilemma* (Federal Publications 1981) 11.

Constitution, a member of a State Legislative Assembly, on appointment as a Federal Minister, must resign from the Assembly before exercising the functions of his ministerial office. To the astute observer of Malaysian politics, the motive was clear. Lim Kit Siang noted:

> Dr Mahathir has finally decided that it would be politically too costly and damaging for UMNO Baru to go through with the Usukan by-election and that it would be easier to amend the Federal Constitution instead. It is indeed scandalous that the Malaysian Constitution should be amended just to enable one person to be a Federal Cabinet Minister and to save UMNO Baru Sabah from the embarrassment of a defeat in the by-election.[41]

As Article 43(8) was an impediment to these political machinations, the simple expedient of repealing Article 43(8) was resorted to.

Tun Mohamed Suffian, in commenting on the provisions of the Constitution (Amendment) (No. 3) Act 1993, explained that another amendment which provides that no by-election caused by death or resignation of an elected Member of Parliament need be called if general elections are due within two years was 'prompted by the hostility of [the Federal government] towards Sabah (and Kelantan).'[42] Accordingly, Article 54(1) was amended by substituting, for the second proviso in that clause, the following new proviso:

> Provided further that, if a casual vacancy in the House of Representatives is established on a date within two years of the date Parliament shall, in accordance with Clause (3) of Article 55, stand dissolved, such casual vacancy shall not be filled unless the Speaker notifies the Election Commission in writing that the numerical strength of the party that constitutes a majority of all the members of the House of Representatives is being affected by such vacancy, in which event such vacancy shall be filled within sixty days from the date of the receipt of that notification.

This means that a constituency can be denied representation in the Parliament for a period of up to 2 years, instead of 6 months as previously required under the second proviso to Article 54(1). A similar change was effected at state level, by a parallel change to Section 9(5) in the Eighth Schedule to the Federal Constitution.

The Separation of Judicial Power Doctrine: Where Has It Gone?

In Chapter 1, it is shown how the Federal Parliament has diminished the judicial power though the constitutional amendment of Article 121(1) and the insertion of a new Article 121(1A). It was also earlier stated that the civil courts squandered the opportunity provided by *Public Prosecutor v Kok Wah Kuan*[43] to enhance the entrenched status of the judicial power and assert a vigorous separation of judicial power doctrine. Professor Andrew Harding said, 'The *Kok Wah Kuan* decision is alarming in its implications for the separation of the judicial power which the Bar

[41] (1993) 13(6) Aliran 6. [42] ibid 8.
[43] [2007] 5 MLJ 174 (CA); [2008] 1 MLJ 1 (FC).

has fought so strongly to defend. It is less alarming if one considers that it may not represent the final word on this matter.'[44]

In *Kok Wah Kuan*,[45] Abdul Hamid Mohamad PCA wrote the majority judgment, and after noting that because of the amendment, there would no longer be a specific provision declaring that the judicial power of the Federation shall be vested in the two High Courts, said:

> What it means is that there is no longer a declaration that 'judicial power of the Federation' as the term was understood prior to the amendment vests in the two High Courts...Thus, to say that the amendment has no effect does not make sense. There must be. The only question is to what extent?[46]

Malanjumm CJSS (in dissent) said:

> The amendment which states that '*the High Courts and inferior courts shall have such jurisdiction and powers as may be conferred by or under federal law*' should by no means be read to mean that the doctrines of separation of powers and independence of the Judiciary are now no more the basic features of our Federal Constitution ... It must be remembered that the Courts, especially the Superior Courts of this country, are a separate and independent pillar of the Federal Constitution and not mere agents of the federal Legislature. In the performance of their function they perform a myriad of roles and interpret and enforce a myriad of laws. Article 121(1) is not, and cannot be, the whole and sole repository of the judicial role in this country ...[47]

Richard Foo, in a critique of the majority decision, said that if *Kok Wah Kuan* were to be taken to its logical conclusion, 'Parliament may now freely vest judicial functions in any entity which is not an Article 121 court, remove any present function of an Article 121 court to non-judicial entities, or even direct that any apparently entrenched function may also be performed by non-judicial entities'.[48] He added that, conversely, 'Parliament may now also subordinate them to the other branches to perform *non*-judicial functions, without this being unconstitutional either'.[49] Andrew Harding remarked, 'Thus in one aspect the amendment was designed in effect to limit and codify judicial powers, taking the power of defining them away from the judiciary itself and vesting it in the legislature.'[50] Harding further observed, 'Whether it succeeded, however, in that objective remained unclear.'[51]

On a mission to Malaysia, the Working Group on Arbitrary Detention observed that the amendment to Clause 1 of Article 121 of the Federal Constitution, which eliminated the term 'judicial power', 'seriously affected the hierarchy between the three powers of the State, as the judiciary is no longer at the same level as the executive or the legislative'.[52] In response to the report, the Government of Malaysia

[44] Andrew Harding, *The Constitution of Malaysia: A Contextual Analysis* (Hart 2012) 204–5.
[45] [2007] 5 MLJ 174 (CA); [2008] 1 MLJ 1 (FC).
[46] [2008] 1 MLJ 1, 15 (FC).
[47] ibid 21.
[48] Richard Foo, 'Malaysia—Death of a Separate Constitutional Judicial Power' [2010] SJLS 253.
[49] ibid 252–3.
[50] *The Constitution of Malaysia: A Contextual Analysis* (Hart 2012) 204.
[51] ibid.
[52] *Report of the Working Group on Arbitrary Detention on its visit to Malaysia* (7–17 June 2010) (A/HRC/16/47/Add.2).

said that the doctrine of separation of powers is 'not a provision' of the Malaysian Constitution. It asserted that neither a provision of the Constitution nor a provision of the law could be struck out on the ground of contravention of the doctrine.[53]

The decision of the majority of the Federal Court in *Kok Wah Kuan* is disappointing. This was an excellent opportunity for the apex court to reinvigorate its role as the guardian of the Constitution. The Malaysian judiciary should draw on the lessons from the Indian Supreme Court. In *Kesavananda Bharati v State of Kerala*,[54] the Indian Supreme Court held that the power of amending the Indian Constitution provided expressly by the Constitution was subject to the implied limitation that the amendment power cannot be used to destroy the basic features of the Constitution. Surely, the separation of powers doctrine must be a key element of the basic structure of the constitutional framework in Malaysia.

The Resurgence of Sedition Laws

In Malaysia, the offence of sedition was given a new meaning in the wake of the 1969 racial riots. In 2011, Prime Minister Najib Razak undertook to abolish the sedition laws. In 2015, he reneged on this undertaking. The sedition legislation was made even more draconian. What is also disconcerting and concerning is the manner in which the sedition laws have been deployed to harass and intimidate members of the opposition.

The Malaysian experience is instructive as to how new hybrid forms of sedition can develop. It also illustrates how a government in power is reluctant to relinquish this law as a legal weapon against dissidents and those who may pose a threat to the political survival of the government. The Malaysian Sedition Act 1948 came into force on 19 July 1948.[55] According to a Malaysian judge, the Malaysian sedition law embodied in the 1948 Act 'had its source, if not its equivalent from English soil'.[56] As far as the right to freedom of speech is concerned,[57] the Sedition Act

[53] ibid. See *Gobind Singh v Yang Dipertua, Dewan Rakyat & Ors* [2010] 2 MLJ 674, 684, where Mohamad Ariff Yusof JC said that the doctrine of separation of powers 'is a feature of our Constitution, and that is recognised even in *Kok Wah Kuan*'.

[54] AIR 1973 1461.

[55] The Sedition Act was enacted originally as Ordinance No.14 of 1948. It was reprinted in 1964 and was revised up to 1 December 1969 as the Sedition Act, 1948. The Act came into force on 14 April 1970. The date of publication in the Gazette was 9 April 1970.

[56] Per Raja Azlan Shah J in *PP v Ooi Kee Saik and Others* [1971] 2 MLJ 108, 111.

[57] Freedom of speech is provided for in Article 10 of the Malaysian Constitution. The whole of Article 10 reads as follows:

> 10. Freedom of speech, assembly and association.
> (1) Subject to Clauses (2) and (3) -
> (a) every citizen has the right to freedom of speech
> (b) all citizens have the right to assemble peaceably and without arms;
> (c) all citizens have the right to form associations
> (2) Parliament may by law impose -
> (a) on the rights conferred by paragraph (a) of Clause (1), such restrictions as it deems necessary or expedient in the interest of the security of the Federation

qualified such a right by making it an offence for any person to utter seditious words or to print or publish any seditious material. Section 2 defines seditious words, when applied to or used in respect of any speech, words, publications, as having a seditious tendency. As to the meaning of 'seditious tendency', section 3(1) provides that it is a tendency

(a) to bring into hatred or contempt or to excite disaffection against any Ruler or against any Government;
(b) to excite the subjects of any Ruler or the inhabitants of any territory governed by any Government to attempt to procure in the territory of the Ruler or governed by the Government, the alteration, otherwise than by lawful means of any matter as by law established;
(c) to bring into hatred or contempt or to excite disaffection against the administration of justice in Malaysia or in any State;
(d) to raise discontent or disaffection amongst the subjects of the Yang di-Pertuan Agong or of the Ruler of any State or amongst the inhabitants of Malaysia or of any State; or
(e) to promote feelings of ill-will and hostility between different races or classes of the population of Malaysia.

In 1970, as a result of an amendment, the Malaysian law developed an offshoot definition of *seditious tendency*, which is peculiar to Malaysia. The Yang di-Pertuan Agong issued a Proclamation of Emergency in the aftermath of the 1969 racial riots and, on 3 August 1970, he promulgated the Emergency (Essential Powers) Ordinance No. 45 of 1970, which came into force on 10 August 1970. In pursuance of Ordinance No. 45, certain sections of the Sedition Act were amended. A new paragraph (f) was added to Section 3(1) of the Sedition Act. The amended section now provides that a 'seditious tendency' is a tendency:

(f) to question any matter, right, status, position, privilege, sovereignty or prerogative established or protected by the provisions of Part III of the Federal Constitution or Article 152, 153 or 181 of the Federal Constitution.

The restrictions were aimed at restricting public discussion on four 'sensitive' issues: citizenship (Part III of the Federal Constitution); the National Language and the languages of other communities (Article 152); the special position and privileges of the Malays, the natives of Sabah and Sarawak, and the legitimate interest

or any part thereof, friendly relations with other countries, public order or morality and restrictions designed to protect the privileges of Parliament or of any Legislative Assembly or to provide against contempt of court, defamation, or incitement to any offence;
(b) on the right conferred by paragraph (b) of Clause (1), such restrictions as it deems necessary or expedient in the interest of the security of the Federation or any part thereof or public order;
(c) on the right conferred by paragraph (c) of Clause (1), such restrictions as it deems necessary or expedient in the interest of the security of the Federation or any part thereof, public order or morality.

(3) Restrictions on the right to form associations conferred by paragraph (c) of Clause (1) may also be imposed by any law relating to labour or education.

of other communities in Malaysia (Article 153); and the sovereignty of the Rulers (Article 181).

Ordinance No. 45 further amended Section 3(2) of the Sedition Act to provide that in respect of any such matter, right, status, position, privilege, sovereignty, or prerogative, an act, speech, words, publication or other thing shall be deemed to be seditious even if it has a tendency:

(i) to persuade the subjects of any Ruler or the inhabitants of any territory governed by the government to attempt to procure by lawful means the alteration of any matter in the territory of the Ruler or governed by such government as by law established; or

(ii) to point out, with a view to their removal, any matters producing or having a tendency to produce feelings of ill will and enmity between different races or classes of the population of Malaysia.

Within a year of the coming into force of the 'new' Sedition law, it was subjected to judicial scrutiny.

Public Prosecutor v Ooi Kee Saik & Ors

In this case,[58] the first accused, Dr Ooi Kee Saik, was charged with an offence under section 4(1)(b)[59] of the Sedition Act 1948, the second accused, Fan Yew Teng, was charged with publishing the alleged seditious words, and the third and fourth accused were charged with printing the alleged seditious words. The presiding judge, Raja Azlan Shah J, held that the speech accused the government of gross partiality in favour of one group and that this was calculated to inspire feelings of enmity and disaffection among the peoples of Malaysia. The judge further held that the speech was also apt to promote feelings of ill will and hostility among the different races in Malaysia, and touched upon the sensitive issue of the special rights of the Malays. The speech, taken as a whole, was considered by the judge as going beyond the limits of freedom of expression. All four accused were convicted and fined RM2000 each in default of 6 months imprisonment.

In arriving at this decision, Raja Azlan Shah J rejected the English and Indian judicial approach to defining the elements necessary to constitute the offence of sedition (i.e. that the offence of sedition requires the ingredient of incitement to violence).[60] (In India, the courts have brought the Indian law of sedition on a par with the English law, notwithstanding the fact that the offence is a statutory one.)[61] Raja Azlan Shah J referred to the 'enlightened view' of Latham CJ in the Australian

[58] [1971] 2 MLJ 108.

[59] Section 4(1)(b) of the Sedition Act, 1948 makes it an offence for any person who 'utters any seditious words'.

[60] *R v Burns* (1886) 16 Cox CC 355.

[61] *Niharendu Majumdar v King Emperor* (1942) FCR 38; *Kedar Nath v State of Bihar* (1962) AIR SC 955. See Indian Law Institute, *The Law of Sedition in India* (New Delhi, 1964) 20–34, for a discussion of the Indian case law.

case of *Burns v Ransley*,[62] wherein the Chief Justice dispensed with the need to consider the common law as the offence in Australia is a statutory offence.[63] *Wallace v Johnson*,[64] which was cited by Latham CJ in *Burns v Ransley*, was also invoked by Raja Azlan Shah J to justify his adoption of a 'strict and literal interpretation' of the Sedition Act 1948. Raja Azlan Shah J concluded that it was impossible to spell out any requirement of intention to incite violence, tumult, or public disorder in order to constitute sedition under the Sedition Act 1948.[65]

In the course of his judgment, Raja Azlan Shah J said that a meaningful understanding of the right to freedom of speech under the Constitution must be based on the realities of the Malaysian society. He said:

> Our sedition law would not necessarily be apt for other people but we ought always to remember that it is a law which suits our temperament. A line must therefore be drawn between the right to freedom of speech and sedition. In this country the court draws the line. The question arises: where is the line to be drawn; when does free political criticism end and sedition begin? In my view, the right to free speech ceases at the point where it comes within the mischief of section 3 of the Sedition Act. The dividing line between lawful criticism of Government and sedition is this - if upon reading the impugned speech as a whole the court finds that it was intended to be a criticism of Government policy or administration with a view to obtain its change or reform, the speech is safe. But if the court comes to the conclusion that the speech used naturally, clearly and indubitably, has the tendency of stirring up hatred, contempt or disaffection against the Government, then it is caught within the ban of paragraph (a) of section 3(1) of the Act. In other contexts the word "disaffection" might have a different meaning, but in the context of the Sedition Act it means more than political criticism; it means the absence of affection, disloyalty, enmity and hostility. To 'excite disaffection' in relation to a Government refers to the implanting or arousing or stimulating in the minds of people a feeling of antagonism, enmity and disloyalty tending to make government insecure. If the natural consequences of the impugned speech is apt to produce conflict and discord amongst the people or to create race hatred, the speech transgresses paragraph (d) and (e) of section 3(1). Again paragraph (f) of section 3(1) comes into

[62] (1949) 79 CLR 101. Cf Campbell and Whitmore, *Freedom in Australia* (Sydney University Press 1973) where the authors regarded the decisions in *Burns v Ramsley* and *R v Sharkey* (1949) 79 CLR 121 as 'unfortunate'.

[63] At that time, the Commonwealth of Australia Crimes Act 1914–1966, ss 24A, B, C, D, and s 25, which was equivalent to the English Incitement to Disaffection Act 1934.

[64] [1940] AC 231.

[65] *Public Prosecutor v Ooi Kee Saik & Ors* [1971] 2 MLJ 108, 111. Raja Azlan Shah J further invoked subsection (3) of section 3 of the Sedition Act 1948 in support of his conclusion. Section 3(3) provides 'For the purpose of proving the commission of any offence against this Act the intention of the person charged at the time he did or attempted to do or made any preparation to do or conspired with any person to do any act or uttered any seditious words or printed, published, sold, offered for sale, distributed, reproduced or imported any publication or did any other thing shall be deemed to be irrelevant if in fact the act had, or would, if done, have had, or the words, publication or thing had a seditious tendency.' It is questionable whether 'intention' in section 3(3) covers the intention to incite violence. In view of the fact that the Malaysian Act employs the term 'seditious tendency' in contrast to 'seditious intention' in other common law countries, it is submitted that the purpose of Section 3(3) is to render irrelevant the intention to effect any of the objects in paragraphs (a)-(f) of Section 3(1). Section 3(3) does not prevent the court from reading (if it wants to follow the English judicial approach) the ingredient of incitement to violence into the Act.

play if the impugned speech has reference to question any of the four sensitive issues - citizenship, national language, special rights of the Malays and the sovereignty of the Rulers.[66]

The statement of the law by Raja Azlan Shah J may give rise to an impression that there is room for a court to manoeuvre; the reality is that a speech which touches upon any of the sensitive issues will be caught by the Act even if 'it was intended to be a criticism of Government policy or administration with a view to obtain its change or reform'. This is because under the amended section 3(2) of the Sedition Act, the moment a speech has even such a tendency, it is *deemed* seditious. The courts have no line to draw. Once a speech touches upon and calls in question any of the 'sensitive' matters it will automatically be caught by the Sedition Act

Melan Bin Abdullah v Public Prosecutor

Ooi Kee Saik was soon followed by *Melan bin Abdullah v PP*,[67] a case held up to show that the government would be even-handed in the operation of the new law. In *Melan bin Abdullah*, the Utusan Melayu newspaper, on 6 April 1971, published a report of a talk given by Musa Hitam, a prominent Malay leader and at the time a Member of Parliament, at the National Educational Congress held in the Dewan Bahasa dan Pustaka, Kuala Lumpur. In the report was an editorial subheading, which, in the English translation read, 'Abolish Tamil or Chinese medium schools in this country'. The first appellant was the editor-in-chief of the Utusan Melayu, and the second appellant, the author of the subheading inserted in the report. Both were tried on a charge of publishing a seditious publication in contravention of section 4(1)(c)[68] of the Sedition Act and were convicted and fined the sum of RM500 and RM1,000, respectively, in default of 1 month and 2 months' imprisonment. Both appealed against their conviction and sentence.

Ong CJ set aside the conviction of the first appellant because he had taken all precautionary measures necessary and that he had not failed in the high standard of care and caution required of him, but the conviction of the second appellant was affirmed.[69] In the course of his judgment, Ong CJ said:

By virtue of the 1970 amendment to the Sedition Act, 'sedition' no longer requires the same judicial approach as the misdemeanour at common law. The amendment was *ad*

[66] *Public Prosecutor v Ooi Kee Saik & Ors* [1971] 2 MLJ 108, 112.

[67] [1971] 2 MLJ 280.

[68] Section 4(1)(c) makes it an offence for any person who 'prints, publishes, sells, offers for sale, distributes or reproduces any seditious publication ...'

[69] Section 6(2) of the Sedition Act provides that 'no person shall be convicted of any offence referred to in Section 4(1)(c) or (d) if the person proves that the publication in respect of which he is charged was printed, published, sold, offered for sale, distributed, reproduced or imported (as the case may be) without his authority, consent and knowledge and without any want of due care or caution on his part, or that he did not know and had no reason to believe that the publication had a seditious tendency'.

In *Public Prosecutor v Ooi Kee Saik and Ors* [1971] 2 MLJ 108, the third and fourth accused said that they did not know the contents of the impugned article was seditious as they did not read nor write English. Neither did they employ English translators. Raja Azlan Shah J. held that they had not satisfied the burden of proof imposed by Section 6(2) as 'bare words to the effect that they did not know the contents of the impugned article was seditious is not even *prima facie* evidence of absence of knowledge or reasonable belief'. ([1971] 2 MLJ 108, 114).

hoc legislation, passed to meet the special needs and circumstances of the time. The duty of the court is to interpret and uphold the law as passed by Parliament. Whether or not paragraph (f) [of section 3(1)] fits into the common law concept of sedition is wholly beside the point. It does give, however, a new and, perhaps, highly artificial meaning to what used to be considered 'seditious tendencies'. English and Indian authorities are, therefore, of little relevance and are not referred to herein. In my view paragraph (f) is unique in that it raises a presumption of law that anything falling squarely within the terms thereof has a seditious tendency, irrespective of whether or not such thing sows any seeds of disaffection ...[70]

Ong CJ was referring specifically to the context of the new paragraph (f) when he rejected the relevance of English and Indian authorities. The Chief Justice stated that the offence of 'sedition', as embodied in paragraph (f), would not require the same judicial approach in relation to the misdemeanour at common law *only by virtue of the 1970 amendment to the Act*. Implied in this remark was the distinct probability that the English judicial approach could be applied in the absence of the 1970 amendment.

The cases of *Dr Ooi Kee Saik* and *Melan* clearly showed that the new sedition laws operated effectively to stifle discussion of the four 'sensitive' issues.

The Constitution (Amendment) Act 1971

The 1970 amendment to the Sedition Act was effected by an emergency ordinance [the Emergency (Essential Powers) Ordinance No. 45 of 1970] and not by an Act of Parliament.[71] If the ordinance is neither revoked nor nullified, the ordinance promulgated in pursuance of the Proclamation of Emergency automatically ceases to have effect at the expiration of 6 months from the date the Proclamation of Emergency ceases to be in force.[72] However, for the Proclamation to cease to be in force, it must again either be revoked by the Yang di-Pertuan Agong or nullified by resolutions passed by both Houses of Parliament once Parliament is convened.

If the Malaysian Parliament wants to prolong the prohibition on the discussion of sensitive matters even after the revocation of the Proclamation of Emergency, the amendment to the Sedition Act will have to be embodied in an Act of Parliament. To pave the way for such a future Act, the Constitution (Amendment) Act 1971[73] was passed by both Houses of the Malaysian Parliament, and it received the royal assent on 9 March 1971 and was gazetted on the same day.[74]

In moving the Second Reading of the Constitution (Amendment) Bill, Prime Minister Tun Abdul Razak referred to the disturbances of 13 May 1969 as marking 'the darkest period in our national history'. After stressing that the 'lessons of

[70] *Melan bin Abdullah v Public Prosecutor* [1971] 2 MLJ 280, 283–4.
[71] Article 150(3) of the Malaysian Constitution.
[72] Article 150(7) of the Malaysian Constitution.
[73] Act A30 of 1971.
[74] For a discussion of this Act, see the Introduction by Professor Ahmad Ibrahim to *Parliamentary Debates on the Constitution Amendment Bill, 1971* (Kuala Lumpur: Government Printers 1972), hereafter referred to as *Parliamentary Debates*.

the May 13 tragedy must never be forgotten', the Prime Minister stated the broad objectives of the Bill:

> Firstly, these amendments are intended to remove certain sensitive issues from the realm of public discussion so as to ensure the smooth and continuing function of parliamentary democracy in this country. Secondly, they are intended to redress the racial imbalance in certain sectors of the nation's life in so far as this imbalance can be rectified by legislation.[75]

In respect of the first objective, the government thought it necessary to empower itself to curtail freedom of speech by amending Article 10 of the Constitution, which expressly declares that 'every citizen has the right to freedom of speech and expression'. Section 2 of the Constitution (Amendment) Act 1971 amended Article 10, to give Parliament power to pass laws prohibiting the questioning of any matter, right, status, position, privilege, sovereignty, or prerogative established or protected by the provisions of Part III (which contained provisions relating to citizenship); Article 152 (relating to the National Language and the languages of the other communities); Article 153 (relating to the special position of the Malays and the legitimate interest of the other communities); and Article 181 (relating to the sovereignty of the Rulers).

No law has so far been enacted by the Malaysian Parliament under the amended Article 10. It has been asserted that if Parliament passes a law under the amended Article 10 of the Malaysian Constitution there is nothing to prohibit the questioning of the implementation, but not the existence or substance of the sensitive matters. In other words, Parliament may not enact laws prohibiting anyone from questioning the implementation of those constitutional provisions that are considered sensitive matters.[76] Such an assertion arises mainly because Section 2 of the Constitution (Amendment) Act 1971 provides that Parliament may pass law prohibiting the questioning of sensitive matters 'otherwise than in relation to the implementation thereof as may be specified in such law'. The scope of the provision is difficult to comprehend. It is doubtful whether such an assertion is altogether tenable as the word 'implementation' is qualified by the phrase 'as may be specified in such law'.

The curtailment on the right to freedom of speech was also extended to Members of Parliament and the Legislative Assemblies of the states. Article 63(2) and Article 72(2) of the Federal Constitution respectively provide, in similar terms, that no person shall be liable to any proceedings in any court in respect of anything said or any vote given by him when taking part in any proceedings of either House of Parliament or any committee thereof, or of the Legislative Assembly of any state or of any committee thereof. These provisions are embodiments of the concept of 'parliamentary privilege'.[77] The effect of the amendments is that these provisions

[75] *Parliamentary Debates* 3.

[76] Tun Mohamed Suffian, *An Introduction to the Constitution of Malaysia* (Government Printers 1972) 40.

[77] See also the Houses of Parliament (Privileges and Powers) Act, 1952, which defines and declares the privileges and powers of the Malaysian Parliament. The Act also states that—'Save as is otherwise expressly provided by this Act the House and the members thereof respectively shall hold, enjoy and

can no longer be invoked so as to make available the defence of privilege by a Member of Parliament or Legislative Assembly of a state who is charged with an offence under any law passed by Parliament under the new Article 10(4) or under the Sedition Act 1948 as amended by the Emergency (Essential Powers) Ordinance No. 45 of 1970.

The essence of parliamentary privilege is the umbrella of protection, which covers Members of Parliament acting in their public capacities, against outside interference. The justification for such protection is to ensure that they can carry out their duties effectively. If the effective performance of their duties and functions is in any way hindered, it will result in detriment to the welfare of the nation. Of the specific rights, powers and immunities conferred by parliamentary privilege, the most crucial is freedom of speech. In England, it took centuries before this freedom of speech found embodiment in Article 9 of the Bill of Rights of 1689 and, thus, provided the basis of the modern law. Article 9 of the Bill of Rights provides 'that the freedom of speech, and debates or the proceedings in Parliament ought not to be impeached or questioned in any court or place out of Parliament'.

In the light of the amendments to the Federal Constitution, this 'modern law' approach as originally reflected in Article 63(2) and Article 72(2) is no longer true in Malaysia. Tun Abdul Razak sought to rationalize the amendments along the following lines: (1) that nobody, not even a Member of Parliament or of a State Legislative Assembly, is above the law, and (2) that press publicity of discussion on the sensitive issues will have adverse effect on national harmony and stability. A concept of unrestrained freedom of speech may pose problems for a multiracial society. In Malaysia, stability, which depends upon the understanding and tolerance among the various racial components of the country, can easily be fractured by inflammatory racist speeches. However, in respect of Parliament, some queries have been raised as to whether some other modes could not have been devised, such as, for example, amending the standing orders to give more 'sting' to the Speaker's power to deal with a recalcitrant member, the clearance of the visitor's galleries of all visitors and even the press, and the conducting of secret sessions of Parliament if it should be necessary to discuss sensitive matters.[78] Such measures perhaps would be more consonant with the language of Article 10(2)(a), which empowers Parliament to impose restrictions designed 'to *protect* the privileges of Parliament or of any Legislative Assembly'. It would be a contradiction in terms to say that lowering the shield of immunity of a Member of Parliament or of the Legislative Assembly amounts to a 'protection' of their privileges.

exercise such and the like privileges and immunities, and powers relating thereto as are held, enjoyed and exercised by the Commons House of Parliament of the United Kingdom and by the members thereof and also such privileges, immunities and powers as are from time to time defined by any law of the Federation but not exceeding those at the commencement of such law held, enjoyed and exercised by the Commons House aforesaid and by the members thereof respectively whether such privileges, immunities or powers were so held, possessed or enjoyed by custom, statute or otherwise.' In *Mark Koding v Public Prosecutor* [1982] 2 MLJ 120, the Federal Court upheld the validity of the amendments made by the Constitution (Amendment) Act 1971 limiting the right of free speech of parliamentarians.

[78] See *Parliamentary Debates* 5, 75.

A Member of Parliament will face another consequence if he or she is convicted of sedition. Under the Constitution he will be disqualified for membership of either House if, inter alia, he or she has been convicted of an offence by a court of law and sentenced to imprisonment for a term of not less than 1 year, or to a fine of not less than RM 2000, and has not received a free pardon.[79] Before the 2015 amendments, a conviction under the Sedition Act rendered a person liable to a fine not exceeding RM 5,000 or to imprisonment for a term not exceeding 3 years or both in respect of a first offence, and to imprisonment for a term not exceeding 5 years for a subsequent offence.[80] The amendments in 2015 have completely removed the court's discretion to impose a fine. Now a person will be liable to imprisonment for a minimum term of 3 years and a maximum of 7 years. However, no person shall be prosecuted for an offence under the Sedition Act without the written consent of the Public Prosecutor.[81] In Malaysia, the Public Prosecutor is the Attorney General himself.[82] The requirement of the Public Prosecutor's consent is a frail protection, given that the post of Attorney General in Malaysia is a political appointment.

There is no doubt that there is no such thing as an absolute or uncontrolled right to freedom of speech. What is more fundamentally at issue is the balance to

[79] Article 48(1)(e) of the Malaysian Constitution. The same applies to a member of a State Legislative Assembly. See 8th Schedule, Part I, s 6(1)(e) of the Malaysian Constitution. The disqualification may be removed by the Yang di-Pertuan Agong. If it is not so removed, it ceases at the expiration of 5 years from the date on which the convicted member was released from custody or the date on which the fine was imposed (see Article 48(3)). The same applies in respect of a member of a State Legislative Assembly except that the disqualification may be removed by the State Ruler (see 8th Schedule, Part I, Section 6(2)). Before 1960, not every conviction will result in disqualification. The convicted member must have been sentenced to imprisonment for a term of not less than two years. However in 1960 the words 'one year or to a fine of not less than two thousand dollars' were substituted for 'two years' in Article 48(1)(e)—see Act No. 10 of 1960, Section 7, in force from 31 May 1960.

[80] Fan Yew Teng, a Member of Parliament, was the second accused in *Ooi Kee Saik*. In an appeal to the Federal Court, it was held that the trial was a nullity and his conviction was accordingly quashed: *Fan Yew Teng v Public Prosecutor* [1971] 2 MLJ 271. He was again convicted after a retrial: *Public Prosecutor v Fan Yew Teng* [1975] 1 MLJ 176. He appealed unsuccessfully to the Federal Court and the privy Council in *Fan Yew Teng v Public Prosecutor* [1975] 2 MLJ 235; [1977] 2 MLJ 125, PC. Two days after Fan's conviction in the second High Court trial, the Election Commission announced that Fan's Menglembu seat had become vacant, as he had been disqualified from being a member of the House of Representatives. The Commission also issued a writ of election to the Returning Officer of the constituency to conduct a by-election to fill the vacancy. Both the nomination day and polling day were fixed. Fan's application for an interim injunction to restrain the Election Commission from holding the by-election was dismissed by Harun Hashim J on 25 February 1975—*New Straits Times* (26 February 1975). On 26 February 1975, Fan applied to the High Court for a declaration asking the High Court to declare that a by-election could not legally be held—*New Straits Times* (27 February 1975). This time he was successful. On 12 March 1975, Azmi J ruled that Fan's conviction on 13 January 1975 did not automatically render his seat in the House of Representatives vacant. In granting Fan's application Azmi J held that the Malaysian Constitution gave Parliament the overriding power to make decisions as to disqualification. Article 53 provides, 'If any question arises whether a member of a House of Parliament has become disqualified for membership, the decision of that House shall be taken and shall be final: Provided that this Article shall not be taken to prevent the practice of the House postponing a decision in order to allow for the taking or determination of any proceedings that may affect the decision (including proceedings for the removal of the disqualification)' (*Fan Yew Teng v Setia Usaha, Dewan Ra'ayat & Ors* [1975] 2 MLJ 41).

[81] Section 5(2) of the Sedition Act.

[82] By virtue of Section 376(i), Criminal Procedure Code (Act 593).

be struck between individual liberty and social control. Too heavy a reliance on a yardstick based on countries with long democratic traditions may be too myopic, and could result in a failure to note the different temperament and the highly volatile mixture of the Malaysian society. On the other hand, the argument may be mounted whether it would not be detrimental to the nation's long-term interest to have such blanket restrictions. The Constitution (Amendment) Act 1971 has not only imposed curbs on the right to freedom of speech but has also sought to 'entrench' them. Ong CJ in *Melan bin Abdullah*, had expressed the hope that, as and when the justification no longer existed for banning fair comment on matters of public interest, the 1970 amendments to the Sedition Act would be removed. Such a decision on when the ban should end is a political decision and not a matter for the courts.

The Constitution (Amendment) Act 1993, which removed the legal immunity of the Rulers, has also partly removed the fetter on parliamentary freedom of speech. A number of statements uttered during the confrontation with the Rulers over their legal immunity could be argued to be seditious. Because criticism of the Rulers was in line with the government's objective, no prosecution was initiated, as the consent of the Attorney General was required. The 1993 amendments now enable federal and state parliamentarians to criticize the Rulers as long as the criticisms do not extend to calling for the abolition of the position of Yang di-Pertuan Agong and that of the State Rulers.

Second phase: Abuse of Sedition Law

In the second phase, any attempt to present an acceptable face to the use of the sedition law was undermined by the deployment of the sedition law to impede the opposition and stifle dissenting voices.

Public Prosecutor v Param Cumaraswamy

In *Public Prosecutor v Param Cumaraswamy*,[83] Dato' Param Cumaraswamy, the then vice-president of the Malaysian Bar Council, was prosecuted for allegedly raising disaffection against the Yang di-Pertuan Agong through a purported suggestion of discrimination on the part of the Pardons Board, which was chaired by the Yang di-Pertuan Agong. The accused was eventually acquitted.

Lim Guan Eng v Public Prosecutor

In *Lim Guan Eng v Public Prosecutor*,[84] the accused, who was then an opposition Member of Parliament and Deputy Secretary of the Democratic Action Party, was charged in 1995 under the Sedition Act and the 'false news' provision of the Printing Presses and Publications Act 1984. The charges arose in 1994, after he publicly

[83] [1986] 1 MLJ 512. [84] [1998] 3 MLJ 34.

criticized the government's handling of statutory rape allegations against a former Chief Minister of Melaka (Tan Sri Rahim Tamby Chik). The central thrust of the criticism was 'an allegation of selective prosecution'. The trial judge, in convicting the accused, sentenced him to a fine of RM 10,000, in default 6 months imprisonment, in respect of the charge relating to publication, and a fine of RM 5,000, in default 3 months imprisonment, in respect of the charge, under the Sedition Act. On appeal, the Court of Appeal raised the sentence to 18 months' imprisonment on each charge.[85] The *Justice in Jeopardy* report commented that the Lim Guan Eng episode 'shows in fact that anyone who dares to criticise the legal or judicial process may have to pay a very high price'.[86]

Sedition prosecutions as ramifications of the Anwar saga

The tensions between Anwar Ibrahim (a former DPM and Minister of Finance, who was once anointed by Dr Mahathir as his potential successor) and Dr Mahathir led to a chain of events that resembled a tragic soap opera with serious ramifications for Anwar's personal safety and liberty and reputation and for the profound impact on the state of constitutionalism in Malaysia. After Dr Mahathir had fired him as DPM and the Minister of Finance, Anwar found himself flung into a legal mesh of a most abominable nature. He was arrested on 20 September 1998 and charged with sodomy under the Penal Code (s 377B). His defence counsel, Karpal Singh, was prosecuted for sedition over certain words he was alleged to have uttered in court on 10 September 1999, while conducting the defence of his client.[87] He had 'expressed the concern that somebody might be trying to murder his client'.[88] The charge against Karpal Singh was eventually withdrawn.[89] How is it possible in this day and age when Malaysia is set on the path to become a first world country that a lawyer can be prosecuted for the offence of sedition for trying his best to carry out his role as a defence lawyer?

In May 2003 Zulkifli Sulong, the editor-in-chief of a publication Harakah, was convicted under s 4(1)(c) of the Sedition Act 1948 'for publishing a seditious article four years ago regarding the trial of ex-deputy premier Anwar Ibrahim'. Sessions Court judge Rosenani Abdul Rahman fined him RM 4,000.[90] The article 'featured

[85] An appeal from the decision of the Court of Appeal was dismissed by the Federal Court: [2000] 2 MLJ 577.

[86] *Justice in Jeopardy* 21–30, 36–9.

[87] See Wu Min Aun, 'Anwar Ibrahim: The Fall and Fall of a Favoured Son' (2000/2001) 46 Lawasia Journal 68, note 44.

[88] See Gail Davidson, Tami Friesen, and Michael Jackson, 'Lawyers and the Rule of law on Trial: Sedition Prosecutions in Malaysia' (2001) 12 *Criminal Law Forum* 1–23, at para 3 (Kluwer Academic Publishers 2001) . The authors explained, 'At the time, the trial judge, Justice Arifin Jaka, the lead prosecutor, Attorney-General Tan Sri Mohtar Abdullah, and Karpal Singh were discussing a report that seemed to indicate that Ibrahim, who had been in custody for over a year, was suffering from arsenic poisoning. Karpal Singh was calling for an inquiry into his client's in-custody treatment.' (ibid 3)

[89] Ian Stewart, *The Mahathir Legacy* (Sydney: Allen & Unwin 2003) 172.

[90] 'Malaysia: Human Rights Report 2003' at 107. The printer of *Harakah*, Chia LimThye, had pleaded guilty and was fined RM 4,000 in May 2000.

the views of prominent academic and then-National Justice Party (KeADilan) deputy president Chandra Muzaffar, who alleged that the police, the AG's chambers, the court and the media were used by Prime Minister Mahathir and his followers to conspire against Anwar'.[91]

On 9 August 2001, a prosecution was initiated against a secondary school teacher (Shamsukamal Abu Bakar) in the northern state of Terengganu, which is controlled by the opposition Parti Islam SeMalaysia (PAS), in relation to the following question he had set for a Form-Two test. 'You have been selected to take part in an elocution contest on the topic: Justice is eroding and lacking in the judiciary system of Malaysia. Prepare the speech.'[92] It was alleged by the prosecution that the test question had a tendency to 'spread hatred against the Government's administration and the judiciary'. On 5 December 2001, he was acquitted by the Sessions Court judge (Ahmad Zaidi) without the need for his defence to be entered. In April 2003, Shamsukamal was convicted of sedition and fined RM 5,000.[93]

The Karpal Singh case

In the midst of the 'Perak crisis', Karpal Singh conducted a press conference in his law firm in Kuala Lumpur. The first segment of the press conference was the reading out of a pre-prepared press statement, while the second segment consisted of responses by Karpal Singh to questions posed by journalists present at the conference. Karpal Singh was subsequently charged with sedition under the Sedition Act 1948 for uttering various remarks including the utterance 'In law, the decision of the Sultan of Perak can be questioned in a court of law' in relation to the 'Perak crisis'. Judge Azman Abdullah of the High Court, at first instance, determined that the prosecution had failed to prove a prima facie case and the charges were dismissed in June 2010.[94] According to the English translation of the judgment rendered in the Malay language by Judge Azman Abdullah, it was held that the 'prosecution had failed to prove the essence required by s 3(1) of the Sedition Act ie the connection or the result of the statement to bring into hatred or contempt or to excite disaffection against any Ruler'. Furthermore, the Court was of the view 'that the media conference of [Karpal Singh] did not amount to a tendency to commit sedition to bring into hatred or contempt or to excite disaffection against any Ruler or against any government' and that 'the anger and hatred' in the complaints to the police against the accused were directed to the accused and not to the Sultan of Perak. Interestingly, the Court also held that the matter fell 'under the exception of s 3(2) of the Act, ie the tendency to show that the Sultan be confused or mistaken in any steps taken'.

However, the Court of Appeal, comprising Mohamad Apandi bin Ali JCA, Clement Allan Skinner JCA, and Ahmad bin Hj Maarop JCA (as he then was), in

[91] ibid.

[92] http://news.bbc.co.uk/2/hi/asia-pacific/1481659.stm; Malaysian Human Reports Report (SUARAM) 98.

[93] Malaysia: Human Rights Report 2003, 108.

[94] *Pendakwa Raya lwn Karpal Singh a/l Ram Singh* (2011) 9 MLJ 54.

January 2012, held that the prosecution had established a prima facie case, and they reversed the decision of the High Court.[95] The Court said that Karpal Singh had more than once uttered words 'which clearly carried the meaning that the DYMM Sultan of Perak did not respect or did not comply with the law'. 'Apart from that, the respondent clearly questioned the power of DYMM Sultan of Perak in the appointment of Mentri Besar under art 18(2)(a) of the laws of the Constitution of Perak. Not only that, but he had also given a stern reminder (warning) to His Royal Highness to cease his act of appointing (sic) the Mentri Besar and the new State Assembly.' The Court of Appeal transmitted the case back to the High Court and Karpal Singh was ordered to enter his defence. An appeal by Karpal Singh to the Federal Court was dismissed.[96] In February 2014, the High Court convicted him. He was fined RM 4,000. Very soon after, Karpal was killed in a car crash.

Elsewhere the author has observed, 'In the early years after the 1970 amendment to the Sedition Act 1948, the government sought to show that it was even-handed in its operation of the new law. Since then, the prosecution of some prominent Malaysian citizens under the Act has generated considerable concern that the law has been used to stifle criticism, whether of the government or of the judiciary.'[97] Stephen Gray and Naomita Royan asserted:

> There is, however, little to suggest that either sedition prosecutions or threats of prosecution were ever used 'even-handedly' against both political opponents and allies alike. Whether or not such 'even-handedness' ever existed in the past, there is increasing evidence that it does not exist now. In particular, in the years since Anwar Ibrahim's arrest and trial, and particularly since the surprise election result of March 2008, the Malaysian government has shown an apparently willingness to use the charge of sedition – among other legal sanctions – against real or potential political opponents. More specifically, it has shown willingness to use sedition charges against those individuals ... who influence public opinion.[98]

Article 19 in calling for a repeal of the Sedition Act said:

> The law simply cannot be justified as a restriction on freedom of expression. It is excessively vague, serves no legitimate aim sanctioned by international law and it cannot be justified as necessary in a democratic society, in particular because of its over breadth and the serious effect it has on open, democratic debate.[99]

The Court of Appeal's decision in reversing the acquittal of Karpal Singh by the High Court judge at first instance and his retrial and conviction make it more difficult for the Malaysian judiciary to traverse the path of restoring pride of place in the eyes of the Malaysian people.

[95] *Pendakwa Raya lwn Karpal Singh a/l Ram Singh* (2012) 4 MLJ 443.

[96] *Karpal Singh a/l Ram Singh v Public Prosecutor* (2012) 5 MLJ 293 (Zulkefli CJ [Malaya], Hashim Yusoff, Abdull Hamid Embong, Suriyadi, and Hasan Lah FCJ). The Federal Court found that as the order of the Court of Appeal was not a final order (and therefore did not come within the definition of 'decision' under s 3 of the Courts of Judicature Act 1964) there was no right of appeal.

[97] HP Lee, 'Competing Conceptions of Rule of Law in Malaysia' in Randall Peerenboom (ed), *Asian Discourses of Rule of Law* (Routledge 2004) 241.

[98] Stephen Gray and Naomita Royan, 'The Blogger Prince and the Cultured Mongolian: Sedition Prosecutions in the Modern Malaysian State' (2009) 14 Media and Arts Law Review 455, 465.

[99] Article 19 Memorandum on the Malaysian Sedition Act 1948 (London 2003).

The third phase: The 'Sedition Dragnet'

The earlier undertaking to abolish the Sedition Act 1948 and the proposal to replace it with a more progressive law was stymied even before it was born. Instead, a dark period of instilling fear in critics of the government through a 'sedition dragnet' began.[100]

It was contemplated that a National Harmony Act would be enacted to replace the Sedition Act 1948.[101] This had clearly been ditched because of the Prime Minister succumbing to pressure from right-wing forces within UMNO. Instead, there is concern of an expanded use of the Sedition Act as a weapon of harassment and intimidation, mainly against government critics, concerned citizens, and opposition members.

PP v Azmi bin Sharom

The Federal Court had occasion to consider a challenge to the validity of the Sedition Act. On 2 September 2014, Azmi Sharom, an associate professor of law from the University of Malaya, was charged under s 4(1)(b) and, alternatively, under s 4(1)(c) of the Sedition Act 1948, for uttering two statements he made in an article titled 'Take Perak crisis route for speedy end to Selangor impasse, Pakatan told'.[102] The specific statements were, 'You don't want a repeat of that, where a secret meeting took place ...' and 'I think what happened in Perak was legally wrong. The best thing to do is do it legally and transparently as possible.' On a reference by way of a special case, the Federal Court was called on to determine two questions posed to it. The first question was 'Whether section 4(1) of the Sedition Act 1948 contravenes Article 10(2) of the Federal Constitution and is therefore void under Article 4(1) of the Federal Constitution'. The second question was 'Whether the Sedition Act 1948 is a valid and enforceable Act under the Federal Constitution'.

The contention of the defendant was that as the Act imposed restrictions on the right of freedom of speech and expression as guaranteed by Article 10 of the Constitution, and as Article 10 provides for Parliament to legislate on such restrictions, only Parliament would have the sole authority to make law to restrict freedom of speech and expression. Since the Sedition Act 1948 was not enacted by Parliament, it was submitted that the Act was not a valid law.

[100] A phrase coined by the Malaysian media to refer to the roundup of critics of the Najib Razak government with a view to investigating and charging them under the Sedition Act 1948.

[101] It was reported that the Minister in the Prime Minister's Department (Nancy Shukri) had stated that the first draft of the National Harmony Bill had been presented by the National Unity Consultative Council (NUCC) to the Cabinet. She also said that the Prime Minister's Department was studying several examples of implementation in countries such as Singapore and the United Kingdom—'Cabinet receives first draft of National Harmony Bill' (28 May 2014) http://www.thesundaily.my/news/1060729 (accessed 14 October 2016).

[102] 'Azmi could have been spared 17 months of misery, Bar says after sedition case dropped'—Malay Mail Online (15 February 2016) http://www.themalaymailonline.com/malaysia/article/azmi-could-have-been-spared-17-months-of-misery-bar-says-after-sedition-cas (accessed 14 October 2016).

The Federal Court dealt with the second question first. The Court noted that the Sedition Act originated from the Sedition Ordinance 1948, which was first enacted by the Federal Legislative Council. The attempt to have the Act invalidated failed. It was pointed out that the Act was a pre-Merdeka law and, therefore, was saved by Article 162 of the Constitution. Article 162(1) provides that laws existing at the time of Merdeka Day shall 'continue in force on and after Merdeka Day, with such modifications as may be made therein under this Article and subject to any amendments made by federal or State law.' Chief Justice Arifin Zakaria, delivering the judgment of the Federal Court, held that the Act came within the phrase 'existing law' and by virtue of Article 162, would continue to be valid and enforceable post-Merdeka Day.

The Federal Court then proceeded to deal with the first question. While the Court's response to the second question is logical and a persuasive application of Article 162, its response to the first question exhibits an inability to rise to the occasion in support of fundamental liberties. Article 10(2) empowers Parliament to legislate to impose on freedom of speech and expression 'such restrictions as it deems necessary or expedient in the interest of the security of the Federation or any part thereof' and other ground enumerated in Article 10(2).[103]

The defendant sought to rely on a 2010 Federal Court decision (*Sivarasa Rasiah v Badan Peguam Malaysia*[104]) where it was held that such restrictions had to be reasonable and proportionate. It was argued that the Sedition Act was not such a law and was therefore unconstitutional. Departing from the earlier decision, the Federal Court rejected the argument on the ground that it was not in a position to determine the reasonableness of such restrictions in absence of an express requirement for reasonableness in Article 10(2) and in view of the intentional omission of the word by the framers of the Constitution. What is perplexing is that the Court, in dismissing the need for reasonableness, concluded (albeit with little analysis) that the Sedition Act was 'proportionate'. The Court upheld the validity of the legislation.

On 12 February 2016, the Attorney-General (Mohamed Apandi Ali) announced his decision to drop the sedition charges against Azmi Sharon.[105] Although the Attorney-General was lauded for exhibiting 'common sense' in dropping the charges, the prosecution should not have been launched in the first place. Why should Azmi Sharom be subjected to over 17 months of combating a prosecution that was perceived as a blatant act designed to stifle public debate on topical public issue?[106]

[103] The other grounds are 'friendly relations with other countries, public order or morality and restrictions designed to protect the privileges of Parliament or of any Legislative Assembly or to provide against contempt of court, defamation, or incitement to any offence'.

[104] [2010] 2 MLJ 333.

[105] 'AG drops sedition case against Azmi Sharom' *Malay Mail Online* (12 February 2016) http://www.themalaymailonline.com/malaysia/article/ag-drops-sedition-case-against-azmi-sharom (accessed 20 July 2016).

[106] 'Azmi could have been spared 17 months of misery, Bar says after sedition case dropped'—*Malaymail* Online (15 February 2016) http://www.themalaymailonline.com/malaysia/article/azmi-could-have-been-spared-17-months-of-misery-bar-says-after-sedition-cas (accessed 14 October 2016).

A constitutional conundrum

As mentioned earlier, the 1969 emergency proclamation was revoked in 2011. This must surely rendered invalid paragraph (f), which was inserted into Section 3(1) of the Sedition Act by the Emergency (Essential Powers) Ordinance No. 45 of 1970. Paragraph (f) removed from the realm of public discussion the four 'sensitive' issues. There does not appear to have been any public discussion of this invalidity issue. However, in reality, offences against paragraph (f) can be prosecuted under the other paragraphs of Section 3(1).

Constitutional Amendments

Many emergent states display their new constitutions proudly. The pride of governments turns to dismay when they realize that the constitutional documents also contain safeguards to ensure the protection of constitutional rule. The familiar refrain of these governments is that these constitutional safeguards are impediments to progress. In truth, these safeguards impede only the progress of unscrupulous leaders who seek to plunder the state coffers. In answer to those who argue that the rule of law is an unnecessary luxury for a developing country, one may ask how many developing countries have truly benefited from dictatorial rule?[107]

In order to secure their own interests and the interests of their relatives and cronies, the governments in many developing countries right at the outset start to undermine the very constitutional constraints that are there to keep a check on abuse of power. The story is familiar: unjustified detention of members and leaders of opposition parties, curbs on the press, expulsion of foreign correspondents, and the use of sedition laws to stifle the voice of reason, and, in a number of instances, resort to torture and murder. Despite all these, there are considerable attempts being made to present a facade of constitutional rule. Dictators have this curious tendency of wanting to be regarded as respecters of the rule of law.

The courts are forced along to give the stamp of legality to such actions that are clearly contrary to the rule of law. In many instances, they are forced along because these actions are sanctioned by amendments to the constitutional framework.[108]

[107] See Claudio Tehankee, 'The Return of Constitutional Democracy in the Philippines' (Tun A Razak Memorial Lecture delivered on 7 July 1988), reproduced in (1988) INSAF 83.

[108] For the Indian people in the darkest hour of the 1975 emergency, things looked very ominous when the Government made extensive amendments to the Constitution, amendments that had far-reaching implications for the rule of law. Just to cite a few examples, the guarantees of fundamental rights in the Constitution were virtually rendered nugatory; the powers of the courts to determine the constitutionality of laws was severely restricted; the President became a figurehead; the life of Parliament was extended from 5 to 6 years; offices of profit under the Central or a State government will no longer disqualify a member of the legislature unless the office is declared by Parliament by law to disqualify its holder, for example. And all these, and many other, amendments were made with the following stated purpose 'to spell out expressly the high ideals of socialism, secularism and the integrity of the nation....' As the ICJ observed, the Gandhi Government was equipping itself with powers that could be used to perpetuate the rule of the Congress Party.

Although Malaysia has fortunately escaped the extensive corruption of the constitutional system characteristic of many developing countries, nevertheless, extensive alterations have been effected to the Malaysian Constitution over its life span since independence in 1957.[109] It is beyond the preview of this book to analyse all the amendments to date. I will highlight a number of these amendments that have weakened the rule of law in Malaysia.

An early amendment impinged on the mechanism designed by the architects of the 1957 Constitution to maintain the independence of the judiciary from the executive and legislative authorities'.[110] Article 122 in its original form stated that in appointing the Chief Justice, the Yang di-Pertuan Agong 'may act in his discretion, but after consulting the Conference of Rulers and considering the advice of the Prime Minister'. The Article also provided that in appointing the other judges of the Supreme Court he shall, after consulting the Conference of Rulers, act on the recommendation of the Judicial and Legal Service Commission'. Before acting on the recommendation of the Judicial and Legal Service Commission, he 'shall consider the advice of the Prime Minister and may once refer the recommendation back to the Commission in order that it may be reconsidered'. Within 3 years of independence, the power of appointing the Chief Justice and other judges was transferred to the Prime Minister by virtue of the Constitution (Amendment) Act 1960.[111] That amendment Act also abolished the Judicial and Legal Service Commission and transferred the power of appointing persons to sit on a tribunal to consider the removal of a judge from the Commission to the Yang di-Pertuan Agong. Pending the outcome of the report of the tribunal, the Yang di-Pertuan Agong had, before the 1960 amendment Act, the power to suspend the judge from the exercise of his functions. After the enactment of the amendment Act, this suspension power was transferred to the Prime Minister.

The National Security Council Act 2016

An event that poses concern for the future of constitutionalism and a 'loaded-gun' threat to the grand vision of a working Malaysian democracy is the passing of the National Security Council Act 2016. Despite concerns relayed by the Conference of Rulers regarding some aspects of the Act, the government was able to use the deeming provision under Article 66(4A) of the Constitution to deem that royal assent had been given to the legislation.[112] The Act establishes a statutory entity called the National Security Council ('NSC') comprising the Prime Minister (Chairman), the Deputy Prime Minister (Deputy Chairman), the Minister of Defence, the Minister of Home Affairs, the Minister of Communication and Multimedia, the

[109] HP Lee, 'Constitutional Amendments in Malaysia' (1976) 18 Malaya LR 59. See, also, Tan Sri Salleh Abas, 'Amendment of the Malaysian Constitution' (1977) 2 MLJ xxxiv.

[110] Federation of Malaya Constitutional Proposals 1957 para 31.

[111] Act 10 of 1960.

[112] Shad Saleem Faruqi, 'A precedent but no blanket pass' *The Star* (23 June 2016) http://www.thestar.com.my/opinion/columnists/reflecting-on-the-law/2016/06/23/a-precedent-but-no-blanket-pass-article-66-4a-permits-the-king-to-be-bypassed-but-cannot-apply-to-ot/ (accessed 24 June 2016).

Chief Secretary of the Government, the Chief of Defence Forces, and the Inspector General of Police.[113] The NSC Act empowers the Prime Minister, on advice of the National Security Council, to declare an area a security area, following which he is able to deploy the security forces and any government agencies in a declared security area. In reality, the Act has given the Prime Minister 'unbridled power' to declare almost any part of Malaysia as a security area'.[114] It is simply left to the NSC to determine what constitutes a matter of national security, as the Act does not provide a definition of this concept. The constitutional validity of the NSC Act is highly questionable. The Malaysian Bar Council commented:

> The NSC Act enables the Prime Minister, either unilaterally or through the NSC, to exercise authoritarian executive powers. These powers are in effect emergency powers, but without the need for a proclamation of an emergency under Article 150 of the Federal Constitution. This usurps the powers vested in the Yang di-Pertuan Agong in, and violates the provisions of, Article 150 of the Federal Constitution. The Act is therefore of questionable constitutional validity.[115]

Should the day come when a challenge to its validity is launched, the fate of the Malaysian nation rests in the hands of the courts of law. The assertion that the NSC Act amounts to a usurpation of the Yang di-Pertuan Agong's constitutional power to proclaim a state of emergency is incontrovertible. For the NSC Act to surmount the argument of invalidity it has to be enacted as an amendment of the Constitution by using the process of Article 159, and not simply enacted by using the ordinary process of law making. This is an issue of such fundamental importance that the advisory opinion jurisdiction of the Federal Court under Article 130 should be invoked. Undoubtedly, the NSC Act provides a threat for possible future invocation in the event an unscrupulous leader seeks to override parliamentary democracy with authoritarian rule, especially when the leader is on the verge of losing political power.

Conclusion

The constitutional conflicts between the Rulers and the government and between the judiciary and the government have eroded those constraints that temper the exercise of executive powers. The various amendments to the emergency powers and preventive detention powers provisions of the Constitution place a greater responsibility on the Rulers and the judiciary to nudge the government along the

[113] NSC Act, s 6.

[114] Steven Thiru, 'Press Release: The National Security Council Bill 2015 is a Lurch Towards an Authoritarian Government' (Malaysian Bar Council, 3 December 2015) http://www.malaysianbar.org.my/press_statements/press_release_%7C_the_national_security_council_bill_2015_is_a_lurch_towards_an_authoritarian_government.html (accessed 21 July 2016).

[115] Steven Thiru, 'Press Comment: National Security Council Act 2015 Has All the Hallmarks of Authoritarianism' (Malaysian Bar Council 15 June 2016) http://www.malaysianbar.org.my/press_statements/press_comment_%7C_national_security_council_act_2015_has_all_the_hallmarks_of_authoritarianism.html (accessed 21 July 2016).

path of constitutional rule. The regrettable aspect of these conflicts is that the influential role of both these institutions has been diminished.

A historical survey of constitutional amendments since 1957 gives credence to the view that the Constitution is treated in a cavalier fashion. Often the amendments are effected to achieve short-term political gains or to facilitate long-term expansion of executive powers. There is an obsession with the need to control at least two-thirds of the seats of the Federal Parliament.

The overview of the three major constitutional conflicts of the past decade yields the compelling conclusion that the constitutional system in Malaysia is tilted in the direction of an overweening executive arm of government. The fine line between constitutional government and outright authoritarian rule gets finer. A desperate government which is in fear of losing its grip on political power may be tempted to breach that fine line and effect a dictatorship; otherwise it will be staring down the barrel of the very legal armoury it has created to stifle its opponents.

The government should seek to improve Malaysian society not only in economic terms but also in constitutional terms. It should embark on a process of strengthening at least the fundamental constitutional values that contribute to the rule of law by re-examining certain constitutional provisions that deal with values common to all the communities in Malaysia. For instance, the emergency powers provisions in Article 150 should be restored to the original terms as recommended by the Reid Commission. The preventive detention powers embodied in Article 149 should be reviewed; there is no reason why the safeguards provided in the original terms of that Article cannot be restored. Those safeguards may serve to restrain abuse of the preventive detention powers.

The powers of the courts should be restored. Article 121(1) should be amended to make it explicit that the courts are the sole repositories of the judicial power. The excision of the courts' jurisdiction in relation to Article 150 is clearly contrary to the rule of law. Constitutional rule is rendered a mockery if emergency powers can be invoked even though there is no factual basis for a Proclamation of Emergency. The courts' inability to intervene means that a government under the current terms of Article 150 can declare a state of emergency in a most blatant fashion.

Professor Shad Faruqi proffers a number of steps that can be taken to improve the role of Parliament. In relation to the role of Parliament over legislation, he observes 'the government has become more important than Parliament'.[116] Describing this as an 'unconstitutional shift of power', he suggests that Members of Parliament 'must be supplied with draft Bills at least two weeks before the beginning of the session'.[117] He lists the following additional steps:

> The secrecy that surrounds Bills should be lifted. The sponsoring departments must be duty-bound to prepare policy papers on proposed Bills to enable non-governmental organisations

[116] Shad Faruqi, 'Making Parliament more effective' *The Star* http://www.thestar.com.my/Opinion/Columnists/Reflecting-On-The-Law/Profile/Articles/2015/05/28/Making-Parliament-more-effective-Decisions-in-which-people-participate-are-decisions-they-are-likely/ (accessed 20 July 2016).

[117] ibid.

and the rakyat to participate in a dialogue at the pre-parliamentary stage. Decisions in which people participate are decisions they are likely to respect. Select Committees for scrutiny of Bills either before the second or after the second reading are common in most democracies. Regrettably, in Malaysia there is a dismal record of appointing them less than 10 times in 57 years!

To lighten the load of the Dewan Rakyat, some politically non-controversial Bills could originate in the Dewan Negara. The Houses should set up a Joint Committee to vet subsidiary legislation which outnumbers parliamentary legislation by 20:1.

MPs should be encouraged to draft Private Members' Bills on issues which the government, for political expediency, wishes to shun. In Malaysia, no private Bill has ever passed Parliament though many were proposed.[118]

According to the World Justice Project Rule of Law Index for 2015, Malaysia was ranked 39 (score of 0.57), whereas the neighbouring country across the Causeway, Singapore, was ranked 9 (Score of 0.81).[119] The suggestions made above can easily be implemented. If these steps are taken, they will enhance the stature of the government and constitutional rule in Malaysia. Contemporary Malaysian society is sophisticated enough to appreciate these reforms. The question is whether its political leaders have the courage to face the situation of reform.

[118] ibid.

[119] Out of 102 countries/jurisdictions. http://worldjusticeproject.org/rule-law-around-world (accessed 15 April 2016).

9
Conclusion

> Abuse of power occurs at all levels of society. It is a part of life today.
>
> Raja Azlan Shah, 'Supremacy of Law in Malaysia' (1984) Journal of Malaysian and Comparative Law 1

In contemporary Malaysia today, there is a deep sense of disenchantment that the constitutional system has been distorted and skewed in favour of an overweening executive. There is ever-increasing unease with the unconstrained enlargement of executive power, and strong distrust in the unbridled exercise of powers in the name of protecting public order and security, particularly, the deployment of the sedition laws and laws relating to prevention of public disorder. The federal Parliament is generally perceived as an instrument, indeed as a rubber stamp, of the ruling Barisan Nasional. The Malay Rulers lost much prestige with the Mahathir administration, but there are signs that they have begun to regain the faith of the Malaysian public. There is recognition by the Malay Rulers that, individually, and collectively, acting as the Conference of Rulers, they could play an important role providing wisdom and a sense of calm in public affairs. Whether that faith could be nourished will depend on their ability to project an image of being independent and neutral 'umpires' in the constitutional system. Malaysian royalty was on an upwards trajectory in the journey to regaining public trust when that faith was dented by the manner in which the Perak crisis was resolved and by the role of the Sultan of Selangor in the appointment of the Menteri Besar, following the capture of that state by the opposition. The judiciary, in pursuit of reputational redemption, continues to struggle to regain public confidence in its integrity and its ability to deliver justice in an impartial and independent manner. The ongoing incarceration of Anwar Ibrahim is a reinforcement of the public perception that his prosecution was politically motivated, and it serves as a constant reminder of the unfair manner in which his trials were handled.

The Malaysian Constitution was conceived with the clear aim of dividing powers among the executive, legislative, and judiciary entities and the Malay Rulers. James Madison said, 'The accumulation of all powers, legislative, executive, and judiciary in the same hands, whether of one, a few, or many, and whether hereditary, self-appointed, or elective, may justly be pronounced the very definition of tyranny.'[1]

[1] James Madison, 'The Federalist No 47', in C Rossiter (ed), The Federalist Papers (New American Library, New York 1961) 301.

In the many struggles, documented in the preceding chapters, to preserve the rule *of* law (as opposed to the rule *by* law), while the main participants have been and are the executive arm of the government, the Parliament, the Malay Rulers, and the judiciary, the Constitution has been the main pivot point. The conflicts between the various arms of government have used the framework of the Constitution, albeit heavily amended, for the struggles for power. Civil society galvanized by the trial saga of Anwar Ibrahim has become highly motivated to ensure a meaningful voice in shaping the future of the country.

The Malaysian nation that grew out of the 1963 enlargement of the Federation of Malaya has continued to operate under a constitutional instrument crafted by a panel of distinguished jurists. There are attempts in contemporary Malaysia to advance a 'revisionist' account of the Constitution. The attempts are mounted particularly by proponents of an Islamization agenda. Joseph Fernando, describing the Malayan Constitution of 1957 as 'a unique document', pointed out that it 'was entirely the work of non-Malayan constitutional advisers from the Commonwealth'.[2] This was unlike the experience of other former British colonies and dependencies, where the constitutions 'were drafted either by local or by a combination of local and foreign (usually British) legal experts'.[3] Contrary to the view advanced by the revisionists, the idea of a commission of foreign legal experts was the choice of the Alliance. Tunku Abdul Rahman told the secretary of state, Alan Lennox-Boyd, 'In our opinion, only such a Commission would be able to exercise complete impartiality in the inquiry into the Constitution.'[4] The revisionists, instead of seeking to disparage the Constitution, should take pride in the fact that the draft constitution emanated from the collective effort of five highly experienced jurists. Fernando said, 'Each member brought with him a vast knowledge and experience of constitutional law and public administration and their contributions are reflected in the final document.'[5]

A 'dominant role'[6] was played by the Alliance in making the Constitution. Joseph Fernando, while noting that the 1957 Constitution was 'drafted by a non-Malayan Commission and enacted by the parliament of the United Kingdom', asserted that 'the predominant role of the Alliance in the constitution-making process accorded an element of autochthony to the document'.[7] Professor Andrew Harding, in similar vein, observed:

> Despite its colonial origins and its continually disputed interpretation and relevance, it has achieved, due to its longevity and in spite of colonial origins, a status quite rare in the contemporary world—that of an autochthonous constitution. It is, in other words, meaningful after half a century to refer to 'Malaysian constitutional traditions'. Where the Constitution

[2] Joseph M Fernando, 'Sir Ivor Jennings and the Malayan Constitution' (2006) 34(4) Journal of Imperial and Commonwealth History 577.

[3] ibid. [4] ibid. [5] ibid.

[6] Joseph M Fernando, *The Making of the Malayan Constitution* (Monograph No 31, MBRAS 2002) 5.

[7] ibid.

used to be referred to, as 'the Constitution', it is now referred to, dispassionately as 'our Constitution'...[8]

In comparison with many emergent countries of the Asia Pacific and the African continent, the constitutional document has never been shunted aside since Malayan independence in 1957. This is indeed a record of which the Malaysian people, despite the various constitutional upheavals recorded, should be considerably proud. However, the dawning of the twenty-first century found the Malaysian nation at a crossroads.

The major constitutional conflicts of the past have both bright and alarming aspects to them. The downwards spiral in the standing of the judiciary since the 1988 judiciary crisis and the Anwar Ibrahim trial saga was aggravated by a number of unpleasant controversies and scandals that resulted in an unfavourable perception of the courts. Yvonne Tew observes, 'The Malaysian courts' journey toward constitutional redemption has, so far, been uneven at best.'[9] She adds, 'In order for the Malaysian judiciary to restore its position as a co-equal branch of government, it will need to take firmer steps to assert its commitment to constitutional supremacy and its willingness to protect the fundamental liberties guaranteed by the Constitution.'[10] The establishment of a Judicial Appointments Commission as a mode to regain public confidence in the Malaysian judiciary fails to garner public enthusiasm.

Apart from the hiccup of the 1969 Kuala Lumpur communal riots, Malaysia has maintained a level of stability that is the envy of many emergent nations. That stability faces a degree of turbulence that has been brought about by the hunger of new generations of Malaysians for a more sophisticated form of government and by an utter distaste for the extensive and blatant corruption and cronyism that appear to go unchecked. Malaysians cannot take comfort from the fact that, according to the Corruption Perceptions Index 2015, Malaysia was ranked 54 out of 168 countries and territories.[11]

The political tsunami of the 2008 general election generated excitement of the real possibility of an alternative government for the first time in the life of the Malaysian nation. In the possibility lurks a danger for the country. At the federal level, Malaysia has never experienced a handover of political power, whereas the largest democracy in the world, India, has seen the reins of power changing hands on a few occasions. The true test will be determined by whether the governing coalition, the Barisan Nasional (especially the dominant United Malays National Organisation [UMNO] party), has the maturity to pass on the reins of power in a peaceful manner, should they be confronted by a devastating loss in a general election.

[8] Andrew Harding, *The Constitution of Malaysia: A Contextual Analysis* (Hart Publishing 2012) 2.

[9] Yvonne Tew, 'On the Uneven Journey to Constitutional Redemption: The Malaysian Judiciary and Constitutional Politics' (2016) 25(3) Washington International Law Journal 1, 2.

[10] ibid.

[11] This index was compiled by Transparency International. Malaysia obtained a score of 50 on a scale of 0 (very corrupt) to 100 (very clean). Neighbouring Singapore was ranked 8 (with a score of 85). http://www.transparency.org/cpi2015 (accessed 15 April 2016).

A comforting aspect is that the federal nature of the Malaysian polity has advantages. It allows political experimentation and experience of peaceful handover of political power to occur at a localized level. Changes of state governments have occurred without violence, and the reins of power have changed hands in the same fashion as in many other democratic countries. This augurs well in the event of a transformation of the national political landscape. Malaysia should look to the 2015 general election in Sri Lanka, where a handover of political power took place in a peaceful manner and with the outgoing government accepting defeat gracefully.

How the Malaysian nation, with such a breathtaking diversity of races, languages, cultures, and religions, can continue to traverse the path of harmony and national advancement in a shrinking world will depend on the fidelity to the principle of constitutional rule of its political leaders and its many peoples. It will also depend on the constitutional understandings embodied in the *Merdeka* Constitution; the constitutional principles of fairness, justice, and equality; and a common subscription to the fundamental importance of upholding the rule of law. The contemporary dark clouds in the growth of the Malaysian nation loom over the attempt at revisionism of the fundamentals of the Constitution by those prosecuting an Islamization agenda. Amanda Whiting remarked:

> UMNO and PAS's ['Parti Islam se-Malaysia'] competitive but erratically inconsistent repudiation or denigration of secularism and the secular in favour of its putative opposite—a Muslim society governed by Islamic law—is arguably leading to increasing tension and polarisation within Malaysian society. This is especially so because the preeminent place of Islam as the 'religion of the federation' (as stipulated by article 3(1) of the Federal Constitution) has become inextricably tied to the political hegemony of the Malay '*bangsa*' (nation) within multicultural Malaysia through the juridical equation of 'Malay' ethnicity with the profession of Islam.[12]

The outcome of the battle to 'de-secularize' what has been generally acknowledged to be a secular instrument of governance will ultimately depend on those who have taken the oath to defend and protect the Constitution, and on courageous voices across the spectrum of civil society. Prime Minister Najib Razak once said: 'I have no doubt we can best foster tolerance and understanding not by silencing the voice of hatred, but by making the voice of reason louder and louder.'[13] The extent to which the voice of reason can withstand the chastisement and intimidation by 'authoritarian elements within both government and the opposition that claim exclusive authority and capacity to interpret Islam'[14] will determine which path the Malaysian nation will traverse.

[12] Amanda J Whiting, 'Secularism, the Islamic State and the Malaysian Legal Profession' (2010) 5(1) Asian Journal of Comparative Law 1, 4.

[13] Dato' Sri Najib Tun Razak, 'Keynote Address', speech delivered at the 10th IISA Asia Security Summit, the Shangri-La Dialogue, Singapore, 3 June 2011, https://www.iiss.org/en/publications/conference%20proceedings/sections/shangri-la-aa36/the-shangri-la-dialogue-2011-fa85/sld11-04-keynote-address-45f9 (accessed 18 October 2016).

[14] Amanda J Whiting, 'Secularism, the Islamic State and the Malaysian Legal Profession' (2010) 5(1) Asian Journal of Comparative Law 5.

In a review of the achievements of the Malaysian polity in the first decade of the twenty-first century, I said:

> The road ahead for the Malaysian nation will not be easy as the polity has to reconcile conflicting notions of *ketuanan Melayu* (primacy of the Malays) and the declaration of equality under the law, creeping 'Islamization' and the guarantee of the right to practise and profess a religion of one's personal choice, and the 'right-to-rule' mentality of entrenched UMNO vested interests and new generations of Malaysians from all races who are technically savvy and who have higher aspirations than their forebears in terms of political liberties.[15]

[15] The Malaysian nation is at a crossroads.

APPENDIX 1

Proclamation of Constitutional Principles (Dated 4 July 1992: *New Straits Times* 6 July 1992)

Whereas by Article 71 of the Federal Constitution it is provided inter alia that the Federation shall guarantee the right of a ruler of a State to succeed and to hold, enjoy and exercise the constitutional rights and privileges of ruler of that State in accordance with the Constitution of that State;

And whereas by Article 181 of the Federal Constitution the sovereignty, prerogatives, powers and jurisdiction of the rulers within their respective territories as hitherto had and enjoyed shall, subject to the provisions of the said Constitution, remain unaffected;

And whereas we are desirous that at all times the Constitution and the laws of Malaysia are upheld in the nation by persons;

And whereas we subscribe to the principles of the rule of law;

And whereas to avoid any misinterpretation as to the nature and extent of their sovereignty, prerogatives and jurisdiction;

Now, therefore, we hereby make the following proclamation on the nature and extent of such prerogatives and powers:

1. *Involvement in Politics*
   1.1 In accordance with established practice and convention, we are not directly or indirectly involved in party politics.
2. *Appointment of Menteri Besar*
   2.1 In accordance with the State Constitution, we shall accept the nomination of a person who commands the confidence of the majority of the members of the Legislative Assembly as the Menteri Besar.
   2.2 Where no party has a clear majority in the Legislative Assembly, we shall exercise our own discretion in such appointment in accordance with accepted constitutional principles.
   2.3 When we have any reservation as to the suitability of any person nominated as Menteri Besar, we may refer the nomination for recommendation by the leader of the appropriate party for a final decision.
3. *Appointment of State Executive Council Members*
   3.1 We accept that the appointment of members of the State Executive council is made on the advice of the Menteri Besar alone and that in accordance with the State Constitution, we shall approve such appointments.
4. *Acting on Advice*
   4.1 We shall, in accordance with the general principle provided in each State Constitution, act on the advice of the State Executive Council or of the Menteri Besar.
   4.2 We recognise that in accordance with established constitutional practice, the terms 'acting on advice' or 'Ruler in Council' and other similar terms mean that we shall accept the advice of the Government of the State as tendered by the Menteri Besar and the State Executive Council.

4.3 In accordance with established constitutional practice, we shall have the right to be consulted, the right to encourage and the right to caution the Government.

4.4 In furtherance of our right to request any further information concerning the Government of the State as provided for in each State Constitution, we shall have the right to be briefed by the Menteri Besar as and when requested by us and also prior to each meeting of the State Executive Council.

5. *Appointment of Senior Government Officers*

5.1 We shall appoint the State Secretary, the State Legal Adviser and the State Financial Officer on the recommendation of the appropriate Public Service Commission, and also in accordance with the practice and the provisions of the State Constitution, after the name of the candidate has been submitted to us by the Menteri Besar.

5.2 In accordance with the present practice, we shall be consulted before appointments are made of all heads of Federal Departments in the State.

5.3 We shall appoint the members of the State Public Service Commission in accordance with the relevant State legislation.

6. *Business*

6.1 We shall not actively engage in any commercial enterprise except by way of trust.

6.2 His Royal Highness the Regent may through trusts/nominees participate in any commercial enterprise.

7. *Expenses of the Royal Household*

7.1 The Controller of the Royal Household shall control and administer the allocation provided in the Civil List, in accordance with the financial procedure.

8. *Religion*

8.1 In accordance with the constitutional principle that we are the heads of the religion of Islam in our respective States, we reaffirm our position that we will uphold the teachings and practice of Islam.

9. *Media*

9.1 We, in accordance with constitutional practice do not disclose to or discuss with the media any matter pertaining to the administration of the State which is likely to give rise to controversy.

10. *His Majesty the Yang di-Pertuan Agong*

10.1 Unless otherwise provided for in the Federal Constitution, this proclamation shall apply, mutatis mutandis, to His Majesty the Yang di-Pertuan Agong.

Saving

This Proclamation is made for the purpose of clarification and assurance and is made without prejudice to the provisions of the Federal Constitution, the State Constitutions and existing convention and prerogatives.

Made at the Istana Negara this July 4, 1992.

By Their Royal Highnesses' Command.

(Engku Datuk Ibrahim bin Engku Ngah)

Keeper of the Rulers' Seal.

APPENDIX 2

The Perak Crisis of 2009 Sultan Azlan Shah's Statement

'Yang Amat Berhormat Datuk Seri Mohammad Nizar Jamaluddin was granted an audience by Duli Yang Maha Mulia Paduka Sultan of Perak Darul Ridzuan on Feb 4, to ask for his Royal Highness's consent to dissolve the Perak State Assembly.

Yang Amat Berhormat Datuk Seri Mohd Najib Razak, Deputy Prime Minister of Malaysia, also requested for an audience with his Royal Highness in his capacity as the Perak Barisan Nasional chairman and consent was granted to be present before his Royal Highness on Feb 5.

Yang Amat Berhormat Datuk Seri Mohd Najib informed that the Barisan Nasional and its supporters, now comprising 31 state assemblymen, had the majority in the State Assembly.

On the order of the Duli Yang Maha Mulia to ascertain that the information given was accurate, all the 31 state assemblyman were to present themselves before Paduka Seri Sultan.

After meeting all the 31 assemblymen, DYMM Paduka Seri Sultan of Perak was convinced that YAB Datuk Seri Mohammad Nizar Jamaluddin had ceased to command the confidence of the majority of the State Assembly members.

DYMM Paduka Seri Sultan of Perak had also considered thoroughly YAB Datuk Seri Mohammad Nizar Jamaluddin's application on Feb 4, 2009 for his Royal Highness's consent to dissolve the Perak State Assembly.

His Royal Highness had used his discretion under Article XVIII (2)(b) of the Perak Darul Ridzuan State Constitution and did not consent to the dissolution of the Perak State Assembly.

YAB Datuk Seri Mohammad Nizar Jamaluddin was summoned to an audience with the Sultan to be informed of his Royal Highness's decision not to dissolve the State Assembly, and in accordance with the provisions of Article XVI (6) of the Perak Darul Ridzuan State Constitution, DYMM Paduka Seri Sultan of Perak ordered YAB Datuk Seri Mohammad Nizar Jamaluddin to resign from his post as Perak Mentri Besar together with the members of the state executive council with immediate effect.

If YAB Datuk Seri Mohammad Nizar Jamaluddin does not resign from his post as Perak Mentri Besar together with the state executive council members, then the posts of Mentri Besar and state executive councillors are regarded as vacant.

This statement is issued with the consent of Duli Yang Maha Mulia Paduka Seri Sultan of Perak Darul Ridzuan.'

(Media statement issued by the office of Duli Yang Maha Mulia Paduka Sultan of Perak, Sultan Azlan Shah, which was signed by the ruler's private secretary, Col Datuk Abd Rahim Mohamad Nor.) Published in *The Star* Online 6 February 2009 http://www.thestar.com.my/news/nation/2009/02/06/sultan-azlan-shahs-statement/(accessed 25 July 2009).

Bibliography

GOVERNMENT PUBLICATIONS

Australia, Parliament, Senate, Select Committee on Allegations Concerning a Judge, *Report to the Senate, October 1984*, Canberra: AGPS, 1984.

———, *Report to the Senate, August 1984*, Canberra: AGPS, 1984.

Commission of Enquiry on the Video Clip Recording of Images of a Person Purported to Be an Advocate and Solicitor Speaking on the Telephone on Matters Regarding the Appointment of Judges, *The Report* (9 May 2008).

Constitutional Proposals for Malaya: Report of the Working Committee Appointed by a Conference of His Excellency the Governor of the Malayan Union, their Highnesses the Rulers of the Malay States and the Representatives of the United Malays National Organisation, Kuala Lumpur: 1946.

Federation of Malaya Constitutional Commission. *Report* Kuala Lumpur: 1957.

Federation of Malaya Constitutional Conference *Report* Cmd 9714 London: HMS0, 1956.

Federation of Malaya, *Parliamentary Debates* (Dewan Ra'ayat), (Monday, 16 October 1961) cols 1590–8.

Federation of Malaya, *Report of the Commission of Enquiry, North Borneo and Sarawak* Kuala Lumpur: 1962.

Great Britain, *Malayan Union and Singapore: Statement of Policy on Future Constitution*, Cmd 6724 London: HMSO, 1946.

Malaysia, Department of Information, *United Nations Malaysia Mission Report* (Kuala Lumpur 1963).

Malaysia: Agreement concluded between the United Kingdom of Great Britain and Northern Ireland, the Federation of Malaya, North Borneo, Sarawak and Singapore, Cmd 2094, London: HMSO, 1963.

Parliamentary Debates on the Constitution Amendment Bill, 1971 (Government Printers 1972).

Report of the Tribunal Established Under Article 125(3) and (4) of the Federal Constitution. Re: YAA Tun Dato' Hj Mohamed Salleh Abas (Government Printer 1988).

———, *Re: YA Tan Sri Wan Suleiman bin Pawan* (Government Printer 1988).

The May 13 Tragedy: A Report of the National Operations Council (Government Printer 1969).

BOOKS AND ARTICLES

Abdul Aziz Bari, 'The 1993 Constitutional Crisis: A Redefinition of the Monarchy's Role and Position?' in Andrew Harding and HP Lee (eds), *Constitutional Landmarks in Malaysia: The First 50 Years 1957–2007* (LexisNexis 2007) 227–42.

———, *The Monarchy, and the Constitution in Malaysia* (IDEAS 2013) 333–50.

Abdul Hamid Mohamad, Chief Justice Dato', 'Speech at the Malaysian Judges' Conference 2008' (Marriott Putrajaya 8–11 April 2008) http://www.malaysianbar.org.my/speeches/cjs_speech_at_the_judges_conference_2008.html. (accessed 2 November 2016).

———, *I Will Never Beg* (CLJ Publications 2016) 135–6.

Abdullah Ahmad Badawi, 'Delivering Justice, Renewing Trust' Speech By: Prime Minister Abdullah Ahmad Badawi, Prime Minister of Malaysia, Malaysian Bar Council Dinner,

JW Marriott Hotel, Kuala Lumpur, 17/04/2008 http://www.malaysianbar.org.my/speeches/prime_minister_delivering_justice_renewing_trust.html (accessed 2 November 2016).

'AG drops sedition case against Azmi Sharom' *Malay Mail Online* (12 February 2016) http://www.themalaymailonline.com/malaysia/article/ag-drops-sedition-case-against-azmi-sharom (accessed 2 November 2016).

'Agong has a moral duty to act, says constitutional expert' *Malaysiakini* (29 March 2016) https://www.malaysiakini.com/news/335642 (accessed 2 November 2016).

Ahmad Fairuz bin Dato' Sheikh Abdul Halim, 'Judicial Independence, Accountability, Integrity and Competence: Some Aspects of the Malaysian Position'—Paper presented at the International Conference and Showcase on Judicial Reforms, Shangri-la Hotel, Makati City, Philippines, 28–30 November 2005.

Ahmad Ibrahim and Tan Sri Datuk, 'Professor Groves' Constitution of Malaysia' (1964) 2 MLJ xcvii–viii.

———, 'The Position of Islam in the Constitution of Malaysia' in Tun Mohamad Suffian, HP Lee, and FA Trindade (eds), *The Constitution of Malaysia: Its Development 1957–1977* (OUP 1978) 41–68.

———, 'The Amendment to Article 121 of the Federal Constitution: Its Effect on Administration of Islamic Law' (1989) 2 Malayan Law Journal xvii.

Aliran, 'The Moorthy Maniam Case: Compassion and Justice Missing' (2005) 25(11) Aliran Monthly http://aliran.com/archives/monthly/2005b/11b.html (accessed 2 November 2016).

Amnesty International, *MALAYSIA Human Rights Undermined: Restrictive Laws in a Parliamentary Democracy* (Amnesty International 1999) 26–7.

Ambiga Sreenevasan, 'Press Statement: Bar Council's immediate response to the Report in the Borneo Post dated June 2008' *The Malaysian Bar* (10 June 2008) http://www.malaysianbar.org.my/press_statements/press_statement_bar_councils_immediate_response_to_the_report_in_the_borneo_post_dated_10_june_2008.html (accessed 2 November 2016).

Anbalagan V 'For now, Najib's fate in the hands of 222 MPs, says ex-A-G' *Malaysian Insider* (9 March 2016) https://sg.news.yahoo.com/now-najib-fate-hands-222-230031144.html (accessed 2 November 2016).

'An independent Judiciary is an indispensable requisite of a free society under the Rule of Law', *Report of Committee IV, The Declaration of Delhi* (10 January 1959).

ARTICLE 19 Memorandum on the Malaysian Sedition Act 1948 (London 2003).

'Asian-Pacific Threat to the Rule of Law' (1988) *Australian Law News* (August) 12–16.

'Aziz Bari: Sultan must appoint Azizah due to 1992 deal' *Malaysia Today* (1992) http://www.malaysia-today.net/sultan-must-appoint-azizah-based-on-1992-deal/ (accessed 2 November 2016).

Azlan Shah, Raja, 'Supremacy of Law in Malaysia' (1984) Journal of Malaysian and Comparative Law 1–9.

———, 'The Role of Constitutional Rulers: A Malaysian Perspective for the Laity' (1982) 9 Journal of Malaysian and Comparative Law 1–18 (reproduced as 'The Role of Constitutional Rulers in Malaysia' in FA Trindade and HP Lee (eds), *The Constitution of Malaysia: Further Perspectives and Developments* (OUP 1986) 76–91).

———, Sultan, '50 Years of Constitutionalism and the Rule of Law' *Opening address by HRH Sultan Azlan Shah at the 14th Malaysian Law Conference* http://www.malaysianbar.org.my/speeches/opening_address_by_hrh_sultan_azlan_shah_at_the_14th_malaysian_law_conference.html (accessed 2 November 2016).

———, Sultan, 'The Role of Constitutional Rulers and the Judiciary Revisited' in V Sinnadurai (ed), *Constitutional Monarchy, Rule of Law and Good Governance* (Professional Law Books 2004) 397–8.

Azmi bin Abdul Khalid, 'Emergency Powers & Constitutional Changes' (1983) 3 Aliran Quarterly 3.

'Azmi could have been spared 17 months of misery, Bar says after sedition case dropped'—*Malay Mail Online* (15 February 2016) <http://www.themalaymailonline.com/malaysia/article/azmi-could-have-been-spared-17-months-of-misery-bar-says-after-sedition-cas>accessed 14 October 2016.

Azrul Mohd Khalib, 'Separation of mosque and state' *The Malaysian Insider* (2 April 2012) <http://www.themalaysianinsider.com/opinion/article/separation-of-mosque-and-state/>

Bar Council, 'Federal constitution must remain supreme' in Nathaniel Tan and John Lee (eds), *Religion under Siege?* (Kinibooks 2008) 34.

Barraclough S and Arudsothy P, 'The 1983 Malaysian Constitutional Crisis: Two Views and Select Documents' *Australia-Asia Papers* No 32 (Centre for the Study of Australian-Asian Relations, Griffith University, 1980).

'Basic Principles on the Independence of the Judiciary', Adopted by the Seventh United Nations Congress on the Prevention of Crime and the Treatment of Offenders, held at Milan from 26 August to 6 September 1985.

Berthelsen John, 'Malaysia's Sultans Return to Power' *Asia Sentinel* (18 September 2014) http://www.asiasentinel.com/politics/malaysia-sultans-regain-power/ (accessed 2 November 2016).

'Bill on Rulers passed with 167 votes' *New Straits Times* (10 March 1993) 1.

Boo Su-Lyn, 'Three things we learned from: The Allah case' http://www.themalaymailonline.com/malaysia/article/three-things-we-learned-from-the-allah-case#sthash.EBwLxIuK.dpuf (accessed 2 November 2016).

———, 'Marina Mahathir: Malaysia undergoing "Arab colonialism"' *Malaymail* Online (23 May 2016) http://www.themalaymailonline.com/malaysia/article/marina-mahathir-malaysia-undergoing-arab-colonialism (accessed 2 November 2016).

Bowen Catherine, *The Lion and the Throne* (Little, Brown 1956) 305.

'Cabinet receives first draft of National Harmony Bill' (28 May 2014) http://www.thesundaily.my/news/1060729 (accessed 2 November 2016).

Campbell Enid and Whitmore Harry, *Freedom in Australia* (Sydney University Press 1973).

Chan NH, 'The Federal Court in Nizar v Zambry: A Critique' *LoyarBurok* (19 February 2010) http://loyarburok.com/selected-judgments/the-federal-court-in-nizar-v-zambry-a-critique/ (accessed 2 November 2016).

Chang Wen-Cheng, Thio Li-ann, Tan Kevin YL, and Yeh Jiunn-rong, *Constitutionalism in Asia: Cases and Materials* (Hart Publishing 2014) 117.

'Change to Take Its Course' *New Straits Times* (19 January 1993) 1.

'Civil Courts Failed Duty, Group Says after Indira Gandhi Case' *Malay Mail* Online (1 January 2016) http://www.themalaymailonline.com/malaysia/article/civil-courts-failed-duty-group-says-after-indira-gandhi-case (accessed 2 November 2016).

'Constitutional Change Passed' *New Straits Times* (19 March 1988) 4.

'Court of Appeal Upholds Lifting of Ban on Book' (27 July 2012) http://www.freemalaysiatoday.com/category/nation/2012/07/27/court-of-appeal-upholds-lifting-of-ban-on-book/ (accessed 2 November 2016).

Cowen Zelman, 'The Emergence of a New Federation in Malaya' (1958) 1 Tasmanian University Law Review 46–67.

———, Derham D, 'The Independence of Judges' (1953) 26 Australian Law Journal 462–7.

Cumaraswamy Dato' Param, 'Role of the Executive' in *Reflections on the Malaysian Constitution* (Persatuan Aliran Resedaran Negara 1987) 135.

Das Cyrus, 'The Monarchy in Malaysia: The Sultanate System—Rights, Privileges, And Relations With The Executive Government'. Paper presented at the first conference of the LAWASIA Comparative Constitutional Law Interest Group, Melbourne, 18–20 November 1992, 1–22.

———, 'The May 13th Riots and Emergency Rule' in Andrew Harding and HP Lee (eds), *Constitutional Landmarks in Malaysia: The First 50 Years 1957–2007* (LexisNexis 2007) 103–13.

———, 'Constitutional Supremacy & The Lina Joy Decision' in Ang Samuel, Lee Min Choon, and Lim Siew Foong (eds), *Religious Liberty After 50 Years of Independence* (NECF Malaysia Research Commission 2008) 41–50.

Das K, *Questionable Conduct* (K Das 1990).

Davidson Gail, Friesen Tami, and Jackson Michael, 'Lawyers and the Rule of law on Trial: Sedition Prosecutions in Malaysia' (2001) 12 Criminal Law Forum 1–23 (Kluwer Academic Publishers 2001).

Dawson B and Thiru S, 'The Lina Joy Case and the Future of religious Freedom in Malaysia' [2007] LAWASIA Journal 151.

'Decision of the Special Meeting of the Conference of Rulers on Jan 18, '93' *New Straits Times* (19 January 1993) 2.

'Doing the Impossible: Quitting Islam in Malaysia' *Asia Sentinel* (27 April 2007) <http://www.asiasentinel.com/society/doing-the-impossible-quitting-islam-in-malaysia/>

'Don: Stop Using Degrading Terms in Royal Presence' *New Straits Times* (27 January 1993) 2.

Downey, 'Judicial Independence in Malaysia' (1988) New Zealand Law Journal 217.

'Fan Fails to Get that Injunction' *New Straits Times* (26 February 1975) 1.

'Fan Seeks "By-Election Is Illegal" Ruling' *New Straits Times* (27 February 1975) 1.

Feldman D, *English Public Law* (2nd edn, OUP 2009) 29

Fernando Joseph, 'Sir Ivor Jennings and the Malayan Constitution' (2006) 34(4) Journal of Imperial and Commonwealth History 577–97.

———, *The Making of the Malayan Constitution* (Monograph No 31, MBRAS 2002) 109.

———, 'The Position of Islam in the Constitution of Malaysia' (2006) 37(2) Journal of Southeast Asian Studies 249.

Foo Richard, 'Malaysia—Death of a Separate Constitutional Judicial Power' [2010] SJLS 253.

Foong J, 'The Effects of Current Judicial Reform in Asean Countries' ASEAN Law Association 10th General Assembly http://www.aseanlawassociation.org/10GAdocs/Malaysia5-2.pdf.

Friedrich Carl J, *Limited Government: A Comparison* (Prentice-Hall, 1974).

Gall Gerald L, *The Canadian Legal System* (2nd edn, Carswell Legal Publications 1983).

Ghai Yash, 'The Politics of the Constitution: Another Look at the Ningkan Litigation' (1986) 7 *Singapore Law Review* 147–73.

Gillen Mark R, 'The Malay Rulers' Loss of Immunity' (1995) 29(1) UBC Law Review 163.

'Goalkeeper Agrees and Accepts $1,000 in Compensation—Majid Case Compounded' *New Straits Times* (27 January 1993) 1.

Goh Cheng Teik, *The May Thirteenth Incident and Democracy in Malaysia* (OUP 1971).

———, *Racial Politics in Malaysia* (FEP International Sendirian Berhad 1989).

Gray Stephen and Royan Naomita, 'The Blogger prince and the cultured Mongolian: Sedition prosecutions in the modern Malaysian state' (2009) 14 Media and Arts Law Review 455

'Group of Prominent Malays Calls for Rational Dialogue on Position of Islam in Malaysia' *The Star* Online (7 December 2014) http://www.thestar.com.my/news/nation/2014/12/07/group-prominent-malays-calls-for-moderation/ (accessed 2 November 2016).

Groves Harry E, 'The Constitution of the Federation of Malaya' (1962) Indian Yearbook of International Affairs 103–37.

———, 'The Constitution of Malaysia—The Malaysia Act' (1963) 5(2) Malaya Law Review 245–75.

'Guidelines on Who Should Get Diplomatic Passports' *New Straits Times* (6 February 1993) 2.

Hafiz Yatim, 'JB City Council Loses Appeal in "Chapel Demolition" Case' *Malaysiakini* (30 July 2012) www.malaysiakini.com/news/204997 (accessed 2 November 2016).

———, 'KC Vohrah: Ex-CJ Eusoff Tried to Subvert Judge' *Malaysiakini* (27 February 2015) <https://www.malaysiakini.com/news/290455>

———, 'Can the Agong act to depose a sitting PM?' *Malaysiakini* (7 July 2015) https://www.malaysiakini.com/news/304338

Harding Andrew, 'Sovereigns Immune? The Malaysian Monarchy in Crisis' (1993) 327 The Round Table 305–14.

———, 'The 1988 Constitutional Crisis in Malaysia' (1990) 39 International and Comparative Law Quarterly 57–81.

———, 'The Constitutional Evolution of the Malaysian Monarchy', Working Paper No. 4, June 1993 (School of Oriental and African Studies, University of London), 1–25.

———, 'Turbulence in the land below the wind: Sabah's constitutional crisis of 1984/5' (1991) XXIX JCCP 86.

———, 'When is a Resignation Not a Resignation? A Crisis of Confidence in Sabah' (1995) The Round Table 353.

———, 'The *Keris*, The Crescent and the Blind Goddess: The State, Islam and the Constitution in Malaysia' (2002) 6 Singapore Journal of International & Comparative Law 154.

———, 'Crises of Confidence and Perak's Constitutional Impasse' Center for Policy Initiatives 7 June 2009 http://www.loyarburok.com/2009/06/07/crises-of-confidence-and-peraks-constitutional-impasse/ (accessed 2 November 2016).

———, 'The Perak Constitutional Crisis: An Epilogue' in Audrey Quay (ed), *Perak: A State of Crisis* (LoyarBurok Publications 2010) 165–70.

———, *The Constitution of Malaysia: A Contextual Analysis* (Hart 2012) 9–50.

———, 'Constitutionalism, Islam and National Identity in Malaysia' in Rainer Grote and Tilman J Roder (eds), *Constitutionalism in Islamic Countries: Between Upheaval and Continuity* (OUP 2012) 201.

'Harun: Some Changes Needed' *New Sunday Times* (6 September 1987) 5.

Hasan Hj Hamzah, *Mahathir—Great Malaysian Hero* (2nd ed, Media Printex 1990).

Hector Charles, 'Towards an Impartial, Incorruptible and Independent Judiciary' *malaysianbar.org* (19 August 2002) http://www.malaysianbar.org.my/members_opinions_and_comments/towards_an_impartial_incorruptible_and_independent_judiciary.html?date=2015-06-01(accessed 2 November 2016).

Hickling RH, 'The Prerogative in Malaysia' (1975) 17 Malaya Law Review 207–32.

———, 'An Overview of Constitutional Changes in Malaysia: 1957–1977' in Tun Mohamed Suffian, HP Lee, and FA Trindade (eds), *The Constitution of Malaysia: Its Development 1957–1977* (OUP 1978) 1.

———, and Wishart David A, 'Malaysia: Dr Mahathir's Thinking on Constitutional Issues' (1988–89) Lawasia 47–79.

———, 'The Malaysian Judiciary in Crisis' (1989) Public Law 20–7.

'Hindu Hubbies on Warpath with Islamic Authorities' *Malaysiakini* (20 April 2007) at https://m.malaysiakini.com/news/66226 (accessed 2 November 2016).

'Hockey Coach Takes a Swipe at JHA' *New Straits Times* (29 November 1992) 1.

'Hockey Coach Summoned to Johor Palace' *New Straits Times* (1 December 1992) 2.

Horowitz D, 'The Qu'ran and the Common Law: Islamic Law Reform and the Theory of Legal Change' (1994) 42 American Journal of Comparative Law 233.

'Human Rights in the World: Malaysia' (1986) 37 Review International Commission of Jurists 12.

'"I Know How the People Feel": Interview with Dr Mahathir bin Mohamed' *Time* (24 November 1986) 18.

Indian Law Institute, *The Law of Sedition in India* (New Delhi 1964).

'Inquiry Finds Vasta's Conduct Warrants Sack' *The Weekend Australian* (13–14 May 1989) 1.

International Commission of Jurists, 'Resolution of 20 January 1989' (1989) MLJ 1 cxxii.

———, *States of Emergency: Their Impact on Human Rights*, Geneva, 1983.

Jayakumar S, 'Emergency Powers in Malaysia' in Tun Mohamed Suffian, HP Lee, and FA Trindade (eds), *The Constitution of Malaysia—Its Development: 1957–1977* (OUP 1978) 328–68.

———, 'Emergency Powers in Malaysia: Can the Yang di-Pertuan Agong act in his personal discretion and capacity?' (1976) 18 Malaya Law Review 149–56.

———, 'Legal Aspects of Emergency Powers in Malaysia' (1969) 2(2) Commentary 17; (1969) 4(3) The Law Times (University of Singapore Law Society) 27–31.

———, 'The Philippine Claim to Sabah and International Law'(1968) 10(2) Malaya Law Review 306–35.

Jeffrey Tyler James Brent, 'Preventive Detention in Malaysia: Constitutional and Judicial Obstacles to Reform and Suggestions for the Future' (2013) 41 Ga J Int'l Comp L 535.

Johan Shamsuddin Sabaruddin, 'The Kelantan Challenge' in Andrew Harding and HP Lee (eds), *Constitutional Landmarks in Malaysia: The First 50 Years 1957–2007* (LexisNexis 2007) chap. 3.

Joseph ALR, 'Unfettered Religious Freedom Hangs by the Thread of Minority Dissent in Malaysia: A Review of the Dissenting Judgment of the Federal Court in the *Lina Joy* Case' (2009) 14(2) Review of Constitutional Studies 205.

'Kadir: Monarchy at the Crossroads' *New Straits Times* (5 February 1993) 2.

'Kelantan Ruler's Acts Started the Criticisms' *New Straits Times* (9 March 1993) 4.

Kent Jonathan, 'Malaysia Club Raid Sparks Row' *BBC* (18 February 2005) http://news.bbc.co.uk/2/hi/asia-pacific/4276077.stm (accessed 1 March 2016).

Kershaw Roger, 'Shattered Symbiosis: The Road to Conflict between Malay Nationalism and Monarchy' (1993) 24 Internationales Asienforum 283–310.

Khoo Boo Teik, *Beyond Mahathir: Malaysian Politics and Its Discontents* (Zed Books Ltd 2003).

Khoo Boo Teong, 'Rule of Law and Fundamental Liberties in Malaysia' (PhD thesis, University of Sydney 1999).

Khoo Kay Kim, 'Succession to the Perak Sultanate' (1983) 56 Journal of the Malaysian Branch of the Royal Asiatic Society 7.

King LJ, 'Minimum Standards of Judicial Independence' (1984) 58 Australian Law Journal 340–5.

Kirby Michael, 'Malaysia — the Judiciary and the Rule of Law' (1988) 41 Review International Commission of Jurists 40.

———, 'Fundamental Human Rights and Religious Apostasy: The Malaysian Case of *Lina Joy*' (2008) 17(1) Griffith Law Review 151.

Kobkua Suwannathat-Pian, 'Thrones, Claimants, Rulers and Rules: The Problem of Succession in the Malay Sultanates' (1993) 66 Journal of the Malaysian Branch of the Royal Asiatic Society 1–27.

———, *Palace, Political Party and Power: A Story of the Socio-Political Development of Malay Kingship* (NUS Press 2011).

Koh Philip TN, 'The Sabah Constitutional Cases 1985-1986: Conventions, Justiciability and Democratic Governance' in Andrew Harding and HP Lee (eds), *Constitutional Landmarks in Malaysia: The First 50 Years 1957–2007* (LexisNexis 2007) 165.

Kua Kia Soong, *May 13: Declassified Documents on the Malaysian Riots of 1969* (Suaram 2007).

Kumarasingham H, *Constitution-Maker: Selected Writings of Sir Ivor Jennings* (Camden Fifth Series, Vol 46, CUP 2014).

Lee HP, 'Constitutional Amendments in Malaysia' (1976) 18 Malaya Law Review 59–74.

———, 'The Process of Constitutional Change in Malaysia' in Tun Mohamed Suffian, HP Lee and FA Trindade (eds), *The Constitution of Malaysia—Its Development: 1957–1977* (OUP 1978) 369–92.

———, 'The Malaysian Constitutional Crisis: King, Rulers and Royal Assent' (1984) Lawasia 22–44.

———, 'Emergency Powers in Malaysia' in FA Trindade and HP Lee (eds), *Constitution of Malaysia: Further Perspectives and Developments* (OUP 1986) 133–56.

———, 'A Fragile Bastion Under Siege—The 1988 Convulsion in the Malaysian Judiciary' (1990) 17 Melbourne University Law Review 386–417.

———, 'Hereditary Rulers and Legal Immunities in Malaysia' (1993) 12 University of Tasmania Law Review 323–36.

———, 'Constitutional Values in Turbulent Asia' (1997) 23(2) Monash University Law Review 375.

———, 'Judges and Constitutional Government' [2000/2001] LAWASIA Journal 30.

———, 'Competing Conceptions of Rule of Law in Malaysia' in Randall Peerenboom (ed), *Asian Discourses of Rule of Law* (Routledge 2004) 241.

———, 'The Judicial Power and Constitutional Government: Convergence and Divergence in the Australian and Malaysian Experience' (2005) 1 Journal of Malaysian and Comparative Law 2–3.

———, 'The Constitution of Malaysia After 50 Years: Retrospective, Prospective and Comparative Perspectives' (2007) 9(2) Australian Journal of Asian Law 307.

———, 'The Ningkan Saga: A Chief Minister in the Eye of a Storm' in Andrew Harding and HP Lee (eds), *Constitutional Landmarks in Malaysia: The First 50 Years 1957–2007* (LexisNexis 2007) 77–87.

———, 'The 1983 Constitutional Crisis' in Andrew Harding and HP Lee (eds), *Constitutional Landmarks in Malaysia: The First 50 Years 1957–2007* (LexisNexis 2007) 157–64.

———, 'Malaysian Royalty and the Special Court' in Andrew Harding and Penelope (Pip) Nicholson (eds), *New Courts in Asia* (Routledge 2010) 317–26.

———, 'Malaysia: The Politics of the Judiciary' in Rainer Grote and Tilman J Roder (eds), *Constitutionalism in Islamic Countries: Between Upheaval and Continuity* (OUP 2012) 305.

———, 'Constitutional Developments in Malaysia in the First Decade of the Twenty-First Century: A Nation at the Crossroads' in Albert HY Chen (ed), *Constitutionalism in Asia in the Early Twenty-First Century* (CUP 2014) 244.

Lee HP and Morabito Vince, 'Removal of Judges—The Australian Experience' (1992) Singapore Journal of Legal Studies 40–55.

———, Lee HP, and Trindade FA (eds), *The Constitution of Malaysia—Its Development: 1957–1977* (OUP 1978).

———, 'Four Decades in the Law – Looking Back' in FA Trindade and HP Lee (eds), *The Constitution of Malaysia: Further Perspectives and Developments* (OUP 1986) 216.

Lee Julian CH, *Islamization and Activism in Malaysia* (Institute of Southeast Asian Studies 2010).

Lee Kuan Yew, *The Battle for Merger* (Government Printing Office 1961).

Levin Bernard, 'Justice Mauled in Malaysia' *The Times* (16 October 1989) 16.

———, 'Mahathir Devours His Prey' *The Times* (23 October 1989) 16.

———, 'Malaysia's Law of the Jungle' *The Times* (19 October 1989) 14.

Lim Ida and Tan Shaun, 'Last Nail in Catholic Church's "Allah" Case as Federal Court again Says No' *Malaymail* Online (21 January 2015) http://www.themalaymailonline.com/malaysia/article/last-nail-in-catholic-churchs-allah-case-as-federal-court-again-says-no (accessed 2 November 2016).

Lim Kit Siang, 'Scandalous and Disastrous' (1993) 13(6) Aliran Monthly 6.

———, *Time Bombs in Malaysia* (Democratic Action Party 1978).

Liow Joseph Chinyong, *Piety and Politics: Islamism in Contemporary Malaysia* (OUP 2009) 192.

Lowe V, 'Redefining the "Constitutionality" of the Monarchy: The 1983 Constitutional Amendment Crisis in Malaysia' (1984) 2(2) Kajian Malaysia 1–15.

Lin Yutang (ed), *The Wisdom of Confucius* (The Modern Library 1938) 198.

Madison James, 'The Federalist No 47' in C Rossiter (ed), *The Federalist Papers* (New American Library, New York 1961) 301.

Mahathir bin Mohamed, *The Malay Dilemma* (Federal Publications, 1981).

'Mahathir's Dilemma' *Star* (29 November 1986) 1.

Malaysia: Assault on the Judiciary (Lawyers Committee for Human Rights 1990).

'Malaysia Backs Down from Yoga Ban Amid Backlash' (26 November 2008) http://www.reuters.com/article/us-malaysia-islam-yoga-idUSTRE4AP2CA20081126 (accessed 2 November 2016).

'Malaysia's Highest Court Backs a Ban on Allah in Christian Bibles' *Guardian* (23 June 2014). http://www.theguardian.com/world/2014/jun/23/malaysia-highest-court-allah-bible-ban (accessed 2 November 2016).

'Malaysia: Human Rights Report 2003' (SUARAM 2003).

Maizatul Nazlina, 'Deepa Case: Civil Courts Should Decide Custody of Converted Children' *The Star* Online (10 February 2016) http://www.thestar.com.my/news/nation/2016/02/10/federal-court-civil-courts-decide-deepa-case/ (accessed 2 November 2016).

Maizatul Nazlina and Camoens Austin, 'Federal Court Orders IGP to Arrest Indira's Ex-Husband' *The Star* (30 April 2016) http://www.thestar.com.my/news/nation/2016/04/30/federal-court-orders-igp-to-arrest-indiras-exhusband/ (accessed 2 November 2016).

Malik Imtiaz Sarwar, 'The Death of Civil Liberties' *Malaysia Today* (23 April 2012) https://www.malaysiakini.com/news/315248 (accessed 2 November 2016).

———, 'Constitutionalism, the Rule of Law and Religious Freedom in Malaysia' in Marco Bünte and Björn Dressel (eds), *Politics and Constitutions in Southeast Asia* (Routledge 2017) 331

Mason Chief Justice, 'The Independence of the Bench: The Independence of the Bar and the Bar's Role in the Judicial System', Keynote address to the 1992 Conference of English, Scottish and Australian Bar Associations, London, 4 July 1992, 3.

Mazwin Nik Anis, 'Fatwa Council Says Yoga with Worshipping, Chanting Is Prohibited' *The Star* Online (22 November 2008) http://www.thestar.com.my/story/?file=%2F2008%2F11%2F22%2Fnation%2F20081122111842 (accessed 2 November 2016).

Means, Gordon P, *Malaysian Politics* (2nd edn, Hodder and Stoughton Ltd 1976).

———, *Malaysian Politics: The Second Generation* (OUP 1991).

Mohamed Ariff, *The Philippines Claim to Sabah: Its Historical, Legal and Political Implications* (OUP 1970).

Mohamed Azam Mohamed Adil, 'Law of Apostasy and Freedom of Religion in Malaysia' (2007) 2(1) Asian Journal of Comparative Law 1.

———, 'Restrictions in Freedom of Religion in Malaysia: A Conceptual Analysis with Special Reference to the Law of Apostasy' (2007) 4(2) Muslim World Journal of Human Rights 1.

Mohamed Nawab Mohamed Osman, Oh Ei Sun, and Afif Pasuni, 'The Selangor Chief Minister Crisis and the Future of Pakatan Rakyat (PR)' *RSIS* (October 2014) https://www.rsis.edu.sg/wp-content/uploads/2014/10/NL141007_Malaysia_Update.pdf (accessed 2 November 2016).

Mohamed Noordin Sopiee, *From Malayan Union to Singapore Separation* (Penerbit Universiti Malaya 1974).

Mohamed Suffian Tun, *An Introduction to the Constitution of Malaysia* (Government Printers 1972).

———, *An Introduction to the Constitution of Malaysia* (2nd ed, Government Printer 1976).

———, *An Introduction to the Legal System of Malaysia* (Penerbit Fajar Bakti Sdn Bhd 1988).

———, *Malaysia and India—Shared Experiences in the Law* (All India Reporter Ltd 1980).

———, 'Role of the Monarchy' in *Reflections on the Malaysian Constitution* (Persatuan Aliran Resedaran Negara 1987) 41.

Montesquieu, *The Spirit of the Laws* (translated by Thomas Nugent) (Hafner Press 1949).

'More Malaysians Will Suffer Deepa, Indira's Fate if Constitution Unamended, DAP MP Says' *The Malaymail* (11 February 2016) http://www.themalaymailonline.com/malaysia/article/more-malaysians-will-suffer-deepa-indiras-fate-if-constitution-unamended-da (accessed 2 November 2016).

Moosdeen A. 'The Tribunal on Tun Salleh Abas—A Hundred Years of Legal Wisdom' (1988) XX (5) INSAF: Journal of the Malaysian Bar 68–73.

Muzaffar Chandra, 'A Blitz of Legal Manoeuvres' *Asiaweek* (22 July 1988) 22.

———, 'A Challenge to the Basic Character of the Malaysian Constitution' *Aliran Press Release*, (16 March 1988).

Najib Tun Razak, 'Keynote Address', speech delivered at the 10th IISA Asia Security Summit, the Shangri-La Dialogue, Singapore (3 June 2011) https://www.iiss.org/en/publications/conference%20proceedings/sections/shangri-la-aa36/the-shangri-la-dialogue-2011-fa85/sld11-04-keynote-address-45f9 (accessed 2 November 2016).

Nariman, 'Justice for Judges?' (1988) New Zealand Law Journal 266–7.

NNP, 'Jumpa Tun' (1994) 14(4) Aliran Monthly 2–3.

Neo Jaclyn Ling-Chien, 'Malay Nationalism, Islamic Supremacy and the Constitutional Bargain in the Multi-ethnic Composition of Malaysia' (2006) 13 International Journal on Minority and Group Rights 95.

———, 'What's In a Name? Malaysia's "Allah" Controversy and the Judicial Intertwining of Islam with Ethnic Identity', NUS Law Working Paper Series, Working Paper 2014/008 (June 2014) http://law.nus.edu.sg/wps (accessed 2 November 2016).

Nwabueze BO, *Constitutionalism in the Emergent States* (C Hurst & Co 1973).

'On the Legality of Emergency Laws Proclaimed in Pursuance of Article 150 of the Federal Constitution' (1969) III (3) INSAF: Journal of the Malaysian Bar 31–9.

O'Neill NKF, 'How the Indian Supreme Court Survived the Emergency' (1981) Lawasia 362–76.

'Orders that Can Be Ignored' *New Straits Times* (5 February 1993) 1.

'Palace Incident an Abuse of Power' *New Straits Times* (11 December 1992) 2.

'Palace Nurses May Be Re-deployed' *New Straits Times* (8 February 1993) 2.

'Parliamentary Commission of Inquiry—Re the Hon. Mr Justice Murphy' (1986) 2 Australian Bar Review 203–49.

Pascoe Daniel, 'What the Rejection of Anwar Ibrahim's Petition for Pardon Tells Us about Malaysia's Royal Pardons System' (2016) 18(1) Asian-Pacific Law & Policy Journal (forthcoming).

Pawancheek Marican, *Anwar on Trial: In the Face of Injustice* (Gerakbudaya Enterprise 2009).

Pillai MGG, 'Judicial Row Splits Malaysia' *The Australian* (8 July 1988) 6.

Pinwill William, 'Malaysia Faces a Constitutional Crisis over Its King's Powers' *National Times* (18–24 November 1983).

'Place Confidence in Judiciary, Says Hamid' *New Straits Times* (8 February 1993) 2.

'Prime Minister: Delivering Justice, Renewing Trust', Speech delivered at the Malaysian Bar Council dinner, JW Marriott Hotel, Kuala Lumpur (17 April 2008) http://www.malaysianbar.org.my/speeches/prime_minister_delivering_justice_renewing_trust.html (accessed 12 July 2016).

'Prime Minister's Message for Malaysia Day 2011' (15 September 2011) https://www.najibrazak.com/bm/official-addresses/perutusan-khas-hari-malaysia/ (accessed 2 November 2016).

Qishin Tariq, 'Federal Court Allows Book by Sisters-In-Islam' (14 March 2013). http://www.thestar.com.my/news/nation/2013/03/14/federal-court-allows-book-by-sistersinislam/ (accessed 2 November 2016).

Rais Yatim, 'The Road to Merdeka' in Andrew Harding and HP Lee (eds), *Constitutional Landmarks in Malaysia: The First 50 Years 1957–2007* (LexisNexis 2007) 1–24.

Raja Aziz Addruse, *Conduct Unbecoming* (Walrus 1990).

Ramakrishnan P, 'Proposed constitutional amendments: no justification' (1993) 13(6) Aliran Monthly 2–4.

———, 'A Royal Commission Is Urgently Needed to Purge the Judiciary of All the Negative Elements Plaguing It' (2005) 25(1) Aliran Monthly http://aliran.com/archives/monthly/2005a/1i.html (accessed 2 November 2016).

Rawlings Hugh F, 'The Malaysian Constitutional Crisis of 1983' (1986) 35 International and Comparative Law Quarterly 237–54.

Reflections on the Malaysian Constitution (Persatuan Aliran Kesedaran Negara 1987).

Ramraj Victor V, 'The Cheng Poh Case' in Andrew Harding and HP Lee, *Constitutional Landmarks in Malaysia: The First 50 Years 1957–2007* (LexisNexis 2007) 145.

'Report and Record of the Committee of Investigation into the Conduct of the Hon. Mr Justice Berger and Resolution of the Canadian Judicial Council' (1983) 28 McGill LJ 378–436.

'Report by the Bar Council on the Report of the Tribunal Established in Respect of Tun Mohamed Salleh Abas' (1988) XX (5) INSAF: Journal of the Malaysian Bar 30–47.

Report of the Working Group on Arbitrary Detention on its visit to Malaysia (7–17 June 2010) (A/HRC/16/47/Add.2).

'RMAF Services for Sultans to End' *New Straits Times* (5 February 1993) 1.

Robertson Geoffrey, 'Justice Hangs in the Balance' *The Observer* (28 August 1988) 22.

'RTM to Scale Down Coverage of Royalty' *New Straits Times* (27 January 1993) 2.

Ruban A, 'Dangerous Precedent, MP Says of Federal Court Custody Ruling in Deepa Case' *The Malaymail* (12 February 2016) http://www.themalaymailonline.com/malaysia/article/dangerous-precedent-mp-says-of-federal-court-custody-ruling-in-deepa-case (accessed 2 November 2016).

Rueban Ratna Balasubramaniam, 'The Karam Singh Case' in Andrew Harding and HP Lee (eds), *Constitutional Landmarks in Malaysia: The First 50 Years 1957–2007* (LexisNexis 2007) 89–102.

'Rulers Can Still Live Well' *New Straits Times* (23 January 1993) 1.

Salah El-Sheikh, 'Implementing Islamic Law within a Modern Constitutional Framework – Challenges and Problems in Contemporary Malaysia' 1.3 Islam and Civilizational Renewal (ICR) http://www.iais.org.my/icr/index.php/icr/article/viewFile/279/271 (accessed 2 November 2016).

Salleh bin Abas Tun, 'Amendment of the Malaysian Constitution' (1977) 2 MLJ msxxxiv–xlix.

———, 'Press Statement Regarding First Tribunal Report' Reproduced in (1988) XX (5) INSAF: Journal of the Malaysian Bar 14–27.

———, *The Role of the Independent Judiciary* (Promarketing Publications 1989).

———, with Das K, *May Day for Justice* (Magnus Books 1989).

Santha Oorjitham, 'Interview with Datuk Syed Ahmad Idid' *New Straits Times* (11 June 2008) available at 'Merdeka' (24 June 2006) http://srenggege.blogspot.com.au/2006/06/interview-with-datuk-syed-ahmad-idid.html (accessed 2 November 2016).

Seervai HM, *Constitutional Law of India* (2nd ed, NM Tripathi Pte Ltd 1979) Vol III.

———, *The Emergency, Future Safeguards and the Habeas Corpus Case: A Criticism* (NM Tripathi Pte Ltd 1978).

Shad Saleem Faruqi, 'The Sceptre, the Sword and the Constitution at a Crossroad (A commentary on the Constitution Amendment Bill 1993)' [1993] 1 CLJ xlv–lix.

———, 'A Precedent but no Blanket Pass' *The Star* (23 June 2016) http://www.thestar.com.my/opinion/columnists/reflecting-on-the-law/2016/06/23/a-precedent-but-no-blanket-pass-article-66-4a-permits-the-king-to-be-bypassed-but-cannot-apply-to-ot/

———, 'Making Parliament more Effective' *The Star* (28 May 2015) http://www.thestar.com.my/Opinion/Columnists/Reflecting-On-The-Law/Profile/Articles/2015/05/28/Making-Parliament-more-effective-Decisions-in-which-people-participate-are-decisions-they-are-likely/(accessed 2 November 2016).

Shaila Koshy, Carvalho Martin, Maizatul Nazlina, and Albakri Danial, 'Federal Court Grants Custody of Boy to Izwan while Deepa Is Given the Daughter' *The Star* Online (11 February 2016) http://www.thestar.com.my/news/nation/2016/02/11/each-parent-gets-one-child-federal-court-grants-custody-of-boy-to-izwan-while-deepa-is-given-the-dau/ (accessed 2 November 2016).

Sheridan Lionel Astor, 'Federation of Malaya's New Constitution' (1957) MLJ lxiii–xv.

———(ed), *Malaya and Singapore, the Borneo Territories: the Development of their Laws and Constitutions* (Stevens and Sons Ltd 1961).

———, *The Constitution of Malaysia* (4th edn, Malayan Law Journal Pte Ltd 1987).

Sheridan Lionel Astor and Groves HE, *The Constitution of Malaysia* (3rd edn, Malayan Law Journal Pte Ltd 1979).

Sim Steven, 'Can a Menteri Besar Be Sacked via a Press Conference?' *FMT News* (22 January 2016) http://www.freemalaysiatoday.com/category/opinion/2016/01/22/can-a-menteri-besar-be-sacked-via-a-press-conference/ (accessed 2 November 2016).

Simandjuntak B, *Malayan Federalism 1945–1963* (OUP 1969).

Sinnadurai Visu, 'The 1988 Judiciary Crisis and its Aftermath' in Andrew Harding and HP Lee (eds), *Constitutional Landmarks in Malaysia: The First 50 Years 1957–2007* (LexisNexis, 2007) 173.

'Statement by David Geddes, Secretary-General of Law Association for Asia and the Pacific' (1988) New Zealand Law Journal 218.

'Statement by Niall McDermott, Secretary-General of the International Commission of Jurists' (1988) New Zealand Law Journal 217–18.

Stewart Ian, *The Mahathir Legacy* (Allen & Unwin 2003) 172.

Stephen Ninian, Sir, 'Southey Memorial Lecture 1981: Judicial Independence—A Fragile Bastion' (1982) 13 Melbourne University Law Review 334–48.

Stilt Kristen, 'Contextualizing constitutional Islam: The Malayan Experience' (2015) 13 ICON 407.

Stockwell AJ, 'Princes and Politicians: The Constitutional Crisis in Malaysia, 1983–4' in DA Low (ed), *Constitutional Heads and Political Crises* (Macmillan 1988) 182–97.

'Stop Aping Arabs, Johor Sultan Tells Malays' *Malaymail* Online (24 March 2016) http://www.themalaymailonline.com/malaysia/article/stop-aping-arabs-johor-sultan-tells-malays (accessed 2 November 2016).

'Sultan Admits Importing Cars without Aps' *New Straits Times* (3 February 1993) 2.

Syed Husin Ali, *The Malay Rulers: Regression or Reform?* (Strategic Information and Research Development Centre 2014).

Sykes Edward, Lanham David, and Tracey Richard, *General Principles of Administrative Law* (3rd edn, Butterworths 1989).

Tan Chee Khoon, *The Monarchy in Malaysia* (Pelanduk Publications 1984).

———, 'The Will of the People Must Prevail' *Star* (4 January 1984) 20.

———, *Sabah: A Triumph for Democracy* (Pelanduk Publications 1986).

———, 'Why Are We Still Being Kept in the Dark?' *Star* (5 January 1984) 20–1.

———, 'Without Fear or Favour' *Star* (4 January 1984) 20.

Tan Kevin YL, 'Recent Developments in the Law and Practice of Preventive Detention' in Wu Min Aun (ed), *Public Law in Contemporary Malaysia* (Longman 1999) 307.

———, 'Singapore: In and Out of the Federation' in Andrew Harding and HP Lee (eds), *Constitutional Landmarks in Malaysia: The First 50 Years 1957–2007* (LexisNexis 2007) 55–75.

———, 'The Final Chapter' in Audrey Quay (ed), *Perak: A State in Crisis* (LoyarBurok Publications 2010) 143–4.

———, Keynote Address at the 'Law and Society in Malaysia: Pluralism, Islam and Development' Conference, University of Victoria, BC, 15 July 2011.

Tan Nathamiel and Lee John (eds), *Religion Under Siege? Lina Joy, the Islamic State and Freedom of Faith* (Kinibooks 2008).

Tan Poh-Ling, 'Paying the Price for Religious freedom: A Non-Muslim Perspective' in Wu Min Aun (ed), *Public law in Contemporary Malaysia* (1999) 134–77.

———, 'From Malaya to Malaysia' in Andrew Harding and HP Lee (eds), *Constitutional Landmarks in Malaysia: The First 50 Years 1957–2007* (LexisNexis 2007) 25–46.

Tay Wilson Tze Vern, 'The Use and Misuse of Article 4(3) and 4(4) of the Federal Constitution' [2015] 2 MLJ cliv.

Tehankee Claudio, 'The Return of Constitutional Democracy in the Philippines' Tun A Razak Memorial Lecture delivered on 7 July 1988, reproduced in (1988) INSAF: Journal of the Malaysian Bar 83–104.

Tew Yvonne, 'On the Uneven Journey to Constitutional Redemption: The Malaysian Judiciary and Constitutional Politics' (2016) 25(3) Washington International Law Journal 1

'The Choosing of a King' *Asiaweek* (24 February 1984) 28–37.

The Federalist Papers (with Introduction by Clinton Rossiter), New York: Mentor, 1961, 301.

'The Real Reason: Operation Lalang ISA Arrests October 27, 1987' (DAP 1988).

Thio Li-ann, 'Jurisdictional Imbroglio: Civil and Religious Courts, Turf Wars and Article 121(1A) of the Federal Constitution' in Andrew Harding and HP Lee (eds), *Constitutional Landmarks in Malaysia: The First 50 Years 1957–2007* (LexisNexis 2007) 197.

———, 'Apostasy and Religious Freedom: Constitutional Issues Arising from the Lina Joy Litigation' (2006) 2 MLJ 1.

———, 'Courting Religion: The Judge between Caesar and God in Asian Courts' [2009] Singapore Journal of Legal Studies 52.

Thio SM, 'Dismissal of Chief Ministers' (1966) 8 Malaya Law Review 283–91.

Thiru Steven, 'Sosma Is Becoming the New ISA' *Malaysiakini* (10 October 2015) https://www.malaysiakini.com/news/315248 (accessed 2 November 2016).

———, 'Press Release: The National Security Council Bill 2015 is a Lurch Towards an Authoritarian Government' (Malaysian Bar Council, 3 December 2015) http://www.malaysianbar.org.my/press_statements/press_release_%7C_the_national_security_council_bill_2015_is_a_lurch_towards_an_authoritarian_government.html (accessed 2 November 2016).

———, 'Press Comment: National Security Council Act 2015 Has All the Hallmarks of Authoritarianism' (Malaysian Bar Council 15 June 2016) http://www.malaysianbar.org.my/press_statements/press_comment_%7C_national_security_council_act_2015_has_all_the_hallmarks_of_authoritarianism.html (accessed 2 November 2016).

'Tomboy Protests a Security Threat: Malaysia Police' (13 November 2008) http://www.reuters.com/article/us-malaysia-tomboys-idUSTRE4AC32Y20081113 (accessed 2 November 2016).

'Top Court Says Lingam Video RCI Findings "Cannot Be Reviewed"' *The Malaysian Insider* (13 September 2011) http://blog.limkitsiang.com/2011/09/13/top-court-says-lingam-video-rci-findings-%E2%80%98cannot-be-reviewed%E2%80%99/ (accessed 2 November 2016).

Trindade FA, 'The Constitutional Position of the Yang di-Pertuan Agong' in Tun Mohamed Suffian, Lee HP Lee, and FA Trindade FA (eds), *The Constitution of Malaysia—Its Development: 1957–1977* (OUP 1978).

———, 'The Removal of the Malaysian Judges' (1990) 106 Law Quarterly Review 51–86.

———and Lee HP, *Constitution of Malaysia: Further Perspectives and Developments* (OUP 1986).

Trowell Mark, 'Anwar's Long Struggle for Justice', Report on Datuk Seri Anwar bin Ibrahim's Appeal against conviction observed on behalf of the Australian Bar Association and International Commission of Jurists. http://www.austbar.asn.au/wp-content/uploads/2014/02/ABA_Anwar_Appeal_25E109_v3.pdf (accessed 2 November 2016).

Tunku Abdul Rahman, *Challenging Times* (Pelanduk Publications 1986).

———, *May 13, Before and After* (Utusan Melayu Press Ltd 1969).

———, 'Proclamation of Independence', reproduced in RH Hickling (ed), *Malayan Constitutional Documents* (Government Printers 1959) 18.

———, *Viewpoints* (Heinemann 1978).

Vanitha Sundra Karean, 'The Malaysian Constitution and its Identity Crisis: Secular or Theocratic?' (2006) LAWASIA Journal 47.

Vasil Raj Kumar, *The Malaysian General Elections of 1969* (OUP 1972).

Vatikiotis Michael, 'King and Country—Government further Clips Rulers' Wings' (19 May 1994) Far Eastern Economic Review 23.

Wain Barry, *Malaysian Maverick – Mahathir Mohamad in Turbulent Times* (2nd edn, Palgrave 2012)

Weeramantry CG, *Equality and Freedom: Some Third World Perspectives* (Hansa 1976).

Wheeler Graham John, 'Royal Assent in the British Constitution' (2016) 132 LQR 493.

Whiting Amanda, 'Secularism, the Islamic State and the Malaysian Legal Profession' (2010) 5(1) Asian Journal of Comparative Law 1.

———, 'Emerging from emergency Rule? Malaysian Law "Reform" 2011-2013' (2013) 14(2) Australian Journal of Asian Law Article *9*, 1–55.

———, 'Anwar Ibrahim's Conviction Lowers the Bar on the Malaysian Legal System'—http://www.eastasiaforum.org/2015/04/13/anwar-ibrahims-conviction-lowers-the-bar-on-the-malaysian-legal-system/ (accessed 2 November 2016).

'Who Will Advise King on Delay: Kit Siang' *Star* (10 January 1984) 2.

Williams Peter Aldridge, *Judicial Misconduct* (Pelanduk Publications 1990).

Wong Chun Wai, 'Stop Trying to Be Like Arabs, Ruler Advises Malays' http://aliran.com/web-specials/2016-web-specials/stop-trying-like-arabs-ruler-advises-malays/ (accessed 2 November 2016).

Wu Min Aun, 'Judiciary at the Crossroads' in Wu Min Aun (ed), *Public Law in Contemporary Malaysia* (Longman 1999) 76–106.

———, 'Anwar Ibrahim: Epilogue' [2002] LAWASIA Journal 45.

———, 'Anwar Ibrahim: The Fall and Fall of a Favoured Son' [2000/2001] LAWASIA Journal 46.

———, 'The Saga of Anwar Ibrahim' in Andrew Harding and HP Lee (eds), *Constitutional Landmarks in Malaysia: The First 50 Years 1957–2007* (LexisNexis 2007) 273.

Index